# PERSUASION

*A Longman Cultural Edition*

# PERSUASION

### by Jane Austen

*Edited by*

## William Galperin

PEARSON
Longman

New York   San Francisco   Boston
London   Toronto   Sydney   Tokyo   Singapore   Madrid
Mexico City   Munich   Paris   Cape Town   Hong Kong   Montreal

Vice President and Editor-in-Chief: Joseph P. Terry
Executive Marketing Manager: Megan Galvin-Fak
Production Manager: Ellen MacElree
Project Coordination and Electronic Page Makeup: TexTech Inc.
Cover Designer/Manager: Wendy Ann Fredericks
Cover Illustration: Getty Images
Manufacturing Buyer: Lucy Hebard
Printer and Binder: RR Donnelley & Sons/Harrisonburg
Cover Printer: Coral Graphics

**Library of Congress Cataloging-in-Publication Data**

Austen, Jane, 1775–1817.
    Persuasion / by Jane Austen; edited by William Galperin.
      p. cm.—(A Longman cultural edition)
    ISBN-13: 978-0-321-19822-8
    ISBN-10:     0-321-19822-0
    1. Austen, Jane, 1775–1817. Persuasion. 2. Young women—Fiction.
3. Motherless families—Fiction. 4. Rejection (Psychology)—Fiction.
5. First loves—Fiction. 6. Problem families—Fiction. 7. Ship captains—
Fiction. 8. England—Fiction. I. Galperin, William H. II. Title.
    PR4034.P4 2008
    823'.7—dc22                                                    2007016561

Please visit us at http://www.ablongman.com

ISBN-13: 978-0-321-19822-8
ISBN-10:     0-321-19822-0

    3 4 5 6 7 8 9 10—DOH—10 09 08

# Contents

# List of Illustrations

# About Longman
# Cultural Editions

Reading always vibrates with the transformations of the day—now, yesterday, and centuries ago when presses first put printed language into circulation. So too, literary culture is always open to change, with new pulses of imagination confronting older practices, texts transforming under new ways of reading and new perspectives of understanding, canons shifting and expanding, traditions reviewed and renewed, recast and reformed. Inspired by the innovative *Longman Anthology of British Literature*, Longman Cultural Editions present key texts in contexts that illuminate the lively intersections of literature, tradition, and culture. In each volume, a principal work gains new dimensions from materials that relate it to its past, present, and future: to informing traditions and debates, to the conversations and controversies of its own historical moment, to later eras of reading and reaction.

The series is designed for several kinds of readers and several situations of reading: the cultural editions offer appealing complements to the *Anthology*, as well as attractive resources for a variety of coursework, or for independent encounters. First-time readers will find productive paths to investigate, while more-seasoned readers will enjoy the fresh perspectives and provocative juxtapositions. The contexts for adventure vary from volume to volume, but the constants (in addition to handsome production and affordable pricing) are an important literary work, expertly edited and helpfully annotated; an inviting introduction; a table of dates to track its composition, publication, and reception in relation to biographical, cultural, and historical events; and a guide for further study. To these common measures and uncommon enhancements, we invite your attention and curiosity.

Susan J. Wolfson, General Editor
Professor of English, Princeton University

# About This Edition

*Persuasion* is the last of Austen's six completed novels. Published posthumously in 1817 along with the much earlier drafted *Northanger Abbey*, the novel contains a number of elements that proved puzzling to Austen's nineteenth-century readers. In addition to its heroine, Anne Elliot, who is considerably older and less prone to being judged or criticized than the heroines who precede her, including *Northanger Abbey*'s famously naïve and suggestible Catherine Morland, *Persuasion* was prefaced by a biographical notice by Austen's brother, Henry—which led many readers and reviewers to regard both the novel and its heroine in a didactic or moralistic light. It is true that Anne's maturity and self-possession make her quite exemplary, not only in comparison to *Persuasion*'s other characters but also in comparison to Austen's previous heroines. At the same time, the novel in which we discover Anne, and where she stands apart on moral or ethical grounds, seems more a meditation on the multiple worlds that *Persuasion* opens onto, including the fictional worlds of Austen's previous novels, than a simple narrative of do's and don'ts.

The supplementary materials to this Longman Cultural Edition collaborate with *Persuasion* in addressing and exploring these interlocking worlds: moral, aesthetic, domestic, political, social, and military. Beginning with the biographical notice, which was so influential in shaping the response to *Persuasion,* especially upon publication, this edition features the two most incisive pieces of literary criticism on Austen written in her lifetime: the reviews of *Emma* in *The Champion* and in the *Quarterly Review* (the latter by Walter Scott, England's most popular novelist at that moment). Both reviews strive to come to terms with a novelistic practice that seemed especially unique at the time and that we refer to now as "realistic." To clarify this force, this Longman edition offers some slightly earlier attempts to define realism by distinguishing the kind of novel that Austen would eventually write from what novelists Frances Burney and Clara Reeve called "romance." Unlike romances, which deal with fantastic or improbable circumstances, and could (these writers feared) lead impressionable female readers to harbor great, if dangerous, expectations regarding their own possibilities in life, novels were defended as more probabilistic in focus, and thus a vehicle through which young women might read about themselves and their milieu in more profitable ways.

The literary criticism that predates *Persuasion* helps frame, too, the substantial sections from the most important reviews of *Persuasion* in the wake of its publication: those in *The British Critic, Blackwood's Edinburgh Magazine* and the *Quarterly Review*. The last of these, written by Richard Whately (Archbishop of Dublin) saw both *Persuasion* and the Austen novels that preceded it as "moral lessons." Along with Henry Austen's biographical notice, Whately helped shape the way Austen was read and understood throughout the nineteenth century. We can see this effect in two examples of the later nineteenth-century response, which stress the regulatory or pedagogical work that Austen's writing was believed to perform.

Regulation is not the only work that Austen's last novel undertakes, however. *Persuasion* both echoes and exceeds Austen's previous fiction in its unrelenting preoccupation with questions of gender, from the proper roles of wives and daughters to the more general divisions of both labor and identity that relegate men and women to separate and at times distant spheres. The preoccupation with gender is most evident in the revisions to the ending that Austen undertook shortly after completing the novel in the summer of 1816. The original ending (included in this edition's "Contexts") is concerned primarily with bringing the narrative to a happy close. The revised ending contains an extended debate on men and women and their respective differences, based in turn on the very different lives they lead and the very different expectations they harbor—a debate that is especially relevant given how the novel concludes.

Austen was not alone in her concerns. Many of her contemporaries, both women and men, were equally struck by gender difference and responded in a variety of ways. As the materials on women and men show, Lord Byron echoes many of the points raised in the revised ending to *Persuasion* in the voice of Donna Julia in Canto I of *Don Juan*. In a passage that Byron's editor, Jerome McGann, thinks may have been influenced by *Persuasion* itself,

Donna Julia remarks on the different spheres that men and women occupy and on the limitations that women, in particular, experience. And Thomas Gisborne, whose two books on the duties of men and women Austen undoubtedly knew, sought to codify gender difference not just with respect to women in their domestic lives but with attention to men, including naval officers, in their professional lives. This edition features important excerpts from Gisborne's two books.

This edition also contains several letters by Austen herself from the time when, like her heroine, she was obliged to join her family in relocating to Bath, as well as a letter written from Lyme, where the novel's heroine undergoes an important physical transformation. There is also a brief description of Austen's life along with a detailed chronology in which the author's life and works are marked in conjunction with important contemporaneous events, both political and cultural. There is a section, too, on money, focusing not only on the peculiarities of the British money system at the time Austen was writing but also on both cost and value and their relationship in turn to everyday practice, all matters of central concern to Austen. A guide of further reading relevant to *Persuasion* and to Austen's achievement in general closes this volume.

# Introduction

*Persuasion* (1818), published posthumously with *Northanger Abbey* in 1817, is the last of Jane Austen's six completed novels and arguably the most modern in its probing representation of its heroine's inner life. Resembling *Mansfield Park* (1814) in its sympathetic treatment of a heroine in her various struggles, both internal and external, *Persuasion* has even stronger affinities with the novel that precedes it, *Emma* (1816). Focusing famously on the disparity between its heroine's perception of things and the world she continually misperceives, *Emma* is about the conflict between self and society and about its heroine's separation from the social world where we discover her and in which she is obliged finally to take her place. A similar distance clearly characterizes Anne Elliot's relationship to her environment in *Persuasion*. But unlike Emma, a "heroine whom no one will much like" (or so Austen predicted), Anne has proven one of the most beloved—and undoubtedly the most sympathetic—of Austen's major characters.

The most mature and reflective of Austen's heroines, Anne is also the saddest, especially in *Persuasion*'s opening phase, where we learn quickly of the marriage proposal she rejected, apparently at her family's behest, and of the "early loss of bloom" that she suffered as a result. And Anne rivals *Mansfield Park*'s Fanny Price in being thoroughly unappreciated—in this case by members of her immediate family, who depend on her good sense and good will even as they ignore her at almost every turn. This lack of appreciation is strongly felt by force of Austen's signature "free indirect discourse"—a mode of narration that commits us to Anne's point of view even as we are able to see beyond her perspective. But here there is no disparity, as there is in *Pride and Prejudice* and *Emma*, between the narrator's authoritative view of things and the heroine's narrower, more personal, view. The only difference is that where the narrator can indulge freely in her dislike of Anne's family, in particular her father, Sir Walter Elliot, and her sisters, Elizabeth and Mary (who are odious at worst and ridiculous at best), Anne has no such luxury. This is, after all, her family, her world, and she must endure it despite what both she and the narrator believe.

But there is a world elsewhere in *Persuasion* where Anne also lives or to where she retreats, and it is this inner world that forms the core of the novel's interest and investment, particularly upon the return of Captain Frederick Wentworth, Anne's former suitor. Readers have often taken Anne's retrospective judgment that she was wrong in rejecting Wentworth as a key to her perturbation throughout much of the novel. But the narrator's suggestion that Anne "learned romance as she grew older"—an observation that transforms love into something of a pedagogical exercise—makes her eventual reconciliation with Wentworth a more complicated negotiation, one in which Anne surrenders her privacy and autonomy in becoming a more conventional and transparent heroine. The famous scene at Lyme, where Anne's "bloom" is restored under the triangulated gaze of Wentworth and her cousin, Mr. Elliot, even as she continues to resist the pull that Wentworth continues to exert, perplexes the very nature of love itself, whose nearly disciplinary force may not be the same thing as desire, or what Anne truly wants.

Such confusion over male/female relations is especially evident with respect to marriage. Although marriage is where the romance narrative typically achieves resolution, the domestic scenes that populate *Persuasion* might well suggest otherwise. Most obviously, there is the neurotic debility of Anne's married sister Mary, whose confinement at home in accord with the "doctrine of separate spheres" is a paradigm and a problem to which Anne is especially attentive. Quite late in the novel, in conversation with Captain Harville over men's and women's constancy, Anne observes that women are more loyal than men not because they are necessarily better or more ethical, but because they "cannot help" themselves:

> We live at home, quiet, confined, and our feelings prey upon us. You are forced on exertion. You have always a profession, pursuits, business of some sort or other, to take you back into the world immediately, and continual occupation and change soon weaken impressions.

The alternative to this scenario in *Persuasion* is represented by Admiral and Mrs. Croft: Mrs. Croft actually accompanies her husband aboard ship, effectively sharing his profession and his pursuits. Their childless, companionate, and remarkably democratic marriage is clearly an exception to the rule, a backdrop for a rather heated debate over the appropriateness of having women aboard ship. It is telling that in this debate the negative and customary position is taken by none other than Captain Wentworth: "I hate to hear of women aboard ship, or to see them on board; and no ship, under my command, shall ever convey a family of ladies any where, if I can help it." In the 1995 film adaptation of *Persuasion* Wentworth relents and allows Anne to accompany him on his voyage. This is a fantasy swerve from a novel that leaves its heroine at home in "dread of a future war," a close that goes a long way in explaining not only Anne's inclination across the narrative to resist Wentworth in some fashion, but also why Austen, almost defiantly, leaves other female characters, including Anne's trusted friend, Lady Russell, unmarried.

While there are at least three marriages in *Persuasion* that bode happy closure, the fact that Lady Russell, in particular, has no interest in remarrying attaches to the force of Anne's wariness to cast an unresolved shadow over the felicity of normative marital relations. While Anne's resistance to her own marital prospects is often attributed to her stoicism in the face of disappointment, there is something almost instinctive in her resignation and in her mysterious "loss of bloom," both of which render her invisible to male attention and thereby free. Anne's private observation, then, upon encountering Wentworth after six years' duration—"It is over! It is over. . . . The worst is over!"—oscillates between embarrassment, in which romantic desire undoubtedly figures, and an equally spontaneous relief over the termination of their attachment. This tension continues in a variety of forms. In noticing at one point that Wentworth is looking at her, Anne speculates that he is "observing her altered features, perhaps, trying to trace in them the ruins of the face which had once charmed him." The "perhaps" that intrudes upon Anne's fantasy certainly flirts with a romantic reunion, but not without an apprehension over the prospect of Wentworth's actually picking up where he left off.

It is too easy to limit Anne's resistance to imagining herself in a courtship narrative to a psychological reflex—a transparent means of steeling herself against Wentworth's suspiciously overt dalliances with the Musgrove sisters, Henrietta and Louisa. A more substantial social logic for Anne's resistance is given succinct, if ironic, confirmation in that walk at Lyme, where she is "caught" in the gaze of both Wentworth and her cousin Mr. Elliot:

> When they came to the steps, leading upwards from the beach, a gentleman at the same moment preparing to come down, politely drew back, and stopped to give them way. They ascended and passed him; and as they passed, Anne's face caught his eye, and he looked at her with a degree of earnest admiration, which she could not be insensible of. She was looking remarkably well; her very regular, very pretty features, having the bloom and freshness of youth restored by the fine wind which had been blowing on her complexion, and by the animation of eye, which it had also produced. It was evident that the gentleman . . . admired her exceedingly. Captain Wentworth looked round at her instantly in a way which shewed his noticing of it. He gave her a momentary glance,—a glance of brightness, which seemed to say, "That man is struck with you,—and even I, at this moment, see something like Anne Elliot again."

It is significant that Anne's designation as an object of beauty is prior, in the narrator's description, to the natural explanation for her transformation. And it is significant because here, as throughout the novel, the question of causality or *persuasion* extends beyond the merely physical. It is not enough that Anne was aware of her cousin's glance, for which the play of wind and physiognomy were responsible. The narrator makes a point of giving Mr. Elliot's glance an equal, if not greater, role in the effect of beauty, whose priority as something that men look for in a woman takes precedence over its embodiment in Anne. If Anne is rendered beautiful by a force apart from nature, or by the animation of eye that she produces in a beholder, it is because that "eye" and the mind behind it are also and already "caught" by an ideal for which Anne is essentially a placeholder. Persuasion here, what Austen also calls "internal persuasion," marks the degree to which coercion and conviction are more or less the same. This equivalence is demonstrated quite nicely by the addition of Wentworth to the scene. Although Wentworth's renewed appreciation of Anne draws on Mr. Elliot's admiration, Wentworth's designation of the object of beauty as "something like Anne Elliot" only obscures the fact that, in regaining her bloom as she has, Anne is more properly like something else. Anne has become a "something" that men wish for, in contrast to what she has been thus far: a human subject of depth and individuality.

In a moment such as this one, we see how *Persuasion,* even as it conveys the gender codes of life and fiction, also reflects a social transformation in the early nineteenth century. Beginning with a sharply satirical account of Sir Walter's preoccupation with rank and lineage as he scans his family's entry in the *Baronetage, Persuasion* is unambiguous and unsparing in marking the decline of the landed aristocracy and the rise of the professional and middle classes. This latter grouping, represented primarily by the Navy, has achieved status and prestige on the basis of accomplishments rather than family pedigree. Wentworth's heroism, both as a military leader and as leading man, is symbolic of a new social hierarchy that the Elliot family has no choice but to accept.

This is similarly the case with marriage. Previously a way to maintain class distinction through the consolidation of property, wealth, and genealogy (for example, the almost destined union of Emma Woodhouse and Mr. Knightley), marriage in *Persuasion* is an arrangement that couples enter into by choice and on the basis of mutual love and esteem: it is who one marries that matters far more—certainly to Anne—than what one marries.

Yet, even as *Persuasion* tracks and celebrates the rise of bourgeois individualism and its system of conferring value, another rising formation, domestic ideology and its doctrine of "separate spheres," brings new distinctions, ones based on gender rather than rank. While in the new century marriage may have been more and more by choice or according to volition, the mutual esteem that formed the core of bourgeois marriage did not necessarily honor the "affective individualism" on which it was based. We see this very clearly in Anne's scenario of neurotic confinement and in the diminished situation of her sister Mary, who is denied all those "pursuits" that take men out of the house and into the world.

The notion of "the separate spheres" did confer on women special prerogatives and a growing moral status in their roles as housewives and mothers. But the domestic sphere also served more dubious purposes on the national scene and was used as a massive and self-legitimating symbol of moral stability that proved a counterweight to Britain's imperial and military activities abroad. If *Persuasion* begins in peacetime with the return of the Navy, which had been so instrumental in Napoleon's defeat, it ends with a horizon of future war, and is peppered throughout by allusions to Britain's continued involvements and adventures in the world at large—notably the West Indies, where Wentworth had previously been active and where the lost "property" of Anne's friend, Mrs. Smith, is also located. Austen's contemporary readers would have readily understood what was meant: in the West Indies slavery was legal. And many family fortunes back home in England, including the one that sustains the Bertram family in Austen's *Mansfield Park,* thrived from the goods produced by slave labor on West Indian plantations. One of the tasks of the Navy in the West Indies was to assist plantation owners in maintaining order with their slaves.

None of this peripheral knowledge deflects the sympathy that virtually all readers have for Anne, who has suffered long and maintained her dignity throughout. Further, when we reflect on the fact that Austen was also terminally ill when writing *Persuasion,* her determined effort to create a likeable heroine, who is ultimately granted a new lease on life, seems both generous and heroic. No other Austen novel is as bittersweet as *Persuasion.* And no other novel is so wistfully optimistic and so disarmingly clear-eyed in its view of both human possibility and social limitation.

# Table of Dates

JA: Jane Austen

| | |
|---|---|
| 1764 | Reverend George Austen marries Cassandra Leigh (JA's parents). |
| | Anne Ward (later, Radcliffe) born. George III is king. |
| 1765 | James (brother) born. |
| | James Fordyce, *Sermons to Young Women* |
| 1766 | George (brother) born. |
| 1767 | Edward (brother) born. |
| 1770 | Oliver Goldsmith, *The Deserted Village*. William Wordsworth born. |
| 1771 | Henry (brother) born |
| | First color fashion plates in *The Lady's Magazine*; Henry Mackenzie, *The Man of Feeling*; Tobias Smollett, *Humphry Clinker*. Walter Scott born. |
| 1772 | Lord Mansfield rules in the case of slave James Somerset that slavery has no legal basis in England. |
| 1773 | Cassandra (sister) born. |
| | Oliver Goldsmith, *She Stoops to Conquer*. Boston Tea Party. |
| 1774 | Frank (brother) born. |
| | Lord Chesterfield, Letter to His Son; Goethe, *The Sorrows of Young Werter*; Dr. John Gregory, *A Father's Legacy to His Daughters*. |

Warren Hastings becomes the first Governor General of India.

1775    **December 16: Jane Austen born**; seventh of eight children, one of two daughters.

1776    July 4: United States declares independence from Britain; Adam Smith, *Wealth of Nations*; Thomas Paine, *Common Sense*; Samuel Johnson, *Journey to the Western Islands of Scotland*; Richard Brinsley Sheridan, *The Rivals* and *The Duenna*.

1777    Sheridan, *The School for Scandal*.

1778    Frances Burney, *Evelina, or, The History of a Young Lady's Entrance into the World*. Siding with the American colonies, France declares war on Britain.

1779    Charles (brother) born; James matriculates at St. John's College, Oxford.

        S. Johnson, *The Lives of the Poets*. Spain declares war on Britain.

1780    Hannah Cowley, *The Belles' Stratagem* produced in London.

        Gordon Riots in London against Catholic civil rights.

1781    Surrender at Yorktown ends British war against U.S. independence.

1782    Burney, *Cecilia, or Memoirs of an Heiress*; William Cowper, *Poems*.

        Treaty of Paris officially ends the U.S. war of independence.

1783    Edward adopted by Mr. and Mrs. Thomas Knight II.

        George Crabbe, *The Village*; Peace of Versailles recognizes U.S. independence.

1783    JA and Cassandra attend schools in Oxford, Southampton, and Reading.

1784    Charlotte Smith, *Elegiac Sonnets*. Samuel Johnson dies.

1785    Warren Hastings (godfather of JA's cousin Eliza) returns from India to England.

William Cowper, *The Task;* James Boswell, *Journal of a Tour to the Hebrides with Samuel Johnson.*

1786    Edward on a Grand Tour, 1786–90; April: Frank enters Royal Naval Academy; November: James goes to Europe; December: JA's and Cassandra's formal schooling ends.

Hannah More, *The Bas Bleu* (a poem in praise of female intellectual culture); Robert Burns, *Poems, Chiefly in the Scottish Dialect;* William Beckford, *Vathek.*

1787    JA begins her literary career, drafting sketches and parodies for family entertainment. Autumn: James returns from Europe; Henry matriculates at Oxford; JA and Cassandra visit Kent and London; Frank sails to the East Indies.

**Persuasion's Anne Elliot is born.**

Edmund Burke takes a leading role in the trial to impeach Hastings for his comportment in India. Member of Parliament William Wilberforce organizes the movement to abolish slave trade and colonial slavery.

1788    C. Smith, *Emmeline, or The Orphan of the Castle;* Mary Wollstonecraft, *Mary, A Fiction.* Edward Gibbon finishes *The Decline and Fall of the Roman Empire.* Lord Byron born.

Mental illness of George III produces the first regency crisis. Hastings impeached in the House of Commons.

1789    James starts the periodical *The Loiterer* at Oxford, to which Henry and Jane will contribute.

Radcliffe, *The Castles of Athlyn and Dunbane;* C. Smith, *Ethelinda, or the Recluse of the Lake;* Blake, *Songs of Innocence.*

July 14: the storming of the Bastille launches the French Revolution. Mutiny on the HMS Bounty.

1790    *The Loiterer* ceases publication in March; James becomes curate; Edward returns from his Grand Tour.

Burke, *Reflections on the Revolution in France;* Wollstonecraft, *A Vindication of the Rights of Men.* Radical Jacobins ascend to power in France.

1791    Charles enters the Royal Naval Academy.

Paine, *The Rights of Man;* Elizabeth Inchbald, *A Simple Story;* James Boswell, *Life of Johnson;* Radcliffe, *The Romance of the Forest.*

Attempt of Louis XVI and Marie Antoinette to flee France is halted at Varennes. In Birmingham, Joseph Priestley's house and library burned by a "King & Church" mob.

1792    James marries; Cassandra becomes engaged to Thomas Fowle.

Helen Maria Williams, *Letters from France* (–1796); Wollstonecraft, *A Vindication of the Rights of Woman;* Hannah More's anti-Painite tract, *Village Politics* ("Burke for beginners"); C. Smith, *Desmond;* William Gilpin, *Essays on Picturesque Beauty.*

France declares itself a republic; massacres of suspected Royalists; arrest of royal family; abolition of the monarchy. Britain, fearing invasion, mobilizes its militia. Petitions to abolish slavery circulate and a boycott of sugar (a product of slave-labor) is organized.

1793    Edward's daughter born; Henry abandons plans for ordination to join the Oxfordshire militia as lieutenant; James's daughter born; Frank returns from the Far East.

William Godwin, *Political Justice;* C. Smith, *The Old Manor House.*

Guillotining of Louis XVI (January) and Marie Antoinette (October); Marat murdered; Reign of Terror; France declares war on Britain; treason trials of radicals in Scotland.

1794    Charles goes to sea; Thomas Knight (Edward's adoptive father) dies; JA begins *Lady Susan.* In France, the French aristocrat husband of the Austens' cousin Eliza (she is staying with them at the time) is guillotined in February.

Wollstonecraft, *Historical and Moral View of the French Revolution;* Paine, *The Age of Reason;* Godwin, *Caleb Williams;* Radcliffe, *The Mysteries of Udolpho;* Uvedale Price, *Essay on the Picturesque;* Thomas Gisborne, *An Enquiry into the Duties of Men in the Higher and Middle Classes of Society in Great Britain.*

Danton and Robespierre executed; the Terror ends. Habeas corpus suspended in Britain.

1795    JA writes *Elinor and Marianne,* an early version of *Sense and Sensibility.* JA meets Tom Lefroy, nephew of a close friend and neighbor; they become interested in one another.

Matthew Lewis, *Ambrosio, or The Monk;* Maria Edgeworth, *Letters for Literary Ladies;* Joseph Strutt, *Dresses and Habits of the English People* (–1799).

Napoleon invades Italy. Hastings acquitted. Mutinies in British militia.

1796    January: Tom Lefroy leaves for London, and he and JA never see each other again; James becomes engaged. JA begins *First Impressions* (an early, probably epistolary version of *Pride and Prejudice*).

Wollstonecraft, *Scandinavian Letters;* Staël, *De l'influence des passions;* Burney, *Camilla, or A Picture of Youth;* Mary Hays, *Memoirs of Emma Courtney.*

Spain allies with France against Britain.

1797    August: Jane Austen finishes *First Impressions.* Comparing it to Burney's *Evelina,* her father offers it in November to publisher Thomas Cadell, who does not even reply. JA begins to transform *Elinor and Marianne* into *Sense and Sensibility.* Cassandra's fiancé Thomas Fowle dies of yellow fever in San Domingo. JA and Cassandra visit their mother in Bath; James marries Mary Lloyd; Henry marries cousin Eliza de Feuillide.

Radcliffe, *The Italian.* Maria and Richard Lovell Edgeworth, *Practical Education;* Gisborne, *An Enquiry into the Duties of the Female Sex. Anti-Jacobin Review* founded. Wollstonecraft dies from infection during childbirth.

May: Napoleon proclaims the end of the Venetian Republic. British naval mutinies.

**1798**   JA may have begun *Susan* (later, *Northanger Abbey*); James's son born.

*Lyrical Ballads,* including William Wordsworth's *Tintern Abbey* and several poems set in the Lake District of northwest England; Joanna Baillie, *Plays on the Passions;* Inchbald, *Lovers' Vows;* Gilpin, *Picturesque Remarks on the West of England;* Hays, *An Appeal to the Men of Great Britain on Behalf of Women;* Godwin, *Memoir of Wollstonecraft;* Wollstonecraft, *Maria, or the Wrongs of Woman.* Scathing attacks on Wollstonecraft in the reactionary press. Richard Polwhele, *The Unsex'd Females.*

Irish Rebellion suppressed; Napoleon invades Rome, then Switzerland, then Egypt, defeated by Horatio Nelson at the Battle of the Nile.

**1799**   Mother, JA, Edward, and Elizabeth spend several spring weeks in Bath; JA finishes *Susan.* Aunt Jane Leigh-Perrot charged with shoplifting and sent to jail.

Hannah More, *Strictures on the Modern System of Female Education,* a best-seller for decades; Hays, *Victim of Prejudice.*

Religious Tract Society founded. Napoleon returns to France and in a coup becomes First Consul.

**1800**   JA's aunt acquitted; Edward visits; father decides to retire.

**Elizabeth Elliot (Anne Elliot's mother) dies.**

Second expanded edition of *Lyrical Ballads* (with Preface). Maria Edgeworth's first novel, *Castle Rackrent,* published to acclaim. Death of Cowper.

Napoleon's army of 4,000 crosses the Alps into Austria; French attempt to land in Ireland and fail.

| | |
|---|---|
| 1801 | Henry resigns his military commission to become a banker and army agent in London; JA's father retires and moves the family to Bath; James and his family move to Steventon. |

Edgeworth, *Belinda*; Joseph Strutt, *Sports and Pastimes of the English People*.

Prime Minister Pitt resigns after George III refuses Catholic Emancipation.

| | |
|---|---|
| 1802 | JA and Cassandra visit Steventon; Harris Bigg-Wither proposes marriage to JA; she accepts, but reneges the next morning. She and Cassandra return to Bath. JA revises *Susan*. |

Baillie, *Plays*, vol. 2; *Edinburgh Review* founded.

Society for the Suppression of Vice. Peace of Amiens between England and France; France reoccupies Switzerland.

| | |
|---|---|
| 1803 | JA sells *Susan* for £10 to London publisher Crosby, who advertises but never publishes it; the Austen family visits Lyme Regis. |

Sidney Owenson, Lady Morgan, *St. Clair, or The Heiress of Desmond*.

England and France resume war. Henry and his wife are barely able to get out of France; Burney and her son fail to return to England. British officer Henry Shrapnel invents a time-triggered bomb filled with shot; Robert Fulton demonstrates a steamship on the Seine but finds no backers.

| | |
|---|---|
| 1804 | JA writes *The Watsons*, leaving it unfinished, and not writing again until 1809. |

Amelia Opie, *Adeline Mowbray*.

Napoleon becomes Emperor. Pitt returns as Prime Minister. U.K. declares war on Spain.

| | |
|---|---|
| 1805 | JA's father dies in Bath in January; James's daughter born at Steventon. JA may have been courted by Edward Bridges during the summer; she, Cassandra, |

and mother leave for Worthing. Frank unable to participate in the Battle of Trafalgar on 21 October, at which Admiral Horatio Nelson vanquishes the French fleet, losing his life to the effort.

Owenson, *The Wild Irish Girl: A National Tale;* William Hazlitt, *The Principles of Human Action.*

Napoleon defeats allied Austrian and Russian forces.

1806    Frank marries.

Napoleon closes the Continent to British trade. Inchbald, The British Theatre (–1809) in 25 volumes.

**Frederick Wentworth serves in "the action off St. Domingo":** French naval forces vanquished by British forces, including Frank Austen. **Anne Elliot refuses Frederick Wentworth's proposal of marriage.**

1807    Mother, JA, and Cassandra settle in Southampton; Charles marries.

Wordsworth, *Poems.* Staël's *Corinne* achieves international success.

France invades Spain and Portugal, and Britain's Peninsular Campaign (supporting Spanish uprisings) begins. Parliament abolishes the slave trade (colonial slavery still legal).

1808    Leigh Hunt founds and edits *The Examiner,* a radical weekly. Hannah More, *Coelebs in Search of a Wife* (a conduct novel). British troops land in Portugal.

1809    JA attempts to find a publisher for *Susan.* Mother, JA, and Cassandra move into Chawton Cottage, on Edward's estate in Hampshire; JA begins to write again, with an eye to publication.

Byron takes his seat in House of Lords. John Murray founds the *Quarterly Review;* edited by William Gifford, it becomes the chief Tory-establishment journal. Maria Edgeworth, *Tales of Fashionable Life* (–1812).

Coronation of Joseph Bonaparte in Madrid; Wellesley (later Duke of Wellington) leads the Peninsular Campaign.

| | |
|---|---|
| 1810 | *Sense and Sensibility* accepted for publication by Thomas Egerton. |
| | December 16 (JA's 35th birthday): Mary Elliot marries Charles Musgrove. |
| | Mary Brunton, *Self-Control*. Anna Barbauld, *The British Novelists*, 50 volumes. |
| 1811 | *Sense and Sensibility* ("By a Lady") published at the Austens' expense. Selling out its 2,000 copies, it requires a second edition. JA reworks *First Impressions* into *Pride and Prejudice*, and begins *Mansfield Park*. |
| | George III is deemed incompetent; Prince of Wales becomes Regent. Luddite riots against the weaving frames in the Midlands. |
| 1812 | On the strength of the success of *Sense and Sensibility*, JA sells copyright of *Pride and Prejudice* to Thomas Egerton for £110. Edward Austen Knight officially takes the name of Knight on the death of Mrs. Knight. |
| | Byron's *Childe Harold's Pilgrimage* an overnight sensation; Baillie, Vol. 3 of *Plays*; Grimm's *Fairy Tales*. Barbauld's long poem, *Eighteen Hundred and Eleven*, a critique of British and European imperialism, skewered in the *Quarterly*. |
| | Capital punishment enacted for frame-breaking. Britain declares war on United States; Napoleon's Grand Army invades Russia in June and retreats in December, with catastrophic losses (500,000 of 600,000). |
| 1813 | *Pride and Prejudice*, "By the Author of *Sense and Sensibility*," published January 28. Reviews in *British Critic* and *Critical Review*. The edition of 1,500 sells out in 6 months, and a second printing is required. Second edition of *Sense and Sensibility*. JA completes *Mansfield Park*; it is accepted for publication by the end of the year. JA spends time in London. |
| | Byron, in the whirl of London Regency society; publishes two sensational "Eastern Tales," *The Giaour* and *The Bride of Abydos*. Southey publishes *Life of Nelson* |

and becomes Poet Laureate. John Murray publishes Staël's *De l'Allemagne* (suppressed by Napoleon in 1810). Mary Russell Mitford, *Narrative Poems on the Female Character.*

Leigh Hunt, editor of *The Examiner,* imprisoned until 1815 for libeling the Regent. Massive Luddite trial in York, with many sentenced to death or transportation. Austria joins the Alliance against France; Napoleon suffers several defeats across Europe.

1814    January: JA begins *Emma. Mansfield Park,* "By the Author of *Pride and Prejudice,*" published at the Austens' expense in May; it sells out by November. JA visits London; Charles's wife dies after childbirth; December: JA and Cassandra visit Winchester.

**The narrative of *Persuasion* commences.**

Byron's *The Corsair* has record-breaking first-day sales; he becomes engaged to heiress Annabella Milbanke. Burney's five-volume novel, *The Wanderer, or Female Difficulties* (begun some time before 1800). Wordsworth, *The Excursion;* Scott, *Waverley.* Edmund Kean's debut at Covent Garden theater, London. *New Monthly Magazine* founded.

European allies invade France; Napoleon abdicates and is exiled to Elba; the French monarchy is restored. U.K. war with United States ends. British develop a steam warship; George Stephenson invents the locomotive.

1815    JA finishes *Emma,* visits London to negotiate publication, **begins *Persuasion* in August,** visits Carlton House (the Prince Regent's residence) in November, and receives an invitation to dedicate a future novel to him. *Emma* ("By the Author of *Pride and Prejudice*") published late December, dedicated to the Prince Regent. Scott's unsigned omnibus essay on Austen's novels, on the occasion of *Emma,* in the *Quarterly Review.*

**The narrative of *Persuasion* concludes.**

Scott, *Waverly* (anonymous). Wordsworth, collected *Poems.*

Napoleon escapes Elba, enters France, is defeated at Waterloo, and exiled to St. Helena; restoration of European monarchies. English national debt exceeds £850,000,000.

1816     JA feels unwell; Henry buys back *Susan* from Crosby, and JA reworks it with an intent to try another publisher. **JA finishes first draft of *Persuasion* on July 18 and revises the ending in August.** Murray loses money on a second edition of *Mansfield Park*. Henry's bank fails, with serious losses to family and friends who had backed it; he leaves London to become curate of Chawton. JA and Cassandra visit Steventon and Cheltenham.

January: In a public scandal, Lady Byron leaves Byron, taking their daughter; April: with a decree of separation, Byron leaves England forever. Byron's *Childe Harold's Pilgrimage III*; Caroline Lamb, *Glenarvon* (with a Satanic/Byronic hero); Coleridge, *Christabel and Kubla Khan*. Elgin Marbles (sculptural fragments removed from the parthenon in Athens) displayed in London; prosecution of William Hone (tried in 1817); economic depression in U.K., Spa Field Riots (December).

1817     JA begins *Sanditon* in January and abandons it in March; makes her will. Cassandra takes her to Winchester. **JA dies July 18.** Buried in Winchester Cathedral July 24. **December: Henry publishes *Northanger Abbey* and *Persuasion*; with his "Biographical Notice," they appear at the end of the year (dated 1818).** Third edition of *Pride and Prejudice*.

Death of Mme. de Staël. Princess Charlotte, sole legitimate child of the Prince Regent (and next king), dies during childbirth, along with the infant.

1821     *Quarterly Review* publishes a major, 22-page essay on Austen's novels.

1871     **JA's nephew publishes part of *Persuasion*'s original ending.**

1926     **Editor R. W. Chapman publishes the entire manuscript of the original ending.**

# Jane Austen Biography

Jane Austen was one of two daughters among eight siblings. Her father was an Anglican clergyman in a village in Hampshire, where she lived until she was 26. With the exception of four years in Bath and numerous trips to London, Kent, and elsewhere, she passed her entire life in this county of England. Her formal education (like most girls') ended at age 9; but her father continued to tutor her, and by her teens, she was writing in earnest. She began an irreverent and hilarious "History of England," and across the 1790s drafted numerous sketches and parodies, along with three novels. Initially, she had trouble getting a publisher. And even when she eventually found one for her novel *Susan* (later retitled *Northanger Abbey*), the publisher backed off. The family eventually published *Sense and Sensibility* in 1811 at their own expense (a common practice at the time), and with modest success. Austen received respectable but modest sums for her novels thereafter—between £110 and 150, when acclaimed writers such as Byron, Edgeworth, and Radcliffe were earning in the thousands. Aware of social strictures on women writers, Austen remained anonymous. The title page of *Sense and Sensibility* properly said "By a Lady"; *Pride and Prejudice* (1813) a little more pridefully advertised itself as a work by "the Author of 'Sense and Sensibility,'" and both *Mansfield Park* (1814) and *Emma* (1816) were signed more proudly yet, "By the Author of 'Pride and Prejudice,' &c. &c." After her death, Austen's brother Henry published *Northanger Abbey* and *Persuasion* in 1818, also anonymously. Despite the stance of anonymity, people in the know knew that Austen was the author. When the Prince Regent declared his admiration for her novels and hinted broadly that he would appreciate a dedication, his librarian knew whom to ask, and the result was the dedication of *Emma* to "His Royal Highness, the Prince Regent."

As the first dates of publication show, Austen's career of lifetime publication was compressed into less than a decade. Although she was always admired by connoisseurs, it was not until well after her death that she received wide acclaim, in the Victorian era and early twentieth century. The appeal has proved durable. Two hundred years after their initial drafting, Austen's novels enjoy international readership and new audiences through television and film. Such popularity might have astonished Austen, whose idiom, by her own admission, is rather confined: "the little bit (two Inches wide) of Ivory on which I work with so fine a Brush" is "3 or 4 families in a Country Village . . . the very thing to work on," as she put it, ironically but still aptly to her nephew and niece (both aspiring novelists).

This "thing" may seem otherworldly today. Its villages, townhouses, and great estates run on gossip and finely calibrated social codes punctuated by dinners, teas, and suppers; dances and recitals; evenings of backgammon and quadrille; afternoons of reading, letter writing, needlework; outings in chaises and barouche landaus. Its preoccupations are social status and display, land, property, and money (debts, prospects, incomes, and dowries). Its residents are given to leisure pursuits or only slightly busy. Servants and laborers are nearly invisible and never complain. Austen's provincial idiom and its conventions are not really narrow, however, for the deeper themes—coming of age, anticipating marriage, adjusting relations to parents, siblings, and friends, learning social protocols and testing boundaries, developing moral and intellectual maturity—are the basic pulse of emerging from adolescence to adulthood. Surrounding these heroines, moreover, is Austen's perdurably keen observation of their world (especially patriarchal society in its domestic and civic forms), given to a critical, at times satirical, scrutiny, beyond what her characters may see.

# PERSUASION

# NORTHANGER ABBEY:

## AND

# PERSUASION.

**BY THE AUTHOR OF "PRIDE AND PREJUDICE,"**

**"MANSFIELD-PARK," &c.**

WITH A BIOGRAPHICAL NOTICE OF THE
AUTHOR.

IN FOUR VOLUMES.

VOL. III.

LONDON:
JOHN MURRAY, ALBEMARLE-STREET.
1818.

# Persuasion

## VOLUME I
## CHAPTER I

Sir Walter Elliot, of Kellynch Hall, in Somersetshire, was a man who, for his own amusement, never took up any book but the Baronetage;[1] there he found occupation for an idle hour, and consolation in a distressed one; there his faculties were roused into admiration and respect, by contemplating the limited remnant of the earliest patents;[2] there any unwelcome sensations, arising from domestic affairs changed naturally into pity and contempt as he turned over the almost endless creations of the last century; and there, if every other leaf were powerless, he could read his own history with an interest which never failed. This was the page at which the favourite volume always opened:

**"ELLIOT OF KELLYNCH HALL.**

*Walter Elliot, born March 1, 1760, married, July 15, 1784, Elizabeth, daughter of James Stevenson, Esq. of South Park, in the county of Gloucester, by which lady (who died 1800) he has issue Elizabeth, born June 1, 1785; Anne, born August 9, 1787; a still-born son, November 5, 1789; Mary, born November 20, 1791.*

Precisely such had the paragraph originally stood from the printer's hands; but Sir Walter had improved it by adding, for the information of himself and his family, these words, after the date of Mary's birth—"Married, December 16, 1810, Charles, son and heir of Charles Musgrove, Esq. of Uppercross, in the county of

---

[1] A list of the order of baronets, who make up the lowest titled hereditary rank. Sir Walter is probably consulting Debrett's *Baronetage of England* (1808).

[2] The first baronets to be so designated.

Somerset," and by inserting most accurately the day of the month on which he had lost his wife.

Then followed the history and rise of the ancient and respectable family, in the usual terms; how it had been first settled in Cheshire; how mentioned in Dugdale,[3] serving the office of high sheriff, representing a borough in three successive parliaments, exertions of loyalty, and dignity of baronet, in the first year of Charles II, with all the Marys and Elizabeths they had married; forming altogether two handsome duodecimo pages,[4] and concluding with the arms and motto: :—"Principal seat, Kellynch Hall, in the county of Somerset," and Sir Walter's handwriting again in this finale: :—"Heir presumptive, William Walter Elliot, Esq., great grandson of the second Sir Walter." Vanity was the beginning and the end of Sir Walter Elliot's character; vanity of person and of situation. He had been remarkably handsome in his youth; and, at fifty-four, was still a very fine man. Few women could think more of their personal appearance than he did, nor could the valet of any new made lord be more delighted with the place he held in society. He considered the blessing of beauty as inferior only to the blessing of a baronetcy; and the Sir Walter Elliot, who united these gifts, was the constant object of his warmest respect and devotion.

His good looks and his rank had one fair claim on his attachment; since to them he must have owed a wife of very superior character to any thing deserved by his own. Lady Elliot had been an excellent woman, sensible and amiable; whose judgement and conduct, if they might be pardoned the youthful infatuation which made her Lady Elliot, had never required indulgence afterwards.— She had humoured, or softened, or concealed his failings, and promoted his real respectability for seventeen years; and though not the very happiest being in the world herself, had found enough in her duties, her friends, and her children, to attach her to life, and make it no matter of indifference to her when she was called on to quit them.—Three girls, the two eldest sixteen and fourteen, was an awful legacy for a mother to bequeath, an awful charge rather, to confide to the authority and guidance of a conceited, silly father.

---

[3] Sir William Dugdale, *The Ancient Usage in Bearing of Such Ensigns of Honour as Are Commonly Call'd Arms, with a Catalogue of the Present Nobility of England . . . Scotland . . . and Ireland* (1682).

[4] Pages sized to one-twelfth of a whole sheet. Austen's *Sense and Sensibility* and *Pride and Prejudice* had been published in this inexpensive form, with 24 pages per sheet, 12 on each side.

She had, however, one very intimate friend, a sensible, deserving woman, who had been brought, by strong attachment to herself, to settle close by her, in the village of Kellynch; and on her kindness and advice, Lady Elliot mainly relied for the best help and maintenance of the good principles and instruction which she had been anxiously giving her daughters.

This friend, and Sir Walter, did not marry, whatever might have been anticipated on that head by their acquaintance. Thirteen years had passed away since Lady Elliot's death, and they were still near neighbours and intimate friends, and one remained a widower, the other a widow.

That Lady Russell, of steady age and character, and extremely well provided for, should have no thought of a second marriage, needs no apology to the public, which is rather apt to be unreasonably discontented when a woman does marry again, than when she does not, but Sir Walter's continuing in singleness requires explanation. Be it known then, that Sir Walter, like a good father, (having met with one or two private disappointments in very unreasonable applications), prided himself on remaining single for his dear daughters' sake. For one daughter, his eldest, he would really have given up any thing, which he had not been very much tempted to do. Elizabeth had succeeded, at sixteen, to all that was possible, of her mother's rights and consequence; and being very handsome, and very like himself, her influence had always been great, and they had gone on together most happily. His two other children were of very inferior value. Mary had acquired a little artificial importance, by becoming Mrs. Charles Musgrove; but Anne, with an elegance of mind and sweetness of character, which must have placed her high with any people of real understanding, was nobody with either father or sister; her word had no weight, her convenience was always to give way— she was only Anne.

To Lady Russell, indeed, she was a most dear and highly valued goddaughter, favourite, and friend. Lady Russell loved them all; but it was only in Anne that she could fancy the mother to revive again.

A few years before, Anne Elliot had been a very pretty girl, but her bloom had vanished early, and as even in its height, her father had found little to admire in her, (so totally different were her delicate features and mild dark eyes from his own), there could be nothing in them, now that she was faded and thin, to excite his esteem. He had never indulged much hope, he had now none, of ever reading her name in any other page of his favourite work. All equality of alliance must rest with Elizabeth, for Mary had merely connected herself with an old country family of respectability and large fortune, and had therefore given all the honour and received none: Elizabeth would, one day or other, marry suitably.

It sometimes happens that a woman is handsomer at twenty-nine[5] than she was ten years before; and, generally speaking, if there has been neither ill health nor anxiety, it is a time of life at which scarcely any charm is lost. It was so with Elizabeth, still the same handsome Miss Elliot that she had begun to be thirteen years ago, and Sir Walter might be excused, therefore, in forgetting her age, or, at least, be deemed only half a fool, for thinking himself and Elizabeth as blooming as ever, amidst the wreck of the good looks of everybody else; for he could plainly see how old all the rest of his family and acquaintance were growing. Anne haggard, Mary coarse, every face in the neighbourhood worsting,[6] and the rapid increase of the crow's foot about Lady Russell's temples had long been a distress to him.

Elizabeth did not quite equal her father in personal contentment. Thirteen years had seen her mistress of Kellynch Hall, presiding and directing with a self-possession and decision which could never have given the idea of her being younger than she was. For thirteen years had she been doing the honours, and laying down the domestic law at home, and leading the way to the chaise and four,[7] and walking immediately after Lady Russell out of all the drawing-rooms and dining-rooms in the country. Thirteen winters' revolving frosts had seen her opening every ball of credit which a scanty neighbourhood afforded, and thirteen springs shewn their blossoms, as she travelled up to London with her father, for a few weeks' annual enjoyment of the great world. She had the remembrance of all this, she had the consciousness of being nine-and-twenty to give her some regrets and some apprehensions; she was fully satisfied of being still quite as handsome as ever, but she felt her approach to the years of danger, and would have rejoiced to be certain of being properly solicited by baronet-blood within the next twelvemonth or two. Then might she again take up the book of books[8] with as much enjoyment as in her early youth, but now she liked it not. Always to be presented with the date of her own birth and see no marriage follow but that of a

---

[5] At age 29, Anne would be deemed a "spinster," that is, a woman unlikely to marry.

[6] Getting worse.

[7] A carriage drawn by four horses—a very expensive conveyance.

[8] The Baronetage.

youngest sister, made the book an evil; and more than once, when her father had left it open on the table near her, had she closed it, with averted eyes, and pushed it away.

She had had a disappointment, moreover, which that book, and especially the history of her own family, must ever present the remembrance of. The heir presumptive, the very William Walter Elliot, Esq., whose rights had been so generously supported by her father, had disappointed her.

She had, while a very young girl, as soon as she had known him to be, in the event of her having no brother, the future baronet,[9] meant to marry him, and her father had always meant that she should. He had not been known to them as a boy; but soon after Lady Elliot's death, Sir Walter had sought the acquaintance, and though his overtures had not been met with any warmth, he had persevered in seeking it, making allowance for the modest drawing-back of youth; and, in one of their spring excursions to London, when Elizabeth was in her first bloom, Mr. Elliot had been forced into the introduction.

He was at that time a very young man, just engaged in the study of the law; and Elizabeth found him extremely agreeable, and every plan in his favour was confirmed. He was invited to Kellynch Hall; he was talked of and expected all the rest of the year; but he never came. The following spring he was seen again in town, found equally agreeable, again encouraged, invited, and expected, and again he did not come; and the next tidings were that he was married. Instead of pushing his fortune in the line marked out for the heir of the house of Elliot, he had purchased independence by uniting himself to a rich woman of inferior birth.

Sir Walter has resented it. As the head of the house, he felt that he ought to have been consulted, especially after taking the young man so publicly by the hand; "For they must have been seen together," he observed, "once at Tattersall's,[10] and twice in the lobby of the House of Commons." His disapprobation was expressed, but apparently very little regarded. Mr. Elliot had attempted no apology, and shewn himself as unsolicitous of being longer noticed by the family, as Sir Walter considered him unworthy of it: all acquaintance between them had ceased.

---

[9] Baronetcies are transferred by lineal descent only when there is a son. Otherwise they devolve upon the nearest male relative.

[10] A betting venue in London.

This very awkward history of Mr. Elliot was still, after an interval of several years, felt with anger by Elizabeth, who had liked the man for himself, and still more for being her father's heir, and whose strong family pride could see only in him a proper match for Sir Walter Elliot's eldest daughter. There was not a baronet from A to Z whom her feelings could have so willingly acknowledged as an equal. Yet so miserably had he conducted himself, that though she was at this present time (the summer of 1814[11]) wearing black ribbons for his wife,[12] she could not admit him to be worth thinking of again. The disgrace of his first marriage might, perhaps, as there was no reason to suppose it perpetuated by offspring, have been got over, had he not done worse; but he had, as by the accustomary intervention of kind friends, they had been informed, spoken most disrespectfully of them all, most slightingly and contemptuously of the very blood he belonged to, and the honours which were hereafter to be his own. This could not be pardoned.

Such were Elizabeth Elliot's sentiments and sensations; such the cares to alloy, the agitations to vary, the sameness and the elegance, the prosperity and the nothingness of her scene of life; such the feelings to give interest to a long, uneventful residence in one country circle, to fill the vacancies which there were no habits of utility abroad, no talents or accomplishments for home, to occupy.

But now, another occupation and solicitude of mind was beginning to be added to these. Her father was growing distressed for money. She knew, that when he now took up the *Baronetage*, it was to drive the heavy bills of his tradespeople,[13] and the unwelcome hints of Mr. Shepherd, his agent, from his thoughts. The Kellynch property was good, but not equal to Sir Walter's apprehension of the state required in its possessor. While Lady Elliot lived, there had been method, moderation, and economy, which had just kept him within his income, but with her had died all such right-mindedness, and from that period he had been constantly exceeding it. It had not been possible for him to spend less; he had done nothing but what Sir Walter

---

[11] The date is significant; England had ended its war with America, and Napoleon had been forced to abdicate his throne in April, and was now an exile on Elba. But from the perspective of the novel's time of composition, this would be viewed as a false security: Napoleon escaped Elba the next spring and marched on Paris. He was finally defeated by Wellington at Waterloo in June 1815.

[12] An indirect reference to Mrs. Elliot's relatively recent demise; black ribbons indicate mourning.

[13] Those in commerce or "trade," such as tailors and milliners.

Elliot was imperiously called on to do; but blameless as he was, he was not only growing dreadfully in debt, but was hearing of it so often, that it became vain to attempt concealing it longer, even partially, from his daughter. He had given her some hints of it the last spring in town; he had gone so far even as to say, "Can we retrench? Does it occur to you that there is any one article in which we can retrench?" and Elizabeth, to do her justice, had, in the first ardour of female alarm, set seriously to think what could be done, and had finally proposed these two branches of economy, to cut off some unnecessary charities, and to refrain from new furnishing the drawing-room; to which expedients she afterwards added the happy thought of their taking no present down to Anne, as had been the usual yearly custom. But these measures, however good in themselves, were insufficient for the real extent of the evil, the whole of which Sir Walter found himself obliged to confess to her soon afterwards. Elizabeth had nothing to propose of deeper efficacy. She felt herself ill-used and unfortunate, as did her father; and they were neither of them able to devise any means of lessening their expenses without compromising their dignity, or relinquishing their comforts in a way not to be borne.

There was only a small part of his estate that Sir Walter could dispose of; but had every acre been alienable,[14] it would have made no difference. He had condescended to mortgage as far as he had the power, but he would never condescend[15] to sell. No; he would never disgrace his name so far. The Kellynch estate should be transmitted whole and entire, as he had received it. Their two confidential friends, Mr. Shepherd, who lived in the neighbouring market town, and Lady Russell, were called to advise them; and both father and daughter seemed to expect that something should be struck out by one or the other to remove their embarrassments and reduce their expenditure, without involving the loss of any indulgence of taste or pride.

# CHAPTER II

Mr. Shepherd, a civil, cautious lawyer, who, whatever might be his hold or his views on Sir Walter, would rather have the disagreeable prompted by anybody else, excused himself from offering the slightest hint, and only begged leave to recommend an implicit

---

[14] Disposable; available to be sold.

[15] To acquiesce to a position or action and/or to lower oneself.

reference to the excellent judgement of Lady Russell, from whose known good sense he fully expected to have just such resolute measures advised as he meant to see finally adopted.

Lady Russell was most anxiously zealous on the subject, and gave it much serious consideration. She was a woman rather of sound than of quick abilities, whose difficulties in coming to any decision in this instance were great, from the opposition of two leading principles. She was of strict integrity herself, with a delicate sense of honour; but she was as desirous of saving Sir Walter's feelings, as solicitous for the credit of the family, as aristocratic in her ideas of what was due to them, as anybody of sense and honesty could well be. She was a benevolent, charitable, good woman, and capable of strong attachments, most correct in her conduct, strict in her notions of decorum, and with manners that were held a standard of good-breeding. She had a cultivated mind, and was, generally speaking, rational and consistent; but she had prejudices on the side of ancestry; she had a value for rank and consequence, which blinded her a little to the faults of those who possessed them. Herself the widow of only a knight,[1] she gave the dignity of a baronet all its due; and Sir Walter, independent of his claims as an old acquaintance, an attentive neighbour, an obliging landlord, the husband of her very dear friend, the father of Anne and her sisters, was, as being Sir Walter, in her apprehension, entitled to a great deal of compassion and consideration under his present difficulties.

They must retrench; that did not admit of a doubt. But she was very anxious to have it done with the least possible pain to him and Elizabeth. She drew up plans of economy, she made exact calculations, and she did what nobody else thought of doing: she consulted Anne, who never seemed considered by the others as having any interest in the question. She consulted, and in a degree was influenced by her in marking out the scheme of retrenchment which was at last submitted to Sir Walter. Every emendation of Anne's had been on the side of honesty against importance. She wanted more vigorous measures, a more complete reformation, a quicker release from debt, a much higher tone of indifference for everything but justice and equity.

"If we can persuade your father to all this," said Lady Russell, looking over her paper, "much may be done. If he will adopt these regulations, in seven years he will be clear; and I hope we may be able

[1] A non-hereditary title conferred on the basis of merit or service.

to convince him and Elizabeth, that Kellynch Hall has a respectability in itself which cannot be affected by these reductions; and that the true dignity of Sir Walter Elliot will be very far from lessened in the eyes of sensible people, by acting like a man of principle. What will he be doing, in fact, but what very many of our first families have done, or ought to do? There will be nothing singular in his case; and it is singularity which often makes the worst part of our suffering, as it always does of our conduct. I have great hope of prevailing. We must be serious and decided; for after all, the person who has contracted debts must pay them; and though a great deal is due to the feelings of the gentleman, and the head of a house, like your father, there is still more due to the character of an honest man."

This was the principle on which Anne wanted her father to be proceeding, his friends to be urging him. She considered it as an act of indispensable duty to clear away the claims of creditors with all the expedition[2] which the most comprehensive retrenchments could secure, and saw no dignity in anything short of it. She wanted it to be prescribed, and felt as a duty. She rated Lady Russell's influence highly; and as to the severe degree of self-denial which her own conscience prompted, she believed there might be little more difficulty in persuading them to a complete, than to half a reformation. Her knowledge of her father and Elizabeth inclined her to think that the sacrifice of one pair of horses would be hardly less painful than of both, and so on, through the whole list of Lady Russell's too gentle reductions.

How Anne's more rigid requisitions might have been taken is of little consequence. Lady Russell's had no success at all: could not be put up with, were not to be borne. "What! every comfort of life knocked off! Journeys, London, servants, horses, table—contractions and restrictions every where! To live no longer with the decencies even of a private gentleman! No, he would sooner quit Kellynch Hall at once, than remain in it on such disgraceful terms."

"Quit Kellynch Hall." The hint was immediately taken up by Mr. Shepherd, whose interest was involved in the reality of Sir Walter's retrenching, and who was perfectly persuaded that nothing would be done without a change of abode. "Since the idea had been started in the very quarter which ought to dictate, he had no scruple," he said, "in confessing his judgement to be entirely on that side. It did not appear to him that Sir Walter could materially alter his style of

[2] Efficiency.

living in a house which had such a character of hospitality and ancient dignity to support. In any other place Sir Walter might judge for himself; and would be looked up to, as regulating the modes of life in whatever way he might choose to model his household."

Sir Walter would quit Kellynch Hall; and after a very few days more of doubt and indecision, the great question of whither he should go was settled, and the first outline of this important change made out.

There had been three alternatives, London, Bath, or another house in the country. All Anne's wishes had been for the latter. A small house in their own neighbourhood, where they might still have Lady Russell's society, still be near Mary, and still have the pleasure of sometimes seeing the lawns and groves of Kellynch, was the object of her ambition. But the usual fate of Anne attended her, in having something very opposite from her inclination fixed on. She disliked Bath, and did not think it agreed with her; and Bath was to be her home.

Sir Walter had at first thought more of London; but Mr. Shepherd felt that he could not be trusted in London, and had been skilful enough to dissuade him from it, and make Bath preferred. It was a much safer place for a gentleman in his predicament: he might there be important at comparatively little expense. Two material advantages of Bath over London had of course been given all their weight: its more convenient distance from Kellynch, only fifty miles, and Lady Russell's spending some part of every winter there; and to the very great satisfaction of Lady Russell, whose first views on the projected change had been for Bath, Sir Walter and Elizabeth were induced to believe that they should lose neither consequence[3] nor enjoyment by settling there.

Lady Russell felt obliged to oppose her dear Anne's known wishes. It would be too much to expect Sir Walter to descend into a small house in his own neighbourhood. Anne herself would have found the mortifications of it more than she foresaw, and to Sir Walter's feelings they must have been dreadful. And with regard to Anne's dislike of Bath, she considered it as a prejudice and mistake arising, first, from the circumstance of her having been three years at school there, after her mother's death; and secondly, from her happening to be not in perfectly good spirits the only winter which she had afterwards spent there with herself.

---

[3] Importance; social standing.

Lady Russell was fond of Bath, in short, and disposed to think it must suit them all; and as to her young friend's health, by passing all the warm months with her at Kellynch Lodge, every danger would be avoided; and it was in fact, a change which must do both health and spirits good. Anne had been too little from home, too little seen. Her spirits were not high. A larger society would improve them. She wanted her to be more known.

The undesirableness of any other house in the same neighbourhood for Sir Walter was certainly much strengthened by one part, and a very material part of the scheme, which had been happily engrafted on the beginning. He was not only to quit his home, but to see it in the hands of others; a trial of fortitude, which stronger heads than Sir Walter's have found too much. Kellynch Hall was to be let.[4] This, however, was a profound secret, not to be breathed beyond their own circle.

Sir Walter could not have borne the degradation of being known to design letting his house. Mr. Shepherd had once mentioned the word "advertise," but never dared approach it again. Sir Walter spurned the idea of its being offered in any manner; forbad the slightest hint being dropped of his having such an intention; and it was only on the supposition of his being spontaneously solicited by some most unexceptionable applicant, on his own terms, and as a great favour, that he would let it at all.

How quick come the reasons for approving what we like! Lady Russell had another excellent one at hand, for being extremely glad that Sir Walter and his family were to remove from the country. Elizabeth had been lately forming an intimacy, which she wished to see interrupted. It was with the daughter of Mr. Shepherd, who had returned, after an unprosperous[5] marriage, to her father's house, with the additional burden of two children. She was a clever young woman, who understood the art of pleasing—the art of pleasing, at least, at Kellynch Hall; and who had made herself so acceptable to Miss Elliot, as to have been already staying there more than once, in spite of all that Lady Russell, who thought it a friendship quite out of place, could hint of caution and reserve.

Lady Russell, indeed, had scarcely any influence with Elizabeth, and seemed to love her, rather because she would love her, than because Elizabeth deserved it. She had never received from her

[4] Leased.
[5] Unsuccessful.

more than outward attention, nothing beyond the observances of complaisance; had never succeeded in any point which she wanted to carry, against previous inclination. She had been repeatedly very earnest in trying to get Anne included in the visit to London, sensibly open to all the injustice and all the discredit of the selfish arrangements which shut her out, and on many lesser occasions had endeavoured to give Elizabeth the advantage of her own better judgement and experience; but always in vain: Elizabeth would go her own way; and never had she pursued it in more decided opposition to Lady Russell than in this selection of Mrs. Clay; turning from the society of so deserving a sister, to bestow her affection and confidence on one who ought to have been nothing to her but the object of distant civility.

From situation, Mrs. Clay was, in Lady Russell's estimate, a very unequal, and in her character she believed a very dangerous companion; and a removal that would leave Mrs. Clay behind, and bring a choice of more suitable intimates within Miss Elliot's reach, was therefore an object of first-rate importance.

## CHAPTER III

"I must take leave to observe, Sir Walter," said Mr. Shepherd one morning at Kellynch Hall, as he laid down the newspaper, "that the present juncture is much in our favour. This peace will be turning all our rich naval officers ashore.[1] They will be all wanting a home. Could not be a better time, Sir Walter, for having a choice of tenants, very responsible tenants. Many a noble fortune has been made during the war.[2] If a rich admiral were to come in our way, Sir Walter—"

"He would be a very lucky man, Shepherd," replied Sir Walter; "that's all I have to remark. A prize indeed would Kellynch Hall be to him; rather the greatest prize of all, let him have taken ever so many before; hey, Shepherd?"

Mr. Shepherd laughed, as he knew he must, at this wit, and then added—

---

[1] With the end of the Napoleonic wars and Britain secure in its peace, many officers were decommissioned.

[2] Ships belonging to the nation of the enemy were routinely taken as "prizes" during the wars with France and merchant ships sailing under the enemy's flag were especially lucrative for the officers who captured them.

"I presume to observe, Sir Walter, that, in the way of business, gentlemen of the navy are well to deal with. I have had a little knowledge of their methods of doing business; and I am free to confess that they have very liberal notions, and are as likely to make desirable tenants as any set of people one should meet with. Therefore, Sir Walter, what I would take leave to suggest is that if in consequence of any rumours getting abroad of your intention, which must be contemplated as a possible thing, because we know how difficult it is to keep the actions and designs of one part of the world from the notice and curiosity of the other, consequence has its tax; I, John Shepherd, might conceal any family-matters that I chose, for nobody would think it worth their while to observe me; but Sir Walter Elliot has eyes upon him which it may be very difficult to elude; and therefore, thus much I venture upon, that it will not greatly surprise me if, with all our caution, some rumour of the truth should get abroad; in the supposition of which, as I was going to observe, since applications will unquestionably follow, I should think any from our wealthy naval commanders particularly worth attending to; and beg leave to add that two hours will bring me over at any time, to save you the trouble of replying."

Sir Walter only nodded. But soon afterwards, rising and pacing the room, he observed sarcastically—

"There are few among the gentlemen of the navy, I imagine, who would not be surprised to find themselves in a house of this description."

"They would look around them, no doubt, and bless their good fortune," said Mrs. Clay, for Mrs. Clay was present: her father had driven her over, nothing being of so much use to Mrs. Clay's health as a drive to Kellynch: "but I quite agree with my father in thinking a sailor might be a very desirable tenant. I have known a good deal of the profession; and besides their liberality, they are so neat and careful in all their ways! These valuable pictures of yours, Sir Walter, if you chose to leave them, would be perfectly safe. Everything in and about the house would be taken such excellent care of! The gardens and shrubberies would be kept in almost as high order as they are now. You need not be afraid, Miss Elliot, of your own sweet flower gardens being neglected."

"As to all that," rejoined Sir Walter coolly, "supposing I were induced to let my house, I have by no means made up my mind as to the privileges to be annexed to it. I am not particularly disposed to favour a tenant. The park would be open to him of course, and few navy officers, or men of any other description, can have had such a range; but what restrictions I might impose on the use of the pleasure-grounds, is another thing.[3] I am not fond of the idea of my shrubberies being always approachable; and I should recommend Miss Elliot to be on her guard with respect to her flower garden. I am very little disposed to grant a tenant of Kellynch Hall any extraordinary favour, I assure you, be he sailor or soldier."

After a short pause, Mr. Shepherd presumed to say—

"In all these cases, there are established usages which make everything plain and easy between landlord and tenant. Your interest, Sir Walter, is in pretty safe hands. Depend upon me for taking care that no tenant has more than his just rights. I venture to hint, that Sir Walter Elliot cannot be half so jealous for his own, as John Shepherd will be for him."

Here Anne spoke—"The navy, I think, who have done so much for us, have at least an equal claim with any other set of men, for all the comforts and all the privileges which any home can give. Sailors work hard enough for their comforts, we must all allow."

"Very true, very true. What Miss Anne says is very true," was Mr. Shepherd's rejoinder, and "Oh! certainly," was his daughter's; but Sir Walter's remark was, soon afterwards—"The profession has its utility, but I should be sorry to see any friend of mine belonging to it." "Indeed!" was the reply, and with a look of surprise. "Yes; it is in two points offensive to me; I have two strong grounds of objection to it. First, as being the means of bringing persons of obscure birth into undue distinction, and raising men to honours which their fathers and grandfathers never dreamt of;[4] and secondly, as it cuts up a man's youth and vigour most horribly; a sailor grows old sooner than any other man. I have observed it all my life. A man is in greater danger in the navy of being insulted by the rise of one whose father, his father might have disdained to speak to, and of

[3] Kellynch "park"—the grounds of the estate—will be available for hunting, touring, and other activities. The "pleasure-grounds," landscaped and maintained for entertainments, might contain gardens, mazes, statuary, and architectural ornaments—the preservation of which is of concern to Sir Walter.

[4] Two of the three traditional "professions"—the law and the Church—required a university education and were generally pursued by younger sons of wealthy families, whose estates were entailed to rules of primogeniture, by which the oldest son was the sole heir. The third profession—the officers' corps of the military—had fewer prerequisites and was more open to members of the "middling" classes. The newest profession, medicine, was just achieving "professional" status.

becoming prematurely an object of disgust himself, than in any other line. One day last spring, in town, I was in company with two men, striking instances of what I am talking of; Lord St Ives, whose father we all know to have been a country curate, without bread to eat; I was to give place to Lord St Ives, and a certain Admiral Baldwin, the most deplorable-looking personage you can imagine; his face the colour of mahogany, rough and rugged to the last degree; all lines and wrinkles, nine grey hairs of a side, and nothing but a dab of powder at top. 'In the name of heaven, who is that old fellow?' said I to a friend of mine who was standing near, (Sir Basil Morley). 'Old fellow!' cried Sir Basil, 'it is Admiral Baldwin. What do you take his age to be?' 'Sixty,' said I, 'or perhaps sixty-two.' 'Forty,' replied Sir Basil, 'forty, and no more.' Picture to yourselves my amazement; I shall not easily forget Admiral Baldwin. I never saw quite so wretched an example of what a sea-faring life can do; but to a degree, I know it is the same with them all: they are all knocked about, and exposed to every climate, and every weather, till they are not fit to be seen. It is a pity they are not knocked on the head at once, before they reach Admiral Baldwin's age."

"Nay, Sir Walter," cried Mrs. Clay, "this is being severe indeed. Have a little mercy on the poor men. We are not all born to be handsome. The sea is no beautifier, certainly; sailors do grow old betimes; I have observed it; they soon lose the look of youth. But then, is not it the same with many other professions, perhaps most other? Soldiers, in active service, are not at all better off: and even in the quieter professions, there is a toil and a labour of the mind, if not of the body, which seldom leaves a man's looks to the natural effect of time. The lawyer plods, quite care-worn; the physician is up at all hours, and travelling in all weather; and even the clergyman"—she stopt a moment to consider what might do for the clergyman;—"and even the clergyman, you know is obliged to go into infected rooms, and expose his health and looks to all the injury of a poisonous atmosphere. In fact, as I have long been convinced, though every profession is necessary and honourable in its turn, it is only the lot of those who are not obliged to follow any, who can live in a regular way, in the country, choosing their own hours, following their own pursuits, and living on their own property, without the torment of trying for more; it is only their lot, I say, to hold the blessings of health and a good appearance to the utmost: I know no other set of men but what lose something of their personableness when they cease to be quite young."

It seemed as if Mr. Shepherd, in this anxiety to bespeak Sir Walter's goodwill towards a naval officer as tenant, had been gifted with foresight; for the very first application for the house was from an Admiral Croft, with whom he shortly afterwards fell into company in attending the quarter sessions at Taunton;[5] and indeed, he had received a hint of the Admiral from a London correspondent. By the report which he hastened over to Kellynch to make, Admiral Croft was a native of Somersetshire, who having acquired a very handsome fortune, was wishing to settle in his own country, and had come down to Taunton in order to look at some advertised places in that immediate neighbourhood, which, however, had not suited him; that accidentally hearing—(it was just as he had foretold, Mr. Shepherd observed, Sir Walter's concerns could not be kept a secret)—accidentally hearing of the possibility of Kellynch Hall being to let, and understanding his (Mr. Shepherd's) connection with the owner, he had introduced himself to him in order to make particular inquiries, and had, in the course of a pretty long conference, expressed as strong an inclination for the place as a man who knew it only by description could feel; and given Mr. Shepherd, in his explicit account of himself, every proof of his being a most responsible, eligible tenant.

"And who is Admiral Croft?" was Sir Walter's cold suspicious inquiry. Mr. Shepherd answered for his being of a gentleman's family, and mentioned a place; and Anne, after the little pause which followed, added—

"He is a rear admiral of the white.[6] He was in the Trafalgar action, and has been in the East Indies since;[7] he was stationed there, I believe, several years."

"Then I take it for granted," observed Sir Walter, "that his face is about as orange as the cuffs and capes of my livery."

Mr. Shepherd hastened to assure him that Admiral Croft was a very hale, hearty, well-looking man, a little weather-beaten, to be

---

[5] A court of limited criminal and civil jurisdiction, and of appeal, held quarterly by justices of the peace (*Oxford English Dictionary*). Austen's maternal aunt, Jane Leigh Perrot, was tried in Taunton in 1800 for shoplifting lace.

[6] The British Navy was divided into three squadrons: the red, the white, and the blue.

[7] In battle of Trafalgar in 1805 the British Navy under Admiral Nelson defeated Napoleon's forces giving Britain naval superiority worldwide. Nelson died during the battle. The author's oldest brother, Francis, served under Nelson at Trafalgar and was also a captain in the East India Company, a private company that was given a monopoly on all trade with the East Indies and in which naval officers typically served.

sure, but not much, and quite the gentleman in all his notions and behaviour; not likely to make the smallest difficulty about terms, only wanted a comfortable home, and to get into it as soon as possible; knew he must pay for his convenience; knew what rent a ready-furnished house of that consequence might fetch; should not have been surprised if Sir Walter had asked more; had inquired about the manor; would be glad of the deputation,[8] certainly, but made no great point of it; said he sometimes took out a gun, but never killed; quite the gentleman.

Mr. Shepherd was eloquent on the subject; pointing out all the circumstances of the Admiral's family, which made him peculiarly desirable as a tenant. He was a married man, and without children; the very state to be wished for. A house was never taken good care of, Mr. Shepherd observed, without a lady: he did not know, whether furniture might not be in danger of suffering as much where there was no lady, as where there were many children. A lady, without a family, was the very best preserver of furniture in the world. He had seen Mrs. Croft, too; she was at Taunton with the admiral, and had been present almost all the time they were talking the matter over.

"And a very well-spoken, genteel, shrewd lady, she seemed to be," continued he; "asked more questions about the house, and terms, and taxes, than the Admiral himself, and seemed more conversant with business; and moreover, Sir Walter, I found she was not quite unconnected in this country, any more than her husband; that is to say, she is sister to a gentleman who did live amongst us once; she told me so herself: sister to the gentleman who lived a few years back at Monkford. Bless me! what was his name? At this moment I cannot recollect his name, though I have heard it so lately. Penelope, my dear, can you help me to the name of the gentleman who lived at Monkford: Mrs. Croft's brother?"

But Mrs. Clay was talking so eagerly with Miss Elliot, that she did not hear the appeal.

"I have no conception whom you can mean, Shepherd; I remember no gentleman resident at Monkford since the time of old Governor Trent."

"Bless me! how very odd! I shall forget my own name soon, I suppose. A name that I am so very well acquainted with; knew the gentleman so well by sight; seen him a hundred times; came to consult me once, I remember, about a trespass of one of his neighbours;

[8] The right to hunt, presumably in the park.

farmer's man breaking into his orchard; wall torn down; apples stolen; caught in the fact; and afterwards, contrary to my judgement, submitted to an amicable compromise. Very odd indeed!"

After waiting another moment—

"You mean Mr. Wentworth, I suppose?" said Anne.

Mr. Shepherd was all gratitude.

"Wentworth was the very name! Mr. Wentworth was the very man. He had the curacy of Monkford,[9] you know, Sir Walter, some time back, for two or three years. Came there about the year—5, I take it. You remember him, I am sure."

"Wentworth? Oh! ay,—Mr. Wentworth, the curate of Monkford. You misled me by the term gentleman. I thought you were speaking of some man of property: Mr. Wentworth was nobody, I remember; quite unconnected; nothing to do with the Strafford family. One wonders how the names of many of our nobility become so common."

As Mr. Shepherd perceived that this connexion of the Crofts did them no service with Sir Walter, he mentioned it no more; returning, with all his zeal, to dwell on the circumstances more indisputably in their favour; their age, and number, and fortune; the high idea they had formed of Kellynch Hall, and extreme solicitude for the advantage of renting it; making it appear as if they ranked nothing beyond the happiness of being the tenants of Sir Walter Elliot: an extraordinary taste, certainly, could they have been supposed in the secret of Sir Walter's estimate of the dues of a tenant.

It succeeded, however; and though Sir Walter must ever look with an evil eye on anyone intending to inhabit that house, and think them infinitely too well off in being permitted to rent it on the highest terms, he was talked into allowing Mr. Shepherd to proceed in the treaty, and authorising him to wait on Admiral Croft, who still remained at Taunton, and fix a day for the house being seen.

Sir Walter was not very wise; but still he had experience enough of the world to feel, that a more unobjectionable tenant, in all essentials, than Admiral Croft bid fair to be, could hardly offer. So far went his understanding; and his vanity supplied a little additional soothing, in the Admiral's situation in life, which was just high enough, and not too high. "I have let my house to Admiral Croft," would sound extremely well; very much better than to any

---

[9] Curacies or clerical positions were typically given to their holders as "livings" by patrons who were typically members of the landed aristocracy.

mere Mr.———; a Mr. (save, perhaps, some half dozen in the nation) always needs a note of explanation. An admiral speaks his own consequence, and, at the same time, can never make a baronet look small. In all their dealings and intercourse, Sir Walter Elliot must ever have the precedence.

Nothing could be done without a reference to Elizabeth: but her inclination was growing so strong for a removal, that she was happy to have it fixed and expedited by a tenant at hand; and not a word to suspend decision was uttered by her.

Mr. Shepherd was completely empowered to act; and no sooner had such an end been reached, than Anne, who had been a most attentive listener to the whole, left the room, to seek the comfort of cool air for her flushed cheeks; and as she walked along a favourite grove, said, with a gentle sigh, "A few months more, and he, perhaps, may be walking here."

# CHAPTER IV

He was not Mr. Wentworth, the former curate of Monkford, however suspicious appearances may be, but a Captain Frederick Wentworth, his brother, who being made commander in consequence of the action off St. Domingo, and not immediately employed, had come into Somersetshire, in the summer of 1806; and having no parent living, found a home for half a year at Monkford. He was, at that time, a remarkably fine young man, with a great deal of intelligence, spirit, and brilliancy; and Anne an extremely pretty girl, with gentleness, modesty, taste, and feeling. Half the sum of attraction, on either side, might have been enough, for he had nothing to do, and she had hardly anybody to love; but the encounter of such lavish recommendations could not fail. They were gradually acquainted, and when acquainted, rapidly and deeply in love. It would be difficult to say which had seen highest perfection in the other, or which had been the happiest: she, in receiving his declarations and proposals, or he in having them accepted.

A short period of exquisite felicity followed, and but a short one. Troubles soon arose. Sir Walter, on being applied to, without actually withholding his consent, or saying it should never be, gave it all the negative of great astonishment, great coldness, great silence, and a professed resolution of doing nothing for his daughter.[1] He thought it a very degrading alliance; and Lady Russell, though with more tempered and pardonable pride, received it as a most unfortunate one.

Anne Elliot, with all her claims of birth, beauty, and mind, to throw herself away at nineteen; involve herself at nineteen in an engagement with a young man, who had nothing but himself to recommend him, and no hopes of attaining affluence, but in the chances of a most uncertain profession,[2] and no connexions to secure even his farther rise in the profession, would be, indeed, a throwing away, which she grieved to think of! Anne Elliot, so young; known to so few, to be snatched off by a stranger without alliance or fortune; or rather sunk by him into a state of most wearing, anxious, youth-killing dependence! It must not be, if by any fair interference of friendship, any representations from one who had almost a mother's love, and mother's rights, it would be prevented.

Captain Wentworth had no fortune. He had been lucky in his profession; but spending freely, what had come freely, had realized nothing. But he was confident that he should soon be rich: full of life and ardor, he knew that he should soon have a ship, and soon be on a station that would lead to everything he wanted.[3] He had always been lucky; he knew he should be so still. Such confidence, powerful in its own warmth, and bewitching in the wit which often expressed it, must have been enough for Anne; but Lady Russell saw it very differently. His sanguine temper, and fearlessness of mind, operated very differently on her. She saw in it but an aggravation of the evil. It only added a dangerous character to himself. He was brilliant, he was headstrong. Lady Russell had little taste for wit, and of anything approaching to imprudence a horror. She deprecated the connexion in every light.

Such opposition, as these feelings produced, was more than Anne could combat. Young and gentle as she was, it might yet have been possible to withstand her father's ill will, though unsoftened by one kind word or look on the part of her sister; but Lady Russell, whom she had always loved and relied on, could not, with such steadiness of opinion, and such tenderness of manner, be continually

---

[1] Although the Elliot estate will devolve upon a male descendent or relative, Anne could have expected a dowry from her father, which he apparently threatened to withhold.

[2] A reference, again, to Wentworth's naval career.

[3] A new command that would allow Wentworth to continue his "lucky" run in achieving victories and prizes.

advising her in vain. She was persuaded to believe the engagement a wrong thing: indiscreet, improper, hardly capable of success, and not deserving it. But it was not a merely selfish caution, under which she acted, in putting an end to it. Had she not imagined herself consulting his good, even more than her own, she could hardly have given him up. The belief of being prudent, and self-denying, principally for his advantage, was her chief consolation, under the misery of a parting, a final parting; and every consolation was required, for she had to encounter all the additional pain of opinions, on his side, totally unconvinced and unbending, and of his feeling himself ill used by so forced a relinquishment. He had left the country in consequence.

A few months had seen the beginning and the end of their acquaintance; but not with a few months ended Anne's share of suffering from it. Her attachment and regrets had, for a long time, clouded every enjoyment of youth, and an early loss of bloom and spirits had been their lasting effect.

More than seven years were gone since this little history of sorrowful interest had reached its close; and time had softened down much, perhaps nearly all of peculiar attachment to him, but she had been too dependent on time alone; no aid had been given in change of place (except in one visit to Bath soon after the rupture), or in any novelty or enlargement of society. No one had ever come within the Kellynch circle, who could bear a comparison with Frederick Wentworth, as he stood in her memory. No second attachment,[4] the only thoroughly natural, happy, and sufficient cure, at her time of life, had been possible to the nice tone of her mind, the fastidiousness of her taste, in the small limits of the society around them. She had been solicited, when about two-and-twenty, to change her name, by the young man, who not long afterwards found a more willing mind in her younger sister;[5] and Lady Russell had lamented her refusal; for Charles Musgrove was the eldest son of a man, whose landed property and general importance were second in that country, only to Sir Walter's, and of good character and appearance; and however Lady Russell might have asked yet for something more, while Anne was nineteen, she would have rejoiced to see her at

[4] On the primacy of "first" vs. "second" attachments, see *Sense and Sensibility*, Chapter 11.

[5] So, too, in *Pride and Prejudice* does the near spinster (age 28) Charlotte Lucas quickly take advantage of her younger friend Elizabeth Bennet's rejection of Mr. Collins' proposal of marriage.

twenty-two so respectably removed from the partialities and injustice of her father's house, and settled so permanently near herself. But in this case, Anne had left nothing for advice to do; and though Lady Russell, as satisfied as ever with her own discretion, never wished the past undone, she began now to have the anxiety which borders on hopelessness for Anne's being tempted, by some man of talents and independence, to enter a state for which she held her to be peculiarly fitted by her warm affections and domestic habits.

They knew not each other's opinion, either its constancy or its change, on the one leading point of Anne's conduct, for the subject was never alluded to; but Anne, at seven-and-twenty, thought very differently from what she had been made to think at nineteen. She did not blame Lady Russell, she did not blame herself for having been guided by her; but she felt that were any young person, in similar circumstances, to apply to her for counsel, they would never receive any of such certain immediate wretchedness, such uncertain future good. She was persuaded that under every disadvantage of disapprobation at home, and every anxiety attending his profession, all their probable fears, delays, and disappointments, she should yet have been a happier woman in maintaining the engagement, than she had been in the sacrifice of it; and this—she fully believed, had the usual share,—had even more than the usual share of all such solicitudes and suspense been theirs, without reference to the actual results of their case, which, as it happened, would have bestowed earlier prosperity than could be reasonably calculated on. All his sanguine expectations, all his confidence had been justified. His genius and ardour had seemed to foresee and to command his prosperous path. He had, very soon after their engagement ceased, got employ: and all that he had told her would follow, had taken place. He had distinguished himself, and early gained the other step in rank, and must now, by successive captures, have made a handsome fortune. She had only navy lists[6] and newspapers for her authority, but she could not doubt his being rich; and, in favour of his constancy, she had no reason to believe him married.

How eloquent could Anne Elliot have been! how eloquent, at least, were her wishes on the side of early warm attachment, and a cheerful confidence in futurity, against that overanxious caution which seems to insult exertion and distrust Providence! She had

[6] Publications of the British Navy, identifying the actions and the leadership of various ships.

been forced into prudence in her youth, she learned romance as she grew older: the natural sequel of an unnatural beginning.

With all these circumstances, recollections and feelings, she could not hear that Captain Wentworth's sister was likely to live at Kellynch without a revival of former pain; and many a stroll, and many a sigh, were necessary to dispel the agitation of the idea. She often told herself it was folly, before she could harden her nerves sufficiently to feel the continual discussion of the Crofts and their business no evil. She was assisted, however, by that perfect indifference and apparent unconsciousness, among the only three of her own friends in the secret of the past, which seemed almost to deny any recollection of it. She could do justice to the superiority of Lady Russell's motives in this, over those of her father and Elizabeth; she could honour all the better feelings of her calmness; but the general air of oblivion among them was highly important from whatever it sprung; and in the event of Admiral Croft's really taking Kellynch Hall, she rejoiced anew over the conviction which had always been most grateful to her, of the past being known to those three only among her connexions, by whom no syllable, she believed, would ever be whispered, and in the trust that among his, the brother only with whom he had been residing, had received any information of their short-lived engagement. That brother had been long removed from the country and being a sensible man, and, moreover, a single man at the time, she had a fond dependence on no human creature's having heard of it from him.

The sister, Mrs. Croft, had then been out of England, accompanying her husband on a foreign station, and her own sister, Mary, had been at school while it all occurred; and never admitted by the pride of some, and the delicacy of others, to the smallest knowledge of it afterwards. With these supports, she hoped that the acquaintance between herself and the Crofts, which, with Lady Russell, still resident in Kellynch and Mary fixed only three miles off, must be anticipated, need not involve any particular awkwardness.

# CHAPTER V

On the morning appointed for Admiral and Mrs. Croft's seeing Kellynch Hall, Anne found it most natural to take her almost daily walk to Lady Russell's, and keep out of the way till all was over; when she found it most natural to be sorry that she had missed the opportunity of seeing them.

This meeting of the two parties proved highly satisfactory, and decided the whole business at once. Each lady was previously well disposed for an agreement, and saw nothing, therefore, but good manners in the other; and with regard to the gentlemen, there was such an hearty good humour, such an open, trusting liberality on the Admiral's side, as could not but influence Sir Walter, who had besides been flattered into his very best and most polished behaviour by Mr. Shepherd's assurances of his being known, by report, to the Admiral, as a model of good breeding.

The house and grounds, and furniture, were approved, the Crofts were approved, terms, time, every thing, and every body, was right; and Mr. Shepherd's clerks were set to work, without there having been a single preliminary difference to modify of all that "This indenture sheweth."

Sir Walter, without hesitation, declared the Admiral to be the best-looking sailor he had ever met with, and went so far as to say, that if his own man might have had the arranging of his hair, he should not be ashamed of being seen with him any where; and the Admiral, with sympathetic cordiality, observed to his wife as they drove back through the park, "I thought we should soon come to a deal, my dear, in spite of what they told us at Taunton. The Baronet will never set the Thames on fire, but there seems to be no harm in him," reciprocal compliments, which would have been esteemed about equal.

The Crofts were to have possession at Michaelmas;[1] and as Sir Walter proposed removing to Bath in the course of the preceding month, there was no time to be lost in making every dependent arrangement.

Lady Russell, convinced that Anne would not be allowed to be of any use or any importance, in the choice of the house which they were going to secure, was very unwilling to have her hurried away so soon, and wanted to make it possible for her to stay behind till she might convey her to Bath herself after Christmas; but having engagements of her own which must take her from Kellynch for several weeks, she was unable to give the full invitation she wished, and Anne though dreading the possible heats of September in all the white glare of Bath, and grieving to forego all the influence so sweet

---

[1] September 29, on which the feast of St. Michael the Archangel is celebrated. This is one of the four quarter-days of the business year, in which, for example, leases would commence.

and so sad of the autumnal months in the country, did not think that, everything considered, she wished to remain. It would be most right, and most wise, and, therefore must involve least suffering to go with the others.

Something occurred, however, to give her a different duty. Mary, often a little unwell, and always thinking a great deal of her own complaints, and always in the habit of claiming Anne when anything was the matter, was indisposed; and foreseeing that she should not have a day's health all the autumn, entreated, or rather required her, for it was hardly entreaty, to come to Uppercross Cottage, and bear her company as long as she should want her, instead of going to Bath.

"I cannot possibly do without Anne," was Mary's reasoning; and Elizabeth's reply was, "Then I am sure Anne had better stay, for nobody will want her in Bath."

To be claimed as a good, though in an improper style, is at least better than being rejected as no good at all; and Anne, glad to be thought of some use, glad to have anything marked out as a duty, and certainly not sorry to have the scene of it in the country, and her own dear country, readily agreed to stay.

This invitation of Mary's removed all Lady Russell's difficulties, and it was consequently soon settled that Anne should not go to Bath till Lady Russell took her, and that all the intervening time should be divided between Uppercross Cottage and Kellynch Lodge.

So far all was perfectly right; but Lady Russell was almost startled by the wrong of one part of the Kellynch Hall plan, when it burst on her, which was, Mrs. Clay's being engaged to go to Bath with Sir Walter and Elizabeth, as a most important and valuable assistant to the latter in all the business before her. Lady Russell was extremely sorry that such a measure should have been resorted to at all, wondered, grieved, and feared; and the affront it contained to Anne, in Mrs. Clay's being of so much use, while Anne could be of none, was a very sore aggravation.

Anne herself was become hardened to such affronts; but she felt the imprudence of the arrangement quite as keenly as Lady Russell. With a great deal of quiet observation, and a knowledge, which she often wished less, of her father's character, she was sensible that results the most serious to his family from the intimacy, were more than possible. She did not imagine that her father had at present an idea of the kind. Mrs. Clay had freckles, and a projecting tooth, and a clumsy wrist, which he was continually making severe remarks upon, in her absence; but she was young, and certainly altogether well-looking, and possessed, in an acute mind and assiduous pleasing manners, infinitely more dangerous attractions than any merely personal might have been. Anne was so impressed by the degree of their danger, that she could not excuse herself from trying to make it perceptible to her sister. She had little hope of success; but Elizabeth, who in the event of such a reverse would be so much more to be pitied than herself, should never, she thought, have reason to reproach her for giving no warning.

She spoke, and seemed only to offend. Elizabeth could not conceive how such an absurd suspicion should occur to her, and indignantly answered for each party's perfectly knowing their situation.

"Mrs. Clay," said she, warmly, "never forgets who she is; and as I am rather better acquainted with her sentiments than you can be, I can assure you, that upon the subject of marriage they are particularly nice, and that she reprobates all inequality of condition and rank more strongly than most people. And as to my father, I really should not have thought that he, who has kept himself single so long for our sakes, need be suspected now. If Mrs. Clay were a very beautiful woman, I grant you, it might be wrong to have her so much with me; not that anything in the world, I am sure, would induce my father to make a degrading match, but he might be rendered unhappy. But poor Mrs. Clay who, with all her merits, can never have been reckoned tolerably pretty, I really think poor Mrs. Clay may be staying here in perfect safety. One would imagine you had never heard my father speak of her personal misfortunes, though I know you must fifty times. That tooth of her's and those freckles. Freckles do not disgust me so very much as they do him. I have known a face not materially disfigured by a few, but he abominates them. You must have heard him notice Mrs. Clay's freckles."

"There is hardly any personal defect," replied Anne, "which an agreeable manner might not gradually reconcile one to."

"I think very differently," answered Elizabeth, shortly; "an agreeable manner may set off handsome features, but can never alter plain ones. However, at any rate, as I have a great deal more at stake on this point than anybody else can have, I think it rather unnecessary in you to be advising me."

Anne had done; glad that it was over, and not absolutely hopeless of doing good. Elizabeth, though resenting the suspicion, might yet be made observant by it.

The last office of the four carriage-horses was to draw Sir Walter, Miss Elliot, and Mrs. Clay to Bath. The party drove off in very good spirits; Sir Walter prepared with condescending bows for all the afflicted tenantry and cottagers who might have had a hint to show themselves, and Anne walked up at the same time, in a sort of desolate tranquillity, to the Lodge, where she was to spend the first week.[2]

Her friend was not in better spirits than herself. Lady Russell felt this break-up of the family exceedingly. Their respectability was as dear to her as her own, and a daily intercourse had become precious by habit. It was painful to look upon their deserted grounds, and still worse to anticipate the new hands they were to fall into; and to escape the solitariness and the melancholy of so altered a village, and be out of the way when Admiral and Mrs. Croft first arrived, she had determined to make her own absence from home begin when she must give up Anne. Accordingly their removal was made together, and Anne was set down at Uppercross Cottage, in the first stage of Lady Russell's journey.

Uppercross was a moderate-sized village, which a few years back had been completely in the old English style, containing only two houses superior in appearance to those of the yeomen and labourers; the mansion of the squire, with its high walls, great gates, and old trees, substantial and unmodernized, and the compact, tight parsonage, enclosed in its own neat garden, with a vine and a pear-tree trained round its casements; but upon the marriage of the young 'squire, it had received the improvement of a farmhouse elevated into a cottage, for his residence, and Uppercross Cottage, with its veranda, French windows, and other prettiness, was quite as likely to catch the traveller's eye as the more consistent and considerable aspect and premises of the Great House, about a quarter of a mile farther on.

Here Anne had often been staying. She knew the ways of Uppercross as well as those of Kellynch. The two families were so continually meeting, so much in the habit of running in and out of each other's house at all hours, that it was rather a surprise to her to find Mary alone; but being alone, her being unwell and out of spirits was almost a matter of course. Though better endowed than the

[2] It is unclear whether these afflictions are the performance of a distressed leave-taking, or are genuine distress. The transformations which the novel reflects—the waning of the landed aristocracy and the rise of the professional classes, particularly the navy—would affect the tenantry, whose protections are tied to the social and paternalistic order now, apparently, in decline.

elder sister, Mary had not Anne's understanding nor temper. While well, and happy, and properly attended to, she had great good humour and excellent spirits; but any indisposition sunk her completely. She had no resources for solitude; and inheriting a considerable share of the Elliot self-importance, was very prone to add to every other distress that of fancying herself neglected and ill-used. In person,[3] she was inferior to both sisters, and had, even in her bloom, only reached the dignity of being "a fine girl." She was now lying on the faded sofa of the pretty little drawing room, the once elegant furniture of which had been gradually growing shabby, under the influence of four summers and two children; and, on Anne's appearing, greeted her with—

"So, you are come at last! I began to think I should never see you. I am so ill I can hardly speak. I have not seen a creature the whole morning!"

"I am sorry to find you unwell," replied Anne. "You sent me such a good account of yourself on Thursday!"

"Yes, I made the best of it; I always do: but I was very far from well at the time; and I do not think I ever was so ill in my life as I have been all this morning: very unfit to be left alone, I am sure. Suppose I were to be seized of a sudden in some dreadful way, and not able to ring the bell! So, Lady Russell would not get out. I do not think she has been in this house three times this summer."

Anne said what was proper, and enquired after her husband. "Oh! Charles is out shooting. I have not seen him since seven o'clock. He would go, though I told him how ill I was. He said he should not stay out long; but he has never come back, and now it is almost one. I assure you, I have not seen a soul this whole long morning."

"You have had your little boys with you?"

"Yes, as long as I could bear their noise; but they are so unmanageable that they do me more harm than good. Little Charles does not mind a word I say, and Walter is growing quite as bad."

"Well, you will soon be better now," replied Anne, cheerfully. "You know I always cure you when I come. How are your neighbours at the Great House?"

"I can give you no account of them. I have not seen one of them to-day, except Mr. Musgrove, who just stopped and spoke through the window, but without getting off his horse; and though I told

---

[3] Physically.

him how ill I was, not one of them have been near me. It did not happen to suit the Miss Musgroves, I suppose, and they never put themselves out of their way."

"You will see them yet, perhaps, before the morning is gone. It is early."

"I never want them, I assure you. They talk and laugh a great deal too much for me. Oh! Anne, I am so very unwell! It was quite unkind of you not to come on Thursday."

"My dear Mary, recollect what a comfortable account you sent me of yourself! You wrote in the cheerfullest manner, and said you were perfectly well, and in no hurry for me; and that being the case, you must be aware that my wish would be to remain with Lady Russell to the last: and besides what I felt on her account, I have really been so busy, have had so much to do, that I could not very conveniently have left Kellynch sooner."

"Dear me! what can you possibly have to do?"

"A great many things, I assure you. More than I can recollect in a moment; but I can tell you some. I have been making a duplicate of the catalogue of my father's books and pictures. I have been several times in the garden with Mackenzie, trying to understand, and make him understand, which of Elizabeth's plants are for Lady Russell. I have had all my own little concerns to arrange, books and music to divide, and all my trunks to repack, from not having understood in time what was intended as to the waggons: and one thing I have had to do, Mary, of a more trying nature: going to almost every house in the parish, as a sort of take-leave. I was told that they wished it. But all these things took up a great deal of time."

"Oh! well!" and after a moment's pause, "but you have never asked me one word about our dinner at the Pooles yesterday."

"Did you go then? I have made no enquiries, because I concluded you must have been obliged to give up the party."

"Oh yes! I went. I was very well yesterday; nothing at all the matter with me till this morning. It would have been strange if I had not gone."

"I am very glad you were well enough, and I hope you had a pleasant party."

"Nothing remarkable. One always knows beforehand what the dinner will be, and who will be there; and it is so very uncomfortable not having a carriage of one's own. Mr. and Mrs. Musgrove took me, and we were so crowded! They are both so very large, and take up so much room; and Mr. Musgrove always sits forward. So, there was I, crowded into the back seat with Henrietta and Louise; and I think it very likely that my illness today may be owing to it."

A little further perseverance in patience and forced cheerfulness on Anne's side produced nearly a cure on Mary's. She could soon sit upright on the sofa, and began to hope she might be able to leave it by dinner-time. Then, forgetting to think of it, she was at the other end of the room, beautifying a nosegay; then, she ate her cold meat; and then she was well enough to propose a little walk.

"Where shall we go?" said she, when they were ready. "I suppose you will not like to call at the Great House before they have been to see you?"

"I have not the smallest objection on that account," replied Anne. "I should never think of standing on such ceremony with people I know so well as Mrs. and the Miss Musgroves."

"Oh! but they ought to call upon you as soon as possible. They ought to feel what is due to you as my sister. However, we may as well go and sit with them a little while, and when we have that over, we can enjoy our walk."

Anne had always thought such a style of intercourse highly imprudent; but she had ceased to endeavour to check it, from believing that, though there were on each side continual subjects of offence, neither family could now do without it. To the Great House accordingly they went, to sit the full half hour in the old-fashioned square parlour, with a small carpet and shining floor, to which the present daughters of the house were gradually giving the proper air of confusion by a grand piano-forte and a harp, flower-stands and little tables placed in every direction. Oh! could the originals of the portraits against the wainscot, could the gentlemen in brown velvet and the ladies in blue satin have seen what was going on, have been conscious of such an overthrow of all order and neatness! The portraits themselves seemed to be staring in astonishment.

The Musgroves, like their houses, were in a state of alteration, perhaps of improvement. The father and mother were in the old English style, and the young people in the new. Mr. and Mrs. Musgrove were a very good sort of people; friendly and hospitable, not much educated, and not at all elegant. Their children had more modern minds and manners. There was a numerous family; but the only two grown up, excepting Charles, were Henrietta and Louisa, young ladies of nineteen and twenty, who had brought from school at Exeter all the usual stock of accomplishments,[4] and were now like thousands of other young ladies, living to be fashionable, happy, and merry. Their dress had every advantage, their faces were rather pretty, their spirits extremely good, their manner unembarrassed and pleasant; they were of consequence at home, and favourites abroad. Anne always contemplated them as some of the happiest creatures of her acquaintance; but still, saved as we all are, by some comfortable feeling of superiority from wishing for the possibility of exchange, she would not have given up her own more elegant and cultivated mind for all their enjoyments; and envied them nothing but that seemingly perfect good understanding and agreement together, that good-humoured mutual affection, of which she had known so little herself with either of her sisters.

They were received with great cordiality. Nothing seemed amiss on the side of the Great House family, which was generally, as Anne very well knew, the least to blame. The half hour was chatted away pleasantly enough; and she was not at all surprised at the end of it, to have their walking party joined by both the Miss Musgroves, at Mary's particular invitation.

# CHAPTER VI

Anne had not wanted this visit to Uppercross, to learn that a removal from one set of people to another, though at a distance of only three miles, will often include a total change of conversation, opinion, and idea. She had never been staying there before, without being struck by it, or without wishing that other Elliots could have her advantage in seeing how unknown, or unconsidered there, were the affairs which at Kellynch Hall were treated as of such general publicity and pervading interest; yet, with all this experience, she believed she must now submit to feel that another lesson, in the art of knowing our own nothingness beyond our own circle, was become necessary for her; for certainly, coming as she did, with a heart full of the subject which had been completely occupying both

---

[4] The sorts of skills that constitute a social asset, and so make a young leisure-class woman marriage-marketable: dancing, singing, piano or harp-playing, needlepoint, flower-arranging, china-painting, screen-painting, and so forth, much satirized by Austen in other novels, and excoriated by advocates of sound female education, from the conservative Hannah More to the progressive Mary Wollstonecraft.

houses in Kellynch for many weeks, she had expected rather more curiosity and sympathy than she found in the separate but very similar remark of Mr. and Mrs. Musgrove: "So, Miss Anne, Sir Walter and your sister are gone; and what part of Bath do you think they will settle in?" and this, without much waiting for an answer; or in the young ladies' addition of, "I hope we shall be in Bath in the winter; but remember, papa, if we do go, we must be in a good situation: none of your Queen Squares for us!"[1] or in the anxious supplement from Mary, of—"Upon my word, I shall be pretty well off, when you are all gone away to be happy at Bath!"

She could only resolve to avoid such self-delusion in future, and think with heightened gratitude of the extraordinary blessing of having one such truly sympathising friend as Lady Russell.

The Mr. Musgroves had their own game to guard, and to destroy, their own horses, dogs, and newspapers to engage them, and the females were fully occupied in all the other common subjects of housekeeping, neighbours, dress, dancing, and music. She acknowledged it to be very fitting, that every little social commonwealth should dictate its own matters of discourse; and hoped, ere long, to become a not unworthy member of the one she was now transplanted into. With the prospect of spending at least two months at Uppercross, it was highly incumbent on her to clothe her imagination, her memory, and all her ideas in as much of Uppercross as possible.

She had no dread of these two months. Mary was not so repulsive and unsisterly as Elizabeth, nor so inaccessible to all influence of hers; neither was there anything among the other component parts of the cottage inimical to comfort. She was always on friendly terms with her brother-in-law; and in the children, who loved her nearly as well, and respected her a great deal more than their mother, she had an object of interest, amusement, and wholesome exertion.

Charles Musgrove was civil and agreeable; in sense and temper he was undoubtedly superior to his wife, but not of powers, or conversation, or grace, to make the past, as they were connected together, at all a dangerous contemplation; though, at the same time, Anne could believe, with Lady Russell, that a more equal match might have greatly improved him; and that a woman of real understanding might have given more consequence to his character,

---

[1] This square, which Henrietta and Louisa deem unfashionable, is where Austen lived briefly in 1799.

and more usefulness, rationality, and elegance to his habits and pursuits. As it was, he did nothing with much zeal, but sport; and his time was otherwise trifled away, without benefit from books or anything else. He had very good spirits, which never seemed much affected by his wife's occasional lowness, bore with her unreasonableness sometimes to Anne's admiration, and upon the whole, though there was very often a little disagreement (in which she had sometimes more share than she wished, being appealed to by both parties), they might pass for a happy couple. They were always perfectly agreed in the want of more money, and a strong inclination for a handsome present from his father; but here, as on most topics, he had the superiority, for while Mary thought it a great shame that such a present was not made, he always contended for his father's having many other uses for his money, and a right to spend it as he liked.

As to the management of their children, his theory was much better than his wife's, and his practice not so bad. "I could manage them very well, if it were not for Mary's interference," was what Anne often heard him say, and had a good deal of faith in; but when listening in turn to Mary's reproach of "Charles spoils the children so that I cannot get them into any order," she never had the smallest temptation to say, "Very true."

One of the least agreeable circumstances of her residence there was her being treated with too much confidence by all parties, and being too much in the secret of the complaints of each house. Known to have some influence with her sister, she was continually requested, or at least receiving hints to exert it, beyond what was practicable. "I wish you could persuade Mary not to be always fancying herself ill," was Charles's language; and, in an unhappy mood, thus spoke Mary: "I do believe if Charles were to see me dying, he would not think there was anything the matter with me. I am sure, Anne, if you would, you might persuade him that I really am very ill—a great deal worse than I ever own."

Mary's declaration was, "I hate sending the children to the Great House, though their grandmamma is always wanting to see them, for she humours and indulges them to such a degree, and gives them so much trash and sweet things, that they are sure to come back sick and cross for the rest of the day." And Mrs. Musgrove took the first opportunity of being alone with Anne, to say, "Oh! Miss Anne, I cannot help wishing Mrs. Charles had a little of your method with those children. They are quite different creatures with you! But to be sure, in general they are so spoilt! It is a pity you cannot put your sister in the way of managing them. They are as fine healthy children as ever were seen, poor little dears! without partiality; but Mrs. Charles knows no more how they should be treated—! Bless me! how troublesome they are sometimes. I assure you, Miss Anne, it prevents my wishing to see them at our house so often as I otherwise should. I believe Mrs. Charles is not quite pleased with my not inviting them oftener; but you know it is very bad to have children with one that one is obligated to be checking every moment; 'don't do this,' and 'don't do that;' or that one can only keep in tolerable order by more cake than is good for them."

She had this communication, moreover, from Mary. "Mrs. Musgrove thinks all her servants so steady, that it would be high treason to call it in question; but I am sure, without exaggeration, that her upper house-maid and laundry-maid, instead of being in their business, are gadding about[2] the village, all day long. I meet them wherever I go; and I declare, I never go twice into my nursery without seeing something of them. If Jemima were not the trustiest, steadiest creature in the world, it would be enough to spoil her; for she tells me, they are always tempting her to take a walk with them." And on Mrs. Musgrove's side, it was, "I make a rule of never interfering in any of my daughter-in-law's concerns, for I know it would not do; but I shall tell you, Miss Anne, because you may be able to set things to rights, that I have no very good opinion of Mrs. Charles's nursery-maid: I hear strange stories of her; she is always upon the gad; and from my own knowledge, I can declare, she is such a fine-dressing lady, that she is enough to ruin any servants she comes near. Mrs. Charles quite swears by her, I know; but I just give you this hint, that you may be upon the watch; because, if you see anything amiss, you need not be afraid of mentioning it."

Again, it was Mary's complaint, that Mrs. Musgrove was very apt not to give her the precedence that was her due, when they dined at the Great House with other families; and she did not see any reason why she was to be considered so much at home as to lose her place. And one day when Anne was walking with only the Musgroves, one of them after talking of rank, people of rank, and jealousy of rank, said, "I have no scruple of observing to you, how nonsensical some persons are about their place, because all the world knows how easy and indifferent you are about it; but I wish anybody could give Mary a hint that it would be a great deal better if she were not so very

---

[2] Doing things to little effect.

tenacious, especially if she would not be always putting herself forward to take place of mamma. Nobody doubts her right to have precedence of mamma, but it would be more becoming in her not to be always insisting on it. It is not that mamma cares about it the least in the world, but I know it is taken notice of by many persons."

How was Anne to set all these matters to rights? She could do little more than listen patiently, soften every grievance, and excuse each to the other; give them all hints of the forbearance necessary between such near neighbours, and make those hints broadest which were meant for her sister's benefit.

In all other respects, her visit began and proceeded very well. Her own spirits improved by change of place and subject, by being removed three miles from Kellynch; Mary's ailments lessened by having a constant companion, and their daily intercourse with the other family, since there was neither superior affection, confidence, nor employment in the cottage, to be interrupted by it, was rather an advantage. It was certainly carried nearly as far as possible, for they met every morning, and hardly ever spent an evening asunder; but she believed they should not have done so well without the sight of Mr. and Mrs. Musgrove's respectable forms in the usual places, or without the talking, laughing, and singing of their daughters.

She played a great deal better than either of the Miss Musgroves, but having no voice, no knowledge of the harp, and no fond parents, to sit by and fancy themselves delighted, her performance was little thought of, only out of civility, or to refresh the others, as she was well aware. She knew that when she played she was giving pleasure only to herself; but this was no new sensation. Excepting one short period of her life, she had never, since the age of fourteen, never since the loss of her dear mother, known the happiness of being listened to, or encouraged by any just appreciation or real taste. In music she had been always used to feel alone in the world; and Mr. and Mrs. Musgrove's fond partiality for their own daughters' performance, and total indifference to any other person's, gave her much more pleasure for their sakes, than mortification for her own.

The party at the Great House was sometimes increased by other company. The neighbourhood was not large, but the Musgroves were visited by everybody, and had more dinner-parties, and more callers, more visitors by invitation and by chance, than any other family. There were more completely popular.

The girls were wild for dancing; and the evenings ended, occasionally, in an unpremeditated little ball. There was a family of cousins within a walk of Uppercross, in less affluent circumstances, who depended on the Musgroves for all their pleasures: they would come at any time, and help play at anything, or dance anywhere; and Anne, very much preferring the office of musician to a more active post, played country dances to them by the hour together; a kindness which always recommended her musical powers to the notice of Mr. and Mrs. Musgrove more than anything else, and often drew this compliment;—"Well done, Miss Anne! very well done indeed! Lord bless me! how those little fingers of yours fly about!"

So passed the first three weeks. Michaelmas came; and now Anne's heart must be in Kellynch again. A beloved home made over to others; all the precious rooms and furniture, groves, and prospects, beginning to own other eyes and other limbs! She could not think of much else on the 29th of September; and she had this sympathetic touch in the evening from Mary, who, on having occasion to note down the day of the month, exclaimed, "Dear me, is not this the day the Crofts were to come to Kellynch? I am glad I did not think of it before. How low it makes me!"

The Crofts took possession with true naval alertness, and were to be visited. Mary deplored the necessity for herself. "Nobody knew how much she should suffer. She should put it off as long as she could;" but was not easy till she had talked Charles into driving her over on an early day, and was in a very animated, comfortable state of imaginary agitation, when she came back. Anne had very sincerely rejoiced in there being no means of her going. She wished, however, to see the Crofts, and was glad to be within when the visit was returned. They came: the master of the house was not at home, but the two sisters were together; and as it chanced that Mrs. Croft fell to the share of Anne, while the Admiral sat by Mary, and made himself very agreeable by his good-humoured notice of her little boys, she was well able to watch for a likeness, and if it failed her in the features, to catch it in the voice, or in the turn of sentiment and expression.

Mrs. Croft, though neither tall nor fat, had a squareness, uprightness, and vigour of form, which gave importance to her person. She had bright dark eyes, good teeth, and altogether an agreeable face; though her reddened and weather-beaten complexion, the consequence of her having been almost as much at sea as her husband, made her seem to have lived some years longer in the world than her real eight-and-thirty. Her manners were open, easy, and decided, like one who had no distrust of herself, and no doubts of what to do; without any approach to coarseness, however, or any want of good humour. Anne gave her credit, indeed, for feelings of great consideration towards herself, in all that related to Kellynch, and it pleased her: especially, as she had satisfied herself in the very first half minute, in the instant even of introduction, that there was not the smallest symptom of any knowledge or suspicion on Mrs. Croft's side, to give a bias of any sort. She was quite easy on that head, and consequently full of strength and courage, till for a moment electrified by Mrs. Croft's suddenly saying,—

"It was you, and not your sister, I find, that my brother had the pleasure of being acquainted with, when he was in this country."

Anne hoped she had outlived the age of blushing; but the age of emotion she certainly had not.

"Perhaps you may not have heard that he is married?" added Mrs. Croft.

She could now answer as she ought; and was happy to feel, when Mrs. Croft's next words explained it to be Mr. Wentworth of whom she spoke, that she had said nothing which might not do for either brother. She immediately felt how reasonable it was, that Mrs. Croft should be thinking and speaking of Edward, and not of Frederick; and with shame at her own forgetfulness applied herself to the knowledge of their former neighbour's present state with proper interest.

The rest was all tranquillity; till, just as they were moving, she heard the Admiral say to Mary—

"We are expecting a brother of Mrs. Croft's here soon; I dare say you know him by name."

He was cut short by the eager attacks of the little boys, clinging to him like an old friend, and declaring he should not go; and being too much engrossed by proposals of carrying them away in his coat pockets, &c., to have another moment for finishing or recollecting what he had begun, Anne was left to persuade herself, as well as she could, that the same brother must still be in question. She could not, however, reach such a degree of certainty, as not to be anxious to hear whether anything had been said on the subject at the other house, where the Crofts had previously been calling.

The folks of the Great House were to spend the evening of this day at the Cottage; and it being now too late in the year for such visits to be made on foot, the coach was beginning to be listened for, when the youngest Miss Musgrove walked in. That she was coming to apologize, and that they should have to spend the evening by themselves, was the first black idea; and Mary was quite ready to be affronted, when Louisa made all right by saying, that she only came on foot, to leave more room for the harp, which was bringing in the carriage.

"And I will tell you our reason," she added, "and all about it. I am come on to give you notice, that papa and mamma are out of spirits this evening, especially mamma; she is thinking so much of poor Richard! And we agreed it would be best to have the harp, for it seems to amuse her more than the piano-forte. I will tell you why she is out of spirits. When the Crofts called this morning, (they called here afterwards, did not they?), they happened to say, that her brother, Captain Wentworth, is just returned to England, or paid off, or something, and is coming to see them almost directly; and most unluckily it came into mamma's head, when they were gone, that Wentworth, or something very like it, was the name of poor Richard's captain at one time; I do not know when or where, but a great while before he died, poor fellow! And upon looking over his letters and things, she found it was so, and is perfectly sure that this must be the very man, and her head is quite full of it, and of poor Richard! So we must be as merry as we can, that she may not be dwelling upon such gloomy things."

The real circumstances of this pathetic piece of family history were, that the Musgroves had had the ill fortune of a very troublesome, hopeless son; and the good fortune to lose him before he reached his twentieth year; that he had been sent to sea because he was stupid and unmanageable on shore; that he had been very little cared for at any time by his family, though quite as much as he deserved; seldom heard of, and scarcely at all regretted, when the intelligence of his death abroad had worked its way to Uppercross, two years before.

He had, in fact, though his sisters were now doing all they could for him, by calling him "poor Richard," been nothing better than a thick-headed, unfeeling, unprofitable Dick Musgrove, who had never done anything to entitle himself to more than the abbreviation of his name, living or dead.

He had been several years at sea, and had, in the course of those removals to which all midshipmen are liable, and especially such midshipmen as every captain wishes to get rid of, been six months on board Captain Frederick Wentworth's frigate, the *Laconia*; and from the *Laconia* he had, under the influence of his captain, written the only two letters which his father and mother had ever received from him during the whole of his absence; that is to say, the only two disinterested letters; all the rest had been mere applications for money.

In each letter he had spoken well of his captain; but yet, so little were they in the habit of attending to such matters, so unobservant and incurious were they as to the names of men or ships, that it had made scarcely any impression at the time; and that Mrs. Musgrove should have been suddenly struck, this very day, with a recollection of the name of Wentworth, as connected with her son, seemed one of those extraordinary bursts of mind which do sometimes occur.

She had gone to her letters, and found it all as she supposed; and the re-perusal of these letters, after so long an interval, her poor son gone for ever, and all the strength of his faults forgotten, had affected her spirits exceedingly, and thrown her into greater grief for him than she had known on first hearing of his death. Mr. Musgrove was, in a lesser degree, affected likewise; and when they reached the cottage, they were evidently in want, first, of being listened to anew on this subject, and afterwards, of all the relief which cheerful companions could give them.

To hear them talking so much of Captain Wentworth, repeating his name so often, puzzling over past years, and at last ascertaining that it might, that it probably would, turn out to be the very same Captain Wentworth whom they recollected meeting, once or twice, after their coming back from Clifton—a very fine young man—but they could not say whether it was seven or eight years ago, was a new sort of trial to Anne's nerves. She found, however, that it was one to which she must inure herself. Since he actually was expected in the country, she must teach herself to be insensible on[3] such points. And not only did it appear that he was expected, and speedily, but the Musgroves, in their warm gratitude for the kindness he had shewn poor Dick, and very high respect for his character, stamped as it was by poor Dick's having been six months under his care, and mentioning him in strong, though not perfectly well-spelt praise, as "a fine dashing felow, only two perticular about the schoolmaster,"[4] were bent on introducing themselves, and seeking his acquaintance, as soon as they could hear of his arrival.

The resolution of doing so helped to form the comfort of their evening.

---

[3] Unaffected by.

[4] A direct quotation from Dick's letter, with shoddy spelling and incorrect usage, describing and demonstrating its author's impatience with the ship's schoolmaster. Crews, at this time, routinely included adolescent boys.

# CHAPTER VII

A very few days more, and Captain Wentworth was known to be at Kellynch, and Mr. Musgrove had called on him, and come back warm in his praise, and he was engaged with the Crofts to dine at Uppercross, by the end of another week. It had been a great disappointment to Mr. Musgrove to find that no earlier day could be fixed, so impatient was he to shew his gratitude, by seeing Captain Wentworth under his own roof, and welcoming him to all that was strongest and best in his cellars. But a week must pass; only a week, in Anne's reckoning, and then, she supposed, they must meet; and soon she began to wish that she could feel secure even for a week.

Captain Wentworth made a very early return to Mr. Musgrove's civility, and she was all but calling there in the same half hour. She and Mary were actually setting forward for the Great House, where, as she afterwards learnt, they must inevitably have found him, when they were stopped by the eldest boy's being at that moment brought home in consequence of a bad fall. The child's situation put the visit entirely aside; but she could not hear of her escape with indifference, even in the midst of the serious anxiety which they afterwards felt on his account.

His collar-bone was found to be dislocated, and such injury received in the back, as roused the most alarming ideas. It was an afternoon of distress, and Anne had every thing to do at once; the apothecary to send for,[1] the father to have pursued and informed, the mother to support and keep from hysterics, the servants to control, the youngest child to banish, and the poor suffering one to attend and soothe; besides sending, as soon as she recollected it, proper notice to the other house, which brought her an accession rather of frightened, enquiring companions, than of very useful assistants.

Her brother's return was the first comfort; he could take best care of his wife; and the second blessing was the arrival of the apothecary. Till he came and had examined the child, their apprehensions were the worse for being vague; they suspected great injury, but knew not where; but now the collar-bone was soon replaced, and though Mr. Robinson felt and felt, and rubbed, and looked grave, and spoke low words both to the father and the aunt, still they were all to hope the best, and to be able to part and eat their dinner in tolerable ease of mind; and then it was, just before they parted, that the two young

---

[1] Druggists routinely performed physicians' duties.

aunts were able so far to digress from their nephew's state, as to give the information of Captain Wentworth's visit; staying five minutes behind their father and mother, to endeavour to express how perfectly delighted they were with him, how much handsomer, how infinitely more agreeable they thought him than any individual among their male acquaintance, who had been at all a favourite before. How glad they had been to hear papa invite him to stay dinner, how sorry when he said it was quite out of his power, and how glad again when he had promised in reply to papa and mamma's farther pressing invitations to come and dine with them on the morrow—actually on the morrow; and he had promised it in so pleasant a manner, as if he felt all the motive of their attention just as he ought. And in short, he had looked and said everything with such exquisite grace, that they could assure them all, their heads were both turned by him; and off they ran, quite as full of glee as of love, and apparently more full of Captain Wentworth than of little Charles.

The same story and the same raptures were repeated, when the two girls came with their father, through the gloom of the evening, to make enquiries; and Mr. Musgrove, no longer under the first uneasiness about his heir, could add his confirmation and praise, and hope there would be now no occasion for putting Captain Wentworth off, and only be sorry to think that the cottage party, probably, would not like to leave the little boy, to give him the meeting. "Oh no; as to leaving the little boy," both father and mother were in much too strong and recent alarm to bear the thought; and Anne, in the joy of the escape, could not help adding her warm protestations to theirs.

Charles Musgrove, indeed, afterwards, shewed more of inclination; "the child was going on so well, and he wished so much to be introduced to Captain Wentworth, that, perhaps, he might join them in the evening; he would not dine from home, but he might walk in for half an hour." But in this he was eagerly opposed by his wife, with "Oh! no, indeed, Charles, I cannot bear to have you go away. Only think if anything should happen?"

The child had a good night, and was going on well the next day. It must be a work of time to ascertain that no injury had been done to the spine; but Mr. Robinson found nothing to increase alarm, and Charles Musgrove began, consequently, to feel no necessity for longer confinement. The child was to be kept in bed and amused as quietly as possible; but what was there for a father to do? This was quite a female case, and it would be highly absurd in him, who could be of no use at home, to shut himself up. His father very much wished him to meet Captain Wentworth, and there being no sufficient reason against it, he ought to go; and it ended in his making a bold, public declaration, when he came in from shooting, of his meaning to dress directly, and dine at the other house.

"Nothing can be going on better than the child," said he; "so I told my father, just now, that I would come, and he thought me quite right. Your sister being with you, my love, I have no scruple at all. You would not like to leave him yourself, but you see I can be of no use. Anne will send for me if anything is the matter."

Husbands and wives generally understand when opposition will be vain. Mary knew, from Charles's manner of speaking, that he was quite determined on going, and that it would be of no use to teaze him. She said nothing, therefore, till he was out of the room, but as soon as there was only Anne to hear—

"So you and I are to be left to shift by ourselves, with this poor sick child; and not a creature coming near us all the evening! I knew how it would be. This is always my luck. If there is anything disagreeable going on men are always sure to get out of it, and Charles is as bad as any of them. Very unfeeling! I must say it is very unfeeling of him to be running away from his poor little boy. Talks of his being going on so well! How does he know that he is going on well, or that there may not be a sudden change half an hour hence? I did not think Charles would have been so unfeeling. So here he is to go away and enjoy himself, and because I am the poor mother, I am not to be allowed to stir; and yet, I am sure, I am more unfit than anybody else to be about the child. My being the mother is the very reason why my feelings should not be tried. I am not at all equal to it. You saw how hysterical I was yesterday."

"But that was only the effect of the suddenness of your alarm—of the shock. You will not be hysterical again. I dare say we shall have nothing to distress us. I perfectly understand Mr. Robinson's directions, and have no fears; and indeed, Mary, I cannot wonder at your husband. Nursing does not belong to a man; it is not his province. A sick child is always the mother's property: her own feelings generally make it so."

"I hope I am as fond of my child as any mother, but I do not know that I am of any more use in the sick-room than Charles, for I cannot be always scolding and teazing the poor child when it is ill; and you saw, this morning, that if I told him to keep quiet, he was sure to begin kicking about. I have not nerves for the sort of thing."

"But, could you be comfortable yourself, to be spending the whole evening away from the poor boy?"

"Yes; you see his papa can, and why should not I? Jemima is so careful; and she could send us word every hour how he was. I really think Charles might as well have told his father we would all come. I am not more alarmed about little Charles now than he is. I was dreadfully alarmed yesterday, but the case is very different to-day."

"Well, if you do not think it too late to give notice for yourself, suppose you were to go, as well as your husband. Leave little Charles to my care. Mr. and Mrs. Musgrove cannot think it wrong while I remain with him."

"Are you serious?" cried Mary, her eyes brightening. "Dear me! that's a very good thought, very good, indeed. To be sure, I may just as well go as not, for I am of no use at home—am I? and it only harasses me. You, who have not a mother's feelings, are a great deal the properest person. You can make little Charles do anything; he always minds you at a word. It will be a great deal better than leaving him only with Jemima. Oh! I shall certainly go; I am sure I ought if I can, quite as much as Charles, for they want me excessively to be acquainted with Captain Wentworth, and I know you do not mind being left alone. An excellent thought of yours, indeed, Anne. I will go and tell Charles, and get ready directly. You can send for us, you know, at a moment's notice, if anything is the matter; but I dare say there will be nothing to alarm you. I should not go, you may be sure, if I did not feel quite at ease about my dear child."

The next moment she was tapping at her husband's dressing-room door, and as Anne followed her up stairs, she was in time for the whole conversation, which began with Mary's saying, in a tone of great exultation—

"I mean to go with you, Charles, for I am of no more use at home than you are. If I were to shut myself up for ever with the child, I should not be able to persuade him to do anything he did not like. Anne will stay; Anne undertakes to stay at home and take care of him. It is Anne's own proposal, and so I shall go with you, which will be a great deal better, for I have not dined at the other house since Tuesday."

"This is very kind of Anne," was her husband's answer, "and I should be very glad to have you go; but it seems rather hard that she should be left at home by herself, to nurse our sick child."

Anne was now at hand to take up her own cause, and the sincerity of her manner being soon sufficient to convince him, where conviction was at least very agreeable, he had no farther scruples as to her being left to dine alone, though he still wanted her to join them in the evening, when the child might be at rest for the night, and kindly urged her to let him come and fetch her, but she was quite unpersuadable; and this being the case, she had ere long the pleasure of seeing them set off together in high spirits. They were gone, she hoped, to be happy, however oddly constructed such happiness might seem; as for herself, she was left with as many sensations of comfort, as were, perhaps, ever likely to be hers. She knew herself to be of the first utility to the child; and what was it to her if Frederick Wentworth were only half a mile distant, making himself agreeable to others?

She would have liked to know how he felt as to a meeting. Perhaps indifferent, if indifference could exist under such circumstances. He must be either indifferent or unwilling. Had he wished ever to see her again, he need not have waited till this time; he would have done what she could not but believe that in his place she should have done long ago, when events had been early giving him the independence which alone had been wanting.

Her brother and sister came back delighted with their new acquaintance, and their visit in general. There had been music, singing, talking, laughing, all that was most agreeable; charming manners in Captain Wentworth, no shyness or reserve; they seemed all to know each other perfectly, and he was coming the very next morning to shoot with Charles. He was to come to breakfast, but not at the Cottage, though that had been proposed at first; but then he had been pressed to come to the Great House instead, and he seemed afraid of being in Mrs. Charles Musgrove's way, on account of the child, and therefore, somehow, they hardly knew how, it ended in Charles's being to meet him to breakfast at his father's.

Anne understood it. He wished to avoid seeing her. He had inquired after her, she found, slightly, as might suit a former slight acquaintance, seeming to acknowledge such as she had acknowledged, actuated, perhaps, by the same view of escaping introduction when they were to meet.

The morning hours of the Cottage were always later than those of the other house, and on the morrow the difference was so great that Mary and Anne were not more than beginning breakfast when Charles came in to say that they were just setting off, that he was come for his dogs, that his sisters were following with Captain Wentworth; his sisters meaning to visit Mary and the child, and Captain Wentworth proposing also to wait on her for a few minutes if not inconvenient; and though Charles had answered for the child's being in no such state as could make it inconvenient, Captain Wentworth would not be satisfied without his running on to give notice.

Mary, very much gratified by this attention, was delighted to receive him, while a thousand feelings rushed on Anne, of which this was the most consoling, that it would soon be over. And it was soon over. In two minutes after Charles's preparation, the others appeared; they were in the drawing-room. Her eye half met Captain Wentworth's, a bow, a curtsey passed; she heard his voice; he talked to Mary, said all that was right, said something to the Miss Musgroves, enough to mark an easy footing; the room seemed full, full of persons and voices, but a few minutes ended it. Charles shewed himself at the window, all was ready, their visitor had bowed and was gone, the Miss Musgroves were gone too, suddenly resolving to walk to the end of the village with the sportsmen: the room was cleared, and Anne might finish her breakfast as she could.

"It is over! it is over!" she repeated to herself again and again, in nervous gratitude. "The worst is over!"

Mary talked, but she could not attend. She had seen him. They had met. They had been once more in the same room.

Soon, however, she began to reason with herself, and try to be feeling less. Eight years, almost eight years had passed, since all had been given up. How absurd to be resuming the agitation which such an interval had banished into distance and indistinctness! What might not eight years do? Events of every description, changes, alienations, removals—all, all must be comprised in it, and oblivion of the past—how natural, how certain too! It included nearly a third part of her own life.

Alas! with all her reasoning, she found, that to retentive feelings eight years may be little more than nothing.

Now, how were his sentiments to be read? Was this like wishing to avoid her? And the next moment she was hating herself for the folly which asked the question.

On one other question which perhaps her utmost wisdom might not have prevented, she was soon spared all suspense; for, after the Miss Musgroves had returned and finished their visit at the Cottage she had this spontaneous information from Mary:—

"Captain Wentworth is not very gallant by you, Anne, though he was so attentive to me. Henrietta asked him what he thought of you, when they went away, and he said, 'You were so altered he should not have known you again.'"

Mary had no feelings to make her respect her sister's in a common way, but she was perfectly unsuspicious of being inflicting any peculiar wound.

"Altered beyond his knowledge." Anne fully submitted, in silent, deep mortification. Doubtless it was so, and she could take no revenge, for he was not altered, or not for the worse. She had already acknowledged it to herself, and she could not think differently, let him think of her as he would. No: the years which had destroyed her youth and bloom had only given him a more glowing, manly, open look, in no respect lessening his personal advantages. She had seen the same Frederick Wentworth.

"So altered that he should not have known her again!" These were words which could not but dwell with her. Yet she soon began to rejoice that she had heard them. They were of sobering tendency; they allayed agitation; they composed, and consequently must make her happier.

Frederick Wentworth had used such words, or something like them, but without an idea that they would be carried round to her. He had thought her wretchedly altered, and in the first moment of appeal, had spoken as he felt. He had not forgiven Anne Elliot. She had used him ill, deserted and disappointed him; and worse, she had shewn a feebleness of character in doing so, which his own decided, confident temper could not endure. She had given him up to oblige others. It had been the effect of over-persuasion. It had been weakness and timidity.

He had been most warmly attached to her, and had never seen a woman since whom he thought her equal; but, except from some natural sensation of curiosity, he had no desire of meeting her again. Her power with him was gone for ever.

It was now his object to marry. He was rich, and being turned on shore, fully intended to settle as soon as he could be properly tempted; actually looking round, ready to fall in love with all the speed which a clear head and a quick taste could allow. He had a heart for either of the Miss Musgroves, if they could catch it; a heart, in short, for any pleasing young woman who came in his way, excepting Anne Elliot. This was his only secret exception, when he said to his sister, in answer to her suppositions:—

"Yes, here I am, Sophia, quite ready to make a foolish match. Anybody between fifteen and thirty may have me for asking. A little beauty, and a few smiles, and a few compliments to the navy, and

I am a lost man. Should not this be enough for a sailor, who has had no society among women to make him nice?"

He said it, she knew, to be contradicted. His bright proud eye spoke the conviction that he was nice; and Anne Elliot was not out of his thoughts, when he more seriously described the woman he should wish to meet with. "A strong mind, with sweetness of manner," made the first and the last of the description.

"This is the woman I want," said he. "Something a little inferior I shall of course put up with, but it must not be much. If I am a fool, I shall be a fool indeed, for I have thought on the subject more than most men."

## CHAPTER VIII

From this time Captain Wentworth and Anne Elliot were repeatedly in the same circle. They were soon dining in company together at Mr. Musgrove's, for the little boy's state could no longer supply his aunt with a pretence for absenting herself; and this was but the beginning of other dinings and other meetings.

Whether former feelings were to be renewed must be brought to the proof; former times must undoubtedly be brought to the recollection of each; they could not but be reverted to; the year of their engagement could not but be named by him, in the little narratives or descriptions which conversation called forth. His profession qualified him, his disposition led him, to talk; and "That was in the year six"; "That happened before I went to sea in the year six," occurred in the course of the first evening they spent together: and though his voice did not falter, and though she had no reason to suppose his eye wandering towards her while he spoke, Anne felt the utter impossibility, from her knowledge of his mind, that he could be unvisited by remembrance any more than herself. There must be the same immediate association of thought, though she was very far from conceiving it to be of equal pain.

They had no conversation together, no intercourse but what the commonest civility required. Once so much to each other! Now nothing! There had been a time, when of all the large party now filling the drawing-room at Uppercross, they would have found it most difficult to cease to speak to one another. With the exception, perhaps, of Admiral and Mrs. Croft, who seemed particularly attached and happy, (Anne could allow no other exceptions even among the married couples), there could have been no two hearts so open, no tastes so similar, no feelings so in unison, no countenances so beloved. Now they were as strangers; nay, worse than strangers, for they could never become acquainted. It was a perpetual estrangement.

When he talked, she heard the same voice, and discerned the same mind. There was a very general ignorance of all naval matters throughout the party; and he was very much questioned, and especially by the two Miss Musgroves, who seemed hardly to have any eyes but for him, as to the manner of living on board, daily regulations, food, hours, &c., and their surprise at his accounts, at learning the degree of accommodation and arrangement which was practicable, drew from him some pleasant ridicule, which reminded Anne of the early days when she too had been ignorant, and she too had been accused of supposing sailors to be living on board without anything to eat, or any cook to dress it if there were, or any servant to wait, or any knife and fork to use.

From thus listening and thinking, she was roused by a whisper of Mrs. Musgrove's who, overcome by fond regrets, could not help saying—

"Ah! Miss Anne, if it had pleased Heaven to spare my poor son, I dare say he would have been just such another by this time."

Anne suppressed a smile, and listened kindly, while Mrs. Musgrove relieved her heart a little more; and for a few minutes, therefore, could not keep pace with the conversation of the others.

When she could let her attention take its natural course again, she found the Miss Musgroves just fetching the Navy List (their own navy list, the first that had ever been at Uppercross), and sitting down together to pore over it, with the professed view of finding out the ships that Captain Wentworth had commanded.

"Your first was the Asp, I remember; we will look for the Asp."

"You will not find her there. Quite worn out and broken up. I was the last man who commanded her. Hardly fit for service then. Reported fit for home service for a year or two, and so I was sent off to the West Indies."

The girls looked all amazement.

"The Admiralty," he continued, "entertain themselves now and then, with sending a few hundred men to sea, in a ship not fit to be employed. But they have a great many to provide for; and among the thousands that may just as well go to the bottom as not, it is impossible for them to distinguish the very set who may be least missed."

"Phoo! phoo!" cried the Admiral, "what stuff these young fellows talk! Never was a better sloop than the Asp in her day. For an old built sloop, you would not see her equal. Lucky fellow to get her! He knows there must have been twenty better men than himself applying for her at the same time. Lucky fellow to get anything so soon, with no more interest[1] than his."

"I felt my luck, Admiral, I assure you," replied Captain Wentworth, seriously. "I was as well satisfied with my appointment as you can desire. It was a great object with me at that time to be at sea; a very great object, I wanted to be doing something."

"To be sure you did. What should a young fellow like you do ashore for half a year together? If a man had not a wife, he soon wants to be afloat again."

"But, Captain Wentworth," cried Louisa, "how vexed you must have been when you came to the Asp, to see what an old thing they had given you."

"I knew pretty well what she was before that day;" said he, smiling. "I had no more discoveries to make than you would have as to the fashion and strength of any old pelisse,[2] which you had seen lent about among half your acquaintance ever since you could remember, and which at last, on some very wet day, is lent to yourself. Ah! she was a dear old Asp to me. She did all that I wanted. I knew she would. I knew that we should either go to the bottom together, or that she would be the making of me; and I never had two days of foul weather all the time I was at sea in her; and after taking privateers enough to be very entertaining, I had the good luck in my passage home the next autumn, to fall in with the very French frigate I wanted. I brought her into Plymouth; and here another instance of luck. We had not been six hours in the Sound, when a gale came on, which lasted four days and nights, and which would have done for poor old Asp in half the time; our touch with the Great Nation[3] not having much improved our condition. Four-and-twenty hours later, and I should only have been a gallant Captain Wentworth, in a small paragraph at one corner of the newspapers; and being lost in only a sloop, nobody would have thought about me." Anne's shudderings were to herself alone; but

---

[1] That is, with the influence of those "interested" in his behalf.

[2] A woman's long cloak or coat generally with fur trimming.

[3] France, with which Britain had been at war since 1793.

the Miss Musgroves could be as open as they were sincere, in their exclamations of pity and horror.

"And so then, I suppose," said Mrs. Musgrove, in a low voice, as if thinking aloud, "so then he went away to the Laconia, and there he met with our poor boy. Charles, my dear," (beckoning him to her), "do ask Captain Wentworth where it was he first met with your poor brother. I always forget."

"It was at Gibraltar, mother, I know. Dick had been left ill at Gibraltar, with a recommendation from his former captain to Captain Wentworth."

"Oh! but, Charles, tell Captain Wentworth, he need not be afraid of mentioning poor Dick before me, for it would be rather a pleasure to hear him talked of by such a good friend."

Charles, being somewhat more mindful of the probabilities of the case, only nodded in reply, and walked away.

The girls were now hunting for the Laconia; and Captain Wentworth could not deny himself the pleasure of taking the precious volume into his own hands to save them the trouble, and once more read aloud the little statement of her name and rate,[4] and present non-commissioned class, observing over it that she too had been one of the best friends man ever had.[5]

"Ah! those were pleasant days when I had the Laconia! How fast I made money in her. A friend of mine and I had such a lovely cruise together off the Western Islands. Poor Harville, sister! You know how much he wanted money: worse than myself. He had a wife. Excellent fellow. I shall never forget his happiness. He felt it all, so much for her sake. I wished for him again the next summer, when I had still the same luck in the Mediterranean."

"And I am sure, Sir." said Mrs. Musgrove, "it was a lucky day for us, when you were put captain into that ship. We shall never forget what you did."

Her feelings made her speak low; and Captain Wentworth, hearing only in part, and probably not having Dick Musgrove at all near his thoughts, looked rather in suspense, and as if waiting for more.

"My brother," whispered one of the girls; "mamma is thinking of poor Richard."

"Poor dear fellow!" continued Mrs. Musgrove; "he was grown so steady, and such an excellent correspondent, while he was under

[4] Classification according to size and other specifications.
[5] Captain Wentworth's pride in this volume rivals Sir Walter's in the *Baronetage*.

your care! Ah! it would have been a happy thing, if he had never left you. I assure you, Captain Wentworth, we are very sorry he ever left you."

There was a momentary expression in Captain Wentworth's face at this speech, a certain glance of his bright eye, and curl of his handsome mouth, which convinced Anne, that instead of sharing in Mrs. Musgrove's kind wishes, as to her son, he had probably been at some pains to get rid of him; but it was too transient an indulgence of self-amusement to be detected by any who understood him less than herself; in another moment he was perfectly collected and serious, and almost instantly afterwards coming up to the sofa, on which she and Mrs. Musgrove were sitting, took a place by the latter, and entered into conversation with her, in a low voice, about her son, doing it with so much sympathy and natural grace, as shewed the kindest consideration for all that was real and unabsurd in the parent's feelings.

They were actually on the same sofa, for Mrs. Musgrove had most readily made room for him; they were divided only by Mrs. Musgrove. It was no insignificant barrier, indeed. Mrs. Musgrove was of a comfortable, substantial size, infinitely more fitted by nature to express good cheer and good humour, than tenderness and sentiment; and while the agitations of Anne's slender form, and pensive face, may be considered as very completely screened, Captain Wentworth should be allowed some credit for the self-command with which he attended to her large fat sighings over the destiny of a son, whom alive nobody had cared for.

Personal size and mental sorrow have certainly no necessary proportions. A large bulky figure has as good a right to be in deep affliction, as the most graceful set of limbs in the world. But, fair or not fair, there are unbecoming conjunctions, which reason will patronize in vain—which taste cannot tolerate—which ridicule will seize.

The Admiral, after taking two or three refreshing turns about the room with his hands behind him, being called to order by his wife, now came up to Captain Wentworth, and without any observation of what he might be interrupting, thinking only of his own thoughts, began with—

"If you had been a week later at Lisbon, last spring, Frederick, you would have been asked to give a passage to Lady Mary Grierson and her daughters."

"Should I? I am glad I was not a week later then."

The Admiral abused him for his want of gallantry. He defended himself; though professing that he would never willingly admit any ladies on board a ship of his, excepting for a ball, or a visit, which a few hours might comprehend.

"But, if I know myself," said he, "this is from no want of gallantry towards them. It is rather from feeling how impossible it is, with all one's efforts, and all one's sacrifices, to make the accommodations on board such as women ought to have. There can be no want of gallantry, Admiral, in rating the claims of women to every personal comfort high, and this is what I do. I hate to hear of women on board, or to see them on board; and no ship under my command shall ever convey a family of ladies anywhere, if I can help it."

This brought his sister upon him.

"Oh! Frederick! But I cannot believe it of you. —All idle refinement!—Women may be as comfortable on board, as in the best house in England. I believe I have lived as much on board as most women, and I know nothing superior to the accommodations of a man-of-war. I declare I have not a comfort or an indulgence about me, even at Kellynch Hall," (with a kind bow to Anne), "beyond what I always had in most of the ships I have lived in; and they have been five altogether."

"Nothing to the purpose," replied her brother. "You were living with your husband, and were the only woman on board."

"But you, yourself, brought Mrs. Harville, her sister, her cousin, and three children, round from Portsmouth to Plymouth. Where was this superfine, extraordinary sort of gallantry of yours then?"

"All merged in my friendship, Sophia. I would assist any brother officer's wife that I could, and I would bring anything of Harville's from the world's end, if he wanted it. But do not imagine that I did not feel it an evil in itself."

"Depend upon it, they were all perfectly comfortable."

"I might not like them the better for that perhaps. Such a number of women and children have no right to be comfortable on board."

"My dear Frederick, you are talking quite idly. Pray, what would become of us poor sailors' wives, who often want to be conveyed to one port or another, after our husbands, if everybody had your feelings?"

"My feelings, you see, did not prevent my taking Mrs. Harville and all her family to Plymouth."

"But I hate to hear you talking so like a fine gentleman, and as if women were all fine ladies, instead of rational creatures. We none of us expect to be in smooth water all our days."

"Ah! my dear," said the Admiral, "when he had got a wife, he will sing a different tune. When he is married, if we have the good luck to live to another war, we shall see him do as you and I, and a great many others, have done. We shall have him very thankful to anybody that will bring him his wife."

"Ay, that we shall."

"Now I have done," cried Captain Wentworth. "When once married people begin to attack me with,—'Oh! you will think very differently, when you are married.' I can only say, 'No, I shall not;' and then they say again, 'Yes, you will,' and there is an end of it."

He got up and moved away.

"What a great traveller you must have been, ma'am!" said Mrs. Musgrove to Mrs. Croft.

"Pretty well, ma'am in the fifteen years of my marriage; though many women have done more. I have crossed the Atlantic four times, and have been once to the East Indies, and back again, and only once; besides being in different places about home: Cork, and Lisbon, and Gibraltar. But I never went beyond the Streights, and never was in the West Indies. We do not call Bermuda or Bahama, you know, the West Indies."

Mrs. Musgrove had not a word to say in dissent; she could not accuse herself of having ever called them anything in the whole course of her life.

"And I do assure you, ma'am," pursued Mrs. Croft, "that nothing can exceed the accommodations of a man-of-war; I speak, you know, of the higher rates. When you come to a frigate, of course, you are more confined; though any reasonable woman may be perfectly happy in one of them; and I can safely say, that the happiest part of my life has been spent on board a ship. While we were together, you know, there was nothing to be feared. Thank God! I have always been blessed with excellent health, and no climate disagrees with me. A little disordered always the first twenty-four hours of going to sea, but never knew what sickness was afterwards. The only time I ever really suffered in body or mind, the only time that I ever fancied myself unwell, or had any ideas of danger, was the winter that I passed by myself at Deal, when the Admiral (Captain Croft then) was in the North Seas. I lived in perpetual fright at that time, and had all manner of imaginary complaints from not knowing what to do with myself, or when I should hear from him next; but as long as we could be together, nothing ever ailed me, and I never met with the smallest inconvenience."

"Aye, to be sure. Yes, indeed, oh yes! I am quite of your opinion, Mrs. Croft," was Mrs. Musgrove's hearty answer. "There is nothing so bad as a separation. I am quite of your opinion. I know what it is, for Mr. Musgrove always attends the assizes,[6] and I am so glad when they are over, and he is safe back again."

The evening ended with dancing. On its being proposed, Anne offered her services, as usual; and though her eyes would sometimes fill with tears as she sat at the instrument, she was extremely glad to be employed, and desired nothing in return but to be unobserved.

It was a merry, joyous party, and no one seemed in higher spirits than Captain Wentworth. She felt that he had every thing to elevate him which general attention and deference, and especially the attention of all the young women, could do. The Miss Hayters, the females of the family of cousins already mentioned, were apparently admitted to the honour of being in love with him; and as for Henrietta and Louisa, they both seemed so entirely occupied by him, that nothing but the continued appearance of the most perfect good-will between themselves could have made it credible that they were not decided rivals. If he were a little spoilt by such universal, such eager admiration, who could wonder?

These were some of the thoughts which occupied Anne, while her fingers were mechanically at work, proceeding for half an hour together, equally without error, and without consciousness. Once she felt that he was looking at herself, observing her altered features, perhaps, trying to trace in them the ruins of the face which had once charmed him; and once she knew that he must have spoken of her; she was hardly aware of it, till she heard the answer; but then she was sure of his having asked his partner whether Miss Elliot never danced? The answer was, "Oh, no; never; she has quite given up dancing. She had rather play. She is never tired of playing." Once, too, he spoke to her. She had left the instrument on the dancing being over, and he had sat down to try to make out an air which he wished to give the Miss Musgroves an idea of. Unintentionally she returned to that part of the room; he saw her, and, instantly rising, said, with studied politeness—

---

[6] Periodical sessions of the superior courts under county jurisdiction to try criminal and civil cases.

"I beg your pardon, madam, this is your seat;" and though she immediately drew back with a decided negative, he was not to be induced to sit down again.

Anne did not wish for more of such looks and speeches. His cold politeness, his ceremonious grace, were worse than anything.

# CHAPTER IX

Captain Wentworth was come to Kellynch as to a home, to stay as long as he liked, being as thoroughly the object of the Admiral's fraternal kindness as of his wife's. He had intended, on first arriving, to proceed very soon into Shropshire, and visit the brother settled in that country, but the attractions of Uppercross induced him to put this off. There was so much of friendliness, and of flattery, and of everything most bewitching in his reception there; the old were so hospitable, the young so agreeable, that he could not but resolve to remain where he was, and take all the charms and perfections of Edward's wife upon credit a little longer.

It was soon Uppercross with him almost every day. The Musgroves could hardly be more ready to invite than he to come, particularly in the morning, when he had no companion at home, for the Admiral and Mrs. Croft were generally out of doors together, interesting themselves in their new possessions, their grass, and their sheep, and dawdling about in a way not endurable to a third person, or driving out in a gig,[1] lately added to their establishment.

Hitherto there had been but one opinion of Captain Wentworth among the Musgroves and their dependencies. It was unvarying, warm admiration everywhere; but this intimate footing was not more than established, when a certain Charles Hayter returned among them, to be a good deal disturbed by it, and to think Captain Wentworth very much in the way.

Charles Hayter was the eldest of all the cousins, and a very amiable, pleasing young man, between whom and Henrietta there had been a considerable appearance of attachment previous to Captain Wentworth's introduction. He was in orders; and having a curacy[2] in the neighbourhood, where residence was not required, lived at his father's house, only two miles from Uppercross. A short absence

---

[1] A two-wheeled, one-horse carriage—a sporty vehicle.

[2] A clerical post subordinate to the rector or vicar.

from home had left his fair one unguarded by his attentions at this critical period, and when he came back he had the pain of finding very altered manners, and of seeing Captain Wentworth.

Mrs. Musgrove and Mrs. Hayter were sisters. They had each had money, but their marriages had made a material difference in their degree of consequence. Mr. Hayter had some property of his own, but it was insignificant compared with Mr. Musgrove's; and while the Musgroves were in the first class of society in the country,[3] the young Hayters would, from their parents' inferior, retired, and unpolished way of living, and their own defective education, have been hardly in any class at all, but for their connexion with Uppercross, this eldest son of course excepted, who had chosen to be a scholar and a gentleman,[4] and who was very superior in cultivation and manners to all the rest.

The two families had always been on excellent terms, there being no pride on one side, and no envy on the other, and only such a consciousness of superiority in the Miss Musgroves, as made them pleased to improve their cousins. Charles's attentions to Henrietta had been observed by her father and mother without any disapprobation. "It would not be a great match for her; but if Henrietta liked him,"—and Henrietta did seem to like him.

Henrietta fully thought so herself, before Captain Wentworth came; but from that time Cousin Charles had been very much forgotten.

Which of the two sisters was preferred by Captain Wentworth was as yet quite doubtful, as far as Anne's observation reached. Henrietta was perhaps the prettiest, Louisa had the higher spirits; and she knew not now, whether the more gentle or the more lively character were most likely to attract him.

Mr. and Mrs. Musgrove, either from seeing little, or from an entire confidence in the discretion of both their daughters, and of all the young men who came near them, seemed to leave everything to take its chance. There was not the smallest appearance of solicitude or remark about them in the Mansion-house; but it was different at the Cottage: the young couple there were more disposed to speculate and wonder; and Captain Wentworth had not been above four or five times in the Miss Musgroves' company, and Charles Hayter had but just reappeared, when Anne had to listen to the opinions of

---

[3] District.

[4] A baccalaureate degree was a prerequisite for gaining a curacy.

her brother and sister, as to which was the one liked best. Charles gave it for Louisa, Mary for Henrietta, but quite agreeing that to have him marry either could be extremely delightful.

Charles "had never seen a pleasanter man in his life; and from what he had once heard Captain Wentworth himself say, was very sure that he had not made less than twenty thousand pounds by the war.[5] Here was a fortune at once; besides which, there would be the chance of what might be done in any future war; and he was sure Captain Wentworth was as likely a man to distinguish himself as any officer in the navy. Oh! it would be a capital match for either of his sisters."

"Upon my word it would," replied Mary. "Dear me! If he should rise to any very great honours! If he should ever be made a baronet! 'Lady Wentworth' sounds very well. That would be a noble thing, indeed, for Henrietta! She would take place of me then, and Henrietta would not dislike that. Sir Frederick and Lady Wentworth! It would be but a new creation, however, and I never think much of your new creations."

It suited Mary best to think Henrietta the one preferred on the very account of Charles Hayter, whose pretensions she wished to see put an end to. She looked down very decidedly upon the Hayters, and thought it would be quite a misfortune to have the existing connection between the families renewed—very sad for herself and her children.

"You know," said she, "I cannot think him at all a fit match for Henrietta; and considering the alliances which the Musgroves have made, she has no right to throw herself away. I do not think any young woman has a right to make a choice that may be disagreeable and inconvenient to the principal part of her family, and be giving bad connections to those who have not been used to them. And, pray, who is Charles Hayter? Nothing but a country curate. A most improper match for Miss Musgrove of Uppercross."

Her husband, however, would not agree with her here; for besides having a regard for his cousin, Charles Hayter was an eldest son, and he saw things as an eldest son himself.

"Now you are taking nonsense, Mary," was therefore his answer. "It would not be a great match for Henrietta, but Charles has a very fair chance, through the Spicers, of getting something from the

---

[5] From the capture of an enemy vessel or one flying an enemy's flag. The income (at 5%) from this sum would give Wentworth the status as a mid-gentry squire.

Bishop in the course of a year or two; and you will please to remember, that he is the eldest son; whenever my uncle dies, he steps into very pretty property.[6] The estate at Winthrop is not less than two hundred and fifty acres, besides the farm near Taunton, which is some of the best land in the country. I grant you, that any of them but Charles would be a very shocking match for Henrietta, and indeed it could not be; he is the only one that could be possible; but he is a very good-natured, good sort of a fellow; and whenever Winthrop comes into his hands, he will make a different sort of place of it, and live in a very different sort of way; and with that property, he will never be a contemptible man—good, freehold property.[7] No, no; Henrietta might do worse than marry Charles Hayter; and if she has him, and Louisa can get Captain Wentworth, I shall be very well satisfied."

"Charles may say what he pleases," cried Mary to Anne, as soon as he was out of the room, "but it would be shocking to have Henrietta marry Charles Hayter; a very bad thing for her, and still worse for me; and therefore it is very much to be wished that Captain Wentworth may soon put him quite out of her head, and I have very little doubt that he has. She took hardly any notice of Charles Hayter yesterday. I wish you had been there to see her behaviour. And as to Captain Wentworth's liking Louisa as well as Henrietta, it is nonsense to say so; for he certainly does like Henrietta a great deal the best. But Charles is so positive! I wish you had been with us yesterday, for then you might have decided between us; and I am sure you would have thought as I did, unless you had been determined to give it against me."

A dinner at Mr. Musgrove's had been the occasion when all these things should have been seen by Anne; but she had staid at home, under the mixed plea of a headache of her own, and some return of indisposition in little Charles. She had thought only of avoiding Captain Wentworth; but an escape from being appealed to as umpire was now added to the advantages of a quiet evening.

As to Captain Wentworth's views, she deemed it of more consequence that he should know his own mind early enough not to be endangering the happiness of either sister, or impeaching his own honour, than that he should prefer Henrietta to Louisa, or Louisa to Henrietta. Either of them would, in all probability, make him an

---

[6] Primogeniture (in which the eldest son, or nearest male relative, is the sole heir) was customary in the gentry, but not mandatory as in the barotonetcy.

[7] Legally held for life.

affectionate, good-humoured wife. With regard to Charles Hayter, she had delicacy which must be pained by any lightness of conduct in a well-meaning young woman, and a heart to sympathize in any of the sufferings it occasioned; but if Henrietta found herself mistaken in the nature of her feelings, the alternation could not be understood too soon.

Charles Hayter had met with much to disquiet and mortify him in his cousin's behaviour. She had too old a regard for him to be so wholly estranged as might in two meetings extinguish every past hope, and leave him nothing to do but to keep away from Uppercross: but there was such a change as became very alarming, when such a man as Captain Wentworth was to be regarded as the probable cause. He had been absent only two Sundays, and when they parted, had left her interested, even to the height of his wishes, in his prospect of soon quitting his present curacy, and obtaining that of Uppercross instead. It had then seemed the object nearest her heart, that Dr. Shirley, the rector, who for more than forty years had been zealously discharging all the duties of his office, but was now growing too infirm for many of them, should be quite fixed on engaging a curate; should make his curacy quite as good as he could afford, and should give Charles Hayter the promise of it. The advantage of his having to come only to Uppercross, instead of going six miles another way; of his having, in every respect, a better curacy; of his belonging to their dear Dr. Shirley, and of dear, good Dr. Shirley's being relieved from the duty which he could no longer get through without most injurious fatigue, had been a great deal, even to Louisa, but had been almost everything to Henrietta. When he came back, alas! the zeal of the business was gone by. Louisa could not listen at all to his account of a conversation which he had just held with Dr. Shirley: she was at a window, looking out for Captain Wentworth; and even Henrietta had at best only a divided attention to give, and seemed to have forgotten all the former doubt and solicitude of the negotiation.

"Well, I am very glad indeed: but I always thought you would have it; I always thought you sure. It did not appear to me that—in short, you know, Dr. Shirley must have a curate, and you had secured his promise. Is he coming, Louisa?"

One morning, very soon after the dinner at the Musgroves, at which Anne had not been present, Captain Wentworth walked into the drawing-room at the Cottage, where were only herself and the little invalid Charles, who was lying on the sofa.

The surprise of finding himself almost alone with Anne Elliot, deprived his manners of their usual composure: he started, and could only say, "I thought the Miss Musgroves had been here: Mrs. Musgrove told me I should find them here," before he walked to the window to recollect himself, and feel how he ought to behave.

"They are up stairs with my sister: they will be down in a few moments, I dare say," had been Anne's reply, in all the confusion that was natural; and if the child had not called her to come and do something for him, she would have been out of the room the next moment, and released Captain Wentworth as well as herself.

He continued at the window; and after calmly and politely saying, "I hope the little boy is better," was silent.

She was obliged to kneel down by the sofa, and remain there to satisfy her patient; and thus they continued a few minutes, when, to her very great satisfaction, she heard some other person crossing the little vestibule. She hoped, on turning her head, to see the master of the house; but it proved to be one much less calculated for making matters easy—Charles Hayter, probably not at all better pleased by the sight of Captain Wentworth than Captain Wentworth had been by the sight of Anne.

She only attempted to say, "How do you do? Will you not sit down? The others will be here presently."

Captain Wentworth, however, came from his window, apparently not ill-disposed for conversation; but Charles Hayter soon put an end to his attempts by seating himself near the table, and taking up the newspaper; and Captain Wentworth returned to his window.

Another minute brought another addition. The younger boy, a remarkable stout, forward child, of two years old, having got the door opened for him by some one without, made his determined appearance among them, and went straight to the sofa to see what was going on, and put in his claim to anything good that might be giving away.

There being nothing to eat, he could only have some play; and as his aunt would not let him tease his sick brother, he began to fasten himself upon her, as she knelt, in such a way that, busy as she was about Charles, she could not shake him off. She spoke to him, ordered, entreated, and insisted in vain. Once she did contrive to push him away, but the boy had the greater pleasure in getting upon her back again directly.

"Walter," said she, "get down this moment. You are extremely troublesome. I am very angry with you."

"Walter," cried Charles Hayter, "why do you not do as you are bid? Do not you hear your aunt speak? Come to me, Walter, come to cousin Charles."

But not a bit did Walter stir.

In another moment, however, she found herself in the state of being released from him; some one was taking him from her, though he had bent down her head so much, that his little sturdy hands were unfastened from around her neck, and he was resolutely borne away, before she knew that Captain Wentworth had done it.

Her sensations on the discovery made her perfectly speechless. She could not even thank him. She could only hang over little Charles, with most disordered feelings. His kindness in stepping forward to her relief, the manner, the silence in which it had passed, the little particulars of the circumstance, with the conviction soon forced on her by the noise he was studiously making with the child, that he meant to avoid hearing her thanks, and rather sought to testify that her conversation was the last of his wants, produced such a confusion of varying, but very painful agitation, as she could not recover from, till enabled by the entrance of Mary and the Miss Musgroves to make over her little patient to their cares, and leave the room. She could not stay. It might have been an opportunity of watching the loves and jealousies of the four—they were now altogether; but she could stay for none of it. It was evident that Charles Hayter was not well inclined towards Captain Wentworth. She had a strong impression of his having said, in a vext tone of voice, after Captain Wentworth's interference, "You ought to have minded me, Walter; I told you not to teaze your aunt;" and could comprehend his regretting that Captain Wentworth should do what he ought to have done himself. But neither Charles Hayter's feelings, nor anybody's feelings, could interest her, till she had a little better arranged her own. She was ashamed of herself, quite ashamed of being so nervous, so overcome by such a trifle; but so it was, and it required a long application of solitude and reflection to recover her.

# CHAPTER X

Other opportunities of making her observations could not fail to occur. Anne had soon been in company with all the four together often enough to have an opinion, though too wise to acknowledge as much at home, where she knew it would have satisfied neither husband nor wife; for while she considered Louisa to be rather the favourite, she could not but think, as far as she might dare to judge from memory and experience, that Captain Wentworth was not in love with either. They were more in love with him; yet there it was not love. It was a little fever of admiration; but it might, probably must, end in love with some. Charles Hayter seemed aware of being slighted, and yet Henrietta had sometimes the air of being divided between them. Anne longed for the power of representing to them all what they were about, and of pointing out some of the evils they were exposing themselves to. She did not attribute guile to any. It was the highest satisfaction to her to believe Captain Wentworth not in the least aware of the pain he was occasioning. There was no triumph, no pitiful triumph in his manner. He had, probably, never heard, and never thought of any claims of Charles Hayter. He was only wrong in accepting the attentions (for accepting must be the word) of two young women at once.

After a short struggle, however, Charles Hayter seemed to quit the field. Three days had passed without his coming once to Uppercross; a most decided change. He had even refused one regular invitation to dinner; and having been found on the occasion by Mr. Musgrove with some large books before him, Mr. and Mrs. Musgrove were sure all could not be right, and talked, with grave faces, of his studying himself to death. It was Mary's hope and belief that he had received a positive dismissal from Henrietta, and her husband lived under the constant dependence of seeing him to-morrow. Anne could only feel that Charles Hayter was wise.

One morning, about this time Charles Musgrove and Captain Wentworth being gone a-shooting together, as the sisters in the Cottage were sitting quietly at work, they were visited at the window by the sisters from the Mansion-house.

It was a very fine November day, and the Miss Musgroves came through the little grounds, and stopped for no other purpose than to say, that they were going to take a long walk, and therefore concluded Mary could not like to go with them; and when Mary immediately replied, with some jealousy at not being supposed a good walker, "Oh, yes, I should like to join you very much, I am very fond of a long walk;" Anne felt persuaded, by the looks of the two girls, that it was precisely what they did not wish, and admired[1] again the

---

[1] Was struck by.

sort of necessity which the family habits seemed to produce, of everything being to be communicated, and everything being to be done together, however undesired and inconvenient. She tried to dissuade Mary from going, but in vain; and that being the case, thought it best to accept the Miss Musgroves' much more cordial invitation to herself to go likewise, as she might be useful in turning back with her sister, and lessening the interference in any plan of their own.

"I cannot imagine why they should suppose I should not like a long walk," said Mary, as she went up stairs. "Everybody is always supposing that I am not a good walker; and yet they would not have been pleased, if we had refused to join them. When people come in this manner on purpose to ask us, how can one say no?"

Just as they were setting off, the gentlemen returned. They had taken out a young dog, who had spoilt their sport, and sent them back early. Their time and strength, and spirits, were, therefore, exactly ready for this walk, and they entered into it with pleasure. Could Anne have foreseen such a junction, she would have staid at home; but, from some feelings of interest and curiosity, she fancied now that it was too late to retract, and the whole six set forward together in the direction chosen by the Miss Musgroves, who evidently considered the walk as under their guidance.

Anne's object was, not to be in the way of anybody; and where the narrow paths across the fields made many separations necessary, to keep with her brother and sister. Her pleasure in the walk must arise from the exercise and the day, from the view of the last smiles of the year upon the tawny leaves, and withered hedges, and from repeating to herself some few of the thousand poetical descriptions extant of autumn, that season of peculiar and inexhaustible influence on the mind of taste and tenderness, that season which had drawn from every poet, worthy of being read, some attempt at description, or some lines of feeling. She occupied her mind as much as possible in such like musings and quotations; but it was not possible, that when within reach of Captain Wentworth's conversation with either of the Miss Musgroves, she should not try to hear it; yet she caught little very remarkable. It was mere lively chat, such as any young persons, on an intimate footing, might fall into. He was more engaged with Louisa than with Henrietta. Louisa certainly put more forward for his notice than her sister. This distinction appeared to increase, and there was one speech of Louisa's which struck her. After one of the many praises of the day, which were continually bursting forth, Captain Wentworth added:—

"What glorious weather for the Admiral and my sister! They meant to take a long drive this morning; perhaps we may hail them from some of these hills. They talked of coming into this side of the country. I wonder whereabouts they will upset to-day. Oh! it does happen very often, I assure you; but my sister makes nothing of it; she would as lieve be tossed out as not."

"Ah! You make the most of it, I know," cried Louisa, "but if it were really so, I should do just the same in her place. If I loved a man, as she loves the Admiral, I would always be with him, nothing should ever separate us, and I would rather be overturned by him, than driven safely by anybody else."

It was spoken with enthusiasm.

"Had you?" cried he, catching the same tone; "I honour you!" And there was silence between them for a little while.

Anne could not immediately fall into a quotation again. The sweet scenes of autumn were for a while put by, unless some tender sonnet, fraught with the apt analogy of the declining year, with declining happiness, and the images of youth and hope, and spring, all gone together, blessed her memory. She roused herself to say, as they struck by order into another path, "Is not this one of the ways to Winthrop?" But nobody heard, or, at least, nobody answered her.

Winthrop, however, or its environs—for young men are, sometimes to be met with, strolling about near home—was their destination; and after another half mile of gradual ascent through large enclosures, where the ploughs at work, and the fresh made path spoke the farmer counteracting the sweets of poetical despondence, and meaning to have spring again, they gained the summit of the most considerable hill, which parted Uppercross and Winthrop, and soon commanded a full view of the latter, at the foot of the hill on the other side.

Winthrop, without beauty and without dignity, was stretched before them; an indifferent house, standing low, and hemmed in by the barns and buildings of a farm-yard.

Mary exclaimed, "Bless me! here is Winthrop. I declare I had no idea! Well now, I think we had better turn back; I am excessively tired."

Henrietta, conscious and ashamed, and seeing no cousin Charles walking along any path, or leaning against any gate, was ready to do as Mary wished; but "No!" said Charles Musgrove, and "No, no!" cried Louisa more eagerly, and taking her sister aside, seemed to be arguing the matter warmly.

Charles, in the meanwhile, was very decidedly declaring his resolution of calling on his aunt, now that he was so near; and very evidently, though more fearfully, trying to induce his wife to go too. But this was one of the points on which the lady shewed her strength; and when he recommended the advantage of resting herself a quarter of an hour at Winthrop, as she felt so tired, she resolutely answered, "Oh! no, indeed! walking up that hill again would do her more harm than any sitting down could do her good;" and, in short, her look and manner declared, that go she would not.

After a little succession of these sort of debates and consultations, it was settled between Charles and his two sisters, that he and Henrietta should just run down for a few minutes, to see their aunt and cousins, while the rest of the party waited for them at the top of the hill. Louisa seemed the principal arranger of the plan; and, as she went a little way with them, down the hill, still talking to Henrietta, Mary took the opportunity of looking scornfully around her, and saying to Captain Wentworth—

"It is very unpleasant, having such connexions! But, I assure you, I have never been in the house above twice in my life."

She received no other answer, than an artificial, assenting smile, followed by a contemptuous glance, as he turned away, which Anne perfectly knew the meaning of.

The brow of the hill, where they remained, was a cheerful spot: Louisa returned; and Mary, finding a comfortable seat for herself on the step of a stile,[2] was very well satisfied so long as the others all stood about her; but when Louisa drew Captain Wentworth away, to try for a gleaning of nuts in an adjoining hedge-row, and they were gone by degrees quite out of sight and sound, Mary was happy no longer; she quarrelled with her own seat, was sure Louisa had got a much better somewhere, and nothing could prevent her from going to look for a better also. She turned through the same gate, but could not see them. Anne found a nice seat for her, on a dry sunny bank, under the hedge-row, in which she had no doubt of their still being, in some spot or other. Mary sat down for a moment, but it would not do; she was sure Louisa had found a better seat somewhere else, and she would go on till she overtook her.

Anne, really tired herself, was glad to sit down; and she very soon heard Captain Wentworth and Louisa in the hedge-row, behind her, as if making their way back along the rough, wild sort

---

[2] A step-ladder for getting over a gate.

of channel, down the centre. They were speaking as they drew near. Louisa's voice was the first distinguished. She seemed to be in the middle of some eager speech. What Anne first heard was—

"And so, I made her go. I could not bear that she should be frightened from the visit by such nonsense. What! would I be turned back from doing a thing that I had determined to do, and that I knew to be right, by the airs and interference of such a person, or of any person I may say? No, I have no idea of being so easily persuaded. When I have made up my mind, I have made it; and Henrietta seemed entirely to have made up hers to call at Winthrop to-day; and yet, she was as near giving it up, out of nonsensical complaisance!"

"She would have turned back then, but for you?"

"She would indeed. I am almost ashamed to say it."

"Happy for her, to have such a mind as yours at hand! After the hints you gave just now, which did but confirm my own observations, the last time I was in company with him, I need not affect to have no comprehension of what is going on. I see that more than a mere dutiful morning visit to your aunt was in question; and woe betide him, and her too, when it comes to things of consequence, when they are placed in circumstances requiring fortitude and strength of mind, if she have not resolution enough to resist idle interference in such a trifle as this. Your sister is an amiable creature; but yours is the character of decision and firmness, I see. If you value her conduct or happiness, infuse as much of your own spirit into her as you can. But this, no doubt, you have been always doing. It is the worst evil of too yielding and indecisive a character, that no influence over it can be depended on. You are never sure of a good impression being durable; everybody may sway it. Let those who would be happy be firm. Here is a nut," said he, catching one down from an upper bough. "To exemplify: a beautiful glossy nut, which, blessed with original strength, has outlived all the storms of autumn. Not a puncture, not a weak spot anywhere. This nut," he continued, with playful solemnity, "while so many of his brethren have fallen and been trodden under foot, is still in possession of all the happiness that a hazel nut can be supposed capable of." Then returning to his former earnest tone—"My first wish for all whom I am interested in, is that they should be firm. If Louisa Musgrove would be beautiful and happy in her November of life, she will cherish all her present powers of mind."

He had done, and was unanswered. It would have surprised Anne if Louisa could have readily answered such a speech: words of such interest, spoken with such serious warmth! She could imagine what Louisa was feeling. For herself, she feared to move, lest she should be seen. While she remained, a bush of low rambling holly protected her, and they were moving on. Before they were beyond her hearing, however, Louisa spoke again.

"Mary is good-natured enough in many respects," said she; "but she does sometimes provoke me excessively, by her nonsense and pride—the Elliot pride. She has a great deal too much of the Elliot pride. We do so wish that Charles had married Anne instead. I suppose you know he wanted to marry Anne?"

After a moment's pause, Captain Wentworth said—

"Do you mean that she refused him?"

"Oh! yes; certainly."

"When did that happen?"

"I do not exactly know, for Henrietta and I were at school at the time; but I believe about a year before he married Mary. I wish she had accepted him. We should all have liked her a great deal better; and papa and mamma always think it was her great friend Lady Russell's doing, that she did not. They think Charles might not be learned and bookish enough to please Lady Russell, and that therefore, she persuaded Anne to refuse him."

The sounds were retreating, and Anne distinguished no more. Her own emotions still kept her fixed. She had much to recover from, before she could move. The listener's proverbial fate was not absolutely hers; she had heard no evil of herself, but she had heard a great deal of very painful import. She saw how her own character was considered by Captain Wentworth, and there had been just that degree of feeling and curiosity about her in his manner which must give her extreme agitation.

As soon as she could, she went after Mary, and having found, and walked back with her to their former station, by the stile, felt some comfort in their whole party being immediately afterwards collected, and once more in motion together. Her spirits wanted the solitude and silence which only numbers could give.

Charles and Henrietta returned, bringing, as may be conjectured, Charles Hayter with them. The minutiae of the business Anne could not attempt to understand; even Captain Wentworth did not seem admitted to perfect confidence here; but that there had been a withdrawing on the gentleman's side, and a relenting on the lady's, and that they were now very glad to be together again, did not admit a doubt. Henrietta looked a little ashamed, but very well pleased;—Charles Hayter exceedingly happy: and they were devoted to each other almost from the first instant of their all setting forward for Uppercross.

Everything now marked out Louisa for Captain Wentworth; nothing could be plainer; and where many divisions were necessary, or even where they were not, they walked side by side nearly as much as the other two. In a long strip of meadow land, where there was ample space for all, they were thus divided, forming three distinct parties; and to that party of the three which boasted least animation, and least complaisance, Anne necessarily belonged. She joined Charles and Mary, and was tired enough to be very glad of Charles's other arm; but Charles, though in very good humour with her, was out of temper with his wife. Mary had shewn herself disobliging to him, and was now to reap the consequence, which consequence was his dropping her arm almost every moment to cut off the heads of some nettles in the hedge with his switch; and when Mary began to complain of it, and lament her being ill-used, according to custom, in being on the hedge side, while Anne was never incommoded[3] on the other, he dropped the arms of both to hunt after a weasel which he had a momentary glance of, and they could hardly get him along at all.

This long meadow bordered a lane, which their footpath, at the end of it was to cross, and when the party had all reached the gate of exit, the carriage advancing in the same direction, which had been some time heard, was just coming up, and proved to be Admiral Croft's gig. He and his wife had taken their intended drive, and were returning home. Upon hearing how long a walk the young people had engaged in, they kindly offered a seat to any lady who might be particularly tired; it would save her a full mile, and they were going through Uppercross. The invitation was general, and generally declined. The Miss Musgroves were not at all tired, and Mary was either offended, by not being asked before any of the others, or what Louisa called the Elliot pride could not endure to make a third in a one horse chaise.

The walking party had crossed the lane, and were surmounting an opposite stile, and the Admiral was putting his horse in motion again, when Captain Wentworth cleared the hedge in a moment to say something to his sister. The something might be guessed by its effects.

---

[3] Inconvenienced.

"Miss Elliot, I am sure you are tired," cried Mrs. Croft. "Do let us have the pleasure of taking you home. Here is excellent room for three, I assure you. If we were all like you, I believe we might sit four. You must, indeed, you must."

Anne was still in the lane; and though instinctively beginning to decline, she was not allowed to proceed. The Admiral's kind urgency came in support of his wife's; they would not be refused; they compressed themselves into the smallest possible space to leave her a corner, and Captain Wentworth, without saying a word, turned to her, and quietly obliged her to be assisted into the carriage.

Yes; he had done it. She was in the carriage, and felt that he had placed her there, that his will and his hands had done it, that she owed it to his perception of her fatigue, and his resolution to give her rest. She was very much affected by the view of his disposition towards her, which all these things made apparent. This little circumstance seemed the completion of all that had gone before. She understood him. He could not forgive her, but he could not be unfeeling. Though condemning her for the past, and considering it with high and unjust resentment, though perfectly careless of her, and though becoming attached to another, still he could not see her suffer, without the desire of giving her relief. It was a remainder of former sentiment; it was an impulse of pure, though unacknowledged friendship; it was a proof of his own warm and amiable heart, which she could not contemplate without emotions so compounded of pleasure and pain, that she knew not which prevailed.

Her answers to the kindness and the remarks of her companions were at first unconsciously given. They had travelled half their way along the rough lane, before she was quite awake to what they said. She then found them talking of "Frederick."

"He certainly means to have one or other of those two girls, Sophy," said the Admiral; "but there is no saying which. He has been running after them, too, long enough, one would think, to make up his mind. Ay, this comes of the peace. If it were war now, he would have settled it long ago. We sailors, Miss Elliot, cannot afford to make long courtships in time of war. How many days was it, my dear, between the first time of my seeing you and our sitting down together in our lodgings at North Yarmouth?"

"We had better not talk about it, my dear," replied Mrs. Croft, pleasantly; "for if Miss Elliot were to hear how soon we came to an understanding, she would never be persuaded that we could be happy together. I had known you by character, however, long before."

"Well, and I had heard of you as a very pretty girl, and what were we to wait for besides? I do not like having such things so long in hand. I wish Frederick would spread a little more canvass,[4] and bring us home one of these young ladies to Kellynch. Then there would always be company for them. And very nice young ladies they both are; I hardly know one from the other."

"Very good humoured, unaffected girls, indeed," said Mrs. Croft, in a tone of calmer praise, such as made Anne suspect that her keener powers might not consider either of them as quite worthy of her brother; "and a very respectable family. One could not be connected with better people. My dear Admiral, that post! we shall certainly take that post."

But by coolly giving the reins a better direction herself they happily passed the danger; and by once afterwards judiciously putting out her hand they neither fell into a rut, nor ran foul of a dung-cart; and Anne, with some amusement at their style of driving, which she imagined no bad representation of the general guidance of their affairs, found herself safely deposited by them at the Cottage.

# CHAPTER XI

The time now approached for Lady Russell's return: the day was even fixed; and Anne, being engaged to join her as soon as she was resettled, was looking forward to an early removal to Kellynch, and beginning to think how her own comfort was likely to be affected by it.

It would place her in the same village with Captain Wentworth, within half a mile of him; they would have to frequent the same church, and there must be intercourse between the two families. This was against her; but on the other hand, he spent so much of his time at Uppercross, that in removing thence she might be considered rather as leaving him behind, than as going towards him; and, upon the whole, she believed she must, on this interesting question, be the gainer, almost as certainly as in her change of domestic society, in leaving poor Mary for Lady Russell.

She wished it might be possible for her to avoid ever seeing Captain Wentworth at the Hall: those rooms had witnessed former meetings which would be brought too painfully before her; but she was yet more anxious for the possibility of Lady Russell and Captain

---

[4] Unfurl a bigger sail, to catch more wind and thus travel more quickly.

Wentworth never meeting anywhere. They did not like each other, and no renewal of acquaintance now could do any good; and were Lady Russell to see them together, she might think that he had too much self-possession, and she too little.

These points formed her chief solicitude in anticipating her removal from Uppercross, where she felt she had been stationed quite long enough. Her usefulness to little Charles would always give some sweetness to the memory of her two months' visit there, but he was gaining strength apace, and she had nothing else to stay for.

The conclusion of her visit, however, was diversified in a way which she had not at all imagined. Captain Wentworth, after being unseen and unheard of at Uppercross for two whole days, appeared again among them to justify himself by a relation of what had kept him away.

A letter from his friend, Captain Harville, having found him out at last, had brought intelligence of Captain Harville's being settled with his family at Lyme for the winter; of their being therefore, quite unknowingly, within twenty miles of each other. Captain Harville had never been in good health since a severe wound which he received two years before, and Captain Wentworth's anxiety to see him had determined him to go immediately to Lyme. He had been there for four-and-twenty hours. His acquittal was complete, his friendship warmly honoured, a lively interest excited for his friend, and his description of the fine country about Lyme so feelingly attended to by the party, that an earnest desire to see Lyme themselves, and a project for going thither was the consequence.

The young people were all wild to see Lyme. Captain Wentworth talked of going there again himself, it was only seventeen miles from Uppercross; though November, the weather was by no means bad; and, in short, Louisa, who was the most eager of the eager, having formed the resolution to go, and besides the pleasure of doing as she liked, being now armed with the idea of merit in maintaining her own way, bore down all the wishes of her father and mother for putting it off till summer; and to Lyme they were to go—Charles, Mary, Anne, Henrietta, Louisa, and Captain Wentworth.

The first heedless scheme had been to go in the morning and return at night; but to this Mr. Musgrove, for the sake of his horses, would not consent; and when it came to be rationally considered, a day in the middle of November would not leave much time for seeing a new place, after deducting seven hours, as the nature of the country required, for going and returning. They were, consequently, to stay the night there, and not to be expected back till the next day's dinner. This was felt to be a considerable amendment; and though they all met at the Great House at rather an early breakfast hour, and set off very punctually, it was so much past noon before the two carriages, Mr. Musgrove's coach containing the four ladies, and Charles's curricle,[1] in which he drove Captain Wentworth, were descending the long hill into Lyme, and entering upon the still steeper street of the town itself, that it was very evident they would not have more than time for looking about them, before the light and warmth of the day were gone.

After securing accommodations, and ordering a dinner at one of the inns, the next thing to be done was unquestionably to walk directly down to the sea. They were come too late in the year for any amusement or variety which Lyme, as a public place, might offer. The rooms[2] were shut up, the lodgers almost all gone, scarcely any family but of the residents left; and, as there is nothing to admire in the buildings themselves, the remarkable situation of the town, the principal street almost hurrying into the water, the walk to the Cobb,[3] skirting round the pleasant little bay, which, in the season, is animated with bathing machines and company; the Cobb itself, its old wonders and new improvements, with the very beautiful line of cliffs stretching out to the east of the town, are what the stranger's eye will seek; and a very strange stranger it must be, who does not see charms in the immediate environs of Lyme, to make him wish to know it better. The scenes in its neighbourhood, Charmouth, with its high grounds and extensive sweeps of country, and still more, its sweet, retired bay, backed by dark cliffs, where fragments of low rock among the sands, make it the happiest spot for watching the flow of the tide, for sitting in unwearied contemplation; the woody varieties of the cheerful village of Up Lyme; and, above all, Pinny, with its green chasms between romantic rocks, where the scattered forest trees and orchards of luxuriant growth, declare that many a generation must have passed away since the first partial falling of the cliff prepared the ground for such a state, where a scene so wonderful and so lovely is exhibited, as may more than equal any of the resembling scenes of the far-famed Isle of Wight: these places must be visited, and visited again, to make the worth of Lyme understood.

---

[1] A sporty open carriage that holds only two.

[2] The assembly rooms, places to be booked for social gatherings, balls, concerts.

[3] A huge breakwater, made of stones, that encloses the harbor.

The party from Uppercross passing down by the now deserted
and melancholy looking rooms, and still descending, soon found
themselves on the sea-shore; and lingering only, as all must linger
and gaze on a first return to the sea, who ever deserved to look on it
at all, proceeded towards the Cobb, equally their object in itself and
on Captain Wentworth's account: for in a small house, near the foot
of an old pier of unknown date, were the Harvilles settled. Captain
Wentworth turned in to call on his friend; the others walked on,
and he was to join them on the Cobb.

They were by no means tired of wondering and admiring; and not
even Louisa seemed to feel that they had parted with Captain Wentworth long, when they saw him coming after them, with three companions, all well known already, by description, to be Captain and
Mrs. Harville, and a Captain Benwick, who was staying with them.

Captain Benwick had some time ago been first lieutenant of the
Laconia; and the account which Captain Wentworth had given of
him, on his return from Lyme before, his warm praise of him as an
excellent young man and an officer, whom he had always valued
highly, which must have stamped him well in the esteem of every
listener, had been followed by a little history of his private life,

LIME-REGIS.

Eighteenth-century Print of Lyme Regis (from Library Company of
Philadelphia.)

which rendered him perfectly interesting in the eyes of all the ladies. He had been engaged to Captain Harville's sister, and was now mourning her loss. They had been a year or two waiting for fortune and promotion. Fortune came, his prize-money as lieutenant being great; promotion, too, came at last; but Fanny Harville did not live to know it. She had died the preceding summer while he was at sea. Captain Wentworth believed it impossible for man to be more attached to woman than poor Benwick had been to Fanny Harville, or to be more deeply afflicted under the dreadful change. He considered his disposition as of the sort which must suffer heavily, uniting very strong feelings with quiet, serious, and retiring manners, and a decided taste for reading, and sedentary pursuits. To finish the interest of the story, the friendship between him and the Harvilles seemed, if possible, augmented by the event which closed all their views of alliance, and Captain Benwick was now living with them entirely. Captain Harville had taken his present house for half a year; his taste, and his health, and his fortune, all directing him to a residence inexpensive, and by the sea; and the grandeur of the country, and the retirement of Lyme in the winter, appeared exactly adapted to Captain Benwick's state of mind. The sympathy and good-will excited towards Captain Benwick was very great.

"And yet," said Anne to herself, as they now moved forward to meet the party, "he has not, perhaps, a more sorrowing heart than I have. I cannot believe his prospects so blighted for ever. He is younger than I am; younger in feeling, if not in fact; younger as a man.[4] He will rally again, and be happy with another."

They all met, and were introduced. Captain Harville was a tall, dark man, with a sensible, benevolent countenance; a little lame; and from strong features and want of health, looking much older than Captain Wentworth. Captain Benwick looked, and was, the youngest of the three, and, compared with either of them, a little man. He had a pleasing face and a melancholy air, just as he ought to have, and drew back from conversation.

Captain Harville, though not equalling Captain Wentworth in manners, was a perfect gentleman, unaffected, warm, and obliging. Mrs. Harville, a degree less polished than her husband, seemed, however, to have the same good feelings; and nothing could be more pleasant than their desire of considering the whole party as friends of their

---

[4] Recall Anne's observation (ch. 7) that the "years which had destroyed her bloom had given [Wentworth] a more glowing, manly, open look, in no respect lessening his personal advantages."

own, because the friends of Captain Wentworth, or more kindly hospitable than their entreaties for their all promising to dine with them. The dinner, already ordered at the inn, was at last, though unwillingly, accepted as a excuse; but they seemed almost hurt that Captain Wentworth should have brought any such party to Lyme, without considering it as a thing of course that they should dine with them.

There was so much attachment to Captain Wentworth in all this, and such a bewitching charm in a degree of hospitality so uncommon, so unlike the usual style of give-and-take invitations, and dinners of formality and display, that Anne felt her spirits not likely to be benefited by an increasing acquaintance among his brother-officers. "These would have been all my friends," was her thought; and she had to struggle against a great tendency to lowness.

On quitting the Cobb, they all went in-doors with their new friends, and found rooms so small as none but those who invite from the heart could think capable of accommodating so many. Anne had a moment's astonishment on the subject herself; but it was soon lost in the pleasanter feelings which sprang from the sight of all the ingenious contrivances and nice arrangements of Captain Harville, to turn the actual space to the best account, to supply the deficiencies of lodging-house furniture, and defend the windows and doors against the winter storms to be expected. The varieties in the fitting-up of the rooms, where the common necessaries provided by the owner, in the common indifferent plight, were contrasted with some few articles of a rare species of wood, excellently worked up, and with something curious and valuable from all the distant countries Captain Harville had visited, were more than amusing to Anne; connected as it all was with his profession, the fruit of its labours, the effect of its influence on his habits, the picture of repose and domestic happiness it presented, made it to her a something more, or less, than gratification.

Captain Harville was no reader; but he had contrived excellent accommodations, and fashioned very pretty shelves, for a tolerable collection of well-bound volumes, the property of Captain Benwick. His lameness prevented him from taking much exercise; but a mind of usefulness and ingenuity seemed to furnish him with constant employment within. He drew, he varnished, he carpentered, he glued; he made toys for the children; he fashioned new netting-needles and pins with improvements; and if everything else was done, sat down to his large fishing-net at one corner of the room.

Anne thought she left great happiness behind her when they quitted the house; and Louisa, by whom she found herself walking, burst forth into raptures of admiration and delight on the character of the navy; their friendliness, their brotherliness, their openness, their uprightness; protesting that she was convinced of sailors having more worth and warmth than any other set of men in England; that they only knew how to live, and they only deserved to be respected and loved.

They went back to dress and dine; and so well had the scheme answered already, that nothing was found amiss; though its being "so entirely out of season," and the "no thoroughfare of Lyme," and the "no expectation of company," had brought many apologies from the heads of the inn.

Anne found herself by this time growing so much more hardened to being in Captain Wentworth's company than she had at first imagined could ever be, that the sitting down to the same table with him now, and the interchange of the common civilities attending on it (they never got beyond), was become a mere nothing.

The nights were too dark for the ladies to meet again till the morrow, but Captain Harville had promised them a visit in the evening; and he came, bringing his friend also, which was more than had been expected, it having been agreed that Captain Benwick had all the appearance of being oppressed by the presence of so many strangers. He ventured among them again, however, though his spirits certainly did not seem fit for the mirth of the party in general.

While Captains Wentworth and Harville led the talk on one side of the room, and by recurring to former days, supplied anecdotes in abundance to occupy and entertain the others, it fell to Anne's lot to be placed rather apart with Captain Benwick; and a very good impulse of her nature obliged her to begin an acquaintance with him. He was shy, and disposed to abstraction; but the engaging mildness of her countenance, and gentleness of her manners, soon had their effect; and Anne was well repaid the first trouble of exertion. He was evidently a young man of considerable taste in reading, though principally in poetry; and besides the persuasion of having given him at least an evening's indulgence in the discussion of subjects, which his usual companions had probably no concern in, she had the hope of being of real use to him in some suggestions as to the duty and benefit of struggling against affliction, which had naturally grown out of their conversation. For, though shy, he did not seem reserved; it had rather the appearance of feelings glad to burst their usual restraints; and having talked of poetry, the richness of the present age, and gone through a brief comparison of opinion as to the first-rate poets, trying to ascertain whether *Marmion* or *The Lady of the Lake* were to be preferred, and how ranked the *Giaour* and *The Bride of Abydos*;[5] and moreover, how the *Giaour* was to be pronounced, he showed himself so intimately acquainted with all the tenderest songs of the one poet, and all the impassioned descriptions of hopeless agony of the other; he repeated, with such tremulous feeling, the various lines which imaged a broken heart, or a mind destroyed by wretchedness, and looked so entirely as if he meant to be understood, that she ventured to hope he did not always read only poetry, and to say, that she thought it was the misfortune of poetry to be seldom safely enjoyed by those who enjoyed it completely; and that the strong feelings which alone could estimate it truly were the very feelings which ought to taste it but sparingly.[6]

His looks shewing him not pained, but pleased with this allusion to his situation, she was emboldened to go on; and feeling in herself the right of seniority of mind, she ventured to recommend a larger allowance of prose in his daily study; and on being requested to particularize, mentioned such works of our best moralists, such collections of the finest letters, such memoirs of characters of worth and suffering, as occurred to her at the moment as calculated to rouse and fortify the mind by the highest precepts, and the strongest examples of moral and religious endurances.

Captain Benwick listened attentively, and seemed grateful for the interest implied; and though with a shake of the head, and sighs which declared his little faith in the efficacy of any books on grief like his, noted down the names of those she recommended, and promised to procure and read them.

When the evening was over, Anne could not but be amused at the idea of her coming to Lyme to preach patience and resignation to a young man whom she had never seen before; nor could she help fearing, on more serious reflection, that, like many other great moralists and preachers, she had been eloquent on a point in which her own conduct would ill bear examination.

[5] *Marmion* (1808) and *The Lady of The Lake* (1810) are poetic romances by Walter Scott; *The Giaour* and *The Bride of Abydos* (1813) are two of Byron's wildly popular "Eastern Tales"; the others are *Lara* and *The Corsair,* both 1814 (Austen read these, too).

[6] One of the very few references in Austen's novels to the writing of her Romantic contemporaries and one of the relatively few engagements with a presumably Romantic "state of mind" that pertains chiefly to Benwick but, quite clearly, to Anne herself.

# CHAPTER XII

Anne and Henrietta, finding themselves the earliest of the party the next morning, agreed to stroll down to the sea before breakfast. They went to the sands, to watch the flowing of the tide, which a fine south-easterly breeze was bringing in with all the grandeur which so flat a shore admitted. They praised the morning; gloried in the sea; sympathized in the delight of the fresh-feeling breeze—and were silent; till Henrietta suddenly began again with—

"Oh! yes,—I am quite convinced that, with very few exceptions, the sea-air always does good. There can be no doubt of its having been of the greatest service to Dr. Shirley, after his illness, last spring twelve-month.[1] He declares himself, that coming to Lyme for a month, did him more good than all the medicine he took; and, that being by the sea, always makes him feel young again. Now, I cannot help thinking it a pity that he does not live entirely by the sea. I do think he had better leave Uppercross entirely, and fix[2] at Lyme. Do not you, Anne? Do not you agree with me, that it is the best thing he could do, both for himself and Mrs. Shirley? She has cousins here, you know, and many acquaintance, which would make it cheerful for her, and I am sure she would be glad to get to a place where she could have medical attendance at hand, in case of his having another seizure. Indeed I think it quite melancholy to have such excellent people as Dr. and Mrs. Shirley, who have been doing good all their lives, wearing out their last days in a place like Uppercross, where, excepting our family, they seem shut out from all the world. I wish his friends would propose it to him. I really think they ought. And, as to procuring a dispensation,[3] there could be no difficulty at his time of life, and with his character. My only doubt is, whether anything could persuade him to leave his parish. He is so very strict and scrupulous in his notions; over-scrupulous I must say. Do not you think, Anne, it is being over-scrupulous? Do not you think it is quite a mistaken point of conscience, when a clergyman sacrifices his health for the sake of duties, which may be just as well performed by another person? And at Lyme too, only seventeen miles off, he would be near enough to hear, if people thought there was anything to complain of."

[1] Twelve months ago, last spring.

[2] Fix his residence at.

[3] That is, to keep his living in absentia while assigning his duties to Charles.

Anne smiled more than once to herself during this speech, and entered into the subject, as ready to do good by entering into the feelings of a young lady as of a young man, though here it was good of a lower standard, for what could be offered but general acquiescence? She said all that was reasonable and proper on the business; felt the claims of Dr. Shirley to repose as she ought; saw how very desirable it was that he should have some active, respectable young man, as a resident curate, and was even courteous enough to hint at the advantage of such resident curate's being married.

"I wish," said Henrietta, very well pleased with her companion, "I wish Lady Russell lived at Uppercross, and were intimate with Dr. Shirley. I have always heard of Lady Russell as a woman of the greatest influence with everybody! I always look upon her as able to persuade a person to anything! I am afraid of her, as I have told you before, quite afraid of her, because she is so very clever; but I respect her amazingly, and wish we had such a neighbour at Uppercross."

Anne was amused by Henrietta's manner of being grateful, and amused also that the course of events and the new interests of Henrietta's views should have placed her friend at all in favour with any of the Musgrove family; she had only time, however, for a general answer, and a wish that such another woman were at Uppercross, before all subjects suddenly ceased, on seeing Louisa and Captain Wentworth coming towards them. They came also for a stroll till breakfast was likely to be ready; but Louisa recollecting, immediately afterwards that she had something to procure at a shop, invited them all to go back with her into the town. They were all at her disposal.

When they came to the steps, leading upwards from the beach, a gentleman, at the same moment preparing to come down, politely drew back, and stopped to give them way. They ascended and passed him; and as they passed, Anne's face caught his eye, and he looked at her with a degree of earnest admiration, which she could not be insensible of. She was looking remarkably well; her very regular, very pretty features, having the bloom and freshness of youth restored by the fine wind which had been blowing on her complexion, and by the animation of eye which it had also produced. It was evident that the gentleman, (completely a gentleman in manner) admired her exceedingly. Captain Wentworth looked round at her instantly in a way which shewed his noticing of it. He gave her a momentary glance, a glance of brightness, which seemed to say, "That man is struck with you, and even I, at this moment, see something like Anne Elliot again."

After attending Louisa through her business, and loitering about a little longer, they returned to the inn; and Anne, in passing afterwards quickly from her own chamber to their dining-room, had nearly run against the very same gentleman, as he came out of an adjoining apartment. She had before conjectured him to be a stranger like themselves, and determined that a well-looking groom, who was strolling about near the two inns as they came back, should be his servant. Both master and man being in mourning assisted the idea. It was now proved that he belonged to the same inn as themselves; and this second meeting, short as it was, also proved again by the gentleman's looks, that he thought hers very lovely, and by the readiness and propriety of his apologies, that he was a man of exceedingly good manners. He seemed about thirty, and though not handsome, had an agreeable person. Anne felt that she should like to know who he was.

They had nearly done breakfast, when the sound of a carriage, (almost the first they had heard since entering Lyme) drew half the party to the window. It was a gentleman's carriage, a curricle, but only coming round from the stable-yard to the front door; somebody must be going away. It was driven by a servant in mourning.

The word curricle made Charles Musgrove jump up that he might compare it with his own; the servant in mourning roused Anne's curiosity, and the whole six were collected to look, by the time the owner of the curricle was to be seen issuing from the door amidst the bows and civilities of the household, and taking his seat, to drive off.

"Ah!" cried Captain Wentworth, instantly, and with half a glance at Anne, "it is the very man we passed."

The Miss Musgroves agreed to it; and having all kindly watched him as far up the hill as they could, they returned to the breakfast table. The waiter came into the room soon afterwards.

"Pray," said Captain Wentworth, immediately, "can you tell us the name of the gentleman who is just gone away?"

"Yes, Sir, a Mr. Elliot, a gentleman of large fortune, came in last night from Sidmouth. Dare say you heard the carriage, sir, while you were at dinner; and going on now for Crewkherne, in his way to Bath and London."

"Elliot!" Many had looked on each other, and many had repeated the name, before all this had been got through, even by the smart rapidity of a waiter.

"Bless me!" cried Mary; "it must be our cousin; it must be our Mr. Elliot, it must, indeed! Charles, Anne, must not it? In mourning, you see, just as our Mr. Elliot must be. How very extraordinary! In the very same inn with us! Anne, must not it be our Mr. Elliot? my father's next heir? Pray sir," turning to the waiter, "did not you hear, did not his servant say whether he belonged to the Kellynch family?"

"No, ma'am, he did not mention no particular family; but he said his master was a very rich gentleman, and would be a baronight some day."

"There! you see!" cried Mary in an ecstasy, "just as I said! Heir to Sir Walter Elliot! I was sure that would come out, if it was so. Depend upon it, that is a circumstance which his servants take care to publish, wherever he goes. But, Anne, only conceive how extraordinary! I wish I had looked at him more. I wish we had been aware in time, who it was, that he might have been introduced to us. What a pity that we should not have been introduced to each other! Do you think he had the Elliot countenance? I hardly looked at him, I was looking at the horses; but I think he had something of the Elliot countenance, I wonder the arms[4] did not strike me! Oh! the great-coat was hanging over the panel, and hid the arms, so it did; otherwise, I am sure, I should have observed them, and the livery too; if the servant had not been in mourning, one should have known him by the livery."

"Putting all these very extraordinary circumstances together," said Captain Wentworth, "we must consider it to be the arrangement of Providence, that you should not be introduced to your cousin."

When she could command Mary's attention, Anne quietly tried to convince her that their father and Mr. Elliot had not, for many years, been on such terms as to make the power of attempting an introduction at all desirable.

At the same time, however, it was a secret gratification to herself to have seen her cousin, and to know that the future owner of Kellynch was undoubtedly a gentleman, and had an air of good sense. She would not, upon any account, mention her having met with him the second time; luckily Mary did not much attend to their having passed close by him in their earlier walk, but she would have felt quite ill-used by Anne's having actually run against him in the passage, and received his very polite excuses, while she had never

[4] The coat of arms, signifying the family's long standing and importance, would appear on the carriage.

been near him at all; no, that cousinly little interview must remain a perfect secret.

"Of course," said Mary, "you will mention our seeing Mr. Elliot, the next time you write to Bath. I think my father certainly ought to hear of it; do mention all about him."

Anne avoided a direct reply, but it was just the circumstance which she considered as not merely unnecessary to be communicated, but as what ought to be suppressed. The offence which had been given her father, many years back, she knew; Elizabeth's particular share in it she suspected; and that Mr. Elliot's idea always produced irritation in both was beyond a doubt. Mary never wrote to Bath herself; all the toil of keeping up a slow and unsatisfactory correspondence with Elizabeth fell on Anne.

Breakfast had not been long over, when they were joined by Captain and Mrs. Harville and Captain Benwick; with whom they had appointed to take their last walk about Lyme. They ought to be setting off for Uppercross by one, and in the mean while were to be all together, and out of doors as long as they could.

Anne found Captain Benwick getting near her, as soon as they were all fairly in the street. Their conversation the preceding evening did not disincline him to seek her again; and they walked together some time, talking as before of Mr. Scott and Lord Byron, and still as unable as before, and as unable as any other two readers, to think exactly alike of the merits of either, till something occasioned an almost general change amongst their party, and instead of Captain Benwick, she had Captain Harville by her side.

"Miss Elliot," said he, speaking rather low, "you have done a good deed in making that poor fellow talk so much. I wish he could have such company oftener. It is bad for him, I know, to be shut up as he is; but what can we do? We cannot part."

"No," said Anne, "that I can easily believe to be impossible; but in time, perhaps—we know what time does in every case of affliction, and you must remember, Captain Harville, that your friend may yet be called a young mourner—only last summer, I understand."

"Ay, true enough," (with a deep sigh) "only June."

"And not known to him, perhaps, so soon."

"Not till the first week of August, when he came home from the Cape, just made into the Grappler.[5] I was at Plymouth dreading to hear of him; he sent in letters, but the Grappler was under orders

[5] Promoted to Captain of a new ship.

for Portsmouth. There the news must follow him, but who was to tell it? not I. I would as soon have been run up to the yard-arm.[6] Nobody could do it, but that good fellow" (pointing to Captain Wentworth). "The Laconia had come into Plymouth the week before; no danger of her being sent to sea again. He stood his chance for the rest; wrote up for leave of absence, but without waiting the return, travelled night and day till he got to Portsmouth, rowed off to the Grappler that instant, and never left the poor fellow for a week. That's what he did, and nobody else could have saved poor James. You may think, Miss Elliot, whether he is dear to us!"

Anne did think on the question with perfect decision, and said as much in reply as her own feeling could accomplish, or as his seemed able to bear, for he was too much affected to renew the subject, and when he spoke again, it was of something totally different.

Mrs. Harville's giving it as her opinion that her husband would have quite walking enough by the time he reached home, determined the direction of all the party in what was to be their last walk; they would accompany them to their door, and then return and set off themselves. By all their calculations there was just time for this; but as they drew near the Cobb, there was such a general wish to walk along it once more, all were so inclined, and Louisa soon grew so determined, that the difference of a quarter of an hour, it was found, would be no difference at all; so with all the kind leave-taking, and all the kind interchange of invitations and promises which may be imagined, they parted from Captain and Mrs. Harville at their own door, and still accompanied by Captain Benwick, who seemed to cling to them to the last, proceeded to make the proper adieus to the Cobb.

Anne found Captain Benwick again drawing near her. Lord Byron's "dark blue seas"[7] could not fail of being brought forward by their present view, and she gladly gave him all her attention as long as attention was possible. It was soon drawn, perforce another way.

---

[6] "I would as soon have been hanged" (the yard-arm was a high horizontal beam, routinely used for such punishment).

[7] A frequent phrase in Byron's poetry, with which Austen is familiar. In *The Bride of Abydos* (mentioned in the previous chapter), the young hero's eye "looked o'er the dark blue water" (1.242); Byron's pirate-romance, *The Corsair* (1814), opens: "O'er the glad waters of the dark blue sea,/Our thoughts as boundless, our souls as free"; in his overnight success, *Childe Harold's Pilgrimage* (1812), Byron greets "Fair Cadiz, rising o'er the dark blue sea" (I.lxxi), and appeals to "He that has sail'd upon the dark blue sea" (II.xvii).

Granny's Teeth, The Cobb, Lyme Steps (Courtesy: Jane Austen Society of Australia.)

There was too much wind to make the high part of the new Cobb pleasant for the ladies, and they agreed to get down the steps to the lower, and all were contented to pass quietly and carefully down the steep flight, excepting Louisa; she must be jumped down them by Captain Wentworth. In all their walks, he had had to jump her from the stiles; the sensation was delightful to her. The hardness of the pavement for her feet, made him less willing upon the present occasion; he did it, however. She was safely down, and instantly, to show her enjoyment, ran up the steps to be jumped down again. He advised her against it, thought the jar too great; but no, he reasoned and talked in vain, she smiled and said, "I am determined I will:" he put out his hands; she was too precipitate by half a second, she fell on the pavement on the Lower Cobb, and was taken up lifeless! There was no wound, no blood, no visible bruise; but her eyes were closed, she breathed not, her face was like death. The horror of the moment to all who stood around!

Captain Wentworth, who had caught her up, knelt with her in his arms, looking on her with a face as pallid as her own, in an agony of silence. "She is dead! she is dead!" screamed Mary, catching hold of her husband, and contributing with his own horror to make him immoveable; and in another moment, Henrietta, sinking under the conviction, lost her senses too, and would have fallen on the steps, but for Captain Benwick and Anne, who caught and supported her between them.

"Is there no one to help me?" were the first words which burst from Captain Wentworth, in a tone of despair, and as if all his own strength were gone.

"Go to him, go to him," cried Anne, "for heaven's sake go to him. I can support her myself. Leave me, and go to him. Rub her hands, rub her temples; here are salts;[8] take them, take them."

Captain Benwick obeyed, and Charles at the same moment, disengaging himself from his wife, they were both with him; and Louisa was raised up and supported more firmly between them, and everything was done that Anne had prompted, but in vain; while Captain Wentworth, staggering against the wall for his support, exclaimed in the bitterest agony—

"Oh God! her father and mother!"

"A surgeon!" said Anne.

He caught the word; it seemed to rouse him at once, and saying only—"True, true, a surgeon this instant," was darting away, when Anne eagerly suggested—

"Captain Benwick, would not it be better for Captain Benwick? He knows where a surgeon is to be found."

Every one capable of thinking felt the advantage of the idea, and in a moment (it was all done in rapid moments) Captain Benwick had resigned the poor corpse-like figure entirely to the brother's care, and was off for the town with the utmost rapidity.

As to the wretched party left behind, it could scarcely be said which of the three, who were completely rational, was suffering most: Captain Wentworth, Anne, or Charles, who, really a very affectionate brother, hung over Louisa with sobs of grief, and could only turn his eyes from one sister, to see the other in a state as insensible, or to witness the hysterical agitations of his wife, calling on him for help which he could not give.

---

[8] Smelling salts, used to revive someone from unconsciousness.

Anne, attending with all the strength and zeal, and thought, which instinct supplied, to Henrietta, still tried, at intervals, to suggest comfort to the others, tried to quiet Mary, to animate Charles, to assuage the feelings of Captain Wentworth. Both seemed to look to her for directions.

"Anne, Anne," cried Charles, "What is to be done next? What, in heaven's name, is to be done next?"

Captain Wentworth's eyes were also turned towards her.

"Had not she better be carried to the inn? Yes, I am sure: carry her gently to the inn."

"Yes, yes, to the inn," repeated Captain Wentworth, comparatively collected, and eager to be doing something. "I will carry her myself. Musgrove, take care of the others."

By this time the report of the accident had spread among the workmen and boatmen about the Cobb, and many were collected near them, to be useful if wanted, at any rate, to enjoy the sight of a dead young lady, nay, two dead young ladies, for it proved twice as fine as the first report. To some of the best-looking of these good people Henrietta was consigned, for, though partially revived, she was quite helpless; and in this manner, Anne walking by her side, and Charles attending to his wife, they set forward, treading back with feelings unutterable, the ground, which so lately, so very lately, and so light of heart, they had passed along.

They were not off the Cobb, before the Harvilles met them. Captain Benwick had been seen flying by their house, with a countenance which showed something to be wrong; and they had set off immediately, informed and directed as they passed, towards the spot. Shocked as Captain Harville was, he brought senses and nerves that could be instantly useful; and a look between him and his wife decided what was to be done. She must be taken to their house; all must go to their house; and await the surgeon's arrival there. They would not listen to scruples: he was obeyed; they were all beneath his roof; and while Louisa, under Mrs. Harville's direction, was conveyed up stairs, and given possession of her own bed, assistance, cordials, restoratives were supplied by her husband to all who needed them.

Louisa had once opened her eyes, but soon closed them again, without apparent consciousness. This had been a proof of life, however, of service to her sister; and Henrietta, though perfectly incapable of being in the same room with Louisa, was kept, by the agitation of hope and fear, from a return of her own insensibility. Mary, too, was growing calmer.

The surgeon was with them almost before it had seemed possible. They were sick with horror, while he examined; but he was not hopeless. The head had received a severe contusion, but he had seen greater injuries recovered from: he was by no means hopeless; he spoke cheerfully.

That he did not regard it as a desperate case, that he did not say a few hours must end it, was at first felt, beyond the hope of most; and the ecstasy of such a reprieve, the rejoicing, deep and silent, after a few fervent ejaculations of gratitude to Heaven had been offered, may be conceived.

The tone, the look, with which "Thank God!" was uttered by Captain Wentworth, Anne was sure could never be forgotten by her; nor the sight of him afterwards, as he sat near a table, leaning over it with folded arms and face concealed, as if overpowered by the various feelings of his soul, and trying by prayer and reflection to calm them.

Louisa's limbs had escaped. There was no injury but to the head.

It now became necessary for the party to consider what was best to be done, as to their general situation. They were now able to speak to each other and consult. That Louisa must remain where she was, however distressing to her friends to be involving the Harvilles in such trouble, did not admit a doubt. Her removal was impossible. The Harvilles silenced all scruples; and, as much as they could, all gratitude. They had looked forward and arranged everything before the others began to reflect. Captain Benwick must give up his room to them, and get another bed elsewhere; and the whole was settled. They were only concerned that the house could accommodate no more; and yet perhaps, by "putting the children away in the maid's room, or swinging a cot somewhere," they could hardly bear to think of not finding room for two or three besides, supposing they might wish to stay; though, with regard to any attendance on Miss Musgrove, there need not be the least uneasiness in leaving her to Mrs. Harville's care entirely. Mrs. Harville was a very experienced nurse, and her nursery-maid, who had lived with her long, and gone about with her everywhere, was just such another. Between these two, she could want no possible attendance by day or night. And all this was said with a truth and sincerity of feeling irresistible.

Charles, Henrietta, and Captain Wentworth were the three in consultation, and for a little while it was only an interchange of perplexity and terror. "Uppercross, the necessity of some one's going to Uppercross; the news to be conveyed; how it could be broken to Mr. and Mrs. Musgrove; the lateness of the morning; an hour already gone since they ought to have been off; the impossibility of being in tolerable time." At first, they were capable of nothing more to the purpose than such exclamations; but, after a while, Captain Wentworth, exerting himself, said—

"We must be decided, and without the loss of another minute. Every minute is valuable. Some one must resolve on being off for Uppercross instantly. Musgrove, either you or I must go."

Charles agreed, but declared his resolution of not going away. He would be as little incumbrance as possible to Captain and Mrs. Harville; but as to leaving his sister in such a state, he neither ought, nor would. So far it was decided; and Henrietta at first declared the same. She, however, was soon persuaded to think differently. The usefulness of her staying! She who had not been able to remain in Louisa's room, or to look at her, without sufferings which made her worse than helpless! She was forced to acknowledge that she could do no good, yet was still unwilling to be away, till, touched by the thought of her father and mother, she gave it up; she consented, she was anxious to be at home.

The plan had reached this point, when Anne, coming quietly down from Louisa's room, could not but hear what followed, for the parlour door was open.

"Then it is settled, Musgrove," cried Captain Wentworth, "that you stay, and that I take care of your sister home. But as to the rest, as to the others, if one stays to assist Mrs. Harville, I think it need be only one. Mrs. Charles Musgrove will, of course, wish to get back to her children; but if Anne will stay, no one so proper, so capable as Anne."

She paused a moment to recover from the emotion of hearing herself so spoken of. The other two warmly agreed with what he said, and she then appeared.

"You will stay, I am sure; you will stay and nurse her;" cried he, turning to her and speaking with a glow, and yet a gentleness, which seemed almost restoring the past. She coloured deeply, and he recollected himself and moved away. She expressed herself most willing, ready, happy to remain. "It was what she had been thinking of, and wishing to be allowed to do. A bed on the floor in Louisa's room would be sufficient for her, if Mrs. Harville would but think so."

One thing more, and all seemed arranged. Though it was rather desirable that Mr. and Mrs. Musgrove should be previously alarmed by some share of delay; yet the time required by the Uppercross horses to take them back, would be a dreadful extension of suspense; and Captain Wentworth proposed, and Charles Musgrove agreed, that it would be much better for him to take a chaise from the inn, and leave Mr. Musgrove's carriage and horses to be sent home the next morning early, when there would be the farther advantage of sending an account of Louisa's night.

Captain Wentworth now hurried off to get everything ready on his part, and to be soon followed by the two ladies. When the plan was made known to Mary, however, there was an end of all peace in it. She was so wretched and so vehement, complained so much of injustice in being expected to go away instead of Anne; Anne, who was nothing to Louisa, while she was her sister, and had the best right to stay in Henrietta's stead! Why was not she to be as useful as Anne? And to go home without Charles, too, without her husband! No, it was too unkind. And in short, she said more than her husband could long withstand, and as none of the others could oppose when he gave way, there was no help for it; the change of Mary for Anne was inevitable.

Anne had never submitted more reluctantly to the jealous and ill-judging claims of Mary; but so it must be, and they set off for the town, Charles taking care of his sister, and Captain Benwick attending to her. She gave a moment's recollection, as they hurried along, to the little circumstances which the same spots had witnessed earlier in the morning. There she had listened to Henrietta's schemes for Dr. Shirley's leaving Uppercross; farther on, she had first seen Mr. Elliot; a moment seemed all that could now be given to any one but Louisa, or those who were wrapt up in her welfare.

Captain Benwick was most considerately attentive to her; and, united as they all seemed by the distress of the day, she felt an increasing degree of good-will towards him, and a pleasure even in thinking that it might, perhaps, be the occasion of continuing their acquaintance.

Captain Wentworth was on the watch for them, and a chaise and four in waiting, stationed for their convenience in the lowest part of the street; but his evident surprise and vexation at the substitution of one sister for the other, the change in his countenance, the astonishment, the expressions begun and suppressed, with which Charles was listened to, made but a mortifying reception of Anne; or must at least convince her that she was valued only as she could be useful to Louisa.

She endeavoured to be composed, and to be just. Without emulating the feelings of an Emma towards her Henry,[9] she would have attended on Louisa with a zeal above the common claims of regard, for his sake; and she hoped he would not long be so unjust as to suppose she would shrink unnecessarily from the office of a friend.

In the mean while she was in the carriage. He had handed them both in, and placed himself between them; and in this manner, under these circumstances, full of astonishment and emotion to Anne, she quitted Lyme. How the long stage would pass; how it was to affect their manners; what was to be their sort of intercourse, she could not foresee. It was all quite natural, however. He was devoted to Henrietta; always turning towards her; and when he spoke at all, always with the view of supporting her hopes and raising her spirits. In general, his voice and manner were studiously calm. To spare Henrietta from agitation seemed the governing principle. Once only, when she had been grieving over the last ill-judged, ill-fated walk to the Cobb, bitterly lamenting that it ever had been thought of, he burst forth, as if wholly overcome—

"Don't talk of it, don't talk of it," he cried. "Oh God! that I had not given way to her at the fatal moment! Had I done as I ought! But so eager and so resolute! Dear, sweet Louisa!"

Anne wondered whether it ever occurred to him now, to question the justness of his own previous opinion as to the universal felicity and advantage of firmness of character; and whether it might not strike him that, like all other qualities of the mind, it should have its proportions and limits. She thought it could scarcely escape him to feel that a persuadable temper might sometimes be as much in favour of happiness as a very resolute character.

They got on fast. Anne was astonished to recognise the same hills and the same objects so soon. Their actual speed, heightened by some dread of the conclusion, made the road appear but half as long as on the day before. It was growing quite dusk, however, before they were in the neighbourhood of Uppercross, and there had been total silence among them for some time, Henrietta leaning back in the corner, with a shawl over her face, giving the hope of her having cried herself to sleep; when, as they were going up their last hill,

---

[9] *Henry and Emma, A Poem, upon the Model of the Nut-Brown Maid,* a poem about the abiding love of the title characters, by Matthew Prior (1644–1721). Prior is also mentioned, somewhat disparagingly, in *Northanger Abbey,* where the narrator complains of his ubiquity in miscellanies and anthologies.

Anne found herself all at once addressed by Captain Wentworth. In a low, cautious voice, he said:—

"I have been considering what we had best do. She must not appear at first. She could not stand it. I have been thinking whether you had not better remain in the carriage with her, while I go in and break it to Mr. and Mrs. Musgrove. Do you think this is a good plan?"

She did: he was satisfied, and said no more. But the remembrance of the appeal remained a pleasure to her, as a proof of friendship, and of deference for her judgement, a great pleasure; and when it became a sort of parting proof, its value did not lessen.

When the distressing communication at Uppercross was over, and he had seen the father and mother quite as composed as could be hoped, and the daughter all the better for being with them, he announced his intention of returning in the same carriage to Lyme; and when the horses were baited,[10] he was off.

[10] Given food.

# Persuasion

## VOLUME II

## CHAPTER I

The remainder of Anne's time at Uppercross, comprehending only
two days, was spent entirely at the Mansion House; and she had the
satisfaction of knowing herself extremely useful there, both as an
immediate companion, and as assisting in all those arrangements
for the future, which, in Mr. and Mrs. Musgrove's distressed state
of spirits, would have been difficulties.

They had an early account from Lyme the next morning. Louisa
was much the same. No symptoms worse than before had appeared.
Charles came a few hours afterwards, to bring a later and more particular account. He was tolerably cheerful. A speedy cure must not
be hoped, but everything was going on as well as the nature of the
case admitted. In speaking of the Harvilles, he seemed unable to satisfy his own sense of their kindness, especially of Mrs. Harville's
exertions as a nurse. "She really left nothing for Mary to do. He and
Mary had been persuaded to go early to their inn last night. Mary
had been hysterical again this morning. When he came away, she
was going to walk out with Captain Benwick, which, he hoped,
would do her good. He almost wished she had been prevailed on to
come home the day before; but the truth was, that Mrs. Harville left
nothing for anybody to do."

Charles was to return to Lyme the same afternoon, and his father
had at first half a mind to go with him, but the ladies could not consent. It would be going only to multiply trouble to the others, and
increase his own distress; and a much better scheme followed and
was acted upon. A chaise was sent for from Crewkherne, and Charles
conveyed back a far more useful person in the old nursery-maid of
the family, one who having brought up all the children, and seen the

very last, the lingering and long-petted Master Harry, sent to school after his brothers, was now living in her deserted nursery to mend stockings and dress all the blains[1] and bruises she could get near her, and who, consequently, was only too happy in being allowed to go and help nurse dear Miss Louisa. Vague wishes of getting Sarah thither, had occurred before to Mrs. Musgrove and Henrietta; but without Anne, it would hardly have been resolved on, and found practicable so soon.

They were indebted, the next day, to Charles Hayter, for all the minute knowledge of Louisa, which it was so essential to obtain every twenty-four hours. He made it his business to go to Lyme, and his account was still encouraging. The intervals of sense and consciousness were believed to be stronger. Every report agreed in Captain Wentworth's appearing fixed in Lyme.

Anne was to leave them on the morrow, an event which they all dreaded. "What should they do without her? They were wretched comforters for one another." And so much was said in this way, that Anne thought she could not do better than impart among them the general inclination to which she was privy, and persuaded them all to go to Lyme at once. She had little difficulty; it was soon determined that they would go; go to-morrow, fix themselves at the inn, or get into lodgings, as it suited, and there remain till dear Louisa could be moved. They must be taking off some trouble from the good people she was with; they might at least relieve Mrs. Harville from the care of her own children; and in short, they were so happy in the decision, that Anne was delighted with what she had done, and felt that she could not spend her last morning at Uppercross better than in assisting their preparations, and sending them off at an early hour, though her being left to the solitary range of the house was the consequence.

She was the last, excepting the little boys at the cottage, she was the very last, the only remaining one of all that had filled and animated both houses, of all that had given Uppercross its cheerful character. A few days had made a change indeed!

If Louisa recovered, it would all be well again. More than former happiness would be restored. There could not be a doubt, to her mind there was none, of what would follow her recovery. A few months hence, and the room now so deserted, occupied but by her silent, pensive self, might be filled again with all that was happy and

---

[1] Sores or swellings.

gay, all that was glowing and bright in prosperous love, all that was most unlike Anne Elliot!

An hour's complete leisure for such reflections as these, on a dark November day, a small thick rain almost blotting out the very few objects ever to be discerned from the windows, was enough to make the sound of Lady Russell's carriage exceedingly welcome; and yet, though desirous to be gone, she could not quit the Mansion House, or look an adieu to the Cottage, with its black, dripping and comfortless veranda, or even notice through the misty glasses the last humble tenements of the village, without a saddened heart. Scenes had passed in Uppercross which made it precious. It stood the record of many sensations of pain, once severe, but now softened; and of some instances of relenting feeling, some breathings of friendship and reconciliation, which could never be looked for again, and which could never cease to be dear. She left it all behind her, all but the recollection that such things had been.

Anne had never entered Kellynch since her quitting Lady Russell's house in September. It had not been necessary, and the few occasions of its being possible for her to go to the Hall she had contrived to evade and escape from. Her first return was to resume her place in the modern and elegant apartments of the Lodge, and to gladden the eyes of its mistress.

There was some anxiety mixed with Lady Russell's joy in meeting her. She knew who had been frequenting Uppercross. But happily, either Anne was improved in plumpness and looks, or Lady Russell fancied her so; and Anne, in receiving her compliments on the occasion, had the amusement of connecting them with the silent admiration of her cousin, and of hoping that she was to be blessed with a second spring of youth and beauty.

When they came to converse, she was soon sensible of some mental change. The subjects of which her heart had been full on leaving Kellynch, and which she had felt slighted, and been compelled to smother among the Musgroves, were now become but of secondary interest. She had lately lost sight even of her father and sister and Bath. Their concerns had been sunk under those of Uppercross; and when Lady Russell reverted to their former hopes and fears, and spoke her satisfaction in the house in Camden Place, which had been taken, and her regret that Mrs. Clay should still be with them, Anne would have been ashamed to have it known how much more she was thinking of Lyme and Louisa Musgrove, and all her acquaintance there; how much more interesting to her was the home and the friendship of the Harvilles and Captain Benwick, than her own father's house in Camden Place, or her own sister's intimacy with Mrs. Clay. She was actually forced to exert herself to meet Lady Russell with anything like the appearance of equal solicitude, on topics which had by nature the first claim on her.

There was a little awkwardness at first in their discourse on another subject. They must speak of the accident at Lyme. Lady Russell had not been arrived five minutes the day before, when a full account of the whole had burst on her; but still it must be talked of, she must make enquiries, she must regret the imprudence, lament the result, and Captain Wentworth's name must be mentioned by both. Anne was conscious of not doing it so well as Lady Russell. She could not speak the name, and look straight forward to Lady Russell's eye, till she had adopted the expedient of telling her briefly what she thought of the attachment between him and Louisa. When this was told, his name distressed her no longer.

Lady Russell had only to listen composedly, and wish them happy, but internally her heart revelled in angry pleasure, in pleased contempt, that the man who at twenty-three had seemed to understand somewhat of the value of an Anne Elliot, should, eight years afterwards, be charmed by a Louisa Musgrove.

The first three or four days passed most quietly, with no circumstance to mark them excepting the receipt of a note or two from Lyme, which found their way to Anne, she could not tell how, and brought a rather improving account of Louisa. At the end of that period, Lady Russell's politeness could repose no longer, and the fainter self-threatenings of the past became in a decided tone, "I must call on Mrs. Croft; I really must call upon her soon. Anne, have you courage to go with me, and pay a visit in that house? It will be some trial to us both."

Anne did not shrink from it; on the contrary, she truly felt as she said, in observing—

"I think you are very likely to suffer the most of the two; your feelings are less reconciled to the change than mine. By remaining in the neighbourhood, I am become inured to it."

She could have said more on the subject; for she had in fact so high an opinion of the Crofts, and considered her father so very fortunate in his tenants, felt the parish to be so sure of a good example, and the poor of the best attention and relief, that however sorry and ashamed for the necessity of the removal, she could not but in conscience feel that they were gone who deserved not to stay, and that

Kellynch Hall had passed into better hands than its owners'. These convictions must unquestionably have their own pain, and severe was its kind; but they precluded that pain which Lady Russell would suffer in entering the house again, and returning through the well-known apartments.

In such moments Anne had no power of saying to herself, "These rooms ought to belong only to us. Oh, how fallen in their destination! How unworthily occupied! An ancient family to be so driven away! Strangers filling their place!" No, except when she thought of her mother, and remembered where she had been used to sit and preside, she had no sigh of that description to heave.

Mrs. Croft always met her with a kindness which gave her the pleasure of fancying herself a favourite, and on the present occasion, receiving her in that house, there was particular attention.

The sad accident at Lyme was soon the prevailing topic, and on comparing their latest accounts of the invalid, it appeared that each lady dated her intelligence from the same hour of yestermorn; that Captain Wentworth had been in Kellynch yesterday (the first time since the accident), had brought Anne the last note, which she had not been able to trace the exact steps of; had staid a few hours and then returned again to Lyme, and without any present intention of quitting it any more. He had enquired after her, she found, particularly; had expressed his hope of Miss Elliot's not being the worse for her exertions, and had spoken of those exertions as great. This was handsome, and gave her more pleasure than almost anything else could have done.

As to the sad catastrophe itself, it could be canvassed[2] only in one style by a couple of steady, sensible women, whose judgements had to work on ascertained events; and it was perfectly decided that it had been the consequence of much thoughtlessness and much imprudence; that its effects were most alarming, and that it was frightful to think, how long Miss Musgrove's recovery might yet be doubtful, and how liable she would still remain to suffer from the concussion hereafter! The Admiral wound it up summarily by exclaiming—

"Ay, a very bad business indeed. A new sort of way this, for a young fellow to be making love, by breaking his mistress's head, is not it, Miss Elliot? This is breaking a head and giving a plaster,[3] truly!"

---

[2] Examined in detail.

[3] A medicated protective dressing. The phrase—breaking someone's head and giving him or her a plaster—is a well-known proverb, dating back to the sixteenth century.

Admiral Croft's manners were not quite of the tone to suit Lady Russell, but they delighted Anne. His goodness of heart and simplicity of character were irresistible.

"Now, this must be very bad for you," said he, suddenly rousing from a little reverie, "to be coming and finding us here. I had not recollected it before, I declare, but it must be very bad. But now, do not stand upon ceremony. Get up and go over all the rooms in the house if you like it."

"Another time, Sir, I thank you, not now."

"Well, whenever it suits you. You can slip in from the shrubbery at any time; and there you will find we keep our umbrellas hanging up by that door. A good place is not it? But," (checking himself), "you will not think it a good place, for yours were always kept in the butler's room. Ay, so it always is, I believe. One man's ways may be as good as another's, but we all like our own best. And so you must judge for yourself, whether it would be better for you to go about the house or not."

Anne, finding she might decline it, did so, very gratefully.

"We have made very few changes either," continued the Admiral, after thinking a moment. "Very few. We told you about the laundry-door, at Uppercross. That has been a very great improvement. The wonder was, how any family upon earth could bear with the inconvenience of its opening as it did, so long! You will tell Sir Walter what we have done, and that Mr. Shepherd thinks it the greatest improvement the house ever had. Indeed, I must do ourselves the justice to say, that the few alterations we have made have been all very much for the better. My wife should have the credit of them, however. I have done very little besides sending away some of the large looking-glasses from my dressing-room, which was your father's. A very good man, and very much the gentleman I am sure: but I should think, Miss Elliot," (looking with serious reflection), "I should think he must be rather a dressy man for his time of life. Such a number of looking-glasses! oh Lord! there was no getting away from one's self. So I got Sophy to lend me a hand, and we soon shifted their quarters; and now I am quite snug, with my little shaving glass in one corner, and another great thing that I never go near."

Anne, amused in spite of herself, was rather distressed for an answer, and the Admiral, fearing he might not have been civil enough, took up the subject again, to say—

"The next time you write to your good father, Miss Elliot, pray give him my compliments and Mrs. Croft's, and say that we are settled here quite to our liking, and have no fault at all to find with the place. The breakfast-room chimney smokes a little, I grant you, but it is only when the wind is due north and blows hard, which may not happen three times a winter. And take it altogether, now that we have been into most of the houses hereabouts and can judge, there is not one that we like better than this. Pray say so, with my compliments. He will be glad to hear it."

Lady Russell and Mrs. Croft were very well pleased with each other: but the acquaintance which this visit began was fated not to proceed far at present; for when it was returned, the Crofts announced themselves to be going away for a few weeks, to visit their connexions in the north of the county, and probably might not be at home again before Lady Russell would be removing to Bath.

So ended all danger to Anne of meeting Captain Wentworth at Kellynch Hall, or of seeing him in company with her friend. Everything was safe enough, and she smiled over the many anxious feelings she had wasted on the subject.

# CHAPTER II

Though Charles and Mary had remained at Lyme much longer after Mr. and Mrs. Musgrove's going than Anne conceived they could have been at all wanted, they were yet the first of the family to be at home again; and as soon as possible after their return to Uppercross they drove over to the Lodge. They had left Louisa beginning to sit up; but her head, though clear, was exceedingly weak, and her nerves susceptible to the highest extreme of tenderness; and though she might be pronounced to be altogether doing very well, it was still impossible to say when she might be able to bear the removal home; and her father and mother, who must return in time to receive their younger children for the Christmas holidays, had hardly a hope of being allowed to bring her with them.

They had been all in lodgings together. Mrs. Musgrove had got Mrs. Harville's children away as much as she could, every possible supply from Uppercross had been furnished, to lighten the inconvenience to the Harvilles, while the Harvilles had been wanting them to come to dinner every day; and in short, it seemed to have been only a struggle on each side as to which should be most disinterested and hospitable.

Mary had had her evils; but upon the whole, as was evident by her staying so long, she had found more to enjoy than to suffer. Charles Hayter had been at Lyme oftener than suited her; and when they dined with the Harvilles there had been only a maid-servant to wait, and at first Mrs. Harville had always given Mrs. Musgrove precedence; but then, she had received so very handsome an apology from her on finding out whose daughter she was, and there had been so much going on every day, there had been so many walks between their lodgings and the Harvilles, and she had got books from the library, and changed them so often, that the balance had certainly been much in favour of Lyme. She had been taken to Charmouth too, and she had bathed,[1] and she had gone to church, and there were a great many more people to look at in the church at Lyme than at Uppercross; and all this, joined to the sense of being so very useful, had made really an agreeable fortnight.

Anne enquired after Captain Benwick, Mary's face was clouded directly. Charles laughed.

"Oh! Captain Benwick is very well, I believe, but he is a very odd young man. I do not know what he would be at. We asked him to come home with us for a day or two: Charles undertook to give him some shooting, and he seemed quite delighted, and, for my part, I thought it was all settled; when behold! on Tuesday night, he made a very awkward sort of excuse; 'he never shot' and he had 'been quite misunderstood,' and he had promised this and he had promised that, and the end of it was, I found, that he did not mean to come. I suppose he was afraid of finding it dull; but upon my word I should have thought we were lively enough at the Cottage for such a heart-broken man as Captain Benwick."

Charles laughed again and said, "Now Mary, you know very well how it really was. It was all your doing," (turning to Anne). "He fancied that if he went with us, he should find you close by: he fancied everybody to be living in Uppercross; and when he discovered that Lady Russell lived three miles off, his heart failed him, and he had not courage to come. That is the fact, upon my honour, Mary knows it is."

But Mary did not give into it very graciously, whether from not considering Captain Benwick entitled by birth and situation to be in love with an Elliot, or from not wanting to believe Anne a greater

---

[1] She had visited the mineral or medicinal baths.

attraction to Uppercross than herself, must be left to be guessed. Anne's good-will, however, was not to be lessened by what she heard. She boldly acknowledged herself flattered, and continued her enquiries.

"Oh! he talks of you," cried Charles, "in such terms—" Mary interrupted him. "I declare, Charles, I never heard him mention Anne twice all the time I was there. I declare, Anne, he never talks of you at all."

"No," admitted Charles, "I do not know that he ever does, in a general way; but however, it is a very clear thing that he admires you exceedingly. His head is full of some books that he is reading upon your recommendation, and he wants to talk to you about them; he has found out something or other in one of them which he thinks— oh! I cannot pretend to remember it, but it was something very fine—I overheard him telling Henrietta all about it; and then 'Miss Elliot' was spoken of in the highest terms! Now Mary, I declare it was so, I heard it myself, and you were in the other room. 'Elegance, sweetness, beauty.' Oh! there was no end of Miss Elliot's charms."

"And I am sure," cried Mary, warmly, "it was a very little to his credit, if he did. Miss Harville only died last June. Such a heart is very little worth having; is it, Lady Russell? I am sure you will agree with me."

"I must see Captain Benwick before I decide," said Lady Russell, smiling.

"And that you are very likely to do very soon, I can tell you, ma'am," said Charles. "Though he had not nerves for coming away with us, and setting off again afterwards to pay a formal visit here, he will make his way over to Kellynch one day by himself, you may depend on it. I told him the distance and the road, and I told him of the church's being so very well worth seeing; for as he has a taste for those sort of things, I thought that would be a good excuse, and he listened with all his understanding and soul; and I am sure from his manner that you will have him calling here soon. So, I give you notice, Lady Russell."

"Any acquaintance of Anne's will always be welcome to me," was Lady Russell's kind answer.

"Oh! as to being Anne's acquaintance," said Mary, "I think he is rather my acquaintance, for I have been seeing him every day this last fortnight."

"Well, as your joint acquaintance, then, I shall be very happy to see Captain Benwick."

"You will not find anything very agreeable in him, I assure you, ma'am. He is one of the dullest young men that ever lived. He has walked with me, sometimes, from one end of the sands to the other, without saying a word. He is not at all a well-bred young man. I am sure you will not like him."

"There we differ, Mary," said Anne. "I think Lady Russell would like him. I think she would be so much pleased with his mind, that she would very soon see no deficiency in his manner."

"So do I, Anne," said Charles. "I am sure Lady Russell would like him. He is just Lady Russell's sort. Give him a book, and he will read all day long."

"Yes, that he will!" exclaimed Mary, tauntingly. "He will sit poring over his book, and not know when a person speaks to him, or when one drops one's scissors, or anything that happens. Do you think Lady Russell would like that?"

Lady Russell could not help laughing. "Upon my word," said she, "I should not have supposed that my opinion of any one could have admitted of such difference of conjecture, steady and matter of fact as I may call myself. I have really a curiosity to see the person who can give occasion to such directly opposite notions. I wish he may be induced to call here. And when he does, Mary, you may depend upon hearing my opinion; but I am determined not to judge him beforehand."

"You will not like him, I will answer for it."

Lady Russell began talking of something else. Mary spoke with animation of their meeting with, or rather missing, Mr. Elliot so extraordinarily.

"He is a man," said Lady Russell, "whom I have no wish to see. His declining to be on cordial terms with the head of his family, has left a very strong impression in his disfavour with me."

This decision checked Mary's eagerness, and stopped her short in the midst of the Elliot countenance.

With regard to Captain Wentworth, though Anne hazarded no enquiries, there was voluntary communication sufficient. His spirits had been greatly recovering lately as might be expected. As Louisa improved, he had improved, and he was now quite a different creature from what he had been the first week. He had not seen Louisa; and was so extremely fearful of any ill consequence to her from an interview, that he did not press for it at all; and, on the contrary, seemed to have a plan of going away for a week or ten days, till her head was stronger. He had talked of going down to Plymouth for a week, and wanted to persuade Captain Benwick to go with him; but, as Charles maintained to the last, Captain Benwick seemed much more disposed to ride over to Kellynch.

There can be no doubt that Lady Russell and Anne were both occasionally thinking of Captain Benwick, from this time. Lady Russell could not hear the door-bell without feeling that it might be his herald; nor could Anne return from any stroll of solitary indulgence in her father's grounds, or any visit of charity in the village, without wondering whether she might see him or hear of him. Captain Benwick came not, however. He was either less disposed for it than Charles had imagined, or he was too shy; and after giving him a week's indulgence, Lady Russell determined him to be unworthy of the interest which he had been beginning to excite.

The Musgroves came back to receive their happy boys and girls from school, bringing with them Mrs. Harville's little children, to improve the noise of Uppercross, and lessen that of Lyme. Henrietta remained with Louisa; but all the rest of the family were again in their usual quarters.

Lady Russell and Anne paid their compliments to them once, when Anne could not but feel that Uppercross was already quite alive again. Though neither Henrietta, nor Louisa, nor Charles Hayter, nor Captain Wentworth were there, the room presented as strong a contrast as could be wished to the last state she had seen it in.

Immediately surrounding Mrs. Musgrove were the little Harvilles, whom she was sedulously guarding from the tyranny of the two children from the Cottage, expressly arrived to amuse them. On one side was a table occupied by some chattering girls, cutting up silk and gold paper; and on the other were tressels[2] and trays, bending under the weight of brawn[3] and cold pies, where riotous boys were holding high revel; the whole completed by a roaring Christmas fire, which seemed determined to be heard, in spite of all the noise of the others. Charles and Mary also came in, of course, during their visit, and Mr. Musgrove made a point of paying his respects to Lady Russell, and sat down close to her for ten minutes, talking with a very raised voice, but from the clamour of the children on his knees, generally in vain. It was a fine family-piece.

Anne, judging from her own temperament, would have deemed such a domestic hurricane a bad restorative of the nerves, which

---

[2] Braced frames for trays so that they can serve as tables.

[3] Pig or boar meat.

Louisa's illness must have so greatly shaken. But Mrs. Musgrove, who got Anne near her on purpose to thank her most cordially, again and again, for all her attentions to them, concluded a short recapitulation of what she had suffered herself by observing, with a happy glance round the room, that after all she had gone through, nothing was so likely to do her good as a little quiet cheerfulness at home.

Louisa was now recovering apace. Her mother could even think of her being able to join their party at home, before her brothers and sisters went to school again. The Harvilles had promised to come with her and stay at Uppercross, whenever she returned. Captain Wentworth was gone, for the present, to see his brother in Shropshire.

"I hope I shall remember, in future," said Lady Russell, as soon as they were reseated in the carriage, "not to call at Uppercross in the Christmas holidays."

Everybody has their taste in noises as well as in other matters; and sounds are quite innoxious,[4] or most distressing, by their sort rather than their quantity. When Lady Russell not long afterwards, was entering Bath on a wet afternoon, and driving through the long course of streets from the Old Bridge to Camden Place, amidst the dash of other carriages, the heavy rumble of carts and drays, the bawling of newspapermen, muffin-men and milkmen, and the ceaseless clink of pattens,[5] she made no complaint. No, these were noises which belonged to the winter pleasures; her spirits rose under their influence; and like Mrs. Musgrove, she was feeling, though not saying, that after being long in the country, nothing could be so good for her as a little quiet cheerfulness.

Anne did not share these feelings. She persisted in a very determined, though very silent disinclination for Bath; caught the first dim view of the extensive buildings, smoking in rain, without any wish of seeing them better; felt their progress through the streets to be, however disagreeable, yet too rapid; for who would be glad to see her when she arrived? And looked back, with fond regret, to the bustles of Uppercross and the seclusion of Kellynch.

Elizabeth's last letter had communicated a piece of news of some interest. Mr. Elliot was in Bath. He had called in Camden Place; had called a second time, a third; had been pointedly attentive. If Elizabeth and her father did not deceive themselves, had been taking much pains to seek the acquaintance, and proclaim the value of the

---

[4] Innocuous.

[5] Clogs or overshoes used when walking in mud.

connection, as he had formerly taken pains to shew neglect. This was very wonderful if it were true; and Lady Russell was in a state of very agreeable curiosity and perplexity about Mr. Elliot, already recanting the sentiment she had so lately expressed to Mary, of his being "a man whom she had no wish to see." She had a great wish to see him. If he really sought to reconcile himself like a dutiful branch, he must be forgiven for having dismembered himself from the paternal tree.

Anne was not animated to an equal pitch by the circumstance, but she felt that she would rather see Mr. Elliot again than not, which was more than she could say for many other persons in Bath.

She was put down in Camden Place; and Lady Russell then drove to her own lodgings, in Rivers Street.

# CHAPTER III

Sir Walter had taken a very good house in Camden Place, a lofty dignified situation, such as becomes a man of consequence; and both he and Elizabeth were settled there, much to their satisfaction.

Anne entered it with a sinking heart, anticipating an imprisonment of many months, and anxiously saying to herself, "Oh! when shall I leave you again?" A degree of unexpected cordiality, however, in the welcome she received, did her good. Her father and sister were glad to see her, for the sake of shewing her the house and furniture, and met her with kindness. Her making a fourth, when they sat down to dinner, was noticed as an advantage.

Mrs. Clay was very pleasant, and very smiling, but her courtesies and smiles were more a matter of course. Anne had always felt that she would pretend what was proper on her arrival, but the complaisance of the others was unlooked for. They were evidently in excellent spirits, and she was soon to listen to the causes. They had no inclination to listen to her. After laying out for[1] some compliments of being deeply regretted[2] in their old neighbourhood, which Anne could not pay, they had only a few faint enquiries to make, before the talk must be all their own. Uppercross excited no interest, Kellynch very little: it was all Bath.

They had the pleasure of assuring her that Bath more than answered their expectations in every respect. Their house was undoubtedly the best in Camden Place; their drawing-rooms had

---

[1] Fishing for.

[2] Missed.

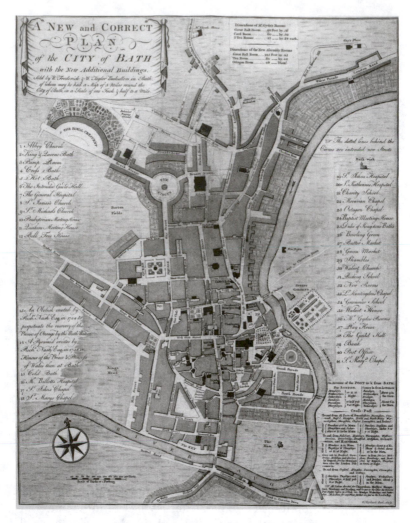

Eighteenth-century Map of Bath (Library Company of Philadelphia.)

many decided advantages over all the others which they had either seen or heard of, and the superiority was not less in the style of the fitting-up,[3] or the taste of the furniture. Their acquaintance was exceedingly sought after. Everybody was wanting to visit them. They had drawn back from many introductions, and still were perpetually having cards left by people of whom they knew nothing.

[3] Interior decorating.

Here were funds of enjoyment. Could Anne wonder that her father and sister were happy? She might not wonder, but she must sigh that her father should feel no degradation in his change, should see nothing to regret in the duties and dignity of the resident land-holder, should find so much to be vain of[4] in the littlenesses of a town; and she must sigh, and smile, and wonder too, as Elizabeth threw open the folding-doors and walked with exultation from one draw-ing-room to the other, boasting of their space; at the possibility of that woman, who had been mistress of Kellynch Hall, finding extent to be proud of between two walls, perhaps thirty feet asunder.[5]

But this was not all which they had to make them happy. They had Mr. Elliot too. Anne had a great deal to hear of Mr. Elliot. He was not only pardoned, they were delighted with him. He had been in Bath about a fortnight; (he had passed through Bath in November, in his way to London, when the intelligence of Sir Walter's being settled there had of course reached him, though only twenty-four hours in the place, but he had not been able to avail himself of it); but he had now been a fortnight in Bath, and his first object on arriving, had been to leave his card in Camden Place, following it up by such assiduous endeavours to meet, and when they did meet, by such great openness of conduct, such readiness to apologize for the past, such solicitude to be received as a relation again, that their former good understanding was completely re-established.

They had not a fault to find in him. He had explained away all the appearance of neglect on his own side. It had originated in misapprehension entirely. He had never had an idea of throwing himself off; he had feared that he was thrown off, but knew not why, and delicacy had kept him silent. Upon the hint of having spoken disrespectfully or carelessly of the family and the family honours, he was quite indig-nant. He, who had ever boasted of being an Elliot, and whose feelings, as to connection, were only too strict to suit the unfeudal tone of the present day.[6] He was astonished, indeed, but his character and general conduct must refute it. He could refer Sir Walter to all who knew him; and certainly, the pains he had been taking on this, the first opportu-nity of reconciliation, to be restored to the footing of a relation and heir-presumptive,[7] was a strong proof of his opinions on the subject.

---

[4] To disdain, out of vanity (self-importance).

[5] Apart.

[6] The waning prestige of the landed aristocracy.

[7] Sir Walter's baronetcy must devolve on his nearest male relative, in this case Mr. Elliot.

The circumstances of his marriage, too, were found to admit of much extenuation. This was an article[8] not to be entered on by himself; but a very intimate friend of his, a Colonel Wallis, a highly respectable man, perfectly the gentleman, (and not an ill-looking man, Sir Walter added), who was living in very good style in Marlborough Buildings, and had, at his own particular request, been admitted to their acquaintance through Mr. Elliot, had mentioned one or two things relative to the marriage, which made a material difference in the discredit of it.

Colonel Wallis had known Mr. Elliot long, had been well acquainted also with his wife, had perfectly understood the whole story. She was certainly not a woman of family, but well educated, accomplished, rich, and excessively in love with his friend. There had been the charm. She had sought him. Without that attraction, not all her money would have tempted Elliot, and Sir Walter was, moreover, assured of her having been a very fine[9] woman. Here was a great deal to soften the business. A very fine woman with a large fortune, in love with him! Sir Walter seemed to admit it as complete apology; and though Elizabeth could not see the circumstance in quite so favourable a light, she allowed it be a great extenuation.

Mr. Elliot had called repeatedly, had dined with them once, evidently delighted by the distinction of being asked, for they gave no dinners in general; delighted, in short, by every proof of cousinly notice, and placing his whole happiness in being on intimate terms in Camden Place.

Anne listened, but without quite understanding it. Allowances, large allowances, she knew, must be made for the ideas of those who spoke. She heard it all under embellishment. All that sounded extravagant or irrational in the progress of the reconciliation might have no origin but in the language of the relators. Still, however, she had the sensation of there being something more than immediately appeared, in Mr. Elliot's wishing, after an interval of so many years, to be well received by them. In a worldly view, he had nothing to gain by being on terms with Sir Walter; nothing to risk by a state of variance. In all probability he was already the richer of the two, and the Kellynch estate would as surely be his hereafter as the title. A sensible man, and he had looked like a very sensible man, why should it be an object to him? She could only offer one solution; it was, perhaps,

---

[8] A matter.

[9] Physically attractive.

for Elizabeth's sake. There might really have been a liking formerly, though convenience and accident had drawn him a different way; and now that he could afford to please himself, he might mean to pay his addresses to her. Elizabeth was certainly very handsome, with well-bred, elegant manners, and her character might never have been penetrated by Mr. Elliot, knowing her but in public, and when very young himself. How her temper and understanding might bear the investigation of his present keener time of life was another concern and rather a fearful one. Most earnestly did she wish that he might not be too nice,[10] or too observant if Elizabeth were his object; and that Elizabeth was disposed to believe herself so, and that her friend Mrs. Clay was encouraging the idea, seemed apparent by a glance or two between them, while Mr. Elliot's frequent visits were talked of.

Anne mentioned the glimpses she had had of him at Lyme, but without being much attended to. "Oh! yes, perhaps, it had been Mr. Elliot. They did not know. It might be him, perhaps." They could not listen to her description of him. They were describing him themselves; Sir Walter especially. He did justice to his very gentle-manlike appearance, his air of elegance and fashion, his good shaped face, his sensible eye; but, at the same time, "must lament his being very much under-hung,[11] a defect which time seemed to have increased; nor could he pretend to say that ten years had not altered almost every feature for the worse. Mr. Elliot appeared to think that he (Sir Walter) was looking exactly as he had done when they last parted;" but Sir Walter had "not been able to return the compliment entirely, which had embarrassed him. He did not mean to complain, however. Mr. Elliot was better to look at than most men, and he had no objection to being seen with him anywhere."

Mr. Elliot, and his friends in Marlborough Buildings, were talked of the whole evening. "Colonel Wallis had been so impatient to be introduced to them! and Mr. Elliot so anxious that he should!" and there was a Mrs. Wallis, at present known only to them by description, as she was in daily expectation of her confinement;[12] but Mr. Elliot spoke of her as "a most charming woman, quite worthy of being known in Camden Place," and as soon as she recovered they were to be acquainted. Sir Walter thought much of Mrs. Wallis; she was said to be an excessively pretty woman, beautiful. "He

[10] Fastidious.

[11] A drooping lower jaw.

[12] Prescribed bed rest during the month prior to childbirth.

longed to see her. He hoped she might make some amends for the many very plain faces he was continually passing in the streets. The worst of Bath was the number of its plain women. He did not mean to say that there were no pretty women, but the number of the plain was out of all proportion. He had frequently observed, as he walked, that one handsome face would be followed by thirty, or five-and-thirty frights; and once, as he had stood in a shop on Bond Street, he had counted eighty-seven women go by, one after another, without there being a tolerable face among them. It had been a frosty morning, to be sure, a sharp frost, which hardly one woman in a thousand could stand the test of. But still, there certainly were a dreadful multitude of ugly women in Bath; and as for the men! they were infinitely worse. Such scarecrows as the streets were full of! It was evident how little the women were used to the sight of anything tolerable, by the effect which a man of decent appearance produced. He had never walked anywhere arm-in-arm with Colonel Wallis (who was a fine military figure, though sandy-haired) without observing that every woman's eye was upon him; every woman's eye was sure to be upon Colonel Wallis." Modest Sir Walter! He was not allowed to escape, however. His daughter and Mrs. Clay united in hinting that Colonel Wallis's companion might have as good a figure as Colonel Wallis, and certainly was not sandy-haired.

"How is Mary looking?" said Sir Walter, in the height of his good humour. "The last time I saw her she had a red nose, but I hope that may not happen every day."

"Oh! no, that must have been quite accidental. In general she has been in very good health and very good looks since Michaelmas."

"If I thought it would not tempt her to go out in sharp winds, and grow coarse, I would send her a new hat and pelisse."

Anne was considering whether she should venture to suggest that a gown, or a cap, would not be liable to any such misuse, when a knock at the door suspended everything. "A knock at the door! and so late! It was ten o'clock. Could it be Mr. Elliot? They knew he was to dine in Lansdown Crescent. It was possible that he might stop in his way home to ask them how they did. They could think of no one else. Mrs. Clay decidedly thought it Mr. Elliot's knock." Mrs. Clay was right. With all the state which a butler and foot-boy could give, Mr. Elliot was ushered into the room.

It was the same, the very same man, with no difference but of dress. Anne drew a little back, while the others received his compliments, and her sister his apologies for calling at so unusual an hour, but "he could not be so near without wishing to know that neither she nor her friend had taken cold the day before," &c. &c; which was all as politely done, and as politely taken, as possible, but her part must follow then. Sir Walter talked of his youngest daughter; "Mr. Elliot must give him leave to present him to his youngest daughter" (there was no occasion for remembering Mary); and Anne, smiling and blushing, very becomingly shewed to Mr. Elliot the pretty features which he had by no means forgotten, and instantly saw, with amusement at his little start of surprise, that he had not been at all aware of who she was. He looked completely astonished, but not more astonished than pleased; his eyes brightened, and with the most perfect alacrity he welcomed the relationship, alluded to the past, and entreated to be received as an acquaintance already. He was quite as good-looking as he had appeared at Lyme, his countenance improved by speaking, and his manners were so exactly what they ought to be, so polished, so easy, so particularly agreeable, that she could compare them in excellence to only one person's manners. They were not the same, but they were, perhaps, equally good.

He sat down with them, and improved their conversation very much. There could be no doubt of his being a sensible man. Ten minutes were enough to certify that. His tone, his expressions, his choice of subject, his knowing where to stop; it was all the operation of a sensible, discerning mind. As soon as he could, he began to talk to her of Lyme, wanting to compare opinions respecting the place, but especially wanting to speak of the circumstance of their happening to be guests in the same inn at the same time; to give his own route, understand something of hers, and regret that he should have lost such an opportunity of paying his respects to her. She gave him a short account of her party and business at Lyme. His regret increased as he listened. He had spent his whole solitary evening in the room adjoining theirs; had heard voices, mirth continually; thought they must be a most delightful set of people, longed to be with them, but certainly without the smallest suspicion of his possessing the shadow of a right to introduce himself. If he had but asked who the party were! The name of Musgrove would have told him enough. "Well, it would serve to cure him of an absurd practice of never asking a question at an inn, which he had adopted, when quite a young man, on the principal of its being very ungenteel to be curious."

"The notions of a young man of one or two and twenty," said he, "as to what is necessary in manners to make him quite the thing, are more absurd, I believe, than those of any other set of beings in the world. The folly of the means they often employ is only to be equalled by the folly of what they have in view."

But he must not be addressing his reflections to Anne alone: he knew it; he was soon diffused again among the others, and it was only at intervals that he could return to Lyme.

His enquiries, however, produced at length an account of the scene she had been engaged in there, soon after his leaving the place. Having alluded to "an accident," he must hear the whole. When he questioned, Sir Walter and Elizabeth began to question also, but the difference in their manner of doing it could not be unfelt. She could only compare Mr. Elliot to Lady Russell, in the wish of really comprehending what had passed, and in the degree of concern for what she must have suffered in witnessing it.

He staid an hour with them. The elegant little clock on the mantel-piece had struck "eleven with its silver sounds,"[13] and the watchman was beginning to be heard at a distance telling the same tale, before Mr. Elliot or any of them seemed to feel that he had been there long.

Anne could not have supposed it possible that her first evening in Camden Place could have passed so well!

# CHAPTER IV

There was one point which Anne, on returning to her family, would have been more thankful to ascertain even than Mr. Elliot's being in love with Elizabeth, which was, her father's not being in love with Mrs. Clay; and she was very far from easy about it, when she had been at home a few hours. On going down to breakfast the next morning, she found there had just been a decent pretence on the lady's side of meaning to leave them. She could imagine Mrs. Clay to have said, that "now Miss Anne was come, she could not suppose herself at all wanted;" for Elizabeth was replying in a sort of whisper, "That must not be any reason, indeed. I assure you I feel it none. She is nothing to me, compared with you;" and she was in full time to hear her father say, "My dear madam, this must not be. As yet, you have seen nothing of Bath. You have been here only to be useful. You must not run away from us now. You must stay to be

---

[13] A likely allusion to Pope's *Rape of the Lock* "And the pressed watch returned a silver sound" (1.18).

View of Bath from Spring Gardens (w/c with pen & grey ink over graphite on wove paper) by Hearne, Thomas (1744–1817) © Yale Center for British Art, Paul Mellon Collection, USA/The Bridgeman Art Library

acquainted with Mrs. Wallis, the beautiful Mrs. Wallis. To your fine mind, I well know the sight of beauty is a real gratification."

He spoke and looked so much in earnest, that Anne was not surprised to see Mrs. Clay stealing a glance at Elizabeth and herself. Her countenance, perhaps, might express some watchfulness; but the praise of the fine mind did not appear to excite a thought in her sister. The lady could not but yield to such joint entreaties, and promise to stay.

In the course of the same morning, Anne and her father chancing to be alone together, he began to compliment her on her improved looks; he thought her "less thin in her person, in her cheeks; her skin, her complexion, greatly improved; clearer, fresher. Had she been using any thing in particular?" "No, nothing." "Merely Gowland,"[1] he supposed. "No, nothing at all." "Ha! he was surprised at that;" and added, "certainly you cannot do better than to continue as

[1] A well-known face cream used to treat facial blemishes, including those from venereal disease.

you are; you cannot be better than well; or I should recommend Gowland, the constant use of Gowland, during the spring months. Mrs. Clay has been using it at my recommendation, and you see what it has done for her. You see how it has carried away her freckles."

If Elizabeth could but have heard this! Such personal praise might have struck her, especially as it did not appear to Anne that the freckles were at all lessened. But everything must take its chance. The evil of a marriage would be much diminished, if Elizabeth were also to marry. As for herself, she might always command a home with Lady Russell.

Lady Russell's composed mind and polite manners were put to some trial on this point, in her intercourse in Camden Place. The sight of Mrs. Clay in such favour, and of Anne so overlooked, was a perpetual provocation to her there; and vexed her as much when she was away, as a person in Bath who drinks the water, gets all the new publications, and has a very large acquaintance, has time to be vexed.

As Mr. Elliot became known to her, she grew more charitable, or more indifferent, towards the others. His manners were an immediate recommendation; and on conversing with him she found the solid so fully supporting the superficial, that she was at first, as she told Anne, almost ready to exclaim, "Can this be Mr. Elliot?" and could not seriously picture to herself a more agreeable or estimable man. Everything united in him; good understanding, correct opinions, knowledge of the world, and a warm heart. He had strong feelings of family attachment and family honour, without pride or weakness; he lived with the liberality of a man of fortune, without display; he judged for himself in everything essential, without defying public opinion in any point of worldly decorum. He was steady, observant, moderate, candid; never run away with by spirits or by selfishness, which fancied itself strong feeling; and yet, with a sensibility to what was amiable and lovely, and a value for all the felicities of domestic life, which characters of fancied enthusiasm and violent agitation seldom really possess. She was sure that he had not been happy in marriage. Colonel Wallis said it, and Lady Russell saw it; but it had been no unhappiness to sour his mind, nor (she began pretty soon to suspect) to prevent his thinking of a second choice. Her satisfaction in Mr. Elliot outweighed all the plague of Mrs. Clay.

It was now some years since Anne had begun to learn that she and her excellent friend could sometimes think differently; and it did not surprise her, therefore, that Lady Russell should see nothing suspicious or inconsistent, nothing to require more motives than appeared, in Mr. Elliot's great desire of a reconciliation. In Lady Russell's view, it was perfectly natural that Mr. Elliot, at a mature time of life, should feel it a most desirable object, and what would very generally recommend him among all sensible people, to be on good terms with the head of his family; the simplest process in the world of time upon a head naturally clear, and only erring in the heyday of youth. Anne presumed, however, still to smile about it, and at last to mention "Elizabeth." Lady Russell listened, and looked, and made only this cautious reply:—"Elizabeth! very well; time will explain."

It was a reference to the future, which Anne, after a little observation, felt she must submit to. She could determine nothing at present. In that house Elizabeth must be first; and she was in the habit of such general observance as "Miss Elliot," that any particularity of attention seemed almost impossible. Mr. Elliot, too, it must be remembered, had not been a widower seven months. A little delay on his side might be very excusable. In fact, Anne could never see the crape round his hat,[2] without fearing that she was the inexcusable one, in attributing to him such imaginations; for though his marriage had not been very happy, still it had existed so many years that she could not comprehend a very rapid recovery from the awful impression of its being dissolved.

However it might end, he was without any question their pleasantest acquaintance in Bath: she saw nobody equal to him; and it was a great indulgence now and then to talk to him about Lyme, which he seemed to have as lively a wish to see again, and to see more of, as herself. They went through the particulars of their first meeting a great many times. He gave her to understand that he had looked at her with some earnestness. She knew it well; and she remembered another person's look also.

They did not always think alike. His value for rank and connexion she perceived was greater than hers. It was not merely complaisance, it must be a liking to the cause, which made him enter warmly into her father and sister's solicitudes on a subject which she thought unworthy to excite them. The Bath paper one morning announced the arrival of the Dowager Viscountess Dalrymple, and her daughter, the Honourable Miss Carteret; and all the comfort of No.—, Camden Place, was swept away for many days; for the Dalrymples (in Anne's opinion, most unfortunately) were cousins of the Elliots; and the agony was how to introduce themselves properly.

[2] Black ribbon, a sign of mourning.

Anne had never seen her father and sister before in contact with nobility, and she must acknowledge herself disappointed. She had hoped better things from their high ideas of their own situation in life, and was reduced to form a wish which she had never foreseen; a wish that they had more pride; for "our cousins Lady Dalrymple and Miss Carteret"; "our cousins, the Dalrymples," sounded in her ears all day long.

Sir Walter had once been in company with the late viscount, but had never seen any of the rest of the family; and the difficulties of the case arose from there having been a suspension of all intercourse by letters of ceremony,[3] ever since the death of that said late viscount, when, in consequence of a dangerous illness of Sir Walter's at the same time, there had been an unlucky omission at Kellynch. No letter of condolence had been sent to Ireland. The neglect had been visited on the head of the sinner; for when poor Lady Elliot died herself, no letter of condolence was received at Kellynch, and, consequently, there was but too much reason to apprehend that the Dalrymples considered the relationship as closed. How to have this anxious business set to rights, and be admitted as cousins again, was the question: and it was a question which, in a more rational manner, neither Lady Russell nor Mr. Elliot thought unimportant. "Family connexions were always worth preserving, good company always worth seeking; Lady Dalrymple had taken a house, for three months, in Laura Place, and would be living in style. She had been at Bath the year before, and Lady Russell had heard her spoken of as a charming woman. It was very desirable that the connexion should be renewed, if it could be done, without any compromise of propriety on the side of the Elliots."

Sir Walter, however, would choose his own means, and at last wrote a very fine letter of ample explanation, regret, and entreaty, to his right honourable cousin. Neither Lady Russell nor Mr. Elliot could admire the letter; but it did all that was wanted, in bringing three lines of scrawl from the Dowager Viscountess. "She was very much honoured, and should be happy in their acquaintance." The toils of the business were over, the sweets began. They visited in Laura Place, they had the cards of Dowager Viscountess Dalrymple, and the Honourable Miss Carteret, to be arranged wherever they might be most visible: and "Our cousins in Laura Place,"—"Our cousin, Lady Dalrymple and Miss Carteret," were talked of to everybody.

[3] Formal letters of condolence, congratulation, etc.

Anne was ashamed. Had Lady Dalrymple and her daughter even been very agreeable, she would still have been ashamed of the agitation they created, but they were nothing. There was no superiority of manner, accomplishment, or understanding. Lady Dalrymple had acquired the name of "a charming woman," because she had a smile and a civil answer for everybody. Miss Carteret, with still less to say, was so plain and so awkward, that she would never have been tolerated in Camden Place but for her birth.

Lady Russell confessed she had expected something better; but yet "it was an acquaintance worth having"; and when Anne ventured to speak her opinion of them to Mr. Elliot, he agreed to their being nothing in themselves, but still maintained that, as a family connexion, as good company, as those who would collect good company around them, they had their value. Anne smiled and said, "My idea of good company, Mr. Elliot, is the company of clever, well-informed people, who have a great deal of conversation; that is what I call good company."

"You are mistaken," said he gently, "that is not good company; that is the best. Good company requires only birth, education, and manners, and with regard to education is not very nice. Birth and good manners are essential; but a little learning is by no means a dangerous thing[4] in good company; on the contrary, it will do very well. My cousin Anne shakes her head. She is not satisfied. She is fastidious. My dear cousin" (sitting down by her), "you have a better right to be fastidious than almost any other woman I know; but will it answer? Will it make you happy? Will it not be wiser to accept the society of those good ladies in Laura Place, and enjoy all the advantages of the connexion as far as possible? You may depend upon it, that they will move in the first set in Bath this winter, and as rank is rank, your being known to be related to them will have its use in fixing your family (our family let me say) in that degree of consideration which we must all wish for."

"Yes," sighed Anne, "we shall, indeed, be known to be related to them!" then recollecting herself, and not wishing to be answered, she added, "I certainly do think there has been by far too much trouble taken to procure the acquaintance. I suppose" (smiling) "I have more pride than any of you; but I confess it does vex me, that we should be so solicitous to have the relationship acknowledged, which we may be very sure is a matter of perfect indifference to them."

---

[4] "A little learning is a dang'rous thing" (Alexander Pope, *Essay on Criticism* l.215).

"Pardon me, dear cousin, you are unjust in your own claims. In London, perhaps, in your present quiet style of living, it might be as you say: but in Bath; Sir Walter Elliot and his family will always be worth knowing: always acceptable as acquaintance."

"Well," said Anne, "I certainly am proud, too proud to enjoy a welcome which depends so entirely upon place."

"I love your indignation," said he; "it is very natural. But here you are in Bath, and the object is to be established here with all the credit and dignity which ought to belong to Sir Walter Elliot. You talk of being proud; I am called proud, I know, and I shall not wish to believe myself otherwise; for our pride, if investigated, would have the same object, I have no doubt, though the kind may seem a little different. In one point, I am sure, my dear cousin," (he continued, speaking lower, though there was no one else in the room) "in one point, I am sure, we must feel alike. We must feel that every addition to your father's society, among his equals or superiors, may be of use in diverting his thoughts from those who are beneath him."

He looked, as he spoke, to the seat which Mrs. Clay had been lately occupying: a sufficient explanation of what he particularly meant; and though Anne could not believe in their having the same sort of pride, she was pleased with him for not liking Mrs. Clay; and her conscience admitted that his wishing to promote her father's getting great acquaintance was more than excusable in the view of defeating her.

# CHAPTER V

While Sir Walter and Elizabeth were assiduously pushing their good fortune in Laura Place, Anne was renewing an acquaintance of a very different description.

She had called on her former governess, and had heard from her of there being an old school-fellow in Bath, who had the two strong claims on her attention of past kindness and present suffering. Miss Hamilton, now Mrs. Smith, had shewn her kindness in one of those periods of her life when it had been most valuable. Anne had gone unhappy to school, grieving for the loss of a mother whom she had dearly loved, feeling her separation from home, and suffering as a girl of fourteen, of strong sensibility and not high spirits, must suffer at such a time; and Miss Hamilton, three years older than herself, but still from the want of near relations and a settled home, remaining another year at school, had been useful and good to her in a way which had considerably lessened her misery, and could never be remembered with indifference.

Miss Hamilton had left school, had married not long afterwards, was said to have married a man of fortune, and this was all that Anne had known of her, till now that their governess's account brought her situation forward in a more decided but very different form.

She was a widow and poor. Her husband had been extravagant; and at his death, about two years before, had left his affairs dreadfully involved. She had had difficulties of every sort to contend with, and in addition to these distresses had been afflicted with a severe rheumatic fever, which, finally settling in her legs, had made her for the present a cripple. She had come to Bath on that account, and was now in lodgings near the hot baths, living in a very humble way, unable even to afford herself the comfort of a servant, and of course almost excluded from society.

Their mutual friend answered for the satisfaction which a visit from Miss Elliot would give Mrs. Smith, and Anne therefore lost no time in going. She mentioned nothing of what she had heard, or what she intended, at home. It would excite no proper interest there. She only consulted Lady Russell, who entered thoroughly into her sentiments, and was most happy to convey her as near to Mrs. Smith's lodgings in Westgate Buildings, as Anne chose to be taken.

The visit was paid, their acquaintance re-established, their interest in each other more than re-kindled. The first ten minutes had its awkwardness and its emotion. Twelve years were gone since they had parted, and each presented a somewhat different person from what the other had imagined. Twelve years had changed Anne from the blooming, silent, unformed girl of fifteen, to the elegant little woman of seven-and twenty, with every beauty except bloom, and with manners as consciously right as they were invariably gentle; and twelve years had transformed the fine-looking, well-grown Miss Hamilton, in all the glow of health and confidence of superiority, into a poor, infirm, helpless widow, receiving the visit of her former protégée as a favour; but all that was uncomfortable in the meeting had soon passed away, and left only the interesting charm of remembering former partialities and talking over old times.

Anne found in Mrs. Smith the good sense and agreeable manners which she had almost ventured to depend on, and a disposition to converse and be cheerful beyond her expectation. Neither the dissipations of the past—and she had lived very much in the world—nor the restrictions of the present, neither sickness nor sorrow seemed to have closed her heart or ruined her spirits.

In the course of a second visit she talked with great openness, and Anne's astonishment increased. She could scarcely imagine a more cheerless situation in itself than Mrs. Smith's. She had been very fond of her husband: she had buried him. She had been used to affluence: it was gone. She had no child to connect her with life and happiness again, no relations to assist in the arrangement of perplexed affairs, no health to make all the rest supportable. Her accommodations were limited to a noisy parlour, and a dark bedroom behind, with no possibility of moving from one to the other without assistance, which there was only one servant in the house to afford, and she never quitted the house but to be conveyed into the warm bath.[1] Yet, in spite of all this, Anne had reason to believe that she had moments only of languor and depression, to hours of occupation and enjoyment. How could it be? She watched, observed, reflected, and finally determined that this was not a case of fortitude or of resignation only. A submissive spirit might be patient, a strong understanding would supply resolution, but here was something more; here was that elasticity of mind, that disposition to be comforted, that power of turning readily from evil to good, and of finding employment which carried her out of herself, which was from nature alone. It was the choicest gift of Heaven; and Anne viewed her friend as one of those instances in which, by a merciful appointment, it seems designed to counterbalance almost every other want.

There had been a time, Mrs. Smith told her, when her spirits had nearly failed. She could not call herself an invalid now, compared with her state on first reaching Bath. Then she had, indeed, been a pitiable object; for she had caught cold on the journey, and had hardly taken possession of her lodgings before she was again confined to her bed and suffering under severe and constant pain; and all this among strangers, with the absolute necessity of having a regular nurse, and finances at that moment particularly unfit to meet any extraordinary expense. She had weathered it, however, and could truly say that it had done her good. It had increased her comforts by making her feel herself to be in good hands. She had seen too much of the world, to expect sudden or disinterested attachment anywhere, but her illness had proved to her that her landlady had a character to preserve, and would not use her ill; and

[1] Bath was so named for its waters which were long thought to promote health.

she had been particularly fortunate in her nurse, as a sister of her landlady, a nurse by profession, and who had always a home in that house when unemployed, chanced to be at liberty just in time to attend her. "And she," said Mrs. Smith, "besides nursing me most admirably, has really proved an invaluable acquaintance. As soon as I could use my hands she taught me to knit, which has been a great amusement; and she put me in the way of making these little thread-cases, pin-cushions and card-racks, which you always find me so busy about, and which supply me with the means of doing a little good to one or two very poor families in this neighbourhood. She had a large acquaintance, of course professionally, among those who can afford to buy, and she disposes of my merchandise. She always takes the right time for applying. Everybody's heart is open, you know, when they have recently escaped from severe pain, or are recovering the blessing of health, and Nurse Rooke thoroughly understands when to speak. She is a shrewd, intelligent, sensible woman. Hers is a line for seeing human nature; and she has a fund of good sense and observation, which, as a companion, make her infinitely superior to thousands of those who having only received 'the best education in the world,' know nothing worth attending to. Call it gossip, if you will, but when Nurse Rooke has half an hour's leisure to bestow on me, she is sure to have something to relate that is entertaining and profitable: something that makes one know one's species better. One likes to hear what is going on, to be au fait[2] as to the newest modes of being trifling and silly. To me, who lives so much alone, her conversation, I assure you, is a treat."

Anne, far from wishing to cavil at the pleasure, replied, "I can easily believe it. Women of that class have great opportunities, and if they are intelligent may be well worth listening to. Such varieties of human nature as they are in the habit of witnessing! And it is not merely in its follies, that they are well read; for they see it occasionally under every circumstance that can be most interesting or affecting. What instances must pass before them of ardent, disinterested, self-denying attachment, of heroism, fortitude, patience, resignation: of all the conflicts and all the sacrifices that ennoble us most. A sick chamber may often furnish the worth of volumes."

"Yes," said Mrs. Smith more doubtingly, "sometimes it may, though I fear its lessons are not often in the elevated style you describe. Here and there, human nature may be great in times of

[2] French: Informed.

trial; but generally speaking, it is its weakness and not its strength that appears in a sick chamber: it is selfishness and impatience rather than generosity and fortitude, that one hears of. There is so little real friendship in the world! and unfortunately" (speaking low and tremulously) "there are so many who forget to think seriously till it is almost too late."

Anne saw the misery of such feelings. The husband had not been what he ought, and the wife had been led among that part of mankind which made her think worse of the world than she hoped it deserved. It was but a passing emotion however with Mrs. Smith; she shook it off, and soon added in a different tone—

"I do not suppose the situation my friend Mrs. Rooke is in at present, will furnish much either to interest or edify me. She is only nursing Mrs. Wallis of Marlborough Buildings; a mere pretty, silly, expensive, fashionable woman, I believe; and of course will have nothing to report but of lace and finery. I mean to make my profit of Mrs. Wallis, however. She has plenty of money, and I intend she shall buy all the high-priced things I have in hand now."[3]

Anne had called several times on her friend, before the existence of such a person was known in Camden Place. At last, it became necessary to speak of her. Sir Walter, Elizabeth and Mrs. Clay, returned one morning from Laura Place, with a sudden invitation from Lady Dalrymple for the same evening, and Anne was already engaged, to spend that evening in Westgate Buildings. She was not sorry for the excuse. They were only asked, she was sure, because Lady Dalrymple being kept at home by a bad cold, was glad to make use of the relationship which had been so pressed on her; and she declined on her own account with great alacrity—"She was engaged to spend the evening with an old schoolfellow." They were not much interested in anything relative to Anne; but still there were questions enough asked, to make it understood what this old schoolfellow was; and Elizabeth was disdainful, and Sir Walter severe.

"Westgate Buildings!" said he, "and who is Miss Anne Elliot to be visiting in Westgate Buildings? A Mrs. Smith. A widow Mrs. Smith; and who was her husband? One of five thousand Mr. Smiths whose names are to be met with everywhere. And what is her attraction? That she is old and sickly. Upon my word, Miss Anne Elliot, you have the most extraordinary taste! Everything that revolts other

---

[3] This statement jibes uneasily with Mrs. Smith's previous claim to be doing "a little good to one or two very poor families in this neighbourhood."

people, low company, paltry rooms, foul air, disgusting associations are inviting to you. But surely you may put off this old lady till to-morrow: she is not so near her end, I presume, but that she may hope to see another day. What is her age? Forty?"

"No, sir, she is not one-and-thirty; but I do not think I can put off my engagement, because it is the only evening for some time which will at once suit her and myself. She goes into the warm bath to-morrow, and for the rest of the week, you know, we are engaged."

"But what does Lady Russell think of this acquaintance?" asked Elizabeth.

"She sees nothing to blame in it," replied Anne; "on the contrary, she approves it, and has generally taken me when I have called on Mrs. Smith."

"Westgate Buildings must have been rather surprised by the appearance of a carriage drawn up near its pavement," observed Sir Walter. "Sir Henry Russell's widow, indeed, has no honours[4] to distinguish her arms, but still it is a handsome equipage, and no doubt is well known to convey a Miss Elliot. A widow Mrs. Smith lodging in Westgate Buildings! A poor widow barely able to live, between thirty and forty; a mere Mrs. Smith, an every-day Mrs. Smith, of all people and all names in the world, to be the chosen friend of Miss Anne Elliot, and to be preferred by her to her own family connections among the nobility of England and Ireland! Mrs. Smith! Such a name!"

Mrs. Clay, who had been present while all this passed, now thought it advisable to leave the room, and Anne could have said much, and did long to say a little in defence of her friend's not very dissimilar claims to theirs, but her sense of personal respect to her father prevented her. She made no reply. She left it to himself to recollect, that Mrs. Smith was not the only widow in Bath between thirty and forty, with little to live on, and no surname of dignity.

Anne kept her appointment; the others kept theirs, and of course she heard the next morning that they had had a delightful evening. She had been the only one of the set absent, for Sir Walter and Elizabeth had not only been quite at her ladyship's service themselves, but had actually been happy to be employed by her in collecting others, and had been at the trouble of inviting both Lady Russell and Mr. Elliot; and Mr. Elliot had made a point of leaving Colonel Wallis early, and Lady Russell had fresh arranged all her

---

[4] Embellishments to a coat of arms signifying special accomplishments.

evening engagements in order to wait on her. Anne had the whole history of all that such an evening could supply from Lady Russell. To her, its greatest interest must be, in having been very much talked of between her friend and Mr. Elliot; in having been wished for, regretted, and at the same time honoured for staying away in such a cause. Her kind, compassionate visits to this old schoolfellow, sick and reduced, seemed to have quite delighted Mr. Elliot. He thought her a most extraordinary young woman; in her temper, manners, mind, a model of female excellence. He could meet even Lady Russell in a discussion of her merits; and Anne could not be given to understand so much by her friend, could not know herself to be so highly rated by a sensible man, without many of those agreeable sensations which her friend meant to create.

Lady Russell was now perfectly decided in her opinion of Mr. Elliot. She was as much convinced of his meaning to gain Anne in time as of his deserving her, and was beginning to calculate the number of weeks which would free him from all the remaining restraints of widowhood,[5] and leave him at liberty to exert his most open powers of pleasing. She would not speak to Anne with half the certainty she felt on the subject, she would venture on little more than hints of what might be hereafter, of a possible attachment on his side, of the desirableness of the alliance, supposing such attachment to be real and returned. Anne heard her, and made no violent exclamations; she only smiled, blushed, and gently shook her head.

"I am no match-maker, as you well know," said Lady Russell, "being much too well aware of the uncertainty of all human events and calculations. I only mean that if Mr. Elliot should some time hence pay his addresses to you, and if you should be disposed to accept him, I think there would be every possibility of your being happy together. A most suitable connection everybody must consider it, but I think it might be a very happy one."

"Mr. Elliot is an exceedingly agreeable man, and in many respects I think highly of him," said Anne; "but we should not suit."

Lady Russell let this pass, and only said in rejoinder, "I own that to be able to regard you as the future mistress of Kellynch, the future Lady Elliot, to look forward and see you occupying your dear mother's place, succeeding to all her rights, and all her popularity, as well as to all her virtues, would be the highest possible

---

[5] The prescribed period of mourning is six months, during which social activity is regarded as inappropriate.

gratification to me. You are your mother's self in countenance and disposition; and if I might be allowed to fancy you such as she was, in situation and name, and home, presiding and blessing in the same spot, and only superior to her in being more highly valued! My dearest Anne, it would give me more delight than is often felt at my time of life!"

Anne was obliged to turn away, to rise, to walk to a distant table, and, leaning there in pretended employment, try to subdue the feelings this picture excited. For a few moments her imagination and her heart were bewitched. The idea of becoming what her mother had been; of having the precious name of "Lady Elliot" first revived in herself; of being restored to Kellynch, calling it her home again, her home for ever, was a charm which she could not immediately resist. Lady Russell said not another word, willing to leave the matter to its own operation; and believing that, could Mr. Elliot at that moment with propriety have spoken for himself!—she believed, in short, what Anne did not believe. The same image of Mr. Elliot speaking for himself[6] brought Anne to composure again. The charm of Kellynch and of "Lady Elliot" all faded away. She never could accept him. And it was not only that her feelings were still adverse to any man save one; her judgement, on a serious consideration of the possibilities of such a case, was against Mr. Elliot.

Though they had now been acquainted a month, she could not be satisfied that she really knew his character. That he was a sensible man, an agreeable man, that he talked well, professed good opinions, seemed to judge properly and as a man of principle, this was all clear enough. He certainly knew what was right, nor could she fix on any one article of moral duty evidently transgressed; but yet she would have been afraid to answer for his conduct. She distrusted the past, if not the present. The names which occasionally dropt of former associates, the allusions to former practices and pursuits, suggested suspicions not favourable of what he had been. She saw that there had been bad habits; that Sunday traveling had been a common thing; that there had been a period of his life (and probably not a short one) when he had been, at least, careless in all serious matters; and, though he might now think very differently, who could answer for the true sentiments of a clever, cautious man, grown old enough to appreciate a fair character? How could it ever be ascertained that his mind was truly cleansed?

[6] As opposed to having his case pleaded by Lady Russell.

Mr. Elliot was rational, discreet, polished, but he was not open. There was never any burst of feeling, any warmth of indignation or delight, at the evil or good of others. This, to Anne, was a decided imperfection. Her early impressions were incurable. She prized the frank, the open-hearted, the eager character beyond all others. Warmth and enthusiasm did captivate her still. She felt that she could so much more depend upon the sincerity of those who sometimes looked or said a careless or a hasty thing, than of those whose presence of mind never varied, whose tongue never slipped.

Mr. Elliot was too generally agreeable. Various as were the tempers in her father's house, he pleased them all. He endured too well, stood too well with every body. He had spoken to her with some degree of openness of Mrs. Clay; had appeared completely to see what Mrs. Clay was about, and to hold her in contempt; and yet Mrs.Clay found him as agreeable as any body.

Lady Russell saw either less or more than her young friend, for she saw nothing to excite distrust. She could not imagine a man more exactly what he ought to be than Mr. Elliot; nor did she ever enjoy a sweeter feeling than the hope of seeing him receive the hand of her beloved Anne in Kellynch church, in the course of the following autumn.

# CHAPTER VI

It was the beginning of February; and Anne, having been a month in Bath, was growing very eager for news from Uppercross and Lyme. She wanted to hear much more than Mary had communicated. It was three weeks since she had heard at all. She only knew that Henrietta was at home again; and that Louisa, though considered to be recovering fast, was still in Lyme; and she was thinking of them all very intently one evening, when a thicker letter than usual from Mary was delivered to her; and, to quicken the pleasure and surprise, with Admiral and Mrs. Croft's compliments.

The Crofts must be in Bath! A circumstance to interest her. They were people whom her heart turned to very naturally.

"What is this?" cried Sir Walter. "The Crofts have arrived in Bath? The Crofts who rent Kellynch? What have they brought you?"

"A letter from Uppercross Cottage, Sir."

"Oh! those letters are convenient passports. They secure an introduction. I should have visited Admiral Croft, however, at any rate. I know what is due to my tenant."

Anne could listen no longer; she could not even have told how the poor Admiral's complexion escaped; her letter engrossed her. It had been begun several days back.

February 1st.

My dear Anne,

I make no apology for my silence, because I know how little people think of letters in such a place as Bath. You must be a great deal too happy to care for Uppercross, which, as you well know, affords little to write about. We have had a very dull Christmas; Mr. and Mrs. Musgrove have not had one dinner party all the holidays. I do not reckon the Hayters as anybody. The holidays, however, are over at last: I believe no children ever had such long ones. I am sure I had not. The house was cleared yesterday, except of the little Harvilles; but you will be surprised to hear they have never gone home. Mrs. Harville must be an odd mother to part with them so long. I do not understand it. They are not at all nice children, in my opinion; but Mrs. Musgrove seems to like them quite as well, if not better, than her grandchildren. What dreadful weather we have had! It may not be felt in Bath, with your nice pavements; but in the country it is of some consequence. I have not had a creature call on me since the second week in January, except Charles Hayter, who had been calling much oftener than was welcome. Between ourselves, I think it a great pity Henrietta did not remain at Lyme as long as Louisa; it would have kept her a little out of his way. The carriage is gone to-day, to bring Louisa and the Harvilles to-morrow. We are not asked to dine with them, however, till the day after, Mrs. Musgrove is so afraid of her being fatigued by the journey, which is not very likely, considering the care that will be taken of her; and it would be much more convenient to me to dine there to-morrow. I am glad you find Mr. Elliot so agreeable, and wish I could be acquainted with him too; but I have my usual luck: I am always out of the way when any thing desirable is going on; always the last of my family to be noticed. What an immense time Mrs. Clay has been staying with Elizabeth! Does she never mean to go away? But perhaps if she were to leave the room vacant, we might not be invited.

Let me know what you think of this. I do not expect my children to be asked, you know. I can leave them at the Great House very well, for a month or six weeks. I have this moment heard that the Crofts are going to Bath almost immediately; they think the Admiral gouty. Charles heard it quite by chance; they have not had the civility to give me any notice, or of offering to take anything. I do not think they improve at all as neighbours. We see nothing of them, and this is really an instance of gross inattention. Charles joins me in love, and everything proper.

Yours affectionately,
Mary M——.

I am sorry to say that I am very far from well; and Jemima has just told me that the butcher says there is a bad sore-throat very much about. I dare say I shall catch it; and my sore-throats, you know, are always worse than anybody's.

So ended the first part, which had been afterwards put into an envelope, containing nearly as much more.

I kept my letter open, that I might send you word how Louisa bore her journey, and now I am extremely glad I did, having a great deal to add. In the first place, I had a note from Mrs. Croft yesterday, offering to convey anything to you; a very kind, friendly note indeed, addressed to me, just as it ought; I shall therefore be able to make my letter as long as I like. The Admiral does not seem very ill, and I sincerely hope Bath will do him all the good he wants. I shall be truly glad to have them back again. Our neighbourhood cannot spare such a pleasant family. But now for Louisa. I have something to communicate that will astonish you not a little. She and the Harvilles came on Tuesday very safely, and in the evening we went to ask her how she did, when we were rather surprised not to find Captain Benwick of the party, for he had been invited as well as the Harvilles; and what do you think was the reason? Neither more nor less than his being in love with Louisa, and not choosing to venture to Uppercross till he had had an answer from Mr. Musgrove; for it was all settled between him and her before she came away, and he had written to her father by Captain Harville. True, upon my honour! Are not you astonished? I shall be surprised at least if you ever received a hint of it, for I never did. Mrs. Musgrove protests solemnly that she knew nothing of the matter. We are all very well pleased, however, for though it is not equal to her marrying Captain Wentworth, it is infinitely better than Charles Hayter; and Mr. Musgrove has written his consent, and Captain

Benwick is expected to-day. Mrs. Harville says her husband feels a good deal on his poor sister's account; but, however, Louisa is a great favourite with both. Indeed, Mrs. Harville and I quite agree that we love her the better for having nursed her. Charles wonders what Captain Wentworth will say; but if you remember, I never thought him attached to Louisa; I never could see anything of it. And this is the end, you see, of Captain Benwick's being supposed to be an admirer of yours. How Charles could take such a thing into his head was always incomprehensible to me. I hope he will be more agreeable now. Certainly not a great match for Louisa Musgrove, but a million times better than marrying among the Hayters.

Mary need not have feared her sister's being in any degree prepared for the news. She had never in her life been more astonished. Captain Benwick and Louisa Musgrove! It was almost too wonderful for belief, and it was with the greatest effort that she could remain in the room, preserve an air of calmness, and answer the common questions of the moment. Happily for her, they were not many. Sir Walter wanted to know whether the Crofts travelled with four horses, and whether they were likely to be situated in such a part of Bath as it might suit Miss Elliot and himself to visit in; but had little curiosity beyond.

"How is Mary?" said Elizabeth; and without waiting for an answer, "And pray what brings the Crofts to Bath?"

"They come on the Admiral's account. He is thought to be gouty."

"Gout and decrepitude!" said Sir Walter. "Poor old gentleman."

"Have they any acquaintance here?" asked Elizabeth.

"I do not know; but I can hardly suppose that, at Admiral Croft's time of life, and in his profession, he should not have many acquaintance in such a place as this."

"I suspect," said Sir Walter coolly, "that Admiral Croft will be best known in Bath as the renter of Kellynch Hall. Elizabeth, may we venture to present him and his wife in Laura Place?"

"Oh, no! I think not. Situated as we are with Lady Dalrymple, cousins, we ought to be very careful not to embarrass her with acquaintance she might not approve. If we were not related, it would not signify; but as cousins, she would feel scrupulous as to any proposal of ours. We had better leave the Crofts to find their own level. There are several odd-looking men walking about here, who, I am told, are sailors. The Crofts will associate with them."

This was Sir Walter and Elizabeth's share of interest in the letter; when Mrs. Clay had paid her tribute of more decent attention, in an enquiry after Mrs. Charles Musgrove, and her fine little boys, Anne was at liberty.

In her own room, she tried to comprehend it. Well might Charles wonder how Captain Wentworth would feel! Perhaps he had quitted the field, had given Louisa up, had ceased to love, had found he did not love her. She could not endure the idea of treachery or levity, or anything akin to ill usage between him and his friend. She could not endure that such a friendship as theirs should be severed unfairly.

Captain Benwick and Louisa Musgrove! The high-spirited, joyous-talking Louisa Musgrove, and the dejected, thinking, feeling, reading, Captain Benwick, seemed each of them everything that would not suit the other. Their minds most dissimilar! Where could have been the attraction? The answer soon presented itself. It had been in situation. They had been thrown together several weeks; they had been living in the same small family party: since Henrietta's coming away, they must have been depending almost entirely on each other, and Louisa, just recovering from illness, had been in an interesting state, and Captain Benwick was not inconsolable. That was a point which Anne had not been able to avoid suspecting before; and instead of drawing the same conclusion as Mary, from the present course of events, they served only to confirm the idea of his having felt some dawning of tenderness toward herself. She did not mean, however, to derive much more from it to gratify her vanity, than Mary might have allowed. She was persuaded that any tolerably pleasing young woman who had listened and seemed to feel for him would have received the same compliment. He had an affectionate heart. He must love somebody.

She saw no reason against their being happy. Louisa had fine naval fervour to begin with, and they would soon grow more alike. He would gain cheerfulness, and she would learn to be an enthusiast for Scott and Lord Byron; nay, that was probably learnt already; of course they had fallen in love over poetry. The idea of Louisa Musgrove turned into a person of literary taste, and sentimental reflection was amusing, but she had no doubt of its being so. The day at Lyme, the fall from the Cobb, might influence her health, her nerves, her courage, her character to the end of her life, as thoroughly as it appeared to have influenced her fate.

The conclusion of the whole was, that if the woman who had been sensible of Captain Wentworth's merits could be allowed to prefer another man, there was nothing in the engagement to excite lasting wonder; and if Captain Wentworth lost no friend by it, certainly nothing to be regretted. No, it was not regret which made Anne's heart beat in spite of herself, and brought the colour into her cheeks when she thought of Captain Wentworth unshackled and free. She had some feelings which she was ashamed to investigate. They were too much like joy, senseless joy!

She longed to see the Crofts; but when the meeting took place, it was evident that no rumour of the news had yet reached them. The visit of ceremony was paid and returned; and Louisa Musgrove was mentioned, and Captain Benwick, too, without even half a smile.

The Crofts had placed themselves in lodgings in Gay Street, perfectly to Sir Walter's satisfaction. He was not at all ashamed of the acquaintance, and did, in fact, think and talk a great deal more about the Admiral, than the Admiral ever thought or talked about him.

The Crofts knew quite as many people in Bath as they wished for, and considered their intercourse with the Elliots as a mere matter of form, and not in the least likely to afford them any pleasure. They brought with them their country habit of being almost always together. He was ordered to walk to keep off the gout, and Mrs. Croft seemed to go shares with him in everything, and to walk for her life to do him good. Anne saw them wherever she went. Lady Russell took her out in her carriage almost every morning, and she never failed to think of them, and never failed to see them. Knowing their feelings as she did, it was a most attractive picture of happiness to her. She always watched them as long as she could, delighted to fancy she understood what they might be talking of, as they walked along in happy independence, or equally delighted to see the Admiral's hearty shake of the hand when he encountered an old friend, and observe their eagerness of conversation when occasionally forming into a little knot of the navy, Mrs. Croft looking as intelligent and keen as any of the officers around her.

Anne was too much engaged with Lady Russell to be often walking herself; but it so happened that one morning, about a week or ten days after the Croft's arrival, it suited her best to leave her friend, or her friend's carriage, in the lower part of the town, and return alone to Camden Place, and in walking up Milsom Street she had the good fortune to meet with the Admiral. He was standing by himself at a printshop window, with his hands behind him, in earnest contemplation of some print, and she not only might have passed him unseen, but was obliged to touch as well as address him before she could catch his notice. When he did perceive and acknowledge her, however, it was done with all his usual frankness and good humour. "Ha! is it you? Thank you, thank you. This is treating me like a friend. Here I am, you see, staring at a picture. I can never get by this shop without stopping. But what a thing here is, by way of a boat! Do look at it. Did you ever see the like? What queer fellows your fine painters must be, to think that anybody would venture their lives in such a shapeless old cockleshell[1] as that? And yet here are two gentlemen stuck up in it mightily at their ease, and looking about them at the rocks and mountains, as if they were not to be upset the next moment, which they certainly must be. I wonder where that boat was built!" (laughing heartily); "I would not venture over a horsepond in it. Well," (turning away), "now, where are you bound? Can I go anywhere for you, or with you? Can I be of any use?"

"None, I thank you, unless you will give me the pleasure of your company the little way our road lies together. I am going home."

"That I will, with all my heart, and farther, too. Yes, yes we will have a snug walk together, and I have something to tell you as we go along. There, take my arm; that's right; I do not feel comfortable if I have not a woman there. Lord! what a boat it is!" taking a last look at the picture, as they began to be in motion.

"Did you say that you had something to tell me, sir?"

"Yes, I have, presently. But here comes a friend, Captain Brigden; I shall only say, 'How d'ye do?' as we pass, however. I shall not stop. 'How d'ye do?' Brigden stares to see anybody with me but my wife. She, poor soul, is tied by the leg. She has a blister on one of her heels, as large as a three-shilling piece. If you look across the street, you will see Admiral Brand coming down and his brother. Shabby fellows, both of them! I am glad they are not on this side of the way. Sophy cannot bear them. They played me a pitiful trick once: got away with some of my best men. I will tell you the whole story another time. There comes old Sir Archibald Drew and his grandson. Look, he sees us; he kisses his hand to you; he takes you for my wife. Ah! the peace has come too soon for that younker.[2] Poor old Sir Archibald! How do you like Bath, Miss Elliot? It suits us very well. We are always meeting with some old friend or other; the streets full of them every morning; sure to have plenty of chat; and

---

[1] A light boat.
[2] A midshipman.

then we get away from them all, and shut ourselves in our lodgings, and draw in our chairs, and are snug as if we were at Kellynch, ay, or as we used to be even at North Yarmouth and Deal. We do not like our lodgings here the worse, I can tell you, for putting us in mind of those we first had at North Yarmouth. The wind blows through one of the cupboards just in the same way."

When they were got a little farther, Anne ventured to press again for what he had to communicate. She hoped when clear of Milsom Street to have her curiosity gratified; but she was still obliged to wait, for the Admiral had made up his mind not to begin till they had gained the greater space and quiet of Belmont; and as she was not really Mrs. Croft, she must let him have his own way. As soon as they were fairly ascending Belmont, he began—

"Well, now you shall hear something that will surprise you. But first of all, you must tell me the name of the young lady I am going to talk about. That young lady, you know, that we have all been so concerned for. The Miss Musgrove, that all this has been happening to. Her Christian name: I always forget her Christian name."

Anne had been ashamed to appear to comprehend so soon as she really did; but now she could safely suggest the name of "Louisa."

"Ay, ay, Miss Louisa Musgrove, that is the name. I wish young ladies had not such a number of fine Christian names. I should never be out if they were all Sophys, or something of that sort. Well, this Miss Louisa, we all thought, you know, was to marry Frederick. He was courting her week after week. The only wonder was, what they could be waiting for, till the business at Lyme came; then, indeed, it was clear enough that they must wait till her brain was set to right. But even then there was something odd in their way of going on. Instead of staying at Lyme, he went off to Plymouth, and then he went off to see Edward. When we came back from Mine-head he was gone down to Edward's, and there he has been ever since. We have seen nothing of him since November. Even Sophy could not understand it. But now, the matter has take the strangest turn of all; for this young lady, the same Miss Musgrove, instead of being to marry Frederick, is to marry James Benwick. You know James Benwick."

"A little. I am a little acquainted with Captain Benwick."

"Well, she is to marry him. Nay, most likely they are married already, for I do not know what they should wait for."

"I thought Captain Benwick a very pleasing young man," said Anne, "and I understand that he bears an excellent character."

"Oh! yes, yes, there is not a word to be said against James Benwick. He is only a commander, it is true, made last summer, and these are bad times for getting on, but he has not another fault that I know of. An excellent, good-hearted fellow, I assure you; a very active, zealous officer too, which is more than you would think for, perhaps, for that soft sort of manner does not do him justice."

"Indeed you are mistaken there, sir; I should never augur want of spirit from Captain Benwick's manners. I thought them particularly pleasing, and I will answer for it, they would generally please."

"Well, well, ladies are the best judges; but James Benwick is rather too piano³ for me; and though very likely it is all our partiality, Sophy and I cannot help thinking Frederick's manners better than his. There is something about Frederick more to our taste."

Anne was caught. She had only meant to oppose the too common idea of spirit and gentleness being incompatible with each other, not at all to represent Captain Benwick's manners as the very best that could possibly be; and, after a little hesitation, she was beginning to say, "I was not entering into any comparison of the two friends," but the Admiral interrupted her with—

"And the thing is certainly true. It is not a mere bit of gossip. We have it from Frederick himself. His sister had a letter from him yesterday, in which he tells us of it, and he had just had it in a letter from Harville, written upon the spot, from Uppercross. I fancy they are all at Uppercross."

This was an opportunity which Anne could not resist; she said, therefore, "I hope, Admiral, I hope there is nothing in the style of Captain Wentworth's letter to make you and Mrs. Croft particularly uneasy. It did seem, last autumn, as if there were an attachment between him and Louisa Musgrove; but I hope it may be understood to have worn out on each side equally, and without violence. I hope his letter does not breathe the spirit of an ill-used man."

"Not at all, not at all; there is not an oath or a murmur from beginning to end."

Anne looked down to hide her smile.

"No, no; Frederick is not a man to whine and complain; he has too much spirit for that. If the girl likes another man better, it is very fit she should have him."

"Certainly. But what I mean is, that I hope there is nothing in Captain Wentworth's manner of writing to make you suppose he

³ Italian: quiet, subdued.

thinks himself ill-used by his friend, which might appear, you know, without its being absolutely said. I should be very sorry that such a friendship as has subsisted between him and Captain Benwick should be destroyed, or even wounded, by a circumstance of this sort."

"Yes, yes, I understand you. But there is nothing at all of that nature in the letter. He does not give the least fling at Benwick; does not so much as say, 'I wonder at it, I have a reason of my own for wondering at it.' No, you would not guess, from his way of writing, that he had ever thought of this Miss (what's her name?) for himself. He very handsomely hopes they will be happy together; and there is nothing very unforgiving in that, I think."

Anne did not receive the perfect conviction which the Admiral meant to convey, but it would have been useless to press the enquiry farther. She therefore satisfied herself with common-place remarks or quiet attention, and the Admiral had it all his own way.

"Poor Frederick!" said he at last. "Now he must begin all over again with somebody else. I think we must get him to Bath. Sophy must write, and beg him to come to Bath. Here are pretty girls enough, I am sure. It would be of no use to go to Uppercross again, for that other Miss Musgrove, I find, is bespoke by[4] her cousin, the young parson. Do not you think, Miss Elliot, we had better try to get him to Bath?"

## CHAPTER VII

While Admiral Croft was taking this walk with Anne, and expressing his wish of getting Captain Wentworth to Bath, Captain Wentworth was already on his way thither. Before Mrs. Croft had written, he was arrived, and the very next time Anne walked out, she saw him.

Mr. Elliot was attending his two cousins and Mrs. Clay. They were in Milsom Street. It began to rain, not much, but enough to make shelter desirable for women, and quite enough to make it very desirable for Miss Elliot to have the advantage of being conveyed home in Lady Dalrymple's carriage, which was seen waiting at a little distance; she, Anne, and Mrs. Clay, therefore, turned into Molland's,[1] while Mr. Elliot stepped to Lady Dalrymple, to request her assistance. He soon joined them again, successful, of course;

[4] Engaged to.

[1] A confection shop.

Lady Dalrymple would be most happy to take them home, and would call for them in a few minutes.

Her ladyship's carriage was a barouche,[2] and did not hold more than four with any comfort. Miss Carteret was with her mother; consequently it was not reasonable to expect accommodation for all the three Camden Place ladies. There could be no doubt as to Miss Elliot. Whoever suffered inconvenience, she must suffer none, but it occupied a little time to settle the point of civility between the other two. The rain was a mere trifle, and Anne was most sincere in preferring a walk with Mr. Elliot. But the rain was also a mere trifle to Mrs. Clay; she would hardly allow it even to drop at all, and her boots were so thick! much thicker than Miss Anne's; and, in short, her civility rendered her quite as anxious to be left to walk with Mr. Elliot as Anne could be, and it was discussed between them with a generosity so polite and so determined, that the others were obliged to settle it for them; Miss Elliot maintaining that Mrs. Clay had a little cold already, and Mr. Elliot deciding on appeal, that his cousin Anne's boots were rather the thickest.

It was fixed accordingly, that Mrs. Clay should be of the party in the carriage; and they had just reached this point, when Anne, as she sat near the window, descried, most decidedly and distinctly, Captain Wentworth walking down the street.

Her start was perceptible only to herself; but she instantly felt that she was the greatest simpleton in the world, the most unaccountable and absurd! For a few minutes she saw nothing before her; it was all confusion. She was lost, and when she had scolded back her senses, she found the others still waiting for the carriage, and Mr. Elliot (always obliging) just setting off for Union Street on a commission of Mrs. Clay's.

She now felt a great inclination to go to the outer door; she wanted to see if it rained. Why was she to suspect herself of another motive? Captain Wentworth must be out of sight. She left her seat, she would go; one half of her should not be always so much wiser than the other half, or always suspecting the other of being worse than it was. She would see if it rained. She was sent back, however, in a moment by the entrance of Captain Wentworth himself, among a party of gentlemen and ladies, evidently his acquaintance, and whom he must have joined a little below Milsom Street. He

---

[2] A four-wheeled carriage with two double seats inside facing each other—a luxury vehicle.

was more obviously struck and confused by the sight of her than she had ever observed before; he looked quite red. For the first time, since their renewed acquaintance, she felt that she was betraying the least sensibility of the two. She had the advantage of him in the preparation of the last few moments. All the overpowering, blinding, bewildering, first effects of strong surprise were over with her. Still, however, she had enough to feel! It was agitation, pain, pleasure, a something between delight and misery.

He spoke to her, and then turned away. The character of his manner was embarrassment. She could not have called it either cold or friendly, or anything so certainly as embarrassed.

After a short interval, however, he came towards her, and spoke again. Mutual enquiries on common subjects passed: neither of them, probably, much the wiser for what they heard, and Anne continuing fully sensible of his being less at ease than formerly. They had by dint of being so very much together, got to speak to each other with a considerable portion of apparent indifference and calmness; but he could not do it now. Time had changed him, or Louisa had changed him. There was consciousness of some sort or other. He looked very well, not as if he had been suffering in health or spirits, and he talked of Uppercross, of the Musgroves, nay, even of Louisa, and had even a momentary look of his own arch significance as he named her; but yet it was Captain Wentworth not comfortable, not easy, not able to feign that he was.

It did not surprise, but it grieved Anne to observe that Elizabeth would not know him.[3] She saw that he saw Elizabeth, that Elizabeth saw him, that there was complete internal recognition on each side; she was convinced that he was ready to be acknowledged as an acquaintance, expecting it, and she had the pain of seeing her sister turn away with unalterable coldness.

Lady Dalrymple's carriage, for which Miss Elliot was growing very impatient, now drew up; the servant came in to announce it. It was beginning to rain again, and altogether there was a delay, and a bustle, and a talking, which must make all the little crowd in the shop understand that Lady Dalrymple was calling to convey Miss Elliot. At last Miss Elliot and her friend, unattended but by the servant, (for there was no cousin returned), were walking off; and Captain Wentworth, watching them, turned again to Anne, and by manner, rather than words, was offering his services to her.

[3] Would not acknowledge him.

"I am much obliged to you," was her answer, "but I am not going with them. The carriage would not accommodate so many. I walk: I prefer walking."

"But it rains."

"Oh! very little, Nothing that I regard."

After a moment's pause he said: "Though I came only yesterday, I have equipped myself properly for Bath already, you see," (pointing to a new umbrella); "I wish you would make use of it, if you are determined to walk; though I think it would be more prudent to let me get you a chair."

She was very much obliged to him, but declined it all, repeating her conviction, that the rain would come to nothing at present, and adding, "I am only waiting for Mr. Elliot. He will be here in a moment, I am sure."

She had hardly spoken the words when Mr. Elliot walked in. Captain Wentworth recollected him perfectly. There was no difference between him and the man who had stood on the steps at Lyme, admiring Anne as she passed, except in the air and look and manner of the privileged relation and friend. He came in with eagerness, appeared to see and think only of her, apologised for his stay, was grieved to have kept her waiting, and anxious to get her away without further loss of time and before the rain increased; and in another moment they walked off together, her arm under his, a gentle and embarrassed glance, and a "Good morning to you!" being all that she had time for, as she passed away.

As soon as they were out of sight, the ladies of Captain Wentworth's party began talking of them.

"Mr. Elliot does not dislike his cousin, I fancy?"

"Oh! no, that is clear enough. One can guess what will happen there. He is always with them; half lives in the family, I believe. What a very good-looking man!"

"Yes, and Miss Atkinson, who dined with him once at the Wallises, says he is the most agreeable man she ever was in company with."

"She is pretty, I think; Anne Elliot; very pretty, when one comes to look at her. It is not the fashion to say so, but I confess I admire her more than her sister."

"Oh! so do I."

"And so do I. No comparison. But the men are all wild after Miss Elliot. Anne is too delicate for them."

Anne would have been particularly obliged to her cousin, if he would have walked by her side all the way to Camden Place, without saying a word. She had never found it so difficult to listen to him, though nothing could exceed his solicitude and care, and though his subjects were principally such as were wont to be always interesting: praise, warm, just, and discriminating, of Lady Russell, and insinuations highly rational against Mrs. Clay. But just now she could think only of Captain Wentworth. She could not understand his present feelings, whether he were really suffering much from disappointment or not; and till that point were settled, she could not be quite herself.

She hoped to be wise and reasonable in time; but alas! alas! she must confess to herself that she was not wise yet.

Another circumstance very essential for her to know, was how long he meant to be in Bath; he had not mentioned it, or she could not recollect it. He might be only passing through. But it was more probable that he should be come to stay. In that case, so liable as every body was to meet every body in Bath, Lady Russell would in all likelihood see him somewhere. Would she recollect him? How would it all be?

She had already been obliged to tell Lady Russell that Louisa Musgrove was to marry Captain Benwick. It had cost her something to encounter Lady Russell's surprise; and now, if she were by any chance to be thrown into company with Captain Wentworth, her imperfect knowledge of the matter might add another shade of prejudice against him.

The following morning Anne was out with her friend, and for the first hour, in an incessant and fearful sort of watch for him in vain; but at last, in returning down Pulteney Street, she distinguished him on the right hand pavement at such a distance as to have him in view the greater part of the street. There were many other men about him, many groups walking the same way, but there was no mistaking him. She looked instinctively at Lady Russell; but not from any mad idea of her recognising him so soon as she did herself. No, it was not to be supposed that Lady Russell would perceive him till they were nearly opposite. She looked at her however, from time to time, anxiously; and when the moment approached which must point him out, though not daring to look again (for her own countenance she knew was unfit to be seen), she was yet perfectly conscious of Lady Russell's eyes being turned exactly in the direction for him—of her being, in short, intently observing him. She could thoroughly comprehend the sort of fascination he must possess over Lady Russell's mind, the difficulty it must be for her to withdraw her eyes, the astonishment she must be feeling that eight or nine years should have passed over him, and in foreign climes and in active service too, without robbing him of one personal grace!

At last, Lady Russell drew back her head. "Now, how would she speak of him?"

"You will wonder," said she, "what has been fixing my eye so long; but I was looking after some window-curtains, which Lady Alicia and Mrs. Frankland were telling me of last night. They described the drawing-room window-curtains of one of the houses on this side of the way, and this part of the street, as being the handsomest and best hung of any in Bath, but could not recollect the exact number, and I have been trying to find out which it could be; but I confess I can see no curtains hereabouts that answer their description."

Anne sighed and blushed and smiled, in pity and disdain, either at her friend or herself. The part which provoked her most, was that in all this waste of foresight and caution, she should have lost the right moment for seeing whether he saw them.

A day or two passed without producing anything. The theatre or the rooms, where he was most likely to be, were not fashionable enough for the Elliots, whose evening amusements were solely in the elegant stupidity of private parties, in which they were getting more and more engaged; and Anne, wearied of such a state of stagnation, sick of knowing nothing, and fancying herself stronger because her strength was not tried, was quite impatient for the concert evening. It was a concert for the benefit of a person patronised by Lady Dalrymple. Of course they must attend. It was really expected to be a good one, and Captain Wentworth was very fond of music. If she could only have a few minutes conversation with him again, she fancied she should be satisfied; and as to the power of addressing him, she felt all over courage if the opportunity occurred. Elizabeth had turned from him, Lady Russell overlooked him; her nerves were strengthened by these circumstances; she felt that she owed him attention.

She had once partly promised Mrs. Smith to spend the evening with her; but in a short hurried call she excused herself and put it off, with the more decided promise of a longer visit on the morrow. Mrs. Smith gave a most good-humoured acquiescence.

"By all means," said she; "only tell me all about it, when you do come. Who is your party?"

Anne named them all. Mrs. Smith made no reply; but when she was leaving her said, and with an expression half serious, half arch, "Well, I heartily wish your concert may answer; and do not fail me to-morrow if you can come; for I begin to have a foreboding that I may not have many more visits from you."

Anne was startled and confused; but after standing in a moment's suspense, was obliged, and not sorry to be obliged, to hurry away.

## CHAPTER VIII

Sir Walter, his two daughters, and Mrs. Clay, were the earliest of all their party at the rooms in the evening; and as Lady Dalrymple must be waited for, they took their station by one of the fires in the Octagon Room. But hardly were they so settled, when the door opened again, and Captain Wentworth walked in alone. Anne was the nearest to him, and making yet a little advance, she instantly spoke. He was preparing only to bow and pass on, but her gentle "How do you do?" brought him out of the straight line to stand near her, and make enquiries in return, in spite of the formidable father and sister in the back ground. Their being in the back ground was a support to Anne; she knew nothing of their looks, and felt equal to everything which she believed right to be done.

While they were speaking, a whispering between her father and Elizabeth caught her ear. She could not distinguish, but she must guess the subject; and on Captain Wentworth's making a distant bow, she comprehended that her father had judged so well as to give him that simple acknowledgement of acquaintance, and she was just in time by a side glance to see a slight curtsey from Elizabeth herself. This, though late, and reluctant, and ungracious, was yet better than nothing, and her spirits improved.

After talking, however, of the weather, and Bath, and the concert, their conversation began to flag, and so little was said at last, that she was expecting him to go every moment, but he did not; he seemed in no hurry to leave her; and presently with renewed spirit, with a little smile, a little glow, he said—

"I have hardly seen you since our day at Lyme. I am afraid you must have suffered from the shock, and the more from its not over-powering you at the time."

She assured him that she had not.

"It was a frightful hour," said he, "a frightful day!" and he passed his hand across his eyes, as if the remembrance were still too painful, but in a moment, half smiling again, added, "The day has produced some effects however; has had some consequences which must be considered as the very reverse of frightful. When you had the presence of mind to suggest that Benwick would be the proper-est person to fetch a surgeon, you could have little idea of his being eventually one of those most concerned in her recovery."

"Certainly I could have none. But it appears—I should hope it would be a very happy match. There are on both sides good principles and good temper."

"Yes," said he, looking not exactly forward; "but there, I think, ends the resemblance. With all my soul I wish them happy, and rejoice over every circumstance in favour of it. They have no difficul-ties to contend with at home, no opposition, no caprice, no delays. The Musgroves are behaving like themselves, most honourably and kindly, only anxious with true parental hearts to promote their daughter's comfort. All this is much, very much in favour of their happiness; more than perhaps—"

He stopped. A sudden recollection seemed to occur, and to give him some taste of that emotion which was reddening Anne's cheeks and fixing her eyes on the ground. After clearing his throat, how-ever, he proceeded thus—

"I confess that I do think there is a disparity, too great a dis-parity, and in a point no less essential than mind. I regard Louisa Musgrove as a very amiable, sweet-tempered girl, and not deficient in understanding, but Benwick is something more. He is a clever man, a reading man; and I confess, that I do consider his attaching himself to her with some surprise. Had it been the effect of gratitude, had he learnt to love her, because he believed her to be preferring him, it would have been another thing. But I have no reason to sup-pose it so. It seems, on the contrary, to have been a perfectly sponta-neous, untaught feeling on his side, and this surprises me. A man like him, in his situation! with a heart pierced, wounded, almost broken! Fanny Harville was a very superior creature, and his attachment to her was indeed attachment. A man does not recover from such a devotion of the heart to such a woman. He ought not; he does not."

Either from the consciousness, however, that his friend had recovered, or from other consciousness, he went no farther; and Anne who, in spite of the agitated voice in which the latter part had been uttered, and in spite of all the various noises of the room, the almost ceaseless slam of the door, and ceaseless buzz of persons walking through, had distinguished every word, was struck, gratified, confused, and beginning to breathe very quick, and feel an hundred things in a moment. It was impossible for her to enter on such a subject; and yet, after a pause, feeling the necessity of speaking, and having not the smallest wish for a total change, she only deviated so far as to say—

"You were a good while at Lyme, I think?"

"About a fortnight. I could not leave it till Louisa's doing well was quite ascertained. I had been too deeply concerned in the mischief to be soon at peace. It had been my doing, solely mine. She would not have been obstinate if I had not been weak. The country round Lyme is very fine. I walked and rode a great deal; and the more I saw, the more I found to admire."

"I should very much like to see Lyme again," said Anne.

"Indeed! I should not have supposed that you could have found anything in Lyme to inspire such a feeling. The horror and distress you were involved in, the stretch of mind, the wear of spirits! I should have thought your last impressions of Lyme must have been strong disgust."

"The last hours were certainly very painful," replied Anne; "but when pain is over, the remembrance of it often becomes a pleasure. One does not love a place the less for having suffered in it, unless it has been all suffering, nothing but suffering, which was by no means the case at Lyme. We were only in anxiety and distress during the last two hours, and previously there had been a great deal of enjoyment. So much novelty and beauty! I have travelled so little, that every fresh place would be interesting to me; but there is real beauty at Lyme; and in short" (with a faint blush at some recollections), "altogether my impressions of the place are very agreeable."

As she ceased, the entrance door opened again, and the very party appeared for whom they were waiting. "Lady Dalrymple, Lady Dalrymple," was the rejoicing sound; and with all the eagerness compatible with anxious elegance, Sir Walter and his two ladies stepped forward to meet her. Lady Dalrymple and Miss Carteret, escorted by Mr. Elliot and Colonel Wallis, who had happened to arrive nearly at the same instant, advanced into the room. The others joined them, and it was a group in which Anne found herself also necessarily included. She was divided from Captain Wentworth. Their interesting, almost too interesting conversation must be broken up for a time, but slight was the penance compared with the happiness which brought it on! She had learnt, in the last ten minutes, more of his feelings towards Louisa, more of all his feelings than she dared to think of; and she gave herself up to the demands of the party, to the needful civilities of the moment, with exquisite, though agitated sensations. She was in good humour with all. She had received ideas which disposed her to be courteous and kind to all, and to pity every one, as being less happy than herself.

The delightful emotions were a little subdued, when on stepping back from the group, to be joined again by Captain Wentworth, she saw that he was gone. She was just in time to see him turn into the Concert Room. He was gone; he had disappeared, she felt a moment's regret. But "they should meet again. He would look for her, he would find her out before the evening were over, and at present, perhaps, it was as well to be asunder. She was in need of a little interval[1] for recollection."

Upon Lady Russell's appearance soon afterwards, the whole party was collected, and all that remained was to marshal themselves, and proceed into the Concert Room; and be of all the consequence in their power, draw as many eyes, excite as many whispers, and disturb as many people as they could.

Very, very happy were both Elizabeth and Anne Elliot as they walked in. Elizabeth arm in arm with Miss Carteret, and looking on the broad back of the dowager Viscountess Dalrymple before her, had nothing to wish for which did not seem within her reach; and Anne—but it would be an insult to the nature of Anne's felicity, to draw any comparison between it and her sister's; the origin of one all selfish vanity, of the other all generous attachment.

Anne saw nothing, thought nothing of the brilliancy of the room. Her happiness was from within. Her eyes were bright and her cheeks glowed; but she knew nothing about it. She was thinking only of the last half hour, and as they passed to their seats, her mind took a hasty range over it. His choice of subjects, his expressions, and still more his manner and look, had been such as she could see in only one light. His opinion of Louisa Musgrove's inferiority, an opinion which he

---

[1] British term for "intermission."

had seemed solicitous to give, his wonder at Captain Benwick, his feelings as to a first, strong attachment; sentences begun which he could not finish, his half averted eyes and more than half expressive glance, all, all declared that he had a heart returning to her at least; that anger, resentment, avoidance, were no more; and that they were succeeded, not merely by friendship and regard, but by the tenderness of the past. Yes, some share of the tenderness of the past. She could not contemplate the change as implying less. He must love her.

These were thoughts, with their attendant visions, which occupied and flurried her too much to leave her any power of observation; and she passed along the room without having a glimpse of him, without even trying to discern him. When their places were determined on, and they were all properly arranged, she looked round to see if he should happen to be in the same part of the room, but he was not; her eye could not reach him; and the concert being just opening, she must consent for a time to be happy in a humbler way.

The party was divided and disposed of on two contiguous benches: Anne was among those on the foremost, and Mr. Elliot had manoeuvred so well, with the assistance of his friend Colonel Wallis, as to have a seat by her. Miss Elliot, surrounded by her cousins, and the principal object of Colonel Wallis's gallantry, was quite contented.

Anne's mind was in a most favourable state for the entertainment of the evening; it was just occupation enough: she had feelings for the tender, spirits for the gay, attention for the scientific, and patience for the wearisome; and had never liked a concert better, at least during the first act. Towards the close of it, in the interval succeeding an Italian song, she explained the words of the song to Mr. Elliot. They had a concert bill[2] between them.

"This," said she, "is nearly the sense, or rather the meaning of the words, for certainly the sense of an Italian love-song must not be talked of,[3] but it is as nearly the meaning as I can give; for I do not pretend to understand the language. I am a very poor Italian scholar."

"Yes, yes, I see you are. I see you know nothing of the matter. You have only knowledge enough of the language to translate at sight these inverted, transposed, curtailed Italian lines, into clear,

[2] Program.

[3] The gist of a love-song is self-evident, and the exact meaning of the words doesn't matter.

comprehensible, elegant English. You need not say anything more of your ignorance. Here is complete proof."

"I will not oppose such kind politeness; but I should be sorry to be examined by a real proficient."

"I have not had the pleasure of visiting in Camden Place so long," replied he, "without knowing something of Miss Anne Elliot; and I do regard her as one who is too modest for the world in general to be aware of half her accomplishments, and too highly accomplished for modesty to be natural in any other woman."

"For shame! for shame! this is too much flattery. I forget what we are to have next," turning to the bill.

"Perhaps," said Mr. Elliot, speaking low, "I have had a longer acquaintance with your character than you are aware of."

"Indeed! How so? You can have been acquainted with it only since I came to Bath, excepting as you might hear me previously spoken of in my own family."

"I knew you by report long before you came to Bath. I had heard you described by those who knew you intimately. I have been acquainted with you by character many years. Your person, your disposition, accomplishments, manner; they were all present to me."

Mr. Elliot was not disappointed in the interest he hoped to raise. No one can withstand the charm of such a mystery. To have been described long ago to a recent acquaintance, by nameless people, is irresistible; and Anne was all curiosity. She wondered, and questioned him eagerly; but in vain. He delighted in being asked, but he would not tell.

"No, no, some time or other, perhaps, but not now. He would mention no names now; but such, he could assure her, had been the fact. He had many years ago received such a description of Miss Anne Elliot as had inspired him with the highest idea of her merit, and excited the warmest curiosity to know her."

Anne could think of no one so likely to have spoken with partiality of her many years ago as the Mr. Wentworth of Monkford, Captain Wentworth's brother. He might have been in Mr. Elliot's company, but she had not courage to ask the question.

"The name of Anne Elliot," said he, "has long had an interesting sound to me. Very long has it possessed a charm over my fancy; and, if I dared, I would breathe my wishes that the name might never change."

Such, she believed, were his words; but scarcely had she received their sound, than her attention was caught by other sounds immediately behind her, which rendered every thing else trivial. Her father and Lady Dalrymple were speaking.

"A well-looking man," said Sir Walter, "a very well-looking man."

"A very fine young man indeed!" said Lady Dalrymple. "More air than one often sees in Bath. Irish, I dare say."

"No, I just know his name. A bowing acquaintance. Wentworth; Captain Wentworth of the navy. His sister married my tenant in Somersetshire, the Croft, who rents Kellynch."

Before Sir Walter had reached this point, Anne's eyes had caught the right direction, and distinguished Captain Wentworth standing among a cluster of men at a little distance. As her eyes fell on him, his seemed to be withdrawn from her. It had that appearance. It seemed as if she had been one moment too late; and as long as she dared observe, he did not look again: but the performance was recommencing, and she was forced to seem to restore her attention to the orchestra and look straight forward.

When she could give another glance, he had moved away. He could not have come nearer to her if he would; she was so surrounded and shut in: but she would rather have caught his eye.

Mr. Elliot's speech, too, distressed her. She had no longer any inclination to talk to him. She wished him not so near her.

The first act was over. Now she hoped for some beneficial change; and, after a period of nothing-saying amongst the party, some of them did decide on going in quest of tea. Anne was one of the few who did not choose to move. She remained in her seat, and so did Lady Russell; but she had the pleasure of getting rid of Mr. Elliot; and she did not mean, whatever she might feel on Lady Russell's account, to shrink from conversation with Captain Wentworth, if he gave her the opportunity. She was persuaded by Lady Russell's countenance that she had seen him.

He did not come however. Anne sometimes fancied she discerned him at a distance, but he never came. The anxious interval wore away unproductively. The others returned, the room filled again, benches were reclaimed and repossessed, and another hour of pleasure or of penance was to be sat out, another hour of music was to give delight or the gapes,[4] as real or affected taste for it prevailed. To Anne, it chiefly wore the prospect of an hour of agitation. She could not quit that room in peace without seeing Captain Wentworth once more, without the interchange of one friendly look.

[4] Yawns.

In re-settling themselves there were now many changes, the result of which was favourable for her. Colonel Wallis declined sitting down again, and Mr. Elliot was invited by Elizabeth and Miss Carteret, in a manner not to be refused, to sit between them; and by some other removals, and a little scheming of her own, Anne was enabled to place herself much nearer the end of the bench than she had been before, much more within reach of a passer-by. She could not do so, without comparing herself with Miss Larolles, the inimitable Miss Larolles;[5] but still she did it, and not with much happier effect; though by what seemed prosperity in the shape of an early abdication in her next neighbours, she found herself at the very end of the bench before the concert closed.

Such was her situation, with a vacant space at hand, when Captain Wentworth was again in sight. She saw him not far off. He saw her too; yet he looked grave, and seemed irresolute, and only by very slow degrees came at last near enough to speak to her. She felt that something must be the matter. The change was indubitable. The difference between his present air and what it had been in the Octagon Room was strikingly great. Why was it? She thought of her father, of Lady Russell. Could there have been any unpleasant glances? He began by speaking of the concert gravely, more like the Captain Wentworth of Uppercross; owned himself disappointed, had expected singing; and in short, must confess that he should not be sorry when it was over. Anne replied, and spoke in defence of the performance so well, and yet in allowance for his feelings so pleasantly, that his countenance improved, and he replied again with almost a smile. They talked for a few minutes more; the improvement held; he even looked down towards the bench, as if he saw a place on it well worth occupying; when at that moment a touch on her shoulder obliged Anne to turn round. It came from Mr. Elliot. He begged her pardon, but she must be applied to, to explain Italian again. Miss Carteret was very anxious to have a general idea of what was next to be sung. Anne could not refuse; but never had she sacrificed to politeness with a more suffering spirit.

A few minutes, though as few as possible, were inevitably consumed; and when her own mistress again, when able to turn and look as she had done before, she found herself accosted by Captain Wentworth, in a reserved yet hurried sort of farewell. "He must

---

[5] A talkative character in Frances Burney's *Cecilia* (1782) who seats herself to gain attention, and for advantage in social contact.

wish her good night; he was going; he should get home as fast as he could."

"Is not this song worth staying for?" said Anne, suddenly struck by an idea which made her yet more anxious to be encouraging.

"No!" he replied impressively, "there is nothing worth my staying for;" and he was gone directly.

Jealousy of Mr. Elliot! It was the only intelligible motive. Captain Wentworth jealous of her affection! Could she have believed it a week ago; three hours ago! For a moment the gratification was exquisite. But, alas! there were very different thoughts to succeed. How was such jealousy to be quieted? How was the truth to reach him? How, in all the peculiar disadvantages of their respective situations, would he ever learn of her real sentiments? It was misery to think of Mr. Elliot's attentions. Their evil was incalculable.

# CHAPTER IX

Anne recollected with pleasure the next morning her promise of going to Mrs. Smith, meaning that it should engage her from home at the time when Mr. Elliot would be most likely to call; for to avoid Mr. Elliot was almost a first object.

She felt a great deal of good-will towards him. In spite of the mischief of his attentions, she owed him gratitude and regard, perhaps compassion. She could not help thinking much of the extraordinary circumstances attending their acquaintance, of the right which he seemed to have to interest her, by everything in situation, by his own sentiments, by his early prepossession. It was altogether very extraordinary; flattering, but painful. There was much to regret. How she might have felt had there been no Captain Wentworth in the case, was not worth enquiry; for there was a Captain Wentworth; and be the conclusion of the present suspense good or bad, her affection would be his for ever. Their union, she believed, could not divide her more from other men, than their final separation.

Prettier musings of high-wrought love and eternal constancy, could never have passed along the streets of Bath, than Anne was sporting with from Camden Place to Westgate Buildings. It was almost enough to spread purification and perfume all the way.

She was sure of a pleasant reception; and her friend seemed this morning particularly obliged to her for coming, seemed hardly to have expected her, though it had been an appointment.

An account of the concert was immediately claimed; and Anne's recollections of the concert were quite happy enough to animate her features and make her rejoice to talk of it. All that she could tell she told most gladly, but the all was little for one who had been there, and unsatisfactory for such an enquirer as Mrs. Smith, who had already heard, through the short cut of a laundress and a waiter, rather more of the general success and produce of the evening than Anne could relate, and who now asked in vain for several particulars of the company. Everybody of any consequence or notoriety in Bath was well known by name to Mrs. Smith.

"The little Durands were there, I conclude," said she, "with their mouths open to catch the music, like unfledged sparrows ready to be fed. They never miss a concert."

"Yes; I did not see them myself, but I heard Mr. Elliot say they were in the room."

"The Ibbotsons, were they there? and the two new beauties, with the tall Irish officer, who is talked of for one of them."

"I do not know. I do not think they were."

"Old Lady Mary Maclean? I need not ask after her. She never misses, I know; and you must have seen her. She must have been in your own circle; for as you went with Lady Dalrymple, you were in the seats of grandeur, round the orchestra, of course."

"No, that was what I dreaded. It would have been very unpleasant to me in every respect. But happily Lady Dalrymple always chooses to be farther off; and we were exceedingly well placed, that is, for hearing; I must not say for seeing, because I appear to have seen very little."

"Oh! you saw enough for your own amusement. I can understand. There is a sort of domestic enjoyment to be known even in a crowd, and this you had. You were a large party in yourselves, and you wanted nothing beyond."

"But I ought to have looked about me more," said Anne, conscious while she spoke that there had in fact been no want of looking about, that the object only had been deficient.

"No, no; you were better employed. You need not tell me that you had a pleasant evening. I see it in your eye. I perfectly see how the hours passed: that you had always something agreeable to listen to. In the intervals of the concert it was conversation."

Anne half smiled and said, "Do you see that in my eye?"

"Yes, I do. Your countenance perfectly informs me that you were in company last night with the person whom you think the most agreeable in the world, the person who interests you at this present time more than all the rest of the world put together."

A blush overspread Anne's cheeks. She could say nothing.

"And such being the case," continued Mrs. Smith, after a short pause, "I hope you believe that I do know how to value your kindness in coming to me this morning. It is really very good of you to come and sit with me, when you must have so many pleasanter demands upon your time."

Anne heard nothing of this. She was still in the astonishment and confusion excited by her friend's penetration, unable to imagine how any report of Captain Wentworth could have reached her. After another short silence—

"Pray," said Mrs. Smith, "is Mr. Elliot aware of your acquaintance with me? Does he know that I am in Bath?"

"Mr. Elliot!" repeated Anne, looking up surprised. A moment's reflection shewed her the mistake she had been under. She caught it instantaneously; and recovering her courage with the feeling of safety, soon added, more composedly, "Are you acquainted with Mr. Elliot?"

"I have been a good deal acquainted with him," replied Mrs. Smith, gravely, "but it seems worn out now. It is a great while since we met."

"I was not at all aware of this. You never mentioned it before. Had I known it, I would have had the pleasure of talking to him about you."

"To confess the truth," said Mrs. Smith, assuming her usual air of cheerfulness, "that is exactly the pleasure I want you to have. I want you to talk about me to Mr. Elliot. I want your interest with him. He can be of essential service to me; and if you would have the goodness, my dear Miss Elliot, to make it an object to yourself, of course it is done."

"I should be extremely happy; I hope you cannot doubt my willingness to be of even the slightest use to you," replied Anne; "but I suspect that you are considering me as having a higher claim on Mr. Elliot, a greater right to influence him, than is really the case. I am sure you have, somehow or other, imbibed such a notion. You must consider me only as Mr. Elliot's relation. If in that light there is anything which you suppose his cousin might fairly ask of him, I beg you would not hesitate to employ me."

Mrs. Smith gave her a penetrating glance, and then, smiling, said—

"I have been a little premature, I perceive; I beg your pardon. I ought to have waited for official information. But now, my dear Miss Elliot, as an old friend, do give me a hint as to when I may speak. Next week? To be sure by next week I may be allowed to think it all settled, and build my own selfish schemes on Mr. Elliot's good fortune."

"No," replied Anne, "nor next week, nor next, nor next. I assure you that nothing of the sort you are thinking of will be settled any week. I am not going to marry Mr. Elliot. I should like to know why you imagine I am?"

Mrs. Smith looked at her again, looked earnestly, smiled, shook her head, and exclaimed—

"Now, how I do wish I understood you! How I do wish I knew what you were at! I have a great idea that you do not design to be cruel, when the right moment occurs. Till it does come, you know, we women never mean to have anybody. It is a thing of course among us, that every man is refused, till he offers. But why should you be cruel? Let me plead for my—present friend I cannot call him, but for my former friend. Where can you look for a more suitable match? Where could you expect a more gentlemanlike, agreeable man? Let me recommend Mr. Elliot. I am sure you hear nothing but good of him from Colonel Wallis; and who can know him better than Colonel Wallis?"

"My dear Mrs. Smith, Mr. Elliot's wife has not been dead much above half a year. He ought not to be supposed to be paying his addresses to any one."

"Oh! if these are your only objections," cried Mrs. Smith, archly, "Mr. Elliot is safe, and I shall give myself no more trouble about him. Do not forget me when you are married, that's all. Let him know me to be a friend of yours, and then he will think little of the trouble required, which it is very natural for him now, with so many affairs and engagements of his own, to avoid and get rid of as he can; very natural, perhaps. Ninety-nine out of a hundred would do the same. Of course, he cannot be aware of the importance to me. Well, my dear Miss Elliot, I hope and trust you will be very happy. Mr. Elliot has sense to understand the value of such a woman. Your peace will not be shipwrecked as mine has been. You are safe in all worldly matters, and safe in his character. He will not be led astray; he will not be misled by others to his ruin."

"No," said Anne, "I can readily believe all that of my cousin. He seems to have a calm decided temper, not at all open to dangerous impressions. I consider him with great respect. I have no reason, from any thing that has fallen within my observation, to do otherwise. But I have not known him long; and he is not a man, I think, to be known intimately soon. Will not this manner of speaking of him, Mrs. Smith, convince you that he is nothing to me? Surely this must be calm enough. And, upon my word, he is nothing to me. Should he ever propose to me (which I have very little reason to imagine he has any thought of doing), I shall not accept him. I assure you I shall not. I assure you, Mr. Elliot had not the share which you have been supposing, in whatever pleasure the concert of last night might afford: not Mr. Elliot; it is not Mr. Elliot that—"

She stopped, regretting with a deep blush that she had implied so much; but less would hardly have been sufficient. Mrs. Smith would hardly have believed so soon in Mr. Elliot's failure, but from the perception of there being a somebody else. As it was, she instantly submitted, and with all the semblance of seeing nothing beyond; and Anne, eager to escape farther notice, was impatient to know why Mrs. Smith should have fancied she was to marry Mr. Elliot; where she could have received the idea, or from whom she could have heard it.

"Do tell me how it first came into your head."

"It first came into my head," replied Mrs. Smith, "upon finding how much you were together, and feeling it to be the most probable thing in the world to be wished for by everybody belonging to either of you; and you may depend upon it that all your acquaintance have disposed of you in the same way. But I never heard it spoken of till two days ago."

"And has it indeed been spoken of?"

"Did you observe the woman who opened the door to you when you called yesterday?"

"No. Was not it Mrs. Speed, as usual, or the maid? I observed no one in particular."

"It was my friend Mrs. Rooke; Nurse Rooke; who, by-the-bye, had a great curiosity to see you, and was delighted to be in the way to let you in. She came away from Marlborough Buildings only on Sunday; and she it was who told me you were to marry Mr. Elliot. She had had it from Mrs. Wallis herself, which did not seem bad authority. She sat an hour with me on Monday evening, and gave me the whole history."

"The whole history," repeated Anne, laughing. "She could not make a very long history, I think, of one such little article of unfounded news."

Mrs. Smith said nothing.

"But," continued Anne, presently, "though there is no truth in my having this claim on Mr. Elliot, I should be extremely happy to be of use to you in any way that I could. Shall I mention to him your being in Bath? Shall I take any message?"

"No, I thank you: no, certainly not. In the warmth of the moment, and under a mistaken impression, I might, perhaps, have endeavoured to interest you in some circumstances; but not now. No, I thank you, I have nothing to trouble you with."

"I think you spoke of having known Mr. Elliot many years?"

"I did."

"Not before he was married, I suppose?"

"Yes; he was not married when I knew him first."

"And—were you much acquainted?"

"Intimately."

"Indeed! Then do tell me what he was at that time of life. I have a great curiosity to know what Mr. Elliot was as a very young man. Was he at all such as he appears now?"

"I have not seen Mr. Elliot these three years," was Mrs. Smith's answer, given so gravely that it was impossible to pursue the subject farther; and Anne felt that she had gained nothing but an increase of curiosity. They were both silent: Mrs. Smith very thoughtful. At last—

"I beg your pardon, my dear Miss Elliot," she cried, in her natural tone of cordiality, "I beg your pardon for the short answers I have been giving you, but I have been uncertain what I ought to do. I have been doubting and considering as to what I ought to tell you. There were many things to be taken into the account. One hates to be officious, to be giving bad impressions, making mischief. Even the smooth surface of family-union seems worth preserving, though there may be nothing durable beneath. However, I have determined; I think I am right; I think you ought to be made acquainted with Mr. Elliot's real character. Though I fully believe that, at present, you have not the smallest intention of accepting him, there is no saying what may happen. You might, some time or other, be differently affected towards him. Hear the truth, therefore, now, while you are unprejudiced. Mr. Elliot is a man without heart or conscience; a designing, wary, cold-blooded being, who thinks only of himself; whom for his own interest or ease, would be guilty of any cruelty, or any treachery, that could be perpetrated without risk of his general character. He has no feeling for others.

Those whom he has been the chief cause of leading into ruin, he can neglect and desert without the smallest compunction. He is totally beyond the reach of any sentiment of justice or compassion. Oh! he is black at heart, hollow and black!"

Anne's astonished air, and exclamation of wonder, made her pause, and in a calmer manner, she added,

"My expressions startle you. You must allow for an injured, angry woman. But I will try to command myself. I will not abuse him. I will only tell you what I have found him. Facts shall speak. He was the intimate friend of my dear husband, who trusted and loved him, and thought him as good as himself. The intimacy had been formed before our marriage. I found them most intimate friends; and I, too, became excessively pleased with Mr. Elliot, and entertained the highest opinion of him. At nineteen, you know, one does not think very seriously; but Mr. Elliot appeared to me quite as good as others, and much more agreeable than most others, and we were almost always together. We were principally in town, living in very good style. He was then the inferior in circumstances; he was then the poor one; he had chambers in the Temple,[1] and it was as much as he could do to support the appearance of a gentleman. He had always a home with us whenever he chose it; he was always welcome; he was like a brother. My poor Charles, who had the finest, most generous spirit in the world, would have divided his last farthing with him; and I know that his purse was open to him; I know that he often assisted him."

"This must have been about that very period of Mr. Elliot's life," said Anne, "which has always excited my particular curiosity. It must have been about the same time that he became known to my father and sister. I never knew him myself; I only heard of him; but there was a something in his conduct then, with regard to my father and sister, and afterwards in the circumstances of his marriage, which I never could quite reconcile with present times. It seemed to announce a different sort of man."

"I know it all, I know it all," cried Mrs. Smith. "He had been introduced to Sir Walter and your sister before I was acquainted with him, but I heard him speak of them for ever. I know he was invited and encouraged, and I know he did not choose to go. I can satisfy you, perhaps, on points which you would little expect; and as to his marriage, I knew all about it at the time. I was privy to all the

[1] One of London's Inns of Court where lawyers work and reside.

fors and againsts; I was the friend to whom he confided his hopes
and plans; and though I did not know his wife previously, her
inferior situation in society, indeed, rendered that impossible, yet
I knew her all her life afterwards, or at least till within the last two
years of her life, and can answer any question you may wish to put."

"Nay," said Anne, "I have no particular enquiry to make about
her. I have always understood they were not a happy couple. But
I should like to know why, at that time of his life, he should slight
my father's acquaintance as he did. My father was certainly disposed
to take very kind and proper notice of him. Why did Mr. Elliot draw
back?"

"Mr. Elliot," replied Mrs. Smith, "at that period of his life, had
one object in view: to make his fortune, and by a rather quicker
process than the law. He was determined to make it by marriage.
He was determined, at least, not to mar it by an imprudent marriage; and I know it was his belief (whether justly or not, of course
I cannot decide), that your father and sister, in their civilities and
invitations, were designing a match between the heir and the young
lady, and it was impossible that such a match should have answered
his ideas of wealth and independence. That was his motive for
drawing back, I can assure you. He told me the whole story. He had
no concealments with me. It was curious, that having just left you
behind me in Bath, my first and principal acquaintance on marrying
should be your cousin; and that, through him, I should be continually hearing of your father and sister. He described one Miss Elliot,
and I thought very affectionately of the other."

"Perhaps," cried Anne, struck by a sudden idea, "you sometimes spoke of me to Mr. Elliot?"

"To be sure I did; very often. I used to boast of my own Anne
Elliot, and vouch for your being a very different creature from—"
She checked herself just in time.

"This accounts for something which Mr. Elliot said last night,"
cried Anne. "This explains it. I found he had been used to hear of
me. I could not comprehend how. What wild imaginations one
forms where dear self is concerned! How sure to be mistaken! But
I beg your pardon; I have interrupted you. Mr. Elliot married then
completely for money? The circumstances, probably, which first
opened your eyes to his character."

Mrs. Smith hesitated a little here. "Oh! those things are too
common. When one lives in the world, a man or woman's marrying
for money is too common to strike one as it ought. I was very

young, and associated only with the young, and we were a thoughtless, gay set, without any strict rules of conduct. We lived for enjoyment. I think differently now; time and sickness and sorrow have
given me other notions; but at that period I must own I saw nothing
reprehensible in what Mr. Elliot was doing. 'To do the best for himself,' passed as a duty."

"But was not she a very low woman?"

"Yes; which I objected to, but he would not regard. Money,
money, was all that he wanted. Her father was a grazier,[2] her grand-
father had been a butcher, but that was all nothing. She was a fine
woman, had had a decent education, was brought forward by some
cousins, thrown by chance into Mr. Elliot's company, and fell in love
with him; and, not a difficulty or a scruple was there on his side,
with respect to her birth. All his caution was spent in being secured
of the real amount of her fortune, before he committed himself.
Depend upon it, whatever esteem Mr. Elliot may have for his own
situation in life now, as a young man he had not the smallest value
for it. His chance for the Kellynch estate was something, but all the
honour of the family he held as cheap as dirt. I have often heard him
declare, that if baronetcies were saleable, anybody should have his
for fifty pounds, arms and motto, name and livery included; but
I will not pretend to repeat half that I used to hear him say on that
subject. It would not be fair; and yet you ought to have proof, for
what is all this but assertion, and you shall have proof."

"Indeed, my dear Mrs. Smith, I want none," cried Anne. "You
have asserted nothing contradictory to what Mr. Elliot appeared to
be some years ago. This is all in confirmation, rather, of what we
used to hear and believe. I am more curious to know why he should
be so different now."

"But for my satisfaction, if you will have the goodness to ring
for Mary; stay: I am sure you will have the still greater goodness of
going yourself into my bedroom, and bringing me the small inlaid
box which you will find on the upper shelf of the closet."

Anne, seeing her friend to be earnestly bent on it, did as she was
desired. The box was brought and placed before her, and Mrs. Smith,
sighing over it as she unlocked it, said—

"This is full of papers belonging to him, to my husband; a small
portion only of what I had to look over when I lost him. The letter
I am looking for was one written by Mr. Elliot to him before our

---

[2] One in charge of grazing sheep or cattle (a farm-worker).

marriage, and happened to be saved; why, one can hardly imagine. But he was careless and immethodical, like other men, about those things; and when I came to examine his papers, I found it with others still more trivial, from different people scattered here and there, while many letters and memorandums of real importance had been destroyed. Here it is; I would not burn it, because being even then very little satisfied with Mr. Elliot, I was determined to preserve every document of former intimacy. I have now another motive for being glad that I can produce it."

This was the letter, directed to "Charles Smith, Esq. Tunbridge Wells," and dated from London, as far back as July, 1803:—

> Dear Smith,
>
> I have received yours. Your kindness almost overpowers me. I wish nature had made such hearts as yours more common, but I have lived three-and-twenty years in the world, and have seen none like it. At present, believe me, I have no need of your services, being in cash again. Give me joy: I have got rid of Sir Walter and Miss. They are gone back to Kellynch, and almost made me swear to visit them this summer; but my first visit to Kellynch will be with a surveyor, to tell me how to bring it with best advantage to the hammer.[3] The baronet, nevertheless, is not unlikely to marry again; he is quite fool enough. If he does, however, they will leave me in peace, which may be a decent equivalent for the reversion.[4] He is worse than last year.
>
> I wish I had any name but Elliot. I am sick of it. The name of Walter I can drop, thank God! and I desire you will never insult me with my second W. again, meaning, for the rest of my life, to be only yours truly,
>
> —Wm. Elliot.

Such a letter could not be read without putting Anne in a glow; and Mrs. Smith, observing the high colour in her face, said—

"The language, I know, is highly disrespectful. Though I have forgot the exact terms, I have a perfect impression of the general meaning. But it shows you the man. Mark his professions to my poor husband. Can any thing be stronger?"

Anne could not immediately get over the shock and mortification of finding such words applied to her father. She was obliged to

---

[3] The gavel at an auction.

[4] The transfer of the baronetcy to Mr. Elliot upon the death of Sir Walter.

recollect that her seeing the letter was a violation of the laws of honour, that no one ought to be judged or to be known by such testimonies, that no private correspondence could bear the eye of others, before she could recover calmness enough to return the letter which she had been meditating over, and say—

"Thank you. This is full proof undoubtedly; proof of every thing you were saying. But why be acquainted with us now?"

"I can explain this too," cried Mrs. Smith, smiling.

"Can you really?"

"Yes. I have shewn you Mr. Elliot as he was a dozen years ago, and I will shew him as he is now. I cannot produce written proof again, but I can give as authentic oral testimony as you can desire, of what he is now wanting, and what he is now doing. He is no hypocrite now. He truly wants to marry you. His present attentions to your family are very sincere: quite from the heart. I will give you my authority: his friend Colonel Wallis."

"Colonel Wallis! you are acquainted with him?"

"No. It does not come to me in quite so direct a line as that; it takes a bend or two, but nothing of consequence. The stream is as good as at first; the little rubbish it collects in the turnings is easily moved away. Mr. Elliot talks unreservedly to Colonel Wallis of his views on you, which said Colonel Wallis, I imagine to be, in himself, a sensible, careful, discerning sort of character; but Colonel Wallis has a very pretty silly wife, to whom he tells things which he had better not, and he repeats it all to her. She in the overflowing spirits of her recovery, repeats it all to her nurse; and the nurse knowing my acquaintance with you, very naturally brings it all to me. On Monday evening, my good friend Mrs. Rooke let me thus much into the secrets of Marlborough Buildings. When I talked of a whole history, therefore, you see I was not romancing so much as you supposed."

"My dear Mrs. Smith, your authority is deficient. This will not do. Mr. Elliot's having any views on me will not in the least account for the efforts he made towards a reconciliation with my father. That was all prior to my coming to Bath. I found them on the most friendly terms when I arrived."

"I know you did; I know it all perfectly, but—"

"Indeed, Mrs. Smith, we must not expect to get real information in such a line. Facts or opinions which are to pass through the hands of so many, to be misconceived by folly in one, and ignorance in another, can hardly have much truth left."

"Only give me a hearing. You will soon be able to judge of the general credit due, by listening to some particulars which you can yourself immediately contradict or confirm. Nobody supposes that you were his first inducement. He had seen you indeed, before he came to Bath, and admired you, but without knowing it to be you. So says my historian, at least. Is this true? Did he see you last summer or autumn, 'somewhere down in the west,' to use her own words, without knowing it to be you?"

"He certainly did. So far it is very true. At Lyme. I happened to be at Lyme."

"Well," continued Mrs. Smith, triumphantly, "grant my friend the credit due to the establishment of the first point asserted. He saw you then at Lyme, and liked you so well as to be exceedingly pleased to meet with you again in Camden Place, as Miss Anne Elliot, and from that moment, I have no doubt, had a double motive in his visits there. But there was another, and an earlier, which I will now explain. If there is anything in my story which you know to be either false or improbable, stop me. My account states, that your sister's friend, the lady now staying with you, whom I have heard you mention, came to Bath with Miss Elliot and Sir Walter as long ago as September (in short when they first came themselves), and has been staying there ever since; that she is a clever, insinuating, handsome woman, poor and plausible, and altogether such in situation and manner, as to give a general idea, among Sir Walter's acquaintance, of her meaning to be Lady Elliot, and as general a surprise that Miss Elliot should be apparently, blind to the danger."

Here Mrs. Smith paused a moment; but Anne had not a word to say, and she continued—

"This was the light in which it appeared to those who knew the family, long before you returned to it; and Colonel Wallis had his eye upon your father enough to be sensible of it, though he did not then visit in Camden Place; but his regard for Mr. Elliot gave him an interest in watching all that was going on there, and when Mr. Elliot came to Bath for a day or two, as he happened to do a little before Christmas, Colonel Wallis made him acquainted with the appearance of things, and the reports beginning to prevail. Now you are to understand, that time had worked a very material change in Mr. Elliot's opinions as to the value of a baronetcy. Upon all points of blood and connexion he is a completely altered man. Having long had as much money as he could spend, nothing to wish for on the side of avarice or indulgence, he has been gradually learning to pin his happiness upon the consequence he is heir to. I thought it coming on before our acquaintance ceased, but it is now a confirmed feeling. He cannot bear the idea of not being Sir William. You may guess, therefore, that the news he heard from his friend could not be very agreeable,[5] and you may guess what it produced; the resolution of coming back to Bath as soon as possible, and of fixing himself here for a time, with the view of renewing his former acquaintance, and recovering such a footing in the family as might give him the means of ascertaining the degree of his danger, and of circumventing the lady if he found it material. This was agreed upon between the two friends as the only thing to be done; and Colonel Wallis was to assist in every way that he could. He was to be introduced, and Mrs. Wallis was to be introduced, and everybody was to be introduced. Mr. Elliot came back accordingly; and on application was forgiven, as you know, and re-admitted into the family; and there it was his constant object, and his only object (till your arrival added another motive), to watch Sir Walter and Mrs. Clay. He omitted no opportunity of being with them, threw himself in their way, called at all hours; but I need not be particular on this subject. You can imagine what an artful man would do; and with this guide, perhaps, may recollect what you have seen him do."

"Yes," said Anne, "you tell me nothing which does not accord with what I have known, or could imagine. There is always something offensive in the details of cunning. The manoeuvres of selfishness and duplicity must ever be revolting, but I have heard nothing which really surprises me. I know those who would be shocked by such a representation of Mr. Elliot, who would have difficulty in believing it; but I have never been satisfied. I have always wanted some other motive for his conduct than appeared. I should like to know his present opinion, as to the probability of the event he has been in dread of; whether he considers the danger to be lessening or not."

"Lessening, I understand," replied Mrs. Smith. "He thinks Mrs. Clay afraid of him, aware that he sees through her, and not daring to proceed as she might do in his absence. But since he must be absent some time or other, I do not perceive how he can ever be secure while she holds her present influence. Mrs. Wallis has an amusing idea, as nurse tells me, that it is to be put into the marriage articles when you

[5] Should Sir Walter remarry and produce a son, William Elliot's expectations would be nil.

and Mr. Elliot marry, that your father is not to marry Mrs. Clay. A scheme, worthy of Mrs. Wallis's understanding, by all accounts; but my sensible nurse Rooke sees the absurdity of it. 'Why, to be sure, ma'am,' said she, 'it would not prevent his marrying anybody else.' And, indeed, to own the truth, I do not think nurse, in her heart, is a very strenuous opposer of Sir Walter's making a second match. She must be allowed to be a favourer of matrimony, you know; and (since self will intrude) who can say that she may not have some flying visions of attending the next Lady Elliot, through Mrs. Wallis's recommendation?"

"I am very glad to know all this," said Anne, after a little thoughtfulness. "It will be more painful to me in some respects to be in company with him, but I shall know better what to do. My line of conduct will be more direct. Mr. Elliot is evidently a disingenuous, artificial, worldly man, who has never had any better principle to guide him than selfishness."

But Mr. Elliot was not done with. Mrs. Smith had been carried away from her first direction, and Anne had forgotten, in the interest of her own family concerns, how much had been originally implied against him; but her attention was now called to the explanation of those first hints, and she listened to a recital which, if it did not perfectly justify the unqualified bitterness of Mrs. Smith, proved him to have been very unfeeling in his conduct towards her; very deficient both in justice and compassion.

She learned that (the intimacy between them continuing unimpaired by Mr. Elliot's marriage) they had been as before always together, and Mr. Elliot had led his friend into expenses much beyond his fortune. Mrs. Smith did not want to take blame to herself, and was most tender of throwing any on her husband; but Anne could collect that their income had never been equal to their style of living, and that from the first there had been a great deal of general and joint extravagance. From his wife's account of him she could discern Mr. Smith to have been a man of warm feelings, easy temper, careless habits, and not strong understanding, much more amiable than his friend, and very unlike him, led by him, and probably despised by him. Mr. Elliot, raised by his marriage to great affluence, and disposed to every gratification of pleasure and vanity which could be commanded without involving himself, (for with all his self-indulgence he had become a prudent man), and beginning to be rich, just as his friend ought to have found himself to be poor, seemed to have had no concern at all for that friend's probable finances, but, on the contrary, had been prompting and encouraging expenses which could end only in ruin; and the Smiths accordingly had been ruined.

The husband had died just in time to be spared the full knowledge of it. They had previously known embarrassments enough to try the friendship of their friends, and to prove that Mr. Elliot's had better not be tried; but it was not till his death that the wretched state of his affairs was fully known. With a confidence in Mr. Elliot's regard, more creditable to his feelings than his judgement, Mr. Smith had appointed him the executor of his will; but Mr. Elliot would not act, and the difficulties and distress which this refusal had heaped on her, in addition to the inevitable sufferings of her situation, had been such as could not be related without anguish of spirit, or listened to without corresponding indignation.

Anne was shewn some letters of his on the occasion, answers to urgent applications from Mrs. Smith, which all breathed the same stern resolution of not engaging in a fruitless trouble, and, under a cold civility, the same hard-hearted indifference to any of the evils it might bring on her. It was a dreadful picture of ingratitude and inhumanity; and Anne felt, at some moments, that no flagrant open crime could have been worse. She had a great deal to listen to; all the particulars of past sad scenes, all the minutiae of distress upon distress, which in former conversations had been merely hinted at, were dwelt on now with a natural indulgence. Anne could perfectly comprehend the exquisite relief, and was only the more inclined to wonder at the composure of her friend's usual state of mind.

There was one circumstance in the history of her grievances of particular irritation. She had good reason to believe that some property of her husband in the West Indies,[6] which had been for many years under a sort of sequestration for the payment of its own incumbrances,[7] might be recoverable by proper measures; and this property, though not large, would be enough to make her comparatively rich. But there was nobody to stir in it. Mr. Elliot would do nothing, and she could do nothing herself, equally disabled from personal exertion by her state of bodily weakness, and from employing others by her want of money. She had no natural connexions to assist

[6] Such property, undoubtedly, either included slaves or was connected to the slave trade.

[7] The appropriation of the income of a property in order to satisfy claims against the owner (*Oxford English Dictionary*).

her even with their counsel, and she could not afford to purchase the assistance of the law. This was a cruel aggravation of actually strait-ened means. To feel that she ought to be in better circumstances, that a little trouble in the right place might do it, and to fear that delay might be even weakening her claims, was hard to bear.

It was on this point that she had hoped to engage Anne's good offices with Mr. Elliot. She had previously, in the anticipation of their marriage, been very apprehensive of losing her friend by it; but on being assured that he could have made no attempt of that nature, since he did not even know her to be in Bath, it immediately occurred, that something might be done in her favour by the influence of the woman he loved, and she had been hastily preparing to interest Anne's feelings, as far as the observances due to Mr. Elliot's character would allow, when Anne's refutation of the supposed engagement changed the face of everything; and while it took from her the new-formed hope of succeeding in the object of her first anxiety, left her at least the comfort of telling the whole story her own way.

After listening to this full description of Mr. Elliot, Anne could not but express some surprise at Mrs. Smith's having spoken of him so favourably in the beginning of their conversation. "She had seemed to recommend and praise him!"

"My dear," was Mrs. Smith's reply, "there was nothing else to be done. I considered your marrying him as certain, though he might not yet have made the offer, and I could no more speak the truth of him, than if he had been your husband. My heart bled for you, as I talked of happiness; and yet he is sensible, he is agreeable, and with such a woman as you, it was not absolutely hopeless. He was very unkind to his first wife. They were wretched together. But she was too ignorant and giddy for respect, and he had never loved her. I was willing to hope that you must fare better."

Anne could just acknowledge within herself such a possibility of having been induced to marry him, as made her shudder at the idea of the misery which must have followed. It was just possible that she might have been persuaded by Lady Russell! And under such a supposition, which would have been most miserable, when time had disclosed all, too late?

It was very desirable that Lady Russell should be no longer deceived; and one of the concluding arrangements of this important conference, which carried them through the greater part of the morn-ing, was, that Anne had full liberty to communicate to her friend everything relative to Mrs. Smith, in which his conduct was involved.

# CHAPTER X

Anne went home to think over all that she had heard. In one point, her feelings were relieved by this knowledge of Mr. Elliot. There was no longer anything of tenderness due to him. He stood as opposed to Captain Wentworth, in all his own unwelcome obtrusiveness; and the evil of his attentions last night, the irremediable mischief he might have done, was considered with sensations unqualified, unperplexed. Pity for him was all over. But this was the only point of relief. In every other respect, in looking around her, or penetrating forward, she saw more to distrust and to apprehend. She was concerned for the disappointment and pain Lady Russell would be feeling; for the mortifications which must be hanging over her father and sister, and had all the distress of foreseeing many evils, without knowing how to avert any one of them. She was most thankful for her own knowledge of him. She had never considered herself as entitled to reward for not slighting an old friend like Mrs. Smith, but here was a reward indeed springing from it! Mrs. Smith had been able to tell her what no one else could have done. Could the knowledge have been extended through her family? But this was a vain idea. She must talk to Lady Russell, tell her, consult with her, and having done her best, wait the event with as much composure as possible; and after all, her greatest want of composure would be in that quarter of the mind which could not be opened to Lady Russell; in that flow of anxieties and fears which must be all to herself.

She found, on reaching home, that she had, as she intended, escaped seeing Mr. Elliot; that he had called and paid them a long morning visit; but hardly had she congratulated herself, and felt safe, when she heard that he was coming again in the evening.

"I had not the smallest intention of asking him," said Elizabeth, with affected carelessness, "but he gave so many hints; so Mrs. Clay says, at least."

"Indeed, I do say it. I never saw anybody in my life spell[1] harder for an invitation. Poor man! I was really in pain for him; for your hard-hearted sister, Miss Anne, seems bent on cruelty."

"Oh!" cried Elizabeth, "I have been rather too much used to the game to be soon overcome by a gentleman's hints. However, when I found how excessively he was regretting that he should miss

---

[1] Angle for.

my father this morning, I gave way immediately, for I would never really omit an opportunity of bringing him and Sir Walter together. They appear to so much advantage in company with each other. Each behaving so pleasantly. Mr. Elliot looking up with so much respect."

"Quite delightful!" cried Mrs. Clay, not daring, however, to turn her eyes towards Anne. "Exactly like father and son! Dear Miss Elliot, may I not say father and son?"

"Oh! I lay no embargo on any body's words. If you will have such ideas! But, upon my word, I am scarcely sensible of his attentions being beyond those of other men."

"My dear Miss Elliot!" exclaimed Mrs. Clay, lifting her hands and eyes, and sinking all the rest of her astonishment in a convenient silence.

"Well, my dear Penelope, you need not be so alarmed about him. I did invite him, you know. I sent him away with smiles. When I found he was really going to his friends at Thornberry Park for the whole day to-morrow, I had compassion on him."

Anne admired the good acting of the friend, in being able to shew such pleasure as she did, in the expectation and in the actual arrival of the very person whose presence must really be interfering with her prime object. It was impossible but that Mrs. Clay must hate the sight of Mr. Elliot; and yet she could assume a most obliging, placid look, and appear quite satisfied with the curtailed license of devoting herself only half as much to Sir Walter as she would have done otherwise.

To Anne herself it was most distressing to see Mr. Elliot enter the room; and quite painful to have him approach and speak to her. She had been used before to feel that he could not be always quite sincere, but now she saw insincerity in everything. His attentive deference to her father, contrasted with his former language, was odious; and when she thought of his cruel conduct towards Mrs. Smith, she could hardly bear the sight of his present smiles and mildness, or the sound of his artificial good sentiments.

She meant to avoid any such alteration of manners as might provoke a remonstrance on his side. It was a great object to her to escape all enquiry or eclat;[2] but it was her intention to be as decidedly cool to him as might be compatible with their relationship; and to retrace, as quietly as she could, the few steps of unnecessary

[2] French: unembarrassed, conspicuous display.

intimacy she had been gradually led along. She was accordingly more guarded, and more cool, than she had been the night before.

He wanted to animate her curiosity again as to how and where he could have heard her formerly praised; wanted very much to be gratified by more solicitation; but the charm was broken: he found that the heat and animation of a public room was necessary to kindle his modest cousin's vanity; he found, at least, that it was not to be done now, by any of those attempts which he could hazard among the too-commanding claims of the others. He little surmised that it was a subject acting now exactly against his interest, bringing immediately to her thoughts all those parts of his conduct which were least excusable.

She had some satisfaction in finding that he was really going out of Bath the next morning, going early, and that he would be gone the greater part of two days. He was invited again to Camden Place the very evening of his return; but from Thursday to Saturday evening his absence was certain. It was bad enough that a Mrs. Clay should be always before her; but that a deeper hypocrite should be added to their party, seemed the destruction of everything like peace and comfort. It was so humiliating to reflect on the constant deception practiced on her father and Elizabeth; to consider the various sources of mortification preparing for them! Mrs. Clay's selfishness was not so complicate nor so revolting as his; and Anne would have compounded[3] for the marriage at once, with all its evils, to be clear of Mr. Elliot's subtleties in endeavouring to prevent it.

On Friday morning she meant to go very early to Lady Russell, and accomplish the necessary communication; and she would have gone directly after breakfast, but that Mrs. Clay was also going out on some obliging purpose of saving her sister trouble, which determined her to wait till she might be safe from such a companion. She saw Mrs. Clay fairly off, therefore, before she began to talk of spending the morning in Rivers Street.

"Very well," said Elizabeth, "I have nothing to send but my love. Oh! you may as well take back that tiresome book she would lend me, and pretend I have read it through. I really cannot be plaguing myself for ever with all the new poems and states of the nation that come out. Lady Russell quite bores one with her new publications. You need not tell her so, but I thought her dress hideous the other

---

[3] Settled happily.

night. I used to think she had some taste in dress, but I was ashamed of her at the concert. Something so formal and *arrangé*[4] in her air! and she sits so upright! My best love, of course."

"And mine," added Sir Walter. "Kindest regards. And you may say, that I mean to call upon her soon. Make a civil message; but I shall only leave my card.[5] Morning visits are never fair by women at her time of life, who make themselves up so little. If she would only wear rouge she would not be afraid of being seen; but last time I called, I observed the blinds were let down immediately."[6]

While her father spoke, there was a knock at the door. Who could it be? Anne, remembering the preconcerted visits, at all hours, of Mr. Elliot, would have expected him, but for his known engagement seven miles off. After the usual period of suspense, the usual sounds of approach were heard, and "Mr. and Mrs. Charles Musgrove" were ushered into the room.

Surprise was the strongest emotion raised by their appearance; but Anne was really glad to see them; and the others were not so sorry but that they could put on a decent air of welcome; and as soon as it became clear that these, their nearest relations, were not arrived with any views of accommodation in that house, Sir Walter and Elizabeth were able to rise in cordiality, and do the honours of it very well. They were come to Bath for a few days with Mrs. Musgrove, and were at the White Hart. So much was pretty soon understood; but till Sir Walter and Elizabeth were walking Mary into the other drawing-room, and regaling themselves with her admiration, Anne could not draw upon Charles's brain for a regular history of their coming, or an explanation of some smiling hints of particular business, which had been ostentatiously dropped by Mary, as well as of some apparent confusion as to whom their party consisted of.

She then found that it consisted of Mrs. Musgrove, Henrietta, and Captain Harville, beside their two selves. He gave her a very plain, intelligible account of the whole; a narration in which she saw a great deal of most characteristic proceeding. The scheme had received its first impulse by Captain Harville's wanting to come to Bath on business. He had begun to talk of it a week ago; and

---

[4] French: contrived.

[5] A calling card, a token one leaves as a sign that one has been by, without requesting a greeting in return.

[6] "Morning" is any time from breakfast to mid afternoon; the blinds would be let down to filter unflattering light.

by way of doing something, as shooting was over, Charles had proposed coming with him, and Mrs. Harville had seemed to like the idea of it very much, as an advantage to her husband; but Mary could not bear to be left, and had made herself so unhappy about it, that for a day or two everything seemed to be in suspense, or at an end. But then, it had been taken up by his father and mother. His mother had some old friends in Bath whom she wanted to see; it was thought a good opportunity for Henrietta to come and buy wedding-clothes for herself and her sister; and, in short, it ended in being his mother's party, that everything might be comfortable and easy to Captain Harville; and he and Mary were included in it by way of general convenience. They had arrived late the night before. Mrs. Harville, her children, and Captain Benwick, remained with Mr. Musgrove and Louisa at Uppercross.

Anne's only surprise was, that affairs should be in forwardness enough for Henrietta's wedding-clothes to be talked of. She had imagined such difficulties of fortune to exist there as must prevent the marriage from being near at hand; but she learned from Charles that, very recently, (since Mary's last letter to herself), Charles Hayter had been applied to by a friend to hold a living for a youth who could not possibly claim it under many years;[7] and that on the strength of his present income, with almost a certainty of something more permanent long before the term in question, the two families had consented to the young people's wishes, and that their marriage was likely to take place in a few months, quite as soon as Louisa's. "And a very good living it was," Charles added: "only five-and-twenty miles from Uppercross, and in a very fine country: fine part of Dorsetshire. In the centre of some of the best preserves[8] in the kingdom, surrounded by three great proprietors, each more careful and jealous than the other; and to two of the three at least, Charles Hayter might get a special recommendation. Not that he will value it as he ought," he observed, "Charles is too cool about sporting. That's the worst of him."

"I am extremely glad, indeed," cried Anne, "particularly glad that this should happen; and that of two sisters, who both deserve

---

[7] Charles Hayter will serve as interim pastor until the young man designated for the post (a "living" granted by patronage of a "proprietor" or landowner) is old enough to assume it. In *Sense and Sensibility*. Colonel Brandon gives such a living to Edward Ferrars.

[8] Private parks for hunting.

equally well, and who have always been such good friends, the pleasant prospect of one should not be dimming those of the other— that they should be so equal in their prosperity and comfort. I hope your father and mother are quite happy with regard to both."

"Oh! yes. My father would be well pleased if the gentlemen were richer, but he has no other fault to find. Money, you know, coming down with money—two daughters at once—it cannot be a very agreeable operation, and it streightens him as to many things.[9] However, I do not mean to say they have not a right to it. It is very fit they should have daughters' shares; and I am sure he has always been a very kind, liberal father to me. Mary does not above half like Henrietta's match. She never did, you know. But she does not do him justice, nor think enough about Winthrop. I cannot make her attend to the value of the property. It is a very fair match, as times go;[10] and I have liked Charles Hayter all my life, and I shall not leave off now."

"Such excellent parents as Mr. and Mrs. Musgrove," exclaimed Anne, "should be happy in their children's marriages. They do everything to confer happiness, I am sure. What a blessing to young people to be in such hands! Your father and mother seem so totally free from all those ambitious feelings which have led to so much misconduct and misery, both in young and old. I hope you think Louisa perfectly recovered now?"

He answered rather hesitatingly, "Yes, I believe I do; very much recovered; but she is altered; there is no running or jumping about, no laughing or dancing; it is quite different. If one happens only to shut the door a little hard, she starts and wriggles like a young dab-chick in the water; and Benwick sits at her elbow, reading verses, or whispering to her, all day long."

Anne could not help laughing. "That cannot be much to your taste, I know," said she; "but I do believe him to be an excellent young man."

"To be sure he is. Nobody doubts it; and I hope you do not think I am so illiberal as to want every man to have the same objects and pleasures as myself. I have a great value for Benwick; and when one can but get him to talk, he has plenty to say. His reading has done him no harm, for he has fought as well as read. He is a brave

---

[9] His finances will be sorely strained in having to provide two dowries.

[10] "As times go," more and more couples were marrying for love and mutual esteem, rather than according to family edict or by way consolidating wealth and property.

fellow. I got more acquainted with him last Monday than ever I did before. We had a famous set-to at rat-hunting all the morning in my father's great barns; and he played his part so well that I have liked him the better ever since."

Here they were interrupted by the absolute necessity of Charles's following the others to admire mirrors and china; but Anne had heard enough to understand the present state of Uppercross, and rejoice in its happiness; and though she sighed as she rejoiced, her sigh had none of the ill-will of envy in it. She would certainly have risen to their blessings if she could, but she did not want to lessen theirs.

The visit passed off altogether in high good humour. Mary was in excellent spirits, enjoying the gaiety and the change, and so well satisfied with the journey in her mother-in-law's carriage with four horses, and with her own complete independence of Camden Place, that she was exactly in a temper to admire everything as she ought, and enter most readily into all the superiorities of the house, as they were detailed to her. She had no demands on her father or sister, and her consequence was just enough increased by their handsome drawing-rooms.

Elizabeth was, for a short time, suffering a good deal. She felt that Mrs. Musgrove and all her party ought to be asked to dine with them; but she could not bear to have the difference of style, the reduction of servants, which a dinner must betray, witnessed by those who had been always so inferior to the Elliots of Kellynch. It was a struggle between propriety and vanity; but vanity got the better, and then Elizabeth was happy again. These were her internal persuasions: "Old fashioned notions; country hospitality; we do not profess to give dinners; few people in Bath do; Lady Alicia never does; did not even ask her own sister's family, though they were here a month: and I dare say it would be very inconvenient to Mrs. Musgrove; put her quite out of her way. I am sure she would rather not come; she cannot feel easy with us. I will ask them all for an evening; that will be much better; that will be a novelty and a treat. They have not seen two such drawing rooms before. They will be delighted to come to-morrow evening. It shall be a regular party, small, but most elegant." And this satisfied Elizabeth: and when the invitation was given to the two present, and promised for the absent, Mary was as completely satisfied. She was particularly asked to meet Mr. Elliot, and be introduced to Lady Dalrymple and Miss Carteret, who were fortunately already engaged to come; and she could not have received a more gratifying attention. Miss Elliot was to have the honour of calling on Mrs. Musgrove in the course of the morning; and Anne walked off with Charles and Mary, to go and see her and Henrietta directly.

Her plan of sitting with Lady Russell must give way for the present. They all three called in Rivers Street for a couple of minutes; but Anne convinced herself that a day's delay of the intended communication could be of no consequence, and hastened forward to the White Hart, to see again the friends and companions of the last autumn, with an eagerness of good-will which many associations contributed to form.

They found Mrs. Musgrove and her daughter within, and by themselves, and Anne had the kindest welcome from each. Henrietta was exactly in that state of recently-improved views, of fresh-formed happiness, which made her full of regard and interest for everybody she had ever liked before at all; and Mrs. Musgrove's real affection had been won by her usefulness when they were in distress. It was a heartiness, and a warmth, and a sincerity which Anne delighted in the more, from the sad want of such blessings at home. She was entreated to give them as much of her time as possible, invited for every day and all day long, or rather claimed as part of the family; and, in return, she naturally fell into all her wonted ways of attention and assistance, and on Charles's leaving them together, was listening to Mrs. Musgrove's history of Louisa, and to Henrietta's of herself, giving opinions on business, and recommendations to shops; with intervals of every help which Mary required, from altering her ribbon to settling her accounts; from finding her keys, and assorting her trinkets, to trying to convince her that she was not ill-used by anybody; which Mary, well amused as she generally was, in her station at a window overlooking the entrance to the Pump Room,[11] could not but have her moments of imagining.

A morning of thorough confusion was to be expected. A large party in an hotel ensured a quick-changing, unsettled scene. One five minutes brought a note, the next a parcel; and Anne had not been there half an hour, when their dining-room, spacious as it was, seemed more than half filled: a party of steady old friends were

---

[11] This central room in the main baths, in which an orchestra played all day long, was primarily a place to socialize as well as drink water pumped from the famous thermal springs.

seated around Mrs. Musgrove, and Charles came back with Captains Harville and Wentworth. The appearance of the latter could not be more than the surprise of the moment. It was impossible for her to have forgotten to feel that this arrival of their common friends must be soon bringing them together again. Their last meeting had been most important in opening his feelings; she had derived from it a delightful conviction; but she feared from his looks, that the same unfortunate persuasion, which had hastened him away from the Concert Room, still governed. He did not seem to want to be near enough for conversation.

She tried to be calm, and leave things to take their course, and tried to dwell much on this argument of rational dependence:— "Surely, if there be constant attachment on each side, our hearts must understand each other ere[12] long. We are not boy and girl, to be captiously irritable, misled by every moment's inadvertence, and wantonly playing with our own happiness." And yet, a few minutes afterwards, she felt as if their being in company with each other, under their present circumstances, could only be exposing them to inadvertencies and misconstructions of the most mischievous kind.

"Anne," cried Mary, still at her window, "there is Mrs. Clay, I am sure, standing under the colonnade, and a gentleman with her. I saw them turn the corner from Bath Street just now. They seemed deep in talk. Who is it? Come, and tell me. Good heavens! I recollect. It is Mr. Elliot himself."

"No," cried Anne, quickly, "it cannot be Mr. Elliot, I assure you. He was to leave Bath at nine this morning, and does not come back till to-morrow."

As she spoke, she felt that Captain Wentworth was looking at her, the consciousness of which vexed and embarrassed her, and made her regret that she had said so much, simple as it was.

Mary, resenting that she should be supposed not to know her own cousin, began talking very warmly about the family features, and protesting still more positively that it was Mr. Elliot, calling again upon Anne to come and look for herself, but Anne did not mean to stir, and tried to be cool and unconcerned. Her distress returned, however, on perceiving smiles and intelligent glances pass between two or three of the lady visitors, as if they believed themselves quite in the secret. It was evident that the report concerning

---

[12] Before.

her had spread, and a short pause succeeded, which seemed to ensure that it would now spread farther.

"Do come, Anne," cried Mary, "come and look yourself. You will be too late if you do not make haste. They are parting; they are shaking hands. He is turning away. Not know Mr. Elliot, indeed! You seem to have forgot all about Lyme."

To pacify Mary, and perhaps screen her own embarrassment, Anne did move quietly to the window. She was just in time to ascertain that it really was Mr. Elliot, which she had never believed, before he disappeared on one side, as Mrs. Clay walked quickly off on the other; and checking the surprise which she could not but feel at such an appearance of friendly conference between two persons of totally opposite interest, she calmly said, "Yes, it is Mr. Elliot, certainly. He has changed his hour of going, I suppose, that is all, or I may be mistaken, I might not attend;" and walked back to her chair, recomposed, and with the comfortable hope of having acquitted herself well.

The visitors took their leave; and Charles, having civilly seen them off, and then made a face at them, and abused them for coming, began with—

"Well, mother, I have done something for you that you will like. I have been to the theatre, and secured a box for to-morrow night. A'n't I a good boy? I know you love a play; and there is room for us all. It holds nine. I have engaged Captain Wentworth. Anne will not be sorry to join us, I am sure. We all like a play. Have not I done well, mother?"

Mrs. Musgrove was good humouredly beginning to express her perfect readiness for the play, if Henrietta and all the others liked it, when Mary eagerly interrupted her by exclaiming—

"Good heavens, Charles! how can you think of such a thing? Take a box for to-morrow night! Have you forgot that we are engaged to Camden Place to-morrow night? and that we were most particularly asked to meet Lady Dalrymple and her daughter, and Mr. Elliot, and all the principal family connexions, on purpose to be introduced to them? How can you be so forgetful?"

"Phoo! phoo!" replied Charles, "what's an evening party? Never worth remembering. Your father might have asked us to dinner, I think, if he had wanted to see us. You may do as you like, but I shall go to the play."

"Oh! Charles, I declare it will be too abominable if you do, when you promised to go."

"No, I did not promise. I only smirked and bowed, and said the word 'happy.' There was no promise."

"But you must go, Charles. It would be unpardonable to fail. We were asked on purpose to be introduced. There was always such a great connexion between the Dalrymples and ourselves. Nothing ever happened on either side that was not announced immediately. We are quite near relations, you know; and Mr. Elliot too, whom you ought so particularly to be acquainted with! Every attention is due to Mr. Elliot. Consider, my father's heir: the future representative of the family."

"Don't talk to me about heirs and representatives," cried Charles. "I am not one of those who neglect the reigning power to bow to the rising sun. If I would not go for the sake of your father, I should think it scandalous to go for the sake of his heir. What is Mr. Elliot to me?" The careless expression was life to Anne, who saw that Captain Wentworth was all attention, looking and listening with his whole soul; and that the last words brought his enquiring eyes from Charles to herself.

Charles and Mary still talked on in the same style; he, half serious and half jesting, maintaining the scheme for the play, and she, invariably serious, most warmly opposing it, and not omitting to make it known that, however determined to go to Camden Place herself, she should not think herself very well used, if they went to the play without her. Mrs. Musgrove interposed.

"We had better put it off. Charles, you had much better go back and change the box for Tuesday. It would be a pity to be divided, and we should be losing Miss Anne, too, if there is a party at her father's; and I am sure neither Henrietta nor I should care at all for the play, if Miss Anne could not be with us."

Anne felt truly obliged to her for such kindness; and quite as much so for the opportunity it gave her of decidedly saying—

"If it depended only on my inclination, ma'am, the party at home (excepting on Mary's account) would not be the smallest impediment. I have no pleasure in the sort of meeting, and should be too happy to change it for a play, and with you. But, it had better not be attempted, perhaps."

She had spoken it; but she trembled when it was done, conscious that her words were listened to, and daring not even to try to observe their effect.

It was soon generally agreed that Tuesday should be the day; Charles only reserving the advantage of still teasing his wife, by persisting that he would go to the play to-morrow if nobody else would.

Captain Wentworth left his seat, and walked to the fire-place; probably for the sake of walking away from it soon afterwards, and taking a station, with less bare-faced design, by Anne.

"You have not been long enough in Bath," said he, "to enjoy the evening parties of the place."

"Oh! no. The usual character of them has nothing for me. I am no card-player."

"You were not formerly, I know. You did not use to like cards; but time makes many changes."

"I am not yet so much changed," cried Anne, and stopped, fearing she hardly knew what misconstruction. After waiting a few moments he said, and as if it were the result of immediate feeling, "It is a period, indeed! Eight years and a half is a period."

Whether he would have proceeded farther was left to Anne's imagination to ponder over in a calmer hour; for while still hearing the sounds he had uttered, she was startled to other subjects by Henrietta, eager to make use of the present leisure for getting out, and calling on her companions to lose no time, lest somebody else should come in.

They were obliged to move. Anne talked of being perfectly ready, and tried to look it; but she felt that could Henrietta have known the regret and reluctance of her heart in quitting that chair, in preparing to quit the room, she would have found, in all her own sensations for her cousin, in the very security of his affection, where-with[13] to pity her.

Their preparations, however, were stopped short. Alarming sounds were heard; other visitors approached, and the door was thrown open for Sir Walter and Miss Elliot, whose entrance seemed to give a general chill. Anne felt an instant oppression, and wherever she looked saw symptoms of the same. The comfort, the freedom, the gaiety of the room was over, hushed into cold composure, determined silence, or insipid talk, to meet the heartless elegance of her father and sister. How mortifying to feel that it was so!

Her jealous eye was satisfied in one particular. Captain Wentworth was acknowledged again by each, by Elizabeth more graciously than before. She even addressed him once, and looked at him more than once. Elizabeth was, in fact, revolving a great measure. The sequel

[13] The means.

explained it. After the waste of a few minutes in saying the proper nothings, she began to give the invitation which was to comprise all the remaining dues of the Musgroves. "To-morrow evening, to meet a few friends: no formal party." It was all said very gracefully, and the cards with which she had provided herself, the "Miss Elliot at home," were laid on the table, with a courteous, comprehensive smile to all, and one smile and one card more decidedly for Captain Wentworth. The truth was, that Elizabeth had been long enough in Bath to under-stand the importance of a man of such an air and appearance as his.[14] The past was nothing. The present was that Captain Wentworth would move about well in her drawing-room. The card was pointedly given, and Sir Walter and Elizabeth arose and disappeared.

The interruption had been short, though severe, and ease and ani-mation returned to most of those they left as the door shut them out, but not to Anne. She could think only of the invitation she had with such astonishment witnessed, and of the manner in which it had been received; a manner of doubtful meaning, of surprise rather than grat-ification, of polite acknowledgement rather than acceptance. She knew him; she saw disdain in his eye, and could not venture to believe that he had determined to accept such an offering, as an atonement for all the insolence of the past. Her spirits sank. He held the card in his hand after they were gone, as if deeply considering it.

"Only think of Elizabeth's including everybody!" whispered Mary very audibly. "I do not wonder Captain Wentworth is delighted! You see he cannot put the card out of his hand."

Anne caught his eye, saw his cheeks glow, and his mouth form itself into a momentary expression of contempt, and turned away, that she might neither see nor hear more to vex her.

The party separated. The gentlemen had their own pursuits, the ladies proceeded on their own business, and they met no more while Anne belonged to them. She was earnestly begged to return and dine, and give them all the rest of the day, but her spirits had been so long exerted that at present she felt unequal to more, and fit only for home, where she might be sure of being as silent as she chose.

Promising to be with them the whole of the following morning, therefore, she closed the fatigues of the present by a toilsome walk to Camden Place, there to spend the evening chiefly in listening to the busy arrangements of Elizabeth and Mrs. Clay for the morrow's

[14] A reference to the growing prestige of the professional classes, in this case naval officers; an "at home" is informal hospitality (an "open house").

party, the frequent enumeration of the persons invited, and the continually improving detail of all the embellishments which were to make it the most completely elegant of its kind in Bath, while harassing herself with the never-ending question, of whether Captain Wentworth would come or not? They were reckoning him as certain, but with her it was a gnawing solicitude never appeased for five minutes together. She generally thought he would come, because she generally thought he ought; but it was a case which she could not so shape into any positive act of duty or discretion, as inevitably to defy the suggestions of very opposite feelings.

She only roused herself from the broodings of this restless agitation, to let Mrs. Clay know that she had been seen with Mr. Elliot three hours after his being supposed to be out of Bath, for having watched in vain for some intimation of the interview from the lady herself, she determined to mention it, and it seemed to her there was guilt in Mrs. Clay's face as she listened. It was transient: cleared away in an instant; but Anne could imagine she read there the consciousness of having, by some complication of mutual trick, or some overbearing authority of his, been obliged to attend (perhaps for half an hour) to his lectures and restrictions on her designs on Sir Walter. She exclaimed, however, with a very tolerable imitation of nature: —

"Oh! dear! very true. Only think, Miss Elliot, to my great surprise I met with Mr. Elliot in Bath Street. I was never more astonished. He turned back and walked with me to the Pump Yard. He had been prevented setting off for Thornberry, but I really forget by what; for I was in a hurry, and could not much attend, and I can only answer for his being determined not to be delayed in his return. He wanted to know how early he might be admitted tomorrow. He was full of 'to-morrow,' and it is very evident that I have been full of it too, ever since I entered the house, and learnt the extension of your plan and all that had happened, or my seeing him could never have gone so entirely out of my head."

## CHAPTER XI

One day only had passed since Anne's conversation with Mrs. Smith; but a keener interest had succeeded, and she was now so little touched by Mr. Elliot's conduct, except by its effects in one quarter, that it became a matter of course the next morning, still to defer her explanatory visit in Rivers Street. She had promised to be with the Musgroves from breakfast to dinner. Her faith was plighted, and Mr. Elliot's character, like the Sultaness Scheherazade's head, must live another day.[1]

She could not keep her appointment punctually, however; the weather was unfavourable, and she had grieved over the rain on her friends' account, and felt it very much on her own, before she was able to attempt the walk. When she reached the White Hart, and made her way to the proper apartment, she found herself neither arriving quite in time, nor the first to arrive. The party before her were, Mrs. Musgrove, talking to Mrs. Croft, and Captain Harville to Captain Wentworth; and she immediately heard that Mary and Henrietta, too impatient to wait, had gone out the moment it had cleared, but would be back again soon, and that the strictest injunctions had been left with Mrs. Musgrove to keep her there till they returned. She had only to submit, sit down, be outwardly composed, and feel herself plunged at once in all the agitations which she had merely laid her account of tasting a little before the morning closed. There was no delay, no waste of time. She was deep in the happiness of such misery, or the misery of such happiness, instantly. Two minutes after her entering the room, Captain Wentworth said—

"We will write the letter we were talking of, Harville, now, if you will give me materials."

Materials were at hand, on a separate table; he went to it, and nearly turning his back to them all, was engrossed by writing.

Mrs. Musgrove was giving Mrs. Croft the history of her eldest daughter's engagement, and just in that inconvenient tone of voice which was perfectly audible while it pretended to be a whisper. Anne felt that she did not belong to the conversation, and yet, as Captain Harville seemed thoughtful and not disposed to talk, she could not avoid hearing many undesirable particulars; such as, "how Mr. Musgrove and my brother Hayter had met again and again to talk it over; what my brother Hayter had said one day, and what Mr. Musgrove had proposed the next, and what had occurred to my sister Hayter, and what the young people had wished, and what I said at first I never could consent to, but was afterwards persuaded to think might do very well," and a great deal in the same

---

[1] The fabled and fictional sultaness in *Arabian Nights' Entertainments* who forestalls her execution by telling stories.

style of open-hearted communication: minutiae which, even with every advantage of taste and delicacy, which good Mrs. Musgrove could not give, could be properly interesting only to the principals. Mrs. Croft was attending with great good-humour, and whenever she spoke at all, it was very sensibly. Anne hoped the gentlemen might each be too much self-occupied to hear.

"And so, ma'am, all these things considered," said Mrs. Musgrove, in her powerful whisper, "though we could have wished it different, yet, altogether, we did not think it fair to stand out any longer, for Charles Hayter was quite wild about it, and Henrietta was pretty near as bad; and so we thought they had better marry at once, and make the best of it, as many others have done before them. At any rate, said I, it will be better than a long engagement."

"That is precisely what I was going to observe," cried Mrs. Croft. "I would rather have young people settle on a small income at once, and have to struggle with a few difficulties together, than be involved in a long engagement. I always think that no mutual—"

"Oh! dear Mrs. Croft," cried Mrs. Musgrove, unable to let her finish her speech, "there is nothing I so abominate for young people as a long engagement. It is what I always protested against for my children. It is all very well, I used to say, for young people to be engaged, if there is a certainty of their being able to marry in six months, or even in twelve; but a long engagement—"

"Yes, dear ma'am," said Mrs. Croft, "or an uncertain engagement, an engagement which may be long. To begin without knowing that at such a time there will be the means of marrying, I hold to be very unsafe and unwise, and what I think all parents should prevent as far as they can."

Anne found an unexpected interest here. She felt its application to herself, felt it in a nervous thrill all over her; and at the same moment that her eyes instinctively glanced towards the distant table, Captain Wentworth's pen ceased to move, his head was raised, pausing, listening, and he turned round the next instant to give a look, one quick, conscious look at her.

The two ladies continued to talk, to re-urge the same admitted truths, and enforce them with such examples of the ill effect of a contrary practice as had fallen within their observation, but Anne heard nothing distinctly; it was only a buzz of words in her ear, her mind was in confusion.

Captain Harville, who had in truth been hearing none of it, now left his seat, and moved to a window, and Anne seeming to watch him, though it was from thorough absence of mind, became gradually sensible that he was inviting her to join him where he stood. He looked at her with a smile, and a little motion of the head, which expressed, "Come to me, I have something to say;" and the unaffected, easy kindness of manner which denoted the feelings of an older acquaintance than he really was, strongly enforced the invitation. She roused herself and went to him. The window at which he stood was at the other end of the room from where the two ladies were sitting, and though nearer to Captain Wentworth's table, not very near. As she joined him, Captain Harville's countenance re-assumed the serious, thoughtful expression which seemed its natural character.

"Look here," said he, unfolding a parcel in his hand, and displaying a small miniature painting, "do you know who that is?"

"Certainly: Captain Benwick."

"Yes, and you may guess who it is for. But," (in a deep tone) "it was not done for her. Miss Elliot, do you remember our walking together at Lyme, and grieving for him? I little thought then—but no matter. This was drawn at the Cape.[2] He met with a clever young German artist at the Cape, and in compliance with a promise to my poor sister, sat to him, and was bringing it home for her; and I have now the charge of getting it properly set for another! It was a commission to me! But who else was there to employ? I hope I can allow for him. I am not sorry, indeed, to make it over to another. He undertakes it;" (looking towards Captain Wentworth,) "he is writing about it now." And with a quivering lip he wound up the whole by adding, "Poor Fanny! she would not have forgotten him so soon!"

"No," replied Anne, in a low, feeling voice. "That I can easily believe."

"It was not in her nature. She doted on him."

"It would not be the nature of any woman who truly loved."

Captain Harville smiled, as much as to say, "Do you claim that for your sex?" and she answered the question, smiling also, "Yes. We certainly do not forget you as soon as you forget us. It is, perhaps, our fate rather than our merit. We cannot help ourselves. We live at home, quiet, confined, and our feelings prey upon us. You are forced on exertion. You have always a profession, pursuits, business of some sort or other, to take you back into the world

---

[2] Presumably the Cape of Good Hope in southern Africa.

immediately, and continual occupation and change soon weaken impressions."

"Granting your assertion that the world does all this so soon for men (which, however, I do not think I shall grant), it does not apply to Benwick. He has not been forced upon any exertion. The peace turned him on shore at the very moment, and he has been living with us, in our little family circle, ever since."

"True," said Anne, "very true; I did not recollect; but what shall we say now, Captain Harville? If the change be not from outward circumstances, it must be from within; it must be nature, man's nature, which has done the business for Captain Benwick."

"No, no, it is not man's nature. I will not allow it to be more man's nature than woman's to be inconstant and forget those they do love, or have loved. I believe the reverse. I believe in a true analogy between our bodily frames and our mental; and that as our bodies are the strongest, so are our feelings; capable of bearing most rough usage, and riding out the heaviest weather."

"Your feelings may be the strongest," replied Anne, "but the same spirit of analogy will authorise me to assert that ours are the most tender. Man is more robust than woman, but he is not longer lived; which exactly explains my view of the nature of their attachments. Nay, it would be too hard upon you, if it were otherwise. You have difficulties, and privations, and dangers enough to struggle with. You are always labouring and toiling, exposed to every risk and hardship. Your home, country, friends, all quitted. Neither time, nor health, nor life, to be called your own. It would be hard, indeed" (with a faltering voice), "if woman's feelings were to be added to all this."

"We shall never agree upon this question," Captain Harville was beginning to say, when a slight noise called their attention to Captain Wentworth's hitherto perfectly quiet division of the room. It was nothing more than that his pen had fallen down; but Anne was startled at finding him nearer than she had supposed, and half inclined to suspect that the pen had only fallen because he had been occupied by them, striving to catch sounds, which yet she did not think he could have caught.

"Have you finished your letter?" said Captain Harville.

"Not quite, a few lines more. I shall have done in five minutes."

"There is no hurry on my side. I am only ready whenever you are. I am in very good anchorage here," (smiling at Anne) "well supplied, and want for nothing. No hurry for a signal at all. Well,

Miss Elliot," (lowering his voice) "as I was saying we shall never agree, I suppose, upon this point. No man and woman, would, probably. But let me observe that all histories are against you—all stories, prose and verse. If I had such a memory as Benwick, I could bring you fifty quotations in a moment on my side the argument, and I do not think I ever opened a book in my life which had not something to say upon woman's inconstancy. Songs and proverbs, all talk of woman's fickleness. But perhaps you will say, these were all written by men."

"Perhaps I shall. Yes, yes, if you please, no reference to examples in books. Men have had every advantage of us in telling their own story. Education has been theirs in so much higher a degree; the pen has been in their hands. I will not allow books to prove anything."

"But how shall we prove anything?"

"We never shall. We never can expect to prove any thing upon such a point. It is a difference of opinion which does not admit of proof. We each begin, probably, with a little bias towards our own sex; and upon that bias build every circumstance in favour of it which has occurred within our own circle; many of which circumstances (perhaps those very cases which strike us the most) may be precisely such as cannot be brought forward without betraying a confidence, or in some respect saying what should not be said."

"Ah!" cried Captain Harville, in a tone of strong feeling, "if I could but make you comprehend what a man suffers when he takes a last look at his wife and children, and watches the boat that he has sent them off in, as long as it is in sight, and then turns away and says, 'God knows whether we ever meet again!' And then, if I could convey to you the glow of his soul when he does see them again; when, coming back after a twelvemonth's absence, perhaps, and obliged to put into another port, he calculates how soon it be possible to get them there, pretending to deceive himself, and saying, 'They cannot be here till such a day,' but all the while hoping for them twelve hours sooner, and seeing them arrive at last, as if Heaven had given them wings, by many hours sooner still! If I could explain to you all this, and all that a man can bear and do, and glories to do, for the sake of these treasures of his existence! I speak, you know, only of such men as have hearts!" pressing his own with emotion.

"Oh!" cried Anne eagerly, "I hope I do justice to all that is felt by you, and by those who resemble you. God forbid that I should undervalue the warm and faithful feelings of any of my fellow-creatures!

I should deserve utter contempt if I dared to suppose that true attachment and constancy were known only by woman. No, I believe you capable of everything great and good in your married lives. I believe you equal to every important exertion, and to every domestic forbearance, so long as—if I may be allowed the expression—so long as you have an object. I mean while the woman you love lives, and lives for you. All the privilege I claim for my own sex (it is not a very enviable one; you need not covet it), is that of loving longest, when existence or when hope is gone."

She could not immediately have uttered another sentence; her heart was too full, her breath too much oppressed.

"You are a good soul," cried Captain Harville, putting his hand on her arm, quite affectionately. "There is no quarrelling with you. And when I think of Benwick, my tongue is tied."

Their attention was called towards the others. Mrs. Croft was taking leave.

"Here, Frederick, you and I part company, I believe," said she. "I am going home, and you have an engagement with your friend. To-night we may have the pleasure of all meeting again at your party," (turning to Anne.) "We had your sister's card yesterday, and I understood Frederick had a card too, though I did not see it; and you are disengaged, Frederick, are you not, as well as ourselves?"

Captain Wentworth was folding up a letter in great haste, and either could not or would not answer fully.

"Yes," said he, "very true; here we separate, but Harville and I shall soon be after you; that is, Harville, if you are ready, I am in half a minute. I know you will not be sorry to be off. I shall be at your service in half a minute."

Mrs. Croft left them, and Captain Wentworth, having sealed his letter with great rapidity, was indeed ready, and had even a hurried, agitated air, which shewed impatience to be gone. Anne knew not how to understand it. She had the kindest "Good morning, God bless you!" from Captain Harville, but from him not a word, nor a look! He had passed out of the room without a look!

She had only time, however, to move closer to the table where he had been writing, when footsteps were heard returning; the door opened, it was himself. He begged their pardon, but he had forgotten his gloves, and instantly crossing the room to the writing table, he drew out a letter from under the scattered paper, placed it before Anne with eyes of glowing entreaty fixed on her for a time, and hastily collecting his gloves, was again out of the room, almost before Mrs. Musgrove was aware of his being in it: the work of an instant!

The revolution which one instant had made in Anne, was almost beyond expression. The letter, with a direction hardly legible, to "Miss A. E.—," was evidently the one which he had been folding so hastily. While supposed to be writing only to Captain Benwick, he had been also addressing her! On the contents of that letter depended all which this world could do for her. Anything was possible, anything might be defied rather than suspense. Mrs. Musgrove had little arrangements of her own at her own table; to their protection she must trust, and sinking into the chair which he had occupied, succeeding to the very spot where he had leaned and written, her eyes devoured the following words:

"I can listen no longer in silence. I must speak to you by such means as are within my reach. You pierce my soul. I am half agony, half hope. Tell me not that I am too late, that such precious feelings are gone for ever. I offer myself to you again with a heart even more your own than when you almost broke it, eight years and a half ago. Dare not say that man forgets sooner than woman, that his love has an earlier death. I have loved none but you. Unjust I may have been, weak and resentful I have been, but never inconstant. You alone have brought me to Bath. For you alone, I think and plan. Have you not seen this? Can you fail to have understood my wishes? I had not waited even these ten days, could I have read your feelings, as I think you must have penetrated mine. I can hardly write. I am every instant hearing something which overpowers me. You sink your voice, but I can distinguish the tones of that voice when they would be lost on others. Too good, too excellent creature! You do us justice, indeed. You do believe that there is true attachment and constancy among men. Believe it to be most fervent, most undeviating, in

F. W.

"I must go, uncertain of my fate; but I shall return hither, or follow your party, as soon as possible. A word, a look, will be enough to decide whether I enter your father's house this evening or never."

Such a letter was not to be soon recovered from. Half an hour's solitude and reflection might have tranquillized her; but the ten minutes only which now passed before she was interrupted, with all the restraints of her situation, could do nothing towards tranquillity. Every moment rather brought fresh agitation. It was overpowering happiness. And before she was beyond the first stage of full sensation, Charles, Mary, and Henrietta all came in.

The absolute necessity of seeming like herself produced then an immediate struggle; but after a while she could do no more. She began not to understand a word they said, and was obliged to plead indisposition and excuse herself. They could then see that she looked very ill, were shocked and concerned, and would not stir without her for the world. This was dreadful. Would they only have gone away, and left her in the quiet possession of that room it would have been her cure; but to have them all standing or waiting around her was distracting, and in desperation, she said she would go home.

"By all means, my dear," cried Mrs. Musgrove, "go home directly, and take care of yourself, that you may be fit for the evening. I wish Sarah was here to doctor you, but I am no doctor myself. Charles, ring and order a chair. She must not walk."

But the chair would never do. Worse than all! To lose the possibility of speaking two words to Captain Wentworth in the course of her quiet, solitary progress up the town (and she felt almost certain of meeting him) could not be borne. The chair was earnestly protested against, and Mrs. Musgrove, who thought only of one sort of illness, having assured herself with some anxiety, that there had been no fall in the case; that Anne had not at any time lately slipped down, and got a blow on her head; that she was perfectly convinced of having had no fall; could part with her cheerfully, and depend on finding her better at night.

Anxious to omit no possible precaution, Anne struggled, and said—

"I am afraid, ma'am, that it is not perfectly understood. Pray be so good as to mention to the other gentlemen that we hope to see your whole party this evening. I am afraid there had been some mistake; and I wish you particularly to assure Captain Harville and Captain Wentworth, that we hope to see them both."

"Oh! my dear, it is quite understood, I give you my word. Captain Harville has no thought but of going."

"Do you think so? But I am afraid; and I should be so very sorry. Will you promise me to mention it, when you see them again? You will see them both this morning, I dare say. Do promise me."

"To be sure I will, if you wish it. Charles, if you see Captain Harville anywhere, remember to give Miss Anne's message. But indeed, my dear, you need not be uneasy. Captain Harville holds himself quite engaged, I'll answer for it; and Captain Wentworth the same, I dare say."

Anne could do no more; but her heart prophesied some mischance to damp the perfection of her felicity. It could not be very lasting, however. Even if he did not come to Camden Place himself, it would be in her power to send an intelligible sentence by Captain Harville. Another momentary vexation occurred. Charles, in his real concern and good nature, would go home with her; there was no preventing him. This was almost cruel. But she could not be long ungrateful; he was sacrificing an engagement at a gunsmith's, to be of use to her; and she set off with him, with no feeling but gratitude apparent.

They were on Union Street, when a quicker step behind, a something of familiar sound, gave her two moments' preparation for the sight of Captain Wentworth. He joined them; but, as if irresolute whether to join or to pass on, said nothing, only looked. Anne could command herself enough to receive that look, and not repulsively. The cheeks which had been pale now glowed, and the movements which had hesitated were decided. He walked by her side. Presently, struck by a sudden thought, Charles said—

"Captain Wentworth, which way are you going? Only to Gay Street, or farther up the town?"

"I hardly know," replied Captain Wentworth, surprised.

"Are you going as high as Belmont? Are you going near Camden Place? Because, if you are, I shall have no scruple in asking you to take my place, and give Anne your arm to her father's door. She is rather done for this morning, and must not go so far without help, and I ought to be at that fellow's in the Market Place. He promised me the sight of a capital gun he is just going to send off; said he would keep it unpacked to the last possible moment, that I might see it; and if I do not turn back now, I have no chance. By his description, a good deal like the second size double-barrel of mine, which you shot with one day round Winthrop."

There could not be an objection. There could be only the most proper alacrity, a most obliging compliance for public view; and smiles reined in and spirits dancing in private rapture. In half a minute Charles was at the bottom of Union Street again, and the other two proceeding together: and soon words enough had passed between them to decide their direction towards the comparatively quiet and retired gravel walk, where the power of conversation would make the present hour a blessing indeed, and prepare it for all the immortality which the happiest recollections of their own future lives could bestow. There they exchanged again those feelings and those promises which had once before seemed to secure everything, but which had been followed by so many, many years of division and estrangement. There they returned again into the past, more exquisitely happy, perhaps, in their re-union, than when it had been first projected; more tender, more tried, more fixed in a knowledge of each other's character, truth, and attachment; more equal to act, more justified in acting. And there, as they slowly paced the gradual ascent, heedless of every group around them, seeing neither sauntering politicians, bustling housekeepers, flirting girls, nor nursery-maids and children, they could indulge in those retrospections and acknowledgements, and especially in those explanations of what had directly preceded the present moment, which were so poignant and so ceaseless in interest. All the little variations of the last week were gone through; and of yesterday and today there could scarcely be an end.

She had not mistaken him. Jealousy of Mr. Elliot had been the retarding weight, the doubt, the torment. That had begun to operate in the very hour of first meeting her in Bath; that had returned, after a short suspension, to ruin the concert; and that had influenced him in everything he had said and done, or omitted to say and do, in the last four-and-twenty hours. It had been gradually yielding to the better hopes which her looks, or words, or actions occasionally encouraged; it had been vanquished at last by those sentiments and those tones which had reached him while she talked with Captain Harville; and under the irresistible governance of which he had seized a sheet of paper, and poured out his feelings.

Of what he had then written, nothing was to be retracted or qualified. He persisted in having loved none but her. She had never been supplanted. He never even believed himself to see her equal. Thus much indeed he was obliged to acknowledge: that he had been constant unconsciously, nay unintentionally; that he had meant to forget her, and believed it to be done. He had imagined himself indifferent, when he had only been angry; and he had been unjust to her merits, because he had been a sufferer from them. Her character was now fixed on his mind as perfection itself, maintaining the loveliest medium of fortitude and gentleness; but he was obliged to

acknowledge that only at Uppercross had he learnt to do her justice, and only at Lyme had he begun to understand himself. At
Lyme, he had received lessons of more than one sort. The passing
admiration of Mr. Elliot had at least roused him, and the scenes on
the Cobb and at Captain Harville's had fixed her superiority.

In his preceding attempts to attach himself to Louisa Musgrove
(the attempts of angry pride), he protested that he had for ever felt
it to be impossible; that he had not cared, could not care, for
Louisa; though till that day, till the leisure for reflection which followed it, he had not understood the perfect excellence of the mind
with which Louisa's could so ill bear a comparison, or the perfect
unrivalled hold it possessed over his own. There, he had learnt to
distinguish between the steadiness of principle and the obstinacy of
self-will, between the darings of heedlessness and the resolution of a
collected mind. There he had seen everything to exalt in his estimation the woman he had lost; and there begun to deplore the pride,
the folly, the madness of resentment, which had kept him from trying to regain her when thrown in his way.

From that period his penance had become severe. He had no
sooner been free from the horror and remorse attending the first
few days of Louisa's accident, no sooner begun to feel himself alive
again, than he had begun to feel himself, though alive, not at liberty.

"I found," said he, "that I was considered by Harville an engaged
man! That neither Harville nor his wife entertained a doubt of our
mutual attachment. I was startled and shocked. To a degree, I could
contradict this instantly; but, when I began to reflect that others
might have felt the same—her own family, nay, perhaps herself—
I was no longer at my own disposal. I was hers in honour if she
wished it. I had been unguarded. I had not thought seriously on this
subject before. I had not considered that my excessive intimacy must
have its danger of ill consequence in many ways; and that I had no
right to be trying whether I could attach myself to either of the girls,
at the risk of raising even an unpleasant report, were there no other ill
effects. I had been grossly wrong, and must abide the consequences."

He found too late, in short, that he had entangled himself; and
that precisely as he became fully satisfied of his not caring for
Louisa at all, he must regard himself as bound to her, if her sentiments for him were what the Harvilles supposed. It determined him
to leave Lyme, and await her complete recovery elsewhere. He
would gladly weaken, by any fair means, whatever feelings or speculations concerning him might exist; and he went, therefore, to his

brother's, meaning after a while to return to Kellynch, and act as circumstances might require.

"I was six weeks with Edward," said he, "and saw him happy. I could have no other pleasure. I deserved none. He enquired after you very particularly; asked even if you were personally altered, little suspecting that to my eye you could never alter."

Anne smiled, and let it pass. It was too pleasing a blunder for a reproach. It is something for a woman to be assured, in her eight-and-twentieth year, that she has not lost one charm of earlier youth; but the value of such homage was inexpressibly increased to Anne, by comparing it with former words, and feeling it to be the result, not the cause of a revival of his warm attachment.

He had remained in Shropshire, lamenting the blindness of his own pride, and the blunders of his own calculations, till at once released from Louisa by the astonishing and felicitous intelligence of her engagement with Benwick.

"Here," said he, "ended the worst of my state; for now I could at least put myself in the way of happiness; I could exert myself; I could do something. But to be waiting so long in inaction, and waiting only for evil, had been dreadful. Within the first five minutes I said, 'I will be at Bath on Wednesday,' and I was. Was it unpardonable to think it worth my while to come? and to arrive with some degree of hope? You were single. It was possible that you might retain the feelings of the past, as I did; and one encouragement happened to be mine. I could never doubt that you would be loved and sought by others, but I knew to a certainty that you had refused one man, at least, of better pretensions than myself; and I could not help often saying, 'Was this for me?'"

Their first meeting in Milsom Street afforded much to be said, but the concert still more. That evening seemed to be made up of exquisite moments. The moment of her stepping forward in the Octagon Room to speak to him: the moment of Mr. Elliot's appearing and tearing her away, and one or two subsequent moments, marked by returning hope or increasing despondency, were dwelt on with energy.

"To see you," cried he, "in the midst of those who could not be my well-wishers; to see your cousin close by you, conversing and smiling, and feel all the horrible eligibilities and proprieties of the match! To consider it as the certain wish of every being who could hope to influence you! Even if your own feelings were reluctant or indifferent, to consider what powerful supports would be his! Was it not enough to make the fool of me which I appeared? How could I look on without agony? Was not the very sight of the friend who sat behind you, was not the recollection of what had been, the knowledge of her influence, the indelible, immoveable impression of what persuasion had once done—was it not all against me?"

"You should have distinguished," replied Anne. "You should not have suspected me now; the case is so different, and my age is so different. If I was wrong in yielding to persuasion once, remember that it was to persuasion exerted on the side of safety, not of risk. When I yielded, I thought it was to duty, but no duty could be called in aid here. In marrying a man indifferent to me, all risk would have been incurred, and all duty violated."

"Perhaps I ought to have reasoned thus," he replied, "but I could not. I could not derive benefit from the late knowledge I had acquired of your character. I could not bring it into play; it was overwhelmed, buried, lost in those earlier feelings which I had been smarting under year after year. I could think of you only as one who had yielded, who had given me up, who had been influenced by any one rather than by me. I saw you with the very person who had guided you in that year of misery. I had no reason to believe her of less authority now. The force of habit was to be added."

"I should have thought," said Anne, "that my manner to yourself might have spared you much or all of this."

"No, no! your manner might be only the ease which your engagement to another man would give. I left you in this belief; and yet, I was determined to see you again. My spirits rallied with the morning, and I felt that I had still a motive for remaining here."

At last Anne was at home again, and happier than any one in that house could have conceived. All the surprise and suspense, and every other painful part of the morning dissipated by this conversation, she re-entered the house so happy as to be obliged to find an alloy in some momentary apprehensions of its being impossible to last. An interval of meditation, serious and grateful, was the best corrective of everything dangerous in such high-wrought felicity; and she went to her room, and grew steadfast and fearless in the thankfulness of her enjoyment.

The evening came, the drawing-rooms were lighted up, the company assembled. It was but a card party, it was but a mixture of those who had never met before, and those who met too often; a commonplace business, too numerous for intimacy, too small for variety; but Anne had never found an evening shorter. Glowing and lovely in sensibility and happiness, and more generally admired than she thought about or cared for, she had cheerful or forbearing feelings for every creature around her. Mr. Elliot was there; she avoided, but she could pity him. The Wallises, she had amusement in understanding them. Lady Dalrymple and Miss Carteret—they would soon be innoxious[3] cousins to her. She cared not for Mrs. Clay, and had nothing to blush for in the public manners of her father and sister. With the Musgroves, there was the happy chat of perfect ease; with Captain Harville, the kind-hearted intercourse of brother and sister; with Lady Russell, attempts at conversation, which a delicious consciousness cut short; with Admiral and Mrs. Croft, everything of peculiar cordiality and fervent interest, which the same consciousness sought to conceal; and with Captain Wentworth, some moments of communications continually occurring, and always the hope of more, and always the knowledge of his being there.

It was in one of these short meetings, each apparently occupied in admiring a fine display of greenhouse plants, that she said—

"I have been thinking over the past, and trying impartially to judge of the right and wrong, I mean with regard to myself; and I must believe that I was right, much as I suffered from it, that I was perfectly right in being guided by the friend whom you will love better than you do now. To me, she was in the place of a parent. Do not mistake me, however. I am not saying that she did not err in her advice. It was, perhaps, one of those cases in which advice is good or bad only as the event decides; and for myself, I certainly never should, in any circumstance of tolerable similarity, give such advice. But I mean, that I was right in submitting to her, and that if I had done otherwise, I should have suffered more in continuing the engagement than I did even in giving it up, because I should have suffered in my conscience. I have now, as far as such a sentiment is allowable in human nature, nothing to reproach myself with; and if I mistake not, a strong sense of duty is no bad part of a woman's portion."

He looked at her, looked at Lady Russell, and looking again at her, replied, as if in cool deliberation—

"Not yet. But there are hopes of her being forgiven in time. I trust to being in charity with her soon. But I too have been thinking over the past, and a question has suggested itself, whether there may not have been one person more my enemy even than that lady? My own self. Tell me if, when I returned to England in the year

---

[3] Innocuous.

eight, with a few thousand pounds, and was posted into the Laconia, if I had then written to you, would you have answered my letter? Would you, in short, have renewed the engagement then?"

"Would I!" was all her answer; but the accent was decisive enough.

"Good God!" he cried, "you would! It is not that I did not think of it, or desire it, as what could alone crown all my other success; but I was proud, too proud to ask again. I did not understand you. I shut my eyes, and would not understand you, or do you justice. This is a recollection which ought to make me forgive every one sooner than myself. Six years of separation and suffering might have been spared. It is a sort of pain, too, which is new to me. I have been used to the gratification of believing myself to earn every blessing that I enjoyed. I have valued myself on honourable toils and just rewards. Like other great men under reverses," he added, with a smile. "I must endeavour to subdue my mind to my fortune. I must learn to brook being happier than I deserve."

## CHAPTER XII

Who can be in doubt of what followed? When any two young people take it into their heads to marry, they are pretty sure by perseverance to carry their point, be they ever so poor, or ever so imprudent, or ever so little likely to be necessary to each other's ultimate comfort. This may be bad morality to conclude with, but I believe it to be truth; and if such parties succeed, how should a Captain Wentworth and an Anne Elliot, with the advantage of maturity of mind, consciousness of right, and one independent fortune between them, fail of bearing down every opposition? They might in fact, have borne down a great deal more than they met with, for there was little to distress them beyond the want of graciousness and warmth. Sir Walter made no objection, and Elizabeth did nothing worse than look cold and unconcerned. Captain Wentworth, with five-and-twenty thousand pounds, and as high in his profession as merit and activity could place him, was no longer nobody. He was now esteemed quite worthy to address[1] the daughter of a foolish, spendthrift baronet, who had not had principle or sense enough to maintain himself in the situation in which Providence had placed him,

---

[1] Court, propose marriage to.

and who could give his daughter at present but a small part of the share of ten thousand pounds which must be hers hereafter.[2]

Sir Walter, indeed, though he had no affection for Anne, and no vanity flattered, to make him really happy on the occasion, was very far from thinking it a bad match for her. On the contrary, when he saw more of Captain Wentworth, saw him repeatedly by daylight, and eyed him well, he was very much struck by his personal claims, and felt that his superiority of appearance might be not unfairly balanced against her superiority of rank; and all this, assisted by his well-sounding name, enabled Sir Walter at last to prepare his pen, with a very good grace, for the insertion of the marriage in the volume of honour.

The only one among them, whose opposition of feeling could excite any serious anxiety was Lady Russell. Anne knew that Lady Russell must be suffering some pain in understanding and relinquishing Mr. Elliot, and be making some struggles to become truly acquainted with, and do justice to Captain Wentworth. This however was what Lady Russell had now to do. She must learn to feel that she had been mistaken with regard to both; that she had been unfairly influenced by appearances in each; that because Captain Wentworth's manners had not suited her own ideas, she had been too quick in suspecting them to indicate a character of dangerous impetuosity; and that because Mr. Elliot's manners had precisely pleased her in their propriety and correctness, their general politeness and suavity, she had been too quick in receiving them as the certain result of the most correct opinions and well-regulated mind. There was nothing less for Lady Russell to do, than to admit that she had been pretty completely wrong, and to take up a new set of opinions and of hopes.

There is a quickness of perception in some, a nicety in the discernment of character, a natural penetration, in short, which no experience in others can equal, and Lady Russell had been less gifted in this part of understanding than her young friend. But she was a very good woman, and if her second object was to be sensible and well-judging, her first was to see Anne happy. She loved Anne better than she loved her own abilities; and when the awkwardness of the beginning was over, found little hardship in attaching herself as a mother to the man who was securing the happiness of her other child.

---

[2] Her expected inheritance (not inconsiderable) at his death. The annual income of £500 would be sufficient to maintain modest, decent circumstances.

Of all the family, Mary was probably the one most immediately gratified by the circumstance. It was creditable to have a sister married, and she might flatter herself with having been greatly instrumental to the connexion, by keeping Anne with her in the autumn; and as her own sister must be better than her husband's sisters, it was very agreeable that Captain Wentworth should be a richer man than either Captain Benwick or Charles Hayter. She had something to suffer, perhaps, when they came into contact again, in seeing Anne restored to the rights of seniority, and the mistress of a very pretty landaulette;[3] but she had a future to look forward to, of powerful consolation. Anne had no Uppercross Hall before her, no landed estate, no headship of a family; and if they could but keep Captain Wentworth from being made a baronet, she would not change situations with Anne.

It would be well for the eldest sister if she were equally satisfied with her situation, for a change is not very probable there. She had soon the mortification of seeing Mr. Elliot withdraw, and no one of proper condition has since presented himself to raise even the unfounded hopes which sunk with him.

The news of his cousin Anne's engagement burst on Mr. Elliot most unexpectedly. It deranged his best plan of domestic happiness, his best hope of keeping Sir Walter single by the watchfulness which a son-in-law's rights would have given.[4] But, though discomfited and disappointed, he could still do something for his own interest and his own enjoyment. He soon quitted Bath; and on Mrs. Clay's quitting it soon afterwards, and being next heard of as established under his protection in London, it was evident how double a game he had been playing, and how determined he was to save himself from being cut out by one artful woman, at least.

Mrs. Clay's affections had overpowered her interest, and she had sacrificed, for the young man's sake, the possibility of scheming longer for Sir Walter. She has abilities, however, as well as affections; and it is now a doubtful point whether his cunning, or hers, may finally carry the day; whether, after preventing her from being the wife of Sir Walter, he may not be wheedled and caressed at last into making her the wife of Sir William.

---

[3] A smaller version of the landau carriage.

[4] Had William married Anne, he would have consolidated his position as heir in several ways, including monitoring Sir Walter's eligibility as a potential mate. However if Anne and Captain Wentworth produce a son, that son is now the designated heir, jumping ahead in line over William.

It cannot be doubted that Sir Walter and Elizabeth were shocked and mortified by the loss of their companion, and the discovery of their deception in her. They had their great cousins, to be sure, to resort to for comfort; but they must long feel that to flatter and follow others, without being flattered and followed in turn, is but a state of half enjoyment.

Anne, satisfied at a very early period of Lady Russell's meaning to love Captain Wentworth as she ought, had no other alloy to the happiness of her prospects than what arose from the consciousness of having no relations to bestow on him which a man of sense could value. There she felt her own inferiority very keenly. The disproportion in their fortune was nothing; it did not give her a moment's regret; but to have no family to receive and estimate him properly, nothing of respectability, of harmony, of good will to offer in return for all the worth and all the prompt welcome which met her in his brothers and sisters, was a source of as lively pain as her mind could well be sensible of under circumstances of otherwise strong felicity. She had but two friends in the world to add to his list, Lady Russell and Mrs. Smith. To those, however, he was very well disposed to attach himself. Lady Russell, in spite of all her former transgressions, he could now value from his heart. While he was not obliged to say that he believed her to have been right in originally dividing them, he was ready to say almost everything else in her favour, and as for Mrs. Smith, she had claims of various kinds to recommend her quickly and permanently.

Her recent good offices by Anne had been enough in themselves, and their marriage, instead of depriving her of one friend, secured her two. She was their earliest visitor in their settled life; and Captain Wentworth, by putting her in the way of recovering her husband's property in the West Indies, by writing for her, acting for her, and seeing her through all the petty difficulties of the case with the activity and exertion of a fearless man and a determined friend, fully requited the services which she had rendered, or ever meant to render, to his wife.

Mrs. Smith's enjoyments were not spoiled by this improvement of income, with some improvement of health, and the acquisition of such friends to be often with, for her cheerfulness and mental alacrity did not fail her; and while these prime supplies of good remained, she might have bid defiance even to greater accessions of worldly prosperity. She might have been absolutely rich and perfectly healthy, and yet be happy. Her spring of felicity was in the glow of her spirits, as her friend Anne's was in the warmth of her heart. Anne was tenderness itself, and she had the full worth of it in Captain Wentworth's affection. His profession was all that could ever make her friends wish that tenderness less, the dread of a future war all that could dim her sunshine. She gloried in being a sailor's wife, but she must pay the tax of quick alarm for belonging to that profession which is, if possible, more distinguished in its domestic virtues than in its national importance.

# Persuasion

## ORIGINAL ENDING

After completing the novel in July 1816, Austen replaced her original, two-chapter ending with the three chapters in the 1817 publication (2: 10–12). After her death, the manuscript of the original ending came into the possession of her niece, Anna Lefroy, and appeared in revised and truncated form in 1871 in the *Memoir of Jane Austen* by her nephew James Edward Austen-Leigh. First published in full in 1926 by R. W. Chapman in *Jane Austen's Autograph*, the original ending, like the alternative ending to Charles Dickens' *Great Expectations*, has become standard in editions of *Persuasion*. In addition to lacking certain details, notably the extended conversation between Anne Elliot and Captain Harville on men's and women's fidelity, the fragment (now in the British Library) is important as the only known extant manuscript of the six Austen novels. It is transcribed here with her abbreviations, ampersands, spellings and other scriptive elements.

## CHAPTER X

With all this knowledge of Mr E—& this authority to impart it, Anne left Westgate Buildgs—her mind deeply busy in revolving what she had heard, feeling, thinking, recalling & foreseeing everything; shocked at Mr. Elliot—sighing over future Kellynch, and pained for Lady Russell, whose confidence in him had been entire.— The Embarrassment which much be felt from this hour in his presence!—How to behave to him?—how to get rid of him?—what to do by any of the Party at home?—where to be blind? where to be active?—It was altogether a confusion of Images & Doubts—a perplexity, an agitation which she could not see the end of—and she was in Gay St & still so much engrossed, that she started on being addressed by Adml Croft, as if he were a person unlikely to be met there. It was within a few steps of his own door.—"You are going to call upon my wife, said he, she will be very glad to see you."—Anne denied it "No—she really had not time, she was in her way home"—but while she spoke, the Adml had stepped back & knocked at the door, calling out, "Yes, yes do go in; she is all alone. go in & rest yourself."—Anne felt so little disposed at this time to be in company of any sort, that it vexed her to be thus constrained—but she was obliged to stop. "Since you are so very kind, said she, I will just ask Mrs Croft how she does, but I really cannot stay 5 minutes.—You are sure she is quite alone."—The possibility of Capt. W. had occurred—and most fearfully anxious was she to be assured—either that he was within or that he was not; *which*, might have been a question.—"Oh! yes, quite alone—Nobody but her Mantua-maker with her, & they have been shut up together this half hour, so it must be over soon."—"Her Mantua maker!—then I am sure my calling now, wd be most inconvenient.—Indeed you must allow me to leave my Card & be so good as to explain it afterwards to Mrs. C." "No, no, not at all, not at all. She will be very happy to see you. Mind—I will not swear that she has not something particular to say to you—but that will all come out in the right place. I give no hints.—Why, Miss Elliot, we begin to hear strange things of you—(smiling in her face)—But you have not much the Look of it—as Grave as a little Judge." —Anne blushed.—"Aye, aye, that will do. Now, it is right. I *thought* we were not mistaken." She was left to guess at the direction of his Suspicions; —the first wild idea had been of some disclosure from his Br in law—but she was ashamed the next moment—& felt how far more probable that he should be meaning Mr. E.—The door was opened—& the Man evidently beginning to *deny* his Mistress, when the sight of his Master stopped him. The Adml enjoyed the joke exceedingly. Anne thought his triumph over Stephen rather too long. At last however, he was able to invite her upstairs, & stepping before her said—"I will just go up with you myself & shew you in—. I cannot stay, because I must go to the P. Office, but if you will only sit down for 5 minutes I am sure Sophy will come—and you will find nobody to disturb you—there is nobody but Frederick here—" opening the door as he spoke.—Such a person to be passed over as a Nobody to *her*!—After being allowed to feel quite secure—indifferent—at her ease, to have it burst on her that she was to be the next moment in the same room with him!—No time for recollection!—for planning behaviour, or regulating manners!—There was time only to turn pale, before she had passed through the door, & met the astonished eyes of Capt. W——. who was sitting by the fire pretending to read & prepared for no greater surprise than the Admiral's hasty return.—Equally unexpected was the meeting, on each side. There was nothing to be done however, but to stifle feelings & be quietly polite;—and the Admiral was too much on the alert, to leave any troublesome pause.— He repeated again what he had said before about his wife & everybody—insisted on Anne's sitting down & being perfectly comfortable, was sorry he must leave her himself, but was sure Mrs. Croft wd be down very soon, & wd go upstairs & give her notice directly.—Anne *was* sitting down, but now she arose again— to entreat him not to interrupt Mrs. C—& re-urge the wish of going away & calling another time.—But the Adml would not hear of it;—and if she did not return to the charge with unconquerable Perseverance, or did not with a more passive Determination walk quietly out of the room—(as certainly she might have done) may she not be pardoned?—If she *had* no horror of a few minutes Tète a Tète with Capt. W——, may she not be pardoned for not wishing to give him the idea that she *had*?—She reseated herself, & the Adml took leave; but on reaching the door, said, "Frederick, a word with you, if you please."—Capt. W—— went to him; and instantly, before they were well out of the room, the Adml continued—"As I am going to leave you together, it is but fair I should give you something to talk of—& so, if you please—" Here the door was very firmly closed; she could guess by which of the two; and she lost entirely what immediately followed; but it was impossible for her not to distinguish parts of the rest, for the Adml on the strength of the Door's being shut was speaking without any management of voice, tho' she cd hear his companion trying to check him.—She could not doubt their being speaking of her. She heard her own name & *Kellynch* repeatedly—she was very much distressed. She knew not what to do, or what to expect—and among other agonies felt the possibility of Capt. W——'s not returning into the room at all, which after *her* consenting to stay would have been—too bad for Language.—They seemed to be talking of the Admls Lease of Kellynch. She heard him say something of "the Lease being signed or not signed"—*that* was not likely to be a very agitating subject—but then followed, "I hate to be at an uncertainty—I must know at once—Sophy thinks the same." Then, in a lower tone, Capt. W—— seemed remonstrating—wanting to be excused—wanting to put something off. "Phoo, Phoo—answered the Admiral now is the Time. If *you* will not speak, I will stop & Speak myself."—"Very well Sir, very well Sir, followed with some impatience from his companion, opening the door as he spoke.—"You will then—you promise you will?" replied the Admiral, in all the power of his natural voice, unbroken even by one thin door.—"Yes—Sir—Yes." And the Adml was hastily left, the door was closed, and the moment arrived in which Anne was alone with Capt. W——. She could not attempt to see how he looked; but he walked immediately to a window, as if irresolute & embarrassed;—and for about the space of 5 seconds, she repented what she had done—censured it as unwise, blushed for it as indelicate.—She longed to be able to speak of the weather or the Concert—but could only compass the releif of taking a Newspaper in her hand.—The distressing pause was soon over however; he turned round in half a minute, and coming towards the table where she sat, said, in a voice of effort & constraint—"You must have heard too much already Madam to be in any doubt of my having promised Adml Croft to speak to you on some particular subject—& this conviction determines me to do it—however repugnant to my—to all my sense of propriety, to be taking so great a liberty.—You will acquit me of Impertinence I trust, by considering me as speaking only for another, and speaking by Necessity;—and the Adml is a Man who can never be thought Impertinent by one who knows him as you do—. His Intentions are always the kindest & the Best;—and you will perceive that he is actuated by none other, in the application which I am now with—with very peculiar feelings—obliged to make."—He stopped—but merely to recover breath;—not seeming to expect any answer.—Anne listened, as if her Life depended on the issue of his Speech.—He proceeded, with a forced alacrity.—"The Adml, Madam, was this morning confidently informed that you were—upon my word I am quite at a loss, ashamed—(breathing & speaking quick)—the awkwardness of *giving* Information of this sort to one of the Parties—You can be at no loss to understand me—It was very confidently said that Mr. Elliot—that everything was settled in the family for an Union between Mr. Elliot—& yourself. It was added that you were to live at Kellynch—that Kellynch was to be given up. This, the Admiral knew could not be correct—But it occurred to him that it might be the wish of the Parties—And my commission from him Madam, is to say, that if the Family wish is such, his Lease of Kellynch shall be cancel'd, & he & my sister will provide themselves with another home, without imagining themselves to be doing anything which under similar circumstances wd not be done for them.—This is all Madam.—A very few words in reply from you will be sufficient.—That *I* should be the person commissioned on this subject is extraordinary!—and beleive me Madam, it is no less painful.—A very few words however will put an end to the awkwardness & distress we may *both* be feeling." Anne spoke a word or two, but they were un-intelligible—And before she could command herself, he replied,—"If you only tell me that the Adml may address a Line to Sir Walter, it will be enough. Pronounce only the words, *he may.*—I shall immediately follow him with your message.—" This was spoken, as with a fortitude which seemed to meet the message.—"No Sir—said Anne—There is no message.—You are misin—the Adml is misinformed.—I do justice to the kindness of his Intentions, but he is quite mistaken. There is no Truth in any such report."—He was a moment silent.— She turned her eyes towards him for the first time since his re-entering the room. His colour was varying—& he was looking at her with all the Power & Keenness, which she beleived no other eyes than his, possessed. "No Truth in any such report!—he repeated.—No Truth in any *part* of it?"—"None."—He had been standing by a chair—enjoying the releif of leaning on it—or of playing with it;— he now sat down—drew it a little nearer to her—& looked, with an expression which had something more than penetration in it, something softer;—Her Countenance did not discourage.—It was a silent, but a very powerful Dialogue;—on his side, Supplication, on her's acceptance.—Still, a little nearer—and a hand taken and pressed—and "Anne, my own dear Anne!"—bursting forth in the fullness of exquisite feeling—and all Suspense & Indecision were over.—They were re-united. They were restored to all that had been lost. They were carried back to the past, with only an increase of attachment & confidence, & only such a flutter of present Delight as made them little fit for the interruption of Mrs Croft, when she joined them not long afterwards.—*She* probably, in the observations of the next ten minutes, saw something to suspect—& tho' it was hardly possible for a woman of her description to wish the Mantuamaker had imprisoned her longer, she might be very likely wishing for some excuse to run about the house, some storm to break the windows above, or a summons to the Admiral's Shoe-maker below.—Fortune favoured them all however in another way—in a gentle, steady rain—just happily set in as the Admiral returned & Anne rose to go.—She was earnestly invited to stay dinner;—a note was dispatched to Camden Place—and she staid, staid till 10 at night. And during that time, the Husband & wife, either by the wife's contrivance, or by simply going on in their usual way, were frequently out of the room together—gone up stairs to hear a noise, or down stairs to settle their accounts, or upon the Landing place to trim the Lamp.—And these precious moments were turned to so good an account that all the most anxious feelings of the past were gone through.—Before they parted at night, Anne had the felicity of being assured in the first place that—(so far from being altered for the worse!)—she had *gained* inexpressibly in personal Loveliness; & that as to Character—her's was now fixed on his Mind as Perfection itself—maintaining the just Medium of Fortitude & Gentleness;—that he had never ceased to love & prefer her, though it had been only at Uppercross that he had learn't to do her Justice—& only at Lyme that he had begun to understand his own sensations;— that at Lyme he had received Lessons of more than one kind;—the passing admiration of Mr Elliot had at least *roused* him, and the scenes on the Cobb & at Capt. Harville's had fixed her superiority. In his preceding *attempts* to attach himself to Louisa Musgrove, (the attempts of Anger & Pique)—he protested that he had continually felt the impossibility of really caring for Louisa, though till *that day*, till the leisure for reflection which followed it, he had not under-stood the perfect excellence of the Mind, with which Louisa's could so ill bear a comparison, or the perfect, the unrivalled hold it pos-sessed over his own.—There he had learnt to distinguish between the steadiness of Principle & the Obstinacy of Self-will, between the Darings of Heedlessness, & the Resolution of a collected Mind— there he had seen everything to exalt in his estimation the Woman he had lost, & there begun to deplore the pride, the folly, the madness of resentment which had kept him from trying to regain her, when thrown in his way. From that period to the present hiad his penance been the most severe.—he found that he was considered by his friend Harville, as an engaged Man. The Harvilles entertained not a doubt of a mutual attachment between him & Louisa—and though this to *a degree*, was contradicted instantly—it yet made him feel that per-haps by *her* family, by everybody, by *herself* even, the same idea might be held—and that he was not *free* in honour—though, if such were to be the conclusion, too free alas! in Heart.—He had never thought justly on this subject before—he had not sufficiently consid-ered that his excessive Intimacy at Uppercross must have it's danger of ill consequence in many ways, and that while trying whether he *cd* attach himself to either of the Girls, he might be exciting unpleasant reports, if not, raising unrequired regard!—He found, too late, that he had entangled hismelf—and that precisely as he became thoroughly satisfied of his not *caring* for Louisa at all, he must regard himself as bound to her, if her feelings for him, were what the Harvilles supposed.—It determined him to leave Lyme—& await her perfect recovery elsewhere. He would gladly weaken, by any *fair* means, whatever sentiments or speculations concerning him might exist; and he went therefore into Shropshire meaning after a while, to return to the Crofts at Kellynch, & act as he found requisite.—He had remained in Shropshire, lamenting the Blindness of his own Pride, & the blunders of his own Calculations, till at once released from Louisa by the astonishing felicity of her engagement with Benwicke. Bath, Bath—had instantly followed, in *Thought*; & not long after, in *fact*. To Bath, to arrive with Hope, to be torn by Jealousy at the first sight of Mr. E——, to experience all the changes of each at the Concert, to be miserable by this morning's circumstantial report, to be now, more happy than Language could express, or any heart but his own be capable of.

He was very eager & very delightful in the description of what he had felt at the Concert.—The Eveng seemed to have been made up of exquisite moments; the moment of her stepping forward in the Octagon Room to speak to him—the moment of Mr. E's appearing & tearing her away, & one or two subsequent moments, marked by returning hope, or increasing Despondence, were all dwelt on with energy. "To see you, cried he, in the midst of those who could not be *my* well-wishers, to see your Cousin close by you—conversing & smiling—& feel all the horrible Eligibilities & Proprieties of the Match!—to consider it as the certain wish of every being who could hope to influence you—even, if your own feelings were reluctant, or indifferent—to consider what powerful supports would be his!— Was not it enough to make the fool of me, which my behaviour expressed?—How could I look on without agony?—Was not the very sight of the *Friend* who sat behind you?—was not the recollection of what *had* been—the knowledge of her Influence—the indelible, immoveable Impression of what *Persuasion* had *once* done, was not it all against me?"—

"You should have distinguished—replied Anne—You should not have suspected me *now*;—The case so different, & my age so different!—If I *was* wrong, in yeilding to Persuasion once, remember that it was to Persuasion exerted on the side of Safety, not of Risk. When I yeilded, I thought it was to *Duty*.—But no *Duty* could be called in aid here.—In marrying a Man indifferent to me, all Risk would have been incurred, & all Duty violated."—"Perhaps I ought to have reasoned thus, he replied, but I could not.—I could not derive benefit from the later knowledge of your Character which I had acquired, I could not bring it into play, it was overwhelmed, buried, lost in those earlier feelings, which I had been smarting under Year after Year.—I could think of you only as one who *had* yeilded, who *had* given me up, who *had* been influenced by any one rather than by *me*—I saw you with the very Person who had guided you in that year of Misery—I had no reason to think her of less authority now;—the force of Habit was to be added."—"I should have thought, said Anne, that my Manner to yourself, might have spared you much, or all of this."—"No—No—Your manner might be only the ease, which your engagement to another Man would give.—I left you with this beleif.—And yet—I was determined to see you again.—My spirits rallied with the morning, & I felt that I had still a motive for remaining here.—The Admirals news indeed, was a revulsion. Since that moment, I have been decided what to do—and had it been confirmed, this would have been my *last day* in Bath."

There was time for all this to pass—with such Interruptions only as enhanced the charm of the communication—and Bath cd scarcely contain any other two Beings at once so rationally & so rapturously happy as during that eveng occupied the Sopha of Mrs Croft's Drawing room in Gay St.

Capt. W.—had taken care to meet the Adml as he returned into the house, to satisfy him as to Mr. E—— & Kellynch;—and the delicacy of the Admiral's good nature kept him from saying another word on the subject to Anne.—He was quite concerned lest he might have been giving her pain by touching a tender part. Who could say?—She might be liking her Cousin, better than he liked her.—And indeed, upon recollection, if they had been to marry at all why should they have waited so long?—

When the Eveng closed, it is probably that the Adml received some new Ideas from his Wife;—whose particularly friendly manner in parting with her, gave Anne the gratifying persuasion of her seeing & approving.

It had been such a day to Anne!—the hours which had passed since her leaving Camden Place, had done so much!—She was almost bewildered, almost too happy in looking back.—It was necessary to sit up half the Night & lie awake the remainder to comprehend with composure her present state, & pay for the over-plus of Bliss, by Headake & Fatigue.—

## CHAPTER XI

WHO can be in doubt of what followed?—When any two Young People take it into their heads to marry, they are pretty sure by per-severance to carry their point—be they ever so poor, or ever so imprudent, or ever so little likely to be necessary to each other's ultimate comfort. This may be bad Morality to conclude with, but I beleive it to be Truth—and if such parties succeed, how should a Capt. W—— & an Anne E——, with the advantage of maturity of Mind, consciousness of Right, & one Independant Fortune between them, fail of bearing down every opposition? They might in fact, have born down a great deal more than they met with, for there was little to distress them beyond the want of Graciousness & Warmth. Sir W. made no objections, & Elizth did nothing worse than look cold & unconcerned.—Capt. W—— with £25,000— & as high in his Profession as Merit & Activity cd place him, was no longer nobody. He was now esteemed quite worthy to address the Daugh-ter of a foolish spendthrift Baronet, who had not the Principle or sense enough to maintain himself in the Situation in which Provi-dence had placed him, & who cd give his Daughter but a small part of the share of ten Thousand pounds which must be her's here-after.—Sir Walter indeed tho' he had no affection for his Daughter & no vanity flattered to make him really happy on the occasion, was very far from thinking it a bad match for her.—On the contrary when he saw more of Capt. W.— & eyed him well, he was very much struck by his personal claims & felt that *his* superiority of appearance might be not unfairly balanced against *her* superiority of Rank; and all this, together with his well-sounding name, enabled Sir W. at last to prepare his pen with a very good grace for the insertion of the Marriage in the volume of Honour.—The only person among them whose opposition of feelings cd excite any seri-ous anxiety, was Lady Russel.—Anne knew that Lady R—— must be suffering some pain in understanding & relinquishing Mr. E—— & be making some struggles to become truly acquainted with & do justice to Capt. W.—This however, was what Lady R—— had now to do. She must learn to feel that she had been mistaken with regard to both—that she had been unfairly influenced by appearances in each—that, because Capt. W.'s manners had not suited her own ideas, she had been too quick in suspecting them to indicate a Character of dangerous Impetuosity, & that because Mr Elliot's manners had precisely pleased her in their propriety & correctness, their general politeness & suavity, she had been to quick in receiving them as the certain result of the most correct opinions & well regulated Mind.—There was nothing less for Lady R. to do than to admit that she had been pretty completely wrong, & to take up a new set of opinions & hopes.—There *is* a quickness of perception in some, a nicety in the discernment of character—a natural Penetration in short which no Experience in others can equal—and Lady R. had been less gifted in this part of Understanding than her young friend;—but she was a very good Woman; & if her second object was to be sensible & well judging, her first was to see Anne happy. She loved Anne better than she loved her own abilities—and when the awkwardness of the Beginning was over, found little hardship in attaching herself as a Mother to the Man who was securing the happiness of her Child. Of all the family, Mary was probably the one most immediately gratified by the circumstance. It was creditable to have a Sister married, and she might flatter herself that she had been greatly instrumental to the connection, by having Anne staying with her in the Autumn; & as her own Sister must be better than her Husbands Sisters, it was very agreable that Captn. W.—— should be a richer Man than either Capt. B. or Charles Hayter.—She had something to suffer perhaps when they came into contact again, in seeing Anne restored to the rights of Seniority & the Mistress of a very pretty Landaulet—but *she* had a *future* to look forward to, of powerful consolation—Anne had no Uppercross Hall before her, no Landed Estate, no Headship of a family, and if they could but keep Capt. W—— from being made a Baronet, she would not change situations with Anne.—It would be well for the *Eldest* Sister if she were equally satisfied with *her* situation, for a change is not very probable there.—She had soon the mortification of seeing Mr. E. withdraw, & no one of proper condition has since presented himself to raise even the unfounded hopes which sunk with *him*. The news of his Cousin Anne's engagement burst on Mr Elliot most unexpectedly. It deranged his best plan of domestic Happiness, his best hopes of keeping Sir Walter single by the watchfulness which a son in law's rights wd have given—But tho' discomfited & disappointed, he cd still do something for his own interest & his own enjoyment. He soon quitted Bath and on Mrs. Clay's quitting it likewise soon afterwards & being next heard of, as established under his Protection in London, it was evident how double a Game he had been playing, & how determined he was to save himself from being cut out by *one* artful woman at least.—Mrs. Clay's affections had overpowered her Interest, & she had sacrificed for the Young Man's sake, the possibility of scheming longer for Sir Walter;—she has Abilities however as well as Affections, and it is now a doubtful point whether his cunning or hers may finally carry the day, whether, after preventing her from being the wife of Sir Walter, he may not be wheedled & caressed at last into making her the wife of Sir William.—

It cannot be doubted that Sir Walter & Eliz: were shocked & mortified by the loss of their companion & the discovery of their deception in her. They had their great cousins to be sure, to resort to for comfort—but they must long feel that to flatter & follow others, without being flattered & followed themselves is but a state of half enjoyment.

Anne, satisfied at a very early period, of Lady Russel's *meaning* to love Capt. W—— as she ought, had no other alloy to the happiness of her prostpects, than what arose from the consciousness of having no relations to bestow on him which a Man of Sense could value.—There, she felt her own Inferiority keenly.—The disproportion in their fortunes was nothing;—it did not give her a moment's regret;—but to have no Family to receive & estimate him properly, nothing of respectability, of Harmony, of Goodwill to offer in return for all the Worth & all the prompt welcome which met her in his Brothers & Sisters, was a source of as lively pain, as her Mind could well be sensible of, under circumstances of otherwise strong felicity.—She had but two friends in the World, to add to his List, Lady R. & Mrs. Smith.—To those, however, he was very well-disposed to attach himself. Lady R—— inspite of all her former transgressions, he could now value from his heart;—while he was not obliged to say that he beleived her to have been right in originally dividing them, he was ready to say almost anything else in her favour;—& as for Mrs Smith, she had claims of various kinds to recommend her quickly & permanently.—Her recent good offices by Anne had been enough in themselves—and their marriage, instead of depriving her of one friend secured her two. She was one of their first visitors in their settled Life—and Capt. Wentworth, by putting her in the way of recovering her Husband's property in the W. Indies, by writing for her, & acting for her, & seeing her through all the petty

Difficulties of the case, with the activity & exertion of a fearless Man, & a determined friend, fully requited the services she had rendered, or had ever meant to render, to his Wife. Mrs Smith's enjoyments were not *spoiled* by this improvement of Income, with some improvement of health, & the acquisition of such friends to be often with, for her chearfulness & mental Activity did not fail her, & while those prime supplies of Good remained, she might have bid defiance even to greater accessions of worldly Prosperity. She might have been absolutely rich & perfectly healthy, & yet be happy.—*Her* spring of Felicity was in the glow of her Spirits—as her friend Anne's was in the warmth of her Heart.—Anne was Tenderness itself;—and she had the full worth of it in Captn Wentworth's affection. His Profession was all that could ever make her friends wish *that* Tenderness less; the dread of a future War, all that could dim her Sunshine.—She gloried in being a Sailor's wife, but she must pay the tax of quick alarm, for belonging to that Profession which is—if possible—more distinguished in it's Domestic Virtues, than in it's National Importance.—

July 18.—1816.

# CONTEXTS

# Henry Austen's "Biographical Notice of the Author"

This notice is the first formal disclosure of Jane Austen's identity as the author of the four novels she had already published. It was written, after her death, by her brother as a preface to the publication in 1817 of *Northanger Abbey* and *Persuasion,* which appeared jointly in a four-volume edition. In addition to featuring Austen's now famous description of her fictional world as "a little bit of ivory, two inches wide," the notice insists that Austen was "thoroughly religious" and a strict moralist.

## Biographical Notice of the Author

The following pages are the production of a pen which has already contributed in no small degree to the entertainment of the public. And when the public, which has not been insensible to the merits of "Sense and Sensibility," "Pride and Prejudice," "Mansfield Park," and "Emma," shall be informed that the hand which guided that pen is now mouldering in the grave, perhaps a brief account of Jane Austen will be read with a kindlier sentiment than simple curiosity.

Short and easy will be the task of the mere biographer. A life of usefulness, literature, and religion, was not by any means a life of event. To those who lament their irreparable loss, it is consolatory to think that, as she never deserved disapprobation, so, in the circle of her family and friends, she never met reproof; that her wishes were not only reasonable, but gratified; and that to the little disappointments incidental to human life was never added, even for a moment, an abatement of good-will from any who knew her.

Jane Austen was born on the 16th of December, 1775, at Steventon, in the county of Hants. Her father was Rector of that parish upwards of forty years. There he resided, in the conscientious and unassisted discharge of his ministerial duties, until he was turned of seventy years. Then he retired with his wife, our authoress, and her sister, to Bath, for the remainder of his life, a period of about four years. Being not only a profound scholar, but possessing a most exquisite taste in every species of literature, it is not wonderful that his daughter Jane should, at a very early age, have become sensible to the charms of style, and enthusiastic in the cultivation of her own language. On the death of her father she removed, with her mother and sister, for a short time, to Southampton, and finally, in 1809, to the pleasant village of Chawton, in the same county. From this place she sent into the world those novels, which by many have been placed on the same shelf as the works of a D'Arblay and an Edgeworth.[1] Some of these novels had been the gradual performances of her previous life. For though in composition she was equally rapid and correct, yet an invincible distrust of her own judgement induced her to withhold her works from the public, till time and many perusals had satisfied her that the charm of recent composition was dissolved. The natural constitution, the regular habits, the quiet and happy occupations of our authoress, seemed to promise a long succession of amusement to the public, and a gradual increase of reputation to herself. But the symptoms of a decay, deep and incurable, began to shew themselves in the commencement of 1816. Her decline was at first deceitfully slow; and until the spring of this present year, those who knew their happiness to be involved in her existence could not endure to despair. But in the month of May, 1817, it was found advisable that she should be removed to Winchester for the benefit of constant medical aid, which none even then dared to hope would be permanently beneficial. She supported,

---

[1] Frances Burney (1752–1840), later Mme D'Arblay after marrying General D'Arblay, a French émigré, wrote four novels: *Evelina* (1778), *Cecilia* (1782), *Camilla* (1796) and *The Wanderer* (1814). She influenced Austen, both as a practitioner of domestic fiction and as an example of what a woman writer could achieve aesthetically and financially. Another influence was prolific writer Maria Edgeworth (1767–1849) whose novels include *Castle Rackrent* (1800), *Belinda* (1801), and *The Absentee* (1812). Austen praises both in the defense of novel-writing in Chapter 5 of *Northanger Abbey* and she sent Edgeworth *Emma* when it appeared in 1816.

during two months, all the varying pain, irksomeness, and tedium, attendant on decaying nature, with more than resignation, with a truly elastic cheerfulness. She retained her faculties, her memory, her fancy, her temper, and her affections, warm, clear, and unimpaired, to the last. Neither her love of God, nor of her fellow creatures flagged for a moment. She made a point of receiving the sacrament before excessive bodily weakness might have rendered her perception unequal to her wishes.

She wrote whilst she could hold a pen, and with a pencil when a pen was become too laborious. The day preceding her death she composed some stanzas replete with fancy and vigour. Her last voluntary speech conveyed thanks to her medical attendant; and to the final question asked of her, purporting to know her wants, she replied, "I want nothing but death."

She expired shortly after, on Friday the 18th of July, 1817, in the arms of her sister, who, as well as the relator of these events, feels too surely that they shall never look upon her like again.

Jane Austen was buried on the 24th of July, 1817, in the cathedral church of Winchester, which, in the whole catalogue of its mighty dead, does not contain the ashes of a brighter genius or a sincerer Christian.

Of personal attractions she possessed a considerable share. Her stature was that of true elegance. It could not have been increased without exceeding the middle height. Her carriage and deportment were quiet, yet graceful. Her features were separately good. Their assemblage produced an unrivalled expression of that cheerfulness, sensibility, and benevolence, which were her real characteristics. Her complexion was of the finest texture. It might with truth be said, that her eloquent blood spoke through her modest cheek. Her voice was extremely sweet. She delivered herself with fluency and precision. Indeed she was formed for elegant and rational society, excelling in conversation as much as in composition. In the present age it is hazardous to mention accomplishments. Our authoress would, probably, have been inferior to few in such acquirements, had she not been so superior to most in higher things. She had not only an excellent taste for drawing, but, in her earlier days, evinced great power of hand in the management of the pencil. Her own musical attainments she held very cheap. Twenty years ago they would have been thought more of, and twenty years hence many a parent will expect their daughters to be applauded for meaner performances. She was fond of dancing, and excelled in it. It remains now to add a few observations on that which her friends deemed more important, on those endowments which sweetened every hour of their lives.

If there be an opinion current in the world, that perfect placidity of temper is not reconcileable to the most lively imagination, and the keenest relish for wit, such an opinion will be rejected for ever by those who have had the happiness of knowing the authoress of the following works. Though the frailties, foibles, and follies of others could not escape her immediate detection, yet even on their vices did she never trust herself to comment with unkindness.

The affectation of candour is not uncommon; but she had no affectation. Faultless herself, as nearly as human nature can be, she always sought, in the faults of others, something to excuse, to forgive or forget. Where extenuation was impossible, she had a sure refuge in silence. She never uttered either a hasty, a silly, or a severe expression. In short, her temper was as polished as her wit. Nor were her manners inferior to her temper. They were of the happiest kind. No one could be often in her company without feeling a strong desire of obtaining her friendship, and cherishing a hope of having obtained it. She was tranquil without reserve or stiffness; and communicative without intrusion or self-sufficiency. She became an authoress entirely from taste and inclination. Neither the hope of fame nor profit mixed with her early motives. Most of her works, as before observed, were composed many years previous to their publication. It was with extreme difficulty that her friends, whose partiality she suspected whilst she honoured their judgement, could prevail on her to publish her first work. Nay, so persuaded was she that its sale would not repay the expense of publication, that she actually made a reserve from her very moderate income to meet the expected loss. She could scarcely believe what she termed her great good fortune when "Sense and Sensibility" produced a clear profit of about £150. Few so gifted were so truly unpretending. She regarded the above sum as a prodigious recompense for that which had cost her nothing. Her readers, perhaps, will wonder that such a work produced so little at a time when some authors have received more guineas than they have written lines. The works of our authoress, however, may live as long as those which have burst on the world with more éclat. But the public has not been unjust; and our authoress was far from thinking it so. Most gratifying to her was the applause which from time to time reached her ears from those who were competent to discriminate. Still, in spite of such applause, so much did she shrink from notoriety, that no accumulation of fame would have induced her, had she lived, to affix her name to any productions of her pen. In the bosom of her own family she talked of them freely, thankful for praise, open to remark, and submissive to criticism. But in public she turned away from any allusion to the character of an authoress. She read aloud with very great taste and effect. Her own works, probably, were never heard to so much advantage as from her own mouth; for she partook largely in all the best gifts of the comic muse. She was a warm and judicious admirer of landscape, both in nature and on canvass. At a very early age she was enamoured of Gilpin on the Picturesque;[2] and she seldom changed her opinions either on books or men.

Her reading was very extensive in history and belles lettres; and her memory extremely tenacious. Her favourite moral writers were Johnson in prose, and Cowper in verse.[3] It is difficult to say at what age she was not intimately acquainted with the merits and defects of the best essays and novels in the English language. Richardson's power of creating, and preserving the consistency of his characters, as particularly exemplified in "Sir Charles Grandison,"[4] gratified the natural discrimination of her mind, whilst her taste secured her from the errors of his prolix style and tedious narrative. She did not rank any work of Fielding quite so high.[5] Without the slightest affectation she recoiled from every thing gross. Neither nature, wit, nor humour, could make her amends for so very low a scale of morals.

Her power of inventing characters seems to have been intuitive, and almost unlimited. She drew from nature; but, whatever may have been surmised to the contrary, never from individuals.

---

[2] Clergyman, writer, and amateur artist William Gilpin (1724–1804) is best known for *Three Essays: On Picturesque Beauty; On Picturesque Travel; and On Sketching Landscape* (1792), which posited a new ideal of natural beauty based on roughness and variety. His aesthetics are treated both seriously and satirically in *Sense and Sensibility, Pride and Prejudice,* and *Northanger Abbey.*

[3] The works of Samuel Johnson (1709–1784), the most influential man of letters in the latter half of the eighteenth century, include *A Dictionary of the English Language* (1755), *Rasselas* (1759), and *Lives of the Poets* (1781). Poet and hymnist William Cowper (1731–1800) is best known for his long poem in blank verse *The Task* (1785), whose striking descriptions of nature were widely admired.

[4] The last of Samuel Richardson's three epistolary novels (1753), whose eponymous hero is especially virtuous. Richardson's status as one of the most important novelists of the eighteenth century was secured with *Pamela* (1740) and *Clarissa* (1748).

[5] Henry Fielding (1707–54), the other important and influential English novelist of the eighteenth century, is the author of *Joseph Andrews* (1742) and *Tom Jones* (1749), both modeled on the picaresque novel that originated in Spain.

The style of her familiar correspondence was in all respects the same as that of her novels. Every thing came finished from her pen; for on all subjects she had ideas as clear as her expressions were well chosen. It is not hazarding too much to say that she never dispatched a note or letter unworthy of publication.

One trait only remains to be touched on. It makes all others unimportant. She was thoroughly religious and devout; fearful of giving offence to God, and incapable of feeling it towards any fellow creature. On serious subjects she was well-instructed, both by reading and meditation, and her opinions accorded strictly with those of our Established Church.[6]

London, Dec. 13, 1817.

## Postscript

Since concluding the above remarks, the writer of them has been put in possession of some extracts from the private correspondence of the authoress. They are few and short; but are submitted to the public without apology, as being more truly descriptive of her temper, taste, feelings, and principles than any thing which the pen of a biographer can produce.

The first extract is a playful defence of herself from a mock charge of having pilfered the manuscripts of a young relation.[7]

"What should I do, my dearest E. with your manly, vigorous sketches, so full of life and spirit? How could I possibly join them on to a little bit of ivory, two inches wide, on which I work with a brush so fine as to produce little effect after much labour?"

The remaining extracts are from various parts of a letter written a few weeks before her death.

"My attendant is encouraging, and talks of making me quite well. I live chiefly on the sofa, but am allowed to walk from one room to the other. I have been out once in a sedan-chair, and am to repeat it, and be promoted to a wheel-chair as the weather serves. On this subject I will only say further that my dearest sister, my tender, watchful, indefatigable nurse, has not been made ill by her exertions. As to what I owe to her, and to the anxious affection of

---

[6] The Anglican Church, The Church of England (that is, not a dissenting sect).

[7] Austen's nephew, James Edward Austen-Leigh, later famous for his *Memoir of Jane Austen (1871)*.

all my beloved family on this occasion, I can only cry over it, and pray to God to bless them more and more."

She next touches with just and gentle animadversion on a subject of domestic disappointment. Of this the particulars do not concern the public. Yet injustice to her characteristic sweetness and resignation, the concluding observation of our authoress thereon must not be suppressed.

"But I am getting too near complaint. It has been the appointment of God, however secondary causes may have operated."

The following and final extract will prove the facility with which she could correct every impatient thought, and turn from complaint to cheerfulness.

You will find Captain ——— a very respectable, well-meaning man, without much manner, his wife and sister all good humour and obligingness, and I hope (since the fashion allows it) with rather longer petticoats than last year.

London, Dec. 20, 1817.

# Jane Austen's Letters to Cassandra Austen

The letters that Jane Austen wrote to her older sister Cassandra in 1801 have special relevance to *Persuasion*. They not only detail the Austen family's move to Bath in 1801 along with many aspects of the city where the novel itself relocates with the Elliot family, but also provide a glimpse of the author's life when she was approximately the same age as her heroine and in a similar state of transition. There is also mention in these letters of Austen's brothers, whose naval careers furnished information that eventually found its way into the characters and descriptions of the many officers who appear in the novel, notably Captain Wentworth. The final three letters, written just before and after Austen's father's death in 1805, are also relevant. The first is from Lyme Regis, the site of Anne's famous walk on the Cobb, where, in an interesting echo of the novelist's own experience at Lyme, she catches the eye of two admiring men. The latter two letters are from Bath with Austen, like her heroine, in a round of social activity, which she describes with an equally characteristic mixture of alacrity and detachment. The letters passed between Austen and Cassandra while the latter was away, mostly at Godmersham Park in Kent, the residence of their wealthy brother, Edward. The text of the letters from 1801 is that of Edward, Lord Brabourne, Edward's grandson, and was published by Richard Bentley in 1884. Bentley had earlier published the first complete reissue of Austen's novels in 1833 in his Standard Novels series. The letters from 1804 and 1805 are from the text in *The Memoir of Jane Austen* by her nephew James Edward Austen-Leigh, published also by Bentley in 1871. The ellipses in square brackets are Austen-Leigh's; all other ellipses are ours unless indicated.

### Steventon: Saturday (January 3, 1801).[1]

MY DEAR CASSANDRA,

As you have by this time received my last letter, it is fit that I should begin another, and I begin with the hope, which is at present uppermost in my mind, that you often wore a white gown in the morning at the time of all the gay parties being with you.

Our visit at Ash Park, last Wednesday, went off in a come-çá way. We met Mr. Lefroy and Tom Chute, played at cards, and came home again. James and Mary dined here on the following day, and at night Henry set off in the mail for London. He was as agreeable as ever during his visit, and has not lost anything in Miss Lloyd's estimation.[2]

Yesterday we were quite alone—only our four selves; but to-day the scene is agreeably varied by Mary's driving Martha to Basingstoke, and Martha's afterwards dining at Deane.

My mother looks forward with as much certainty as you can do to our keeping two maids; my father is the only one not in the secret. We plan having a steady cook and a young, giddy housemaid, with a sedate, middle-aged man, who is to undertake the double office of husband to the former and sweetheart to the latter. No children, of course, to be allowed on either side.

You feel more for John Bond than John Bond deserves. I am sorry to lower his character, but he is not ashamed to own himself that he has no doubt at all of getting a good place, and that he had even an offer many years ago from a Farmer Paine of taking him into his service whenever he might quit my father's.[3]

There are three parts of Bath which we have thought of as likely to have houses in them—Westgate Buildings, Charles Street, and some of the short streets leading from Laura Place or Pulteney Street.[4]

---

[1] Austen was born in Steventon, Hampshire, and lived there until 1801 when her family relocated to Bath.

[2] Henry and James are older brothers; Mary is James's second wife. The others are friends and acquaintances: Rev. Issac Lefroy, Rector of Ashe, Rev. Thomas Chute and Martha Lloyd, Austen's closest friend and the older sister of James's wife. Martha later married Austen's older brother Francis-William in 1828.

[3] John Bond was the bailiff at Steventon Parsonage, where the Rev. George Austen (Austen's father) was rector.

[4] These Bath locations are named in *Persuasion*. Laura Place is the exclusive address of Lady Dalrymple and Miss Carteret; the Westgate Buildings are where Anne's friend, Mrs. Smith, resides humbly to Sir Walter's considerable disdain.

Westgate Buildings, though quite in the lower part of the town, are not badly situated themselves. The street is broad, and has rather a good appearance. Charles Street, however, I think, is preferable. The buildings are new, and its nearness to Kingsmead Fields would be a pleasant circumstance. Perhaps you may remember, or perhaps you may forget, that Charles Street leads from the Queen Square Chapel to the two Green Park Streets.

The houses in the streets near Laura Place I should expect to be above our price. Gay Street would be too high, except only the lower house on the left-hand side as you ascend. Towards that my mother has no disinclination; it used to be lower rented than any other house in the row, from some inferiority in the apartments. But above all others her wishes are at present fixed on the corner house in Chapel Row, which opens into Prince's Street. Her knowledge of it, however, is confined only to the outside, and therefore she is equally uncertain of its being really desirable as of its being to be had. In the meantime she assures you that she will do everything in her power to avoid Trim Street, although you have not expressed the fearful presentiment of it which was rather expected.

We know that Mrs. Perrot will want to get us into Oxford Buildings, but we all unite in particular dislike of that part of the town, and therefore hope to escape.[5] Upon all these different situations you and Edward may confer together, and your opinion of each will be expected with eagerness.

As to our pictures, the battle-piece, Mr. Nibbs, Sir William East, and all the old heterogeneous miscellany, manuscript, Scriptural pieces dispersed over the house, are to be given to James. Your own drawings will not cease to be your own, and the two paintings on tin will be at your disposal. My mother says that the French agricultural prints in the best bedroom were given by Edward to his two sisters. Do you or he know anything about it?[6]

She has written to my aunt, and we are all impatient for the answer. I do not know how to give up the idea of our both going to Paragon in May. Your going I consider as indispensably necessary,

---

[5] Austen's wealthy aunt Jane Leigh-Perrot was a nuisance and an embarrassment to the family, having been arrested in 1799 in Bath and subsequently tried for shoplifting. She was eventually acquitted in 1800 in a much-publicized trial.

[6] George Nibbs, a college friend of Rev. Austen, and Sir William East, the father of one of Rev. Austen's pupils, each of whom appears to have donated the pictures that Austen mentions. Edward was another of Austen's brothers.

and I shall not like being left behind; there is no place here or hereabouts that I shall want to be staying at, and though, to be sure, the keep of two will be more than of one, I will endeavour to make the difference less by disordering my stomach with Bath buns; and as to the trouble of accommodating us, whether there are one or two, it is much the same.

According to the first plan, my mother and our two selves are to travel down together, and my father follow us afterwards in about a fortnight or three weeks. We have promised to spend a couple of days at Ibthorp in our way. We must all meet at Bath, you know, before we set out for the sea, and, everything considered, I think the first plan as good as any.

My father and mother, wisely aware of the difficulty of finding in all Bath such a bed as their own, have resolved on taking it with them; all the beds, indeed, that we shall want are to be removed— viz., besides theirs, our own two, the best for a spare one, and two for servants; and these necessary articles will probably be the only material ones that it would answer to send down. I do not think it will be worth while to remove any of our chests of drawers; we shall be able to get some of a much more commodious sort, made of deal,[7] and painted to look very neat; and I flatter myself that for little comforts of all kinds our apartment will be one of the most complete things of the sort all over Bath, Bristol included.

We have thought at times of removing the sideboard, or a Pembroke table, or some other piece of furniture, but, upon the whole, it has ended in thinking that the trouble and risk of the removal would be more than the advantage of having them at a place where everything may be purchased. Pray send your opinion.

Martha has as good as promised to come to us again in March. Her spirits are better than they were.

I have now attained the true art of letter-writing, which we are always told is to express on paper exactly what one would say to the same person by word of mouth. I have been talking to you almost as fast as I could the whole of this letter.

Your Christmas gaieties are really quite surprising; I think they would satisfy even Miss Walter herself. I hope the ten shillings won by Miss Foote may make everything easy between her and her cousin Frederick.[8]

---

[7] Pine.

[8] Ten shillings was the daily wage for a seamstress at the time.

So Lady Bridges, in the delicate language of Coulson Wallop, is in for it![9] I am very glad to hear of the Pearsons' good fortune. It is a piece of promotion which I know they looked forward to as very desirable some years ago, on Captain Lockyer's illness. It brings them a considerable increase of income and a better house.

My mother bargains for having no trouble at all in furnishing our house in Bath, and I have engaged for your willingly undertaking to do it all. I get more and more reconciled to the idea of our removal. We have lived long enough in this neighbourhood: the Basingstoke balls are certainly on the decline, there is something interesting in the bustle of going away, and the prospect of spending future summers by the sea or in Wales is very delightful. For a time we shall now possess many of the advantages which I have often thought of with envy in the wives of sailors or soldiers. It must not be generally known, however, that I am not sacrificing a great deal in quitting the country, or I can expect to inspire no tenderness, no interest, in those we leave behind.

The threatened Act of Parliament does not seem to give any alarm.[10]

My father is doing all in his power to increase his income, by raising his tithes, &c., and I do not despair of getting very nearly six hundred a year.[11]

In what part of Bath do you mean to place your bees? We are afraid of the South Parade's being too hot.

Monday.—Martha desires her best love, and says a great many kind things about spending some time with you in March, and depending on a large return from us both in the autumn. Perhaps I may not write again before Sunday.

Yours affectionately,
J. A.

---

[9] Pregnant.

[10] The Corn Laws that Parliament enacted to protect the artificially inflated prices for local grains during wartime, when imports were impossible. The landlords did not want prices to decline in peacetime—a benefit to them, and a misery to the poor, who faced starvation for lack of bread.

[11] Tithes are the amount due from the crops of tenant, typically one-tenth of their yield.

**Steventon: Wednesday (January 14, 1801).**

{. . . .}Last Friday was a very busy day with us. We were visited by Miss Lyford and Mr. Bayle.[12] The latter began his operations in the house, but had only time to finish the four sitting-rooms; the rest is deferred till the spring is more advanced and the days longer. He took his paper of appraisement away with him, and therefore we only know the estimate he has made of one or two articles of furniture which my father particularly inquired into. I understand, however, that he was of opinion that the whole would amount to more than two hundred pounds, and it is not imagined that this will comprehend the brewhouse and many other, &c., &c.

Miss Lyford was very pleasant, and gave my mother such an account of the houses in Westgate Buildings, where Mrs. Lyford lodged four years ago, as made her think of a situation there with great pleasures but your opposition will be without difficulty decisive, and my father, in particular, who was very well inclined towards the Row before, has now ceased to think of it entirely. At present the environs of Laura Place seem to be his choice. His views on the subject are much advanced since I came home; he grows quite ambitious, and actually requires now a comfortable and a creditable-looking house.

On Saturday Miss Lyford went to her long home that is to say, it was a long way off—and soon afterwards a party of fine ladies issuing from a well-known commodious green vehicle, their heads full of Bantam cocks and Galinies, entered the house—Mrs. Heathcote, Mrs. Harwood, Mrs. James Austen, Miss Bigg, Miss Jane Blachford. Hardly a day passes in which we do not have some visitor or other: yesterday came Mrs. Bramstone, who is very sorry that she is to lose us, and afterwards Mr. Holder, who was shut up for an hour with my father and James in a most awful manner. John Bond est a lui.[13]

Mr. Holder was perfectly willing to take him on exactly the same terms with my father, and John seems exceedingly well satisfied. The comfort of not changing his home is a very material one to him, and since such are his unnatural feelings, his belonging to Mr. Holder is the every thing needful; but otherwise there would have been a situation offering to him, which I had thought of with particular satisfaction, viz., under Harry Digweed, who, if John had quitted Cheesedown, would have been eager to engage him as

[12] Mary Susannah Lyford, a contemporary of Austen, and James Bayle, a cabinetmaker.
[13] Various friends, family members, and acquaintances.

superintendent at Steventon, would have kept a horse for him to ride about on, would probably have supplied him with a more permanent home, and I think would certainly have been a more desirable master altogether.

John and Corbett are not to have any concern with each other—there are to be two farms and two bailiffs. We are of opinion that it would be better in only one.

This morning brought my aunt's reply, and most thoroughly affectionate is its tenor. She thinks with the greatest pleasure of our being settled in Bath—it is an event which will attach her to the place more than anything else could do, &c., &c. She is, moreover, very urgent with my mother not to delay her visit in Paragon, if she should continue unwell, and even recommends her spending the whole winter with them. At present and for many days past my mother has been quite stout, and she wishes not to be obliged by any relapse to alter her arrangements.

Mr. and Mrs. Chamberlayne are in Bath, lodging at the Charitable Repository; I wish the scene may suggest to Mrs. C. the notion of selling her black beaver bonnet for the relief of the poor. Mrs. Welby has been singing duets with the Prince of Wales.[14]

My father has got above 500 volumes to dispose of; I want James to take them at a venture at half a guinea a volume. The whole repairs of the parsonage at Deane, inside and out, coachbox, basket and dickey will not much exceed £100.

Have you seen that Major Byng, a nephew of Lord Torrington, is dead? That must be Edmund.[15]

Friday.—I thank you for yours, though I should have been more grateful for it if it had not been charged 8d. instead of 6d., which has given me the torment of writing to Mr. Lambould on the occasion. I am rather surprised at the revival of the London visit; but Mr. Doricourt has travelled—he knows best.

That James Digweed has refused Deane curacy I suppose he has told you himself, though probably the subject has never been mentioned between you. Mrs. Milles flatters herself falsely, it has never been Mrs. Rice's wish to have her son settled near herself; and there is now a hope entertained of her relenting in favour of Deane.

---

[14] An allusion to an article in *The Morning Post* reporting on the Prince's activities while visiting Hampshire.

[15] A reference to a report in *The Times* of the death of Major Byng.

Mrs. Lefroy and her son-in-law were here yesterday; she tries not to be sanguine, but he was in excellent spirits. I rather wish they may have the curacy. It would be an amusement to Mary to superintend their household management, and abuse them for expense, especially as Mrs. L. means to advise them to put their washing out.[16]

Yours affectionately,
J. A.

**Steventon: Wednesday (January 21, 1801).**

Expect a most agreeable letter, for not being overburdened with subject (having nothing at all to say), I shall have no check to my genius from beginning to end. Well, and so Frank's letters has made you very happy, but you are afraid he would not have patience to stay for the "Haarlem,"[17] which you wish him to have done as being safer than the merchantman Poor fellow! to wait from the middle of November to the end of December, and perhaps even longer, it must be sad work; especially in a place where the ink is so abominably pale. What a surprise to him it must have been on October 20, to be visited, collared, and thrust out of the "Petterell" by Captain Inglis. He kindly passes over the poignancy of his feelings in quitting his ship, his officers, and his men.

What a pity it is that he should not be in England at the time of this promotion, because he certainly would have had an appointment, so everybody says, and therefore it must be right for me to say it too. Had he been really here, the certainty of the appointment, I dare say, would not have been half so great, but as it could not be brought to the proof his absence will be always a lucky source of regret.

Eliza talks of having read in a newspaper that all the 1st lieutenants of the frigates whose captains were to be sent into line-of-battle ships were to be promoted to the rank of commanders. If it be true, Mr. Valentine may afford himself a fine Valentine's knot, and Charles may perhaps become 1st of the "Endymion," though

[16] Anne Lefroy, a close friend.

[17] Austen's older brother Francis-William (Frank) had a long and distinguished naval career eventually achieving the rank of Admiral of the Fleet in 1863. At this point he probably holds the rank of Post-Captain, which he achieved in 1800, and is evidently between commands. The "merchantman" was a ship used exclusively in commerce and less safe than the Haarlem, which was probably larger and more heavily armed.

I suppose Captain Durham is too likely to bring a villain with him under that denomination.[18]

I dined at Deane yesterday, as I told you I should, and met the two Mr. Holders. We played at vingt-un, which, as Fulwar was unsuccessful, gave him an opportunity of exposing himself as usual.[19] Eliza says she is quite well, but she is thinner than when we saw her last, and not in very good looks. I suppose she has not recovered from the effects of her illness in December. She cuts her hair too short over her forehead, and does not wear her cap far enough upon her head; in spite of these many disadvantages, however, I can still admire her beauty.[20] They all dine here to-day; much good may it do us all.

William and Tom are much as usual; Caroline is improved in her person; I think her now really a pretty child. She is still very shy, and does not talk much.

Fulwar goes next month into Gloucestershire, Leicestershire, and Warwickshire, and Eliza spends the time of his absence at Ibthorp and Deane; she hopes, therefore, to see you before it is long.

Lord Craven was prevented by company at home from paying his visit at Kintbury, but, as I told you before, Eliza is greatly pleased with him, and they seem likely to be on the most friendly terms.

Martha returns into this country next Tuesday, and then begins her two visits at Deane.

I expect to see Miss Bigg every day to fix the time for my going to Manydown; I think it will be next week, and I shall give you notice of it, if I can, that you may direct to me there.

The neighbourhood have quite recovered the death of Mrs. Rider; so much so, that I think they are rather rejoiced at it now; her things were so very dear! and Mrs. Rogers is to be all that is desirable. Not even death itself can fix the friendship of the world.

---

[18] Austen's only younger sibling, Charles-John, was a naval officer as well, at this point serving on the *Endymion* and, like his brother Frank, made a career of it, both in the Navy and later in the East India Company.

[19] Fulwar-Craven Fowle, whose bad reaction at having lost a card game is apparently typical, was the brother of Tom Fowle, who was engaged to Austen's sister when he died of fever in the West Indies in 1797. Eliza is Fulwar's wife. Several of their children—Caroline, Tom, and William—are also mentioned. Twenty-one is a card game very similar to blackjack. "To expose oneself" is to be embarrassed financially in public or otherwise known to be in debt.

[20] "To wear a cap" was to be demure and to signal that one was not socially "out" (as Mary Crawford puts it in *Mansfield Park*) or otherwise on the marriage market.

You are not to give yourself the trouble of going to Penlingtons when you are in town; my father is to settle the matter when he goes there himself; you are only to take special care of the bills of his in your hands, and I dare say will not be sorry to be excused the rest of the business.

Thursday.—Our party yesterday was very quietly pleasant. Today we all attack Ashe Park, and to-morrow I dine again at Deane. What an eventful week!

Eliza left me a message for you, which I have great pleasure in delivering: she will write to you and send you your money next Sunday. Mary has likewise a message: she will be much obliged to you if you can bring her the pattern of the jacket and trousers, or whatever it is that Elizabeth's boys wear when they are first put into breeches; so if you could bring her an old suit itself, she would be very glad, but that I suppose is hardly done.

I am happy to hear of Mrs. Knight's amendment, whatever might be her complaint {. . . .}[21] The Wylmots being robbed must be an amusing thing to their acquaintance, and I hope it is as much their pleasure as it seems their avocation to be subjects of general entertainment.

I have a great mind not to acknowledge the receipt of your letter, which I have just had the pleasure of reading, because I am so ashamed to compare the sprawling lines of this with it. But if I say all that I have to say, I hope I have no reason to hang myself.

Caroline was only brought to bed on the 7th of this month, so that her recovery does seem pretty rapid. I have heard twice from Edward on the occasion, and his letters have each been exactly what they ought to be—cheerful and amusing. He dares not write otherwise to me, but perhaps he might be obliged to purge himself from the guilt of writing nonsense by filling his shoes with whole peas for a week afterwards. Mrs. G. has left him £100, his wife and son £500 each.[22] I join with you in wishing for the environs of Laura Place, but do not venture to expect it. My mother hankers

---

[21] "Complaint" means a physical ailment in this context. Brabourne's edition omits the following sentence: "I cannot think so ill of her however, in spite of your insinuations, as to suspect her of having lain-in—I do not think she would be betrayed beyond an accident at the utmost." "Lying-in" means taking to bed in the month prior to childbirth.

[22] Caroline Cooper, who married Edward Cooper Jr., a member of a large family with ties to the Austens. Austen also mentions Caroline's grandmother, Mrs. Girle.

after the Square dreadfully,[23] and it is but natural to suppose that my uncle will take her part. It would be very pleasant to be near Sydney Gardens; we might go into the labyrinth every day.[24]

You need not endeavour to match my mother's morning calico; she does not mean to make it up any more.

Why did not J. D. make his proposals to you? I suppose he went to see the cathedral, that he might know how he should like to be married in it.

Fanny shall have the boarding-school, as soon as her papa gives me an opportunity of sending it;[25] and I do not know whether I may not by that time have worked myself into so generous a fit as to give it to her forever.

We have a ball on Thursday too; I expect to go to it from Many-down. Do not be surprised, or imagine that Frank is come, if I write again soon; it will only be to say that I am going to M., and to answer your question about my gown.

### Paragon: Tuesday (May 5, 1801).[26]

My Dear Cassandra,

I have the pleasure of writing from my own room up two pair of stairs, with everything very comfortable about me.

Our journey here was perfectly free from accident or event; we changed horses at the end of every stage, and paid at almost every turn-pike. We had charming weather, hardly any dust, and were exceedingly agreeable, as we did not speak above once in three miles.

Between Luggershall and Everley we made our grand meal, and then with admiring astonishment perceived in what a magnificent manner our support had been provided for. We could not with the utmost exertion consume above the twentieth part of the beef. The cucumber will, I believe, be a very acceptable present, as my uncle

---

[23] Probably Queen's Square in Bath.

[24] Sydney Gardens in Bath featured a labyrinth.

[25] Fanny Knight, Austen's beloved niece and daughter of her brother Edward. The "boarding-school" is likely a children's book that Austen had read as a young girl and is passing on to her relative.

[26] Paragon were a set of buildings in Bath.

talks of having inquired the price of one lately, when he was told a shilling.[27]

We had a very neat chaise from Devizes;[28] it looked almost as well as a gentleman's, at least as a very shabby gentleman's; in spite of this advantage, however, we were above three hours coming from thence to Paragon, and it was half after seven by your clocks before we entered the house.

Frank, whose black head was in waiting in the Hall window, received us very kindly; and his master and mistress did not show less cordiality. They both look very well, though my aunt has a violent cough.[29] We drank tea as soon as we arrived, and so ends the account of our journey, which my mother bore without any fatigue.[30]

How do you do to-day? I hope you improve in sleeping—I think you must, because I fall off; I have been awake ever since five and sooner; I fancy I had too much clothes over me; I thought I should by the feel of them before I went to bed, but I had not courage to alter them. I am warmer here without any fire than I have been lately with an excellent one.

Well, and so the good news is confirmed, and Martha triumphs. My uncle and aunt seemed quite surprised that you and my father were not coming sooner.

I have given the soap and the basket, and each have been kindly received. One thing only among all our concerns has not arrived in safety: when I got into the chaise at Devizes I discovered that your drawing ruler was broke in two; it is just at the top where the cross-piece is fastened on. I beg pardon.

There is to be only one more ball—next Monday is the day. The Chamberlaynes are still here. I begin to think better of Mrs. C___, and upon recollection believe she has rather a long chin than otherwise, as she remembers us in Gloucestershire when we were very charming young women.

The first view of Bath in fine weather does not answer my expectations; I think I see more distinctly through rain. The sun was

[27] Cucumbers were a luxury and an acceptable gift.

[28] A chaise is a four-wheeled closed carriage drawn by either two or four horses.

[29] Austen's maternal uncle James Leigh-Perrot and his wife Jane, with whom the Austens lived temporarily when they were house-hunting in Bath.

[30] Drinking tea involved light refreshments as well, which would have been appropriate under the circumstances.

got behind everything, and the appearance of the place from the top of Kingsdown was all vapour, shadow, smoke, and confusion.

I fancy we are to have a house in Seymour Street, or thereabouts.

My uncle and aunt both like the situation. I was glad to hear the former talk of all the houses in New King Street as too small; it was my own idea of them. I had not been two minutes in the dining-room before he questioned me with all his accustomary eager interest about Frank and Charles, their views and intentions. I did my best to give information.

I am not without hopes of tempting Mrs. Lloyd to settle in Bath; meat is only 8d. per pound, butter 12d., and cheese 9½d. You must carefully conceal from her, however, the exorbitant price of fish: a salmon has been sold at 2s. 9d. per pound the whole fish.[31] The Duchess of York's removal is expected to make that article more reasonable—and till it really appears so, say nothing about salmon.

Tuesday night.—When my uncle went to take his second glass of water I walked with him, and in our morning's circuit we looked at two houses in Green Park Buildings, one of which pleased me very well. We walked all over it except into the garret; the dining-room is of a comfortable size, just as large as you like to fancy it; the second room about 14 ft. square. The apartment over the drawing-room pleased me particularly, because it is divided into two, the smaller one a very nice-sized dressing-room, which upon occasion might admit a bed. The aspect is south-east. The only doubt is about the dampness of the offices, of which there were symptoms.

Wednesday.—Mrs. Mussell has got my gown, and I will endeavour to explain what her intentions are. It is to be a round gown, with a jacket and a frock front, like Cath. Bigg's, to open at the side. The jacket is all in one with the body, and comes as far as the pocket-holes—about half a quarter of a yard deep, I suppose, all the way round, cut off straight at the corners with a broad hem. No fulness appears either in the body or the flap; the back is quite plain in this form [hourglass shape], and the sides equally so. The front is sloped round to the bosom and drawn in, and there is to be a frill of the same to put on occasionally when all one's handkerchiefs are dirty—which frill must fall back. She is to put two breadths and a-half in the tail, and no gores—gores not being so much worn as

---

[31] *d* is the sign for pence, *s* for shillings. There are 12 pence per shilling, 20 shillings per pound, and 21 shillings per guinea.

Sydney Place, Bath (Photo Courtesy of Allan Soedring.)

they were. There is nothing new in the sleeves: they are to be plain, with a fulness of the same falling down and gathered up under-neath, just like some of Martha's, or perhaps a little longer. Low in the back behind, and a belt of the same.[32] I can think of nothing more, though I am afraid of not being particular enough.

My mother has ordered a new bonnet, and so have I; both white strip, trimmed with white ribbon. I find my straw bonnet looking very much like other people's, and quite as smart. Bonnets of

---

[32] A gown typical for the period, featuring a high waist among other details.

The 1 Paragon, Bath (Photo Courtesy of Allan Soedring.)

cambric muslin on the plan of Lady Bridges' are a good deal worn, and some of them are very pretty; but I shall defer one of that sort till your arrival. Bath is getting so very empty that I am not afraid of doing too little. Black gauze cloaks are worn as much as anything. I shall write again in a day or two. Best love.

Yours ever,
J. A.

We have had Mrs. Lillingstone and the Chamberlaynes to call on us. My mother was very much struck with the odd looks of the two latter; I have only seen her. Mrs. Busby drinks tea and plays at cribbage here to-morrow; and on Friday, I believe, we go to the Chamberlaynes'. Last night we walked by the Canal.

**Paragon: Tuesday (May 12, 1801).**

MY DEAR CASSANDRA,

My mother has heard from Mary, and I have heard from Frank; we therefore know something now of our concerns in distant quarters; and you, I hope, by some means or other are equally instructed, for I do not feel inclined to transcribe the letter of either.[33]

You know from Elizabeth, I dare say, that my father and Frank, deferring their visit to Kippington on account of Mr. M. Austen's absence, are to be at Godmersham to-day; and James, I dare say, has been over to Ibthorp by this time to inquire particularly after Mrs. Lloyd's health, and forestall whatever intelligence of the sale I might attempt to give; sixty-one guineas and a-half for the three cows gives one some support under the blow of only eleven guineas for the tables. Eight for my pianoforte is about what I really expected to get; I am more anxious to know the amount of my books, especially as they are said to have sold well.

My adventures since I wrote last have not been numerous; but such as they are, they are much at your service.

We met not a creature at Mrs. Lillingstone's, and yet were not so very stupid, as I expected, which I attribute to my wearing my new bonnet and being in good looks. On Sunday we went to church twice, and after evening service walked a little in the Crescent fields, but found it too cold to stay long.

Yesterday morning we looked into a house in Seymour Street, which there is reason to suppose will soon be empty; and as we are assured from many quarters that no inconvenience from the river is felt in those buildings, we are at liberty to fix in them if we can. But this house was not inviting; the largest room downstairs was not much more than fourteen feet square, with a western aspect.

In the evening, I hope you honoured my toilette and ball with a thought;[34] I dressed myself as well as I could, and had all my finery much admired at home. By nine o'clock my uncle, aunt, and I entered the rooms, and linked Miss Winstone on to us. Before tea it was rather

---

[33] Austen's brother Francis and her brother James's wife Mary.

[34] A toilette is the dressing and grooming in preparation for a public appearance.

a dull affair; but then the before tea did not last long, for there was only one dance, danced by four couple. Think of four couple, surrounded by about an hundred people, dancing in the Upper Rooms at Bath. After tea we cheered up; the breaking up of private parties sent some scores more to the ball, and though it was shockingly and inhumanly thin for this place, there were people enough, I suppose, to have made five or six very pretty Basingstoke assemblies.[35]

I then got Mr. Evelyn to talk to, and Miss T. to look at; and I am proud to say that[36] {. . . } though repeatedly assured that another in the same party was the She, I fixed upon the right one from the first. A resemblance to Mrs. L. was my guide. She is not so pretty as I expected; her face has the same defect of baldness as her sisters, and her features not so handsome; she was highly rouged, and looked rather quietly and contentedly silly than anything else.

Mrs. B. and two young women were of the same party, except when Mrs. B. thought herself obliged to leave them to run round the room after her drunken husband. His avoidance, and her pursuit, with the probable intoxication of both, was an amusing scene.

The Evelyns returned our visit on Saturday; we were very happy to meet, and all that; they are going to-morrow into Gloucestershire to the Dolphins for ten days. Our acquaintance, Mr. Woodward, is just married to a Miss Rowe, a young lady rich in money and music {. . . .}

Wednesday.—Another stupid party last night; perhaps if larger they might be less intolerable, but here there were only just enough to make one card-table, with six people to look on and talk nonsense to each other. Lady Fust, Mrs. Busby, and a Mrs. Owen sat down with my uncle to whist, within five minutes after the three old Toughs came in, and there they sat, with only the exchange of Adm. Stanhope for my uncle, till their chairs were announced.

I cannot anyhow continue to find people agreeable; I respect Mrs. Chamberlayne for doing her hair well, but cannot feel a more tender sentiment. Miss Langley is like any other short girl, with a broad nose and wide mouth, fashionable dress and exposed bosom. Adm. Stanhope is a gentleman-like man, but then his legs are too short and his tail too long. Mrs. Stanhope could not come; I fancy she

---

[35] Assemblies are public gatherings for dancing, playing cards, dining, and social circulating, for which tickets are sold.

[36] Brabourne omits the following sentence: "I have a very good eye at an adulteress, for." His suppressions here and elsewhere reflect Victorian sqeamishness over Austen's candor.

had a private appointment with Mr. Chamberlayne, whom I wished to see more than all the rest.

My uncle has quite got the better of his lameness, or at least his walking with a stick is the only remains of it. He and I are soon to take the long-planned walk to the Cassoon,[37] and on Friday we are all to accompany Mrs. Chamberlayne and Miss Langley to Weston.

My mother had a letter yesterday from my father; it seems as if the W. Kent Scheme was entirely given up. He talks of spending a fortnight at Godmersham, and then returning to town.

Yours ever,
J. A.

Excepting a slight cold, my mother is very well; she has been quite free from feverish or bilious complaints since her arrival here.

**Paragon: Thursday (May 21, 1801).**

My Dear Cassandra,

To make long sentences upon unpleasant subjects is very odious, and I shall therefore get rid of the one now uppermost in my thoughts as soon as possible.

Our views on G. P. Buildings seem all at an end; the observation of the damps still remaining in the offices of an house which has been only vacated a week, with reports of discontented families and putrid fevers, has given the coup de grace. We have now nothing in view. When you arrive, we will at least have the pleasure of examining some of these putrefying houses again; they are so very desirable in size and situation, that there is some satisfaction in spending ten minutes within them.

I will now answer the inquiries in your last letter. I cannot learn any other explanation of the coolness between my aunt and Miss Bond than that the latter felt herself slighted by the former's leaving Bath last summer without calling to see her before she went. It seems the oddest kind of quarrel in the world. They never visit, but I believe they speak very civilly if they meet. My uncle and Miss Bond certainly do.

The four boxes of lozenges, at 1s. 1½d. per box, amount, as I was told, to 4s. 6d., and as the sum was so trifling, I thought it better to pay at once than contest the matter.

---

[37] A lock on the Somerset Canal that transported boats to a lower level.

I have just heard from Frank. My father's plans are now fixed; you will see him at Kintbury on Friday, and, unless inconvenient to you, we are to see you both here on Monday, the 1st of June. Frank has an invitation to Milgate, which I believe he means to accept.

Our party at Ly. Fust's was made up of the same set of people that you have already heard of—the Winstones, Mrs. Chamberlayne, Mrs. Busby, Mrs. Franklyn, and Mrs. Maria Somerville; yet I think it was not quite so stupid as the two preceding parties here.

The friendship between Mrs. Chamberlayne and me which you predicted has already taken place, for we shake hands whenever we meet. Our grand walk to Weston was again fixed for yesterday, and was accomplished in a very striking manner. Every one of the party declined it under some pretence or other except our two selves, and we had therefore a tête-à-tête, but that we should equally have had after the first two yards had half the inhabitants of Bath set off with us.[38]

It would have amused you to see our progress. We went up by Sion Hill, and returned across the fields. In climbing a hill Mrs. Chamberlayne is very capital; I could with difficulty keep pace with her, yet would not flinch for the world. On plain ground I was quite her equal. And so we posted away under a fine hot sun, she without any parasol or any shade to her hat, stopping for nothing, and crossing the churchyard at Weston with as much expedition as if we were afraid of being buried alive. After seeing what she is equal to, I cannot help feeling a regard for her. As to agreeableness, she is much like other people.

Yesterday evening we had a short call from two of the Miss Arnolds, who came from Chippenham on business. They are very civil, and not too genteel, and upon hearing that we wanted a house, recommended one at Chippenham.

This morning we have been visited again by Mrs. and Miss Holder; they wanted us to fix an evening for drinking tea with them, but my mother's still remaining cold allows her to decline everything of the kind. As I had a separate invitation, however, I believe I shall go some afternoon. It is the fashion to think them both very detestable, but they are so civil, and their gowns look so white and so nice (which, by the bye, my aunt thinks an absurd pretension in this place), that I cannot utterly abhor them, especially as Miss Holder owns that she has no taste for music.

[38] The walk to Weston was a popular promenade in Bath.

After they left us I went with my mother to help look at some houses in New King Street, towards which she felt some kind of inclination, but their size has now satisfied her. They were smaller than I expected to find them; one in particular out of the two was quite monstrously little; the best of the sitting-rooms not so large as the little parlour at Steventon, and the second room in every floor about capacious enough to admit a very small single bed.

We are to have a tiny party here to-night. I hate tiny parties, they force one into constant exertion. Miss Edwards and her father, Mrs. Busby and her nephew, Mr. Maitland, and Mrs. Lillingstone are to be the whole; and I am prevented from setting my black cap at Mr. Maitland by his having a wife and ten children.

My aunt has a very bad cough—do not forget to have heard about that when you come—and I think she is deafer than ever. My mother's cold disordered her for some days, but she seems now very well. Her resolution as to remaining here begins to give way a little; she will not like being left behind, and will be glad to compound matters with her enraged family.

You will be sorry to hear that Marianne Mapleton's disorder has ended fatally. She was believed out of danger on Sunday, but a sudden relapse carried her off the next day. So affectionate a family must suffer severely; and many a girl on early death has been praised into an angel, I believe, on slighter pretensions to beauty, sense, and merit than Marianne.

Mr. Bent seems bent upon being very detestable, for he values the books at only £70. The whole world is in a conspiracy to enrich one part of our family at the expense of another. Ten shillings for Dodsley's Poems, however, please me to the quick, and I do not care how often I sell them for as much.[39] When Mrs. Bramston has read them through I will sell them again. I suppose you can hear nothing of your magnesia?

Friday.—You have a nice day for your journey, in whatever way it is to be performed, whether in the Debary's coach or on your own twenty toes.

When you have made Martha's bonnet you must make her a cloak of the same sort of materials; they are very much worn here, in different forms—many of them just like her black silk spencer, with a trimming round the armholes instead of sleeves, some are

---

[39] A well-known edition of eighteenth-century verse edited by Robert Dodsley.

long before, and some long all round, like C. Bigg's. Our party last night supplied me with no new idea for my letter.

Yours ever,

J. A.

The Pickfords are in Bath, and have called here. She is the most elegant-looking woman I have seen since I left Martha; he is as raffish in his appearance as I would wish every disciple of Godwin to be.[40] We drink tea to-night with Mrs. Busby. I scandalised her nephew cruelly; he has but three children instead of ten.

Best love to everybody.

## Lyme, Friday, Sept. 14 (1804).

My dear Cassandra,—I take the first sheet of fine striped paper to thank you for your letter from Weymouth, and express my hopes of your being at Ibthorp before this time. I expect to hear that you reached it yesterday evening, being able to get as far as Blandford on Wednesday. Your account of Weymouth contains nothing which strikes me so forcibly as there being no ice in the town.[41] For every other vexation I was in some measure prepared, and particularly for your disappointment in not seeing the Royal Family go on board on Tuesday, having already heard from Mr. Crawford that he had seen you in the very act of being too late. But for there being no ice, what could prepare me? [. . .] You found my letter at Andover, I hope, yesterday, and have now for many hours been satisfied that your kind anxiety on my behalf was as much thrown away as kind anxiety usually is. I continue quite well; in proof of which I have bathed again this morning. It was absolutely necessary that I should have the little fever and indisposition which I had: it has been all the fashion this week in Lyme. [. . .] We are quite settled in our lodgings by this time, as you may suppose, and everything goes on in the usual order. The servants behave very well, and make no difficulties, though nothing

---

[40] William Godwin (1756–1836) was a radical writer and philosopher best known for his novel *Caleb Williams* (1794) and his *Enquiry Concerning Political Justice* (1793). He was also the husband of the great women's rights advocate Mary Wollstonecraft. His *Memoir* of her, published just after her death in 1798, exposed several scandals (premarital affairs, pregnancy out of wedlock, suicide attempts) that ruined her reputation, and tarnished the argument for women's rights as the philosophy of a whore.

[41] Weymouth, like Lyme Regis, was a fashionable seaside resort in southwest England. In *Emma,* it is where Frank Churchill and Jane Fairfax first met.

certainly can exceed the inconvenience of the offices, except the general dirtiness of the house and furniture, and all its inhabitants. [. . .] I endeavour, as far as I can, to supply your place, and be useful, and keep things in order. I detect dirt in the water decanter as fast as I can, and give the cook physic which she throws off her stomach. I forget whether she used to do this under your administration. [. . .] The ball last night was pleasant, but not full for Thursday. My father staid contentedly till half-past nine (we went a little after eight), and then walked home with James and a lanthorn,[42] though I believe the lanthorn was not lit, as the moon was up, but sometimes this lanthorn may be a great convenience to him. My mother and I staid about an hour later. Nobody asked me the two first dances; the next two I danced with Mr. Crawford, and had I chosen to stay longer might have danced with Mr. Granville, Mrs. Granville's son, whom my dear friend Miss A. offered to introduce to me, or with a new odd-looking man who had been eyeing me for some time, and at last, without any introduction, asked me if I meant to dance again. I think he must be Irish by his ease, and because I imagine him to belong to the honbl. B.'s, who are son, and son's wife of an Irish viscount, bold queer-looking people, just fit to be quality at Lyme. I called yesterday morning (ought it not in strict propriety to be termed yester-morning?) on Miss A. and was introduced to her father and mother. Like other young ladies she is considerably genteeler than her parents. Mrs. A. sat darning a pair of stockings the whole of my visit. But do not mention this at home, lest a warning should act as an example. We afterwards walked together for an hour on the Cobb; she is very conversable in a common way; I do not perceive wit or genius, but she has sense and some degree of taste, and her manners are very engaging. She seems to like people rather too easily. [. . .]

Your's affectionately,
J. A.

**25 Gay Street (Bath), Monday, April 8, 1805.**

My dear Cassandra,—Here is a day for you! Did Bath or Ibthorp ever see a finer 8th of April? It is March and April together; the glare of the one and the warmth of the other. We do nothing but walk about. As far as your means will admit, I hope you profit by

[42] Lantern.

such weather too. I dare say you are already the better for change of place. We were out again last night. Miss Irvine invited us, when I met her in the Crescent, to drink tea with them, but I rather declined it, having no idea that my mother would be disposed for another evening visit there so soon; but when I gave her the message, I found her very well inclined to go; and accordingly, on leaving Chapel, we walked to Lansdown. This morning we have been to see Miss Chamberlaine look hot on horseback. Seven years and four months ago we went to the same riding-house to see Miss Lefroy's performance! What a different set are we now moving in! But seven years, I suppose, are enough to change every pore of one's skin and every feeling of one's mind. We did not walk long in the Crescent yesterday.[43]

It was hot and not crowded enough; so we went into the field, and passed close by S. T. and Miss S. again. I have not yet seen her face, but neither her dress nor air have anything of the dash or stylishness which the Browns talked of; quite the contrary; indeed, her dress is not even smart, and her appearance very quiet. Miss Irvine says she is never speaking a word. Poor wretch; I am afraid she is en pénitence.[44] Here has been that excellent Mrs. Coulthard calling, while my mother was out, and I was believed to be so. I always respected her, as a good-hearted friendly woman. And the Browns have been here; I find their affidavits on the table. The "Ambuscade" reached Gibraltar on the 9th of March, and found all well; so say the papers.[45] We have had no letters from anybody, but we expect to hear from Edward to-morrow, and from you soon afterwards. How happy they are at Godmersham now! I shall be very glad of a letter from Ibthorp, that I may know how you all are there, and particularly yourself. This is nice weather for Mrs. J. Austen's going to Speen, and I hope she will have a pleasant visit there. I expect a prodigious account of the christening dinner; perhaps it brought you at last into the company of Miss Dundas again.

Tuesday. —I received your letter last night, and wish it may be soon followed by another to say that all is over; but I cannot help

---

[43] A crescent was often the best part of a town or city and so named because its hilltop townhouses are formed as a continuous crescent at the top end of a park. It is the best place to promenade, to see, and to be seen.

[44] French: In a state of shame.

[45] A frigate on which Frank Austen sailed en route to the Mediterranean, where he served under Admiral Nelson in the war with France.

thinking that nature will struggle again, and produce a revival. Poor woman! May her end be peaceful and easy as the exit we have witnessed![46] And I dare say it will. If there is no revival, suffering must be all over; even the consciousness of existence, I suppose, was gone when you wrote. The nonsense I have been writing in this and in my last letter seems out of place at such a time, but I will not mind it; it will do you no harm, and nobody else will be attacked by it. I am heartily glad that you can speak so comfortably of your own health and looks, though I can scarcely comprehend the latter being really approved. Could traveling fifty miles produce such an immediate change? You were looking very poorly here, and everybody seemed sensible of it. Is there a charm in a hack postchaise?[47] But if there were, Mrs. Craven's carriage might have undone it all. I am much obliged to you for the time and trouble you have bestowed on Mary's cap, and am glad it pleases her; but it will prove a useless gift at present, I suppose. Will not she leave Ibthorp on her mother's death? As a companion you are all that Martha can be supposed to want, and in that light, under these circumstances, your visit will indeed have been well timed, and your presence and support have the utmost value. [. . .]

Thursday.—I was not able to go on yesterday; all my wit and leisure were bestowed on letters to Charles and Henry. To the former I wrote in consequence of my mother's having seen in papers that the "Urania" was waiting at Portsmouth for convoy for Halifax. This is nice, as it is only three weeks ago that you wrote by the "Camilla." I wrote to Henry because I had a letter from him in which he desired to hear from me very soon. His to me was most affectionate and kind, as well as entertaining; there is no merit to him in that; he cannot help being amusing. [. . .] He offers to meet us on the sea coast, if the plan of which Edward gave him some hint takes place. Will not this be making the execution of such a plan more desirable and delightful than ever? He talks of the rambles we took together last summer with pleasing affection. [. . .]

Yours ever,<br>
J. A.

---

[46] A reference to the death of Martha Lloyd, the mother of Austen's closest friend Mary Lloyd.

[47] A closed carriage seating no more than three persons with the driver outside.

**Gay St., Sunday Evening, April 21 (1805).**

My dear Cassandra,—I am much obliged to you for writing to me
again so soon; your letter yesterday was quite an unexpected pleasure. Poor Mrs. Stent! it has been her lot to be always in the way;
but we must be merciful, for perhaps in time we may come to be
Mrs. Stents ourselves, unequal to anything, and unwelcome to
everybody. [. . .] My morning engagement was with the Cookes,
and our party consisted of George and Mary, a Mr. and Miss B.,
who had been with us at the concert, and the youngest Miss W. Not
Julia; we have done with her; she is very ill, but Mary. Mary W.'s
turn is actually come to be grown up, and have a fine complexion,
and wear great square muslin shawls. I have not expressly enumerated myself among the party, but there I was, and my cousin George
was very kind, and talked sense to me every now and then, in the
intervals of his more animated fooleries with Miss B., who is very
young, and rather handsome, and whose gracious manners, ready
wit, and solid remarks, put me somewhat in mind of my old
acquaintance L. L. There was a monstrous deal of stupid quizzing,
and common-place nonsense talked, but scarcely any wit;[48] all that
bordered on it or on sense came from my cousin George, whom
altogether I like very well. Mr. B. seems nothing more than a tall
young man. My evening engagement and walk was with Miss A.,
who had called on me the day before, and gently upbraided me in
her turn with a change of manners to her since she had been in
Bath, or at least of late. Unlucky me! that my notice should be of
such consequence, and my manners so bad! She was so well disposed, and so reasonable, that I soon forgave her, and made this
engagement with her in proof of it. She is really an agreeable girl, so
I think I may like her; and her great want of a companion at home,
which may well make any tolerable acquaintance important to her,
gives her another claim on my attention. I shall endeavour as much
as possible to keep my intimacies in their proper place, and prevent
their clashing. [. . .] Among so many friends, it will be well if I do
not get into a scrape; and now here is Miss Blachford come. I should
have gone distracted if the Bullers had staid. [. . .] When I tell you
I have been visiting a countess this morning, you will immediately,
with great justice, but no truth, guess it to be Lady Roden. No: it is
Lady Leven, the mother of Lord Balgonie. On receiving a message

---

[48] "Quizzing" means teasing rather than questioning.

from Lord and Lady Leven through the Mackays, declaring their intention of waiting on us, we thought it right to go to them. I hope we have not done too much, but the friends and admirers of Charles must be attended to. They seem very reasonable, good sort of people, very civil, and full of his praise.[49] We were shewn at first into an empty drawing-room, and presently in came his lordship, not knowing who we were, to apologise for the servant's mistake, and tell a lie himself, that Lady Leven was not within. He is a tall gentlemanlike looking man, with spectacles, and rather deaf. After sitting with him ten minutes we walked away; but Lady Leven coming out of the dining parlour as we passed the door, we were obliged to attend her back to it, and pay our visit over again. She is a stout woman, with a very handsome face. By this means we had the pleasure of hearing Charles's praises twice over. They think themselves excessively obliged to him, and estimate him so highly as to wish Lord Balgonie, when he is quite recovered, to go out to him. There is a pretty little Lady Marianne of the party to be shaken hands with, and asked if she remembered Mr. Austen. [. . .]

I shall write to Charles by the next packet, unless you tell me in the meantime of your intending to do it.

Believe me, if you chuse,
Your affectionate Sister.

---

[49] Charles Austen may have been of some assistance to the son of Lord and Lady Leven, Lord Balgonie, who was also in the navy. Lady Roden was related to people in Hampshire with whom the Austens were sufficiently close to justify Austen's visiting her.

# Money from the 1790s to the Regency (1811–1820)

## Who Has It?

Income could be earned by salaried work, by a "living" (stipend plus income), by speculative investment of capital and labor (say farming or livestock with expectations of a market price, but prey to vicissitudes of weather, disease, and market volatility in times of war or depression) or by interest on principal (savings, an inheritance, or a dowry); government funds paid 5%.

In *English Landed Society in the Eighteenth Century* (London, 1963), G. E. Mingay reports that in Austen's day only 400 families had annual incomes in the range of £5000–50,000, with £10,000 (Mr. Darcy's income) the average (£ is the sign for pound, the basic unit of currency, analogous to the $US). Mingay gives the annual incomes among the upper ranks (no more than 10% of the population in 1800) as follows: gentlemen: £300–1000; squires: £1000–3000; wealthy gentry (landowners): £3000–5000; great landlords: £5000–10,000.

The population of the United Kingdom during the Regency (the decade during which Austen's novels were published) was around 12,000,000. Only 250,000—a bit more than 2%—had incomes of more than £700 per year. The Prince Regent, funded by taxes, spent £260,000 in 3 years on furniture for his residence, £23,000 per year on plate and jewels, and £12,000 per year on china and glassware.

WHAT'S IT WORTH?

Since 1971, the pound has been decimal, equaling 100 pence. Before then, it was divided into 20 shillings, and shillings into 12 pence. As with U.S. currency, there were coins: a crown was 5 shillings; a half crown was half that; there was also a sixpence, and a farthing (a quarter penny). At the high end, there was a guinea, an upscale coin worth a pound and a shilling. Figures up to £5 were often given in shillings only.

There is no stable equivalence between dollars and pounds. In 2001, £1 is equal to about $1.60; in 1970, about $2.20; in 1912, about $5. It makes more sense to look at purchasing power within the system.

MONEY IN *PERSUASION*

When incomes, inheritances, and dowries are not directly computed, the "worth" of an individual or family may be read by real estate— houses (town and country), grounds, gardens—carriages and horses, number of servants, pianos, plate, furnishings, clothes and jewels, ability to travel and where, food served, the frequency and style of entertainment, consumer power, and the ratio of labor to leisure (who works, who does not have to). A house in London, as Edward Copeland notes, signified an annual income of at least £5000. In *Persuasion*, Copeland observes, debt and credit are the key issues. Sir Walter Elliot, his daughter Elizabeth, and his nephew William Walter Elliot are all encumbered by debt, whereas Captain Wentworth, a member of the new professional class, has both substantial savings and substantial credit. Captain and Mrs. Wentworth will be able to live on the income from 30,000 pounds, or on about 1500 pounds a year—enough to maintain a horse and carriage, enough to belong to the upper professional classes, and enough to move in all social circles.

### Men

Captain Wentworth's profits from his career at sea, including prize money (spoils from captured ships), total £25,000.

By comparison, Mr. Darcy in *Pride and Prejudice* has an annual income of £10,000 from his inherited estate, rents from tenant farmers and other investments.

## Women

The women have "fortunes": dowries brought to a marriage and/or lump-sum inheritances. A wife's fortune becomes her husband's (hence the term "fortune-hunter"), unless there are legal provisions to the contrary. An unmarried woman's inheritance was not enjoyed as a lump sum, but was invested in the government funds, at 5% interest. Anne Elliot's fortune of £10,000 would have yielded an annual income of £500.

Georgiana Darcy and Emma Woodhouse (in *Pride and Prejudice* and *Emma* respectively) have fortunes of £30,000 (two of Austen's wealthiest young women, both unmarried).

## What about Everyone Else?

When Jane Austen's father married in 1764, his living as a reverend was £100 a year, plus whatever he could realize from 200 acres of land.

In 1805, Jane Austen, her mother, her sister Cassandra, and the sister of her brother's wife were living together on £450 per year.

Sample annual incomes at the time *Pride and Prejudice* was published:

- 2 million skilled laborers (artisans): £55 (£50 is the poverty line.)
- 1.5 million agriculture laborers: £30
- 1 million clergy, farm owners, and schoolmasters: £120
- 0.5 million shopkeepers: £150
- miners: £40
- seamstresses: £20
- governesses: £12–20 (with room and board); Jane Fairfax in *Emma* might be paid a bit more than £20, should she accept the handsome offer Mrs. Elton has arranged for her.

After her first novel, *Sense and Sensibility*, which Austen published at her own expense and on which she realized £140 net, she made between £110 and 150 per novel. She sold the copyright for *Pride and Prejudice* for £110.

In October 1815, the establishment publisher John Murray offered Austen £450 for *Emma* and the copyrights of *Mansfield Park* and *Sense and Sensibility*. Austen turned this down, hoping to do better by paying Murray a commission to print the novel and then realize the profits herself. This turned out to be a bad decision.

In 1816, Murray paid £2000 for Byron's *Childe Harold's Pilgrimage III* and *The Prisoner of Chillon*, improving on the £600 he had paid for *Childe Harold I–II* (1812). Byron's asking price for *Childe Harold IV* was 2500 guineas (£2625). Murray offered poet Thomas Campbell 3000 guineas for an anthology of British poetry, and poet Thomas Moore received this same sum from Longman for *Lalla Rookh*. At about this time John Chetwode Eustace had been promised 2000 guineas for a long poem on education.

### What Does It Cost?

Lady Catherine de Bourgh in *Pride and Prejudice* has her own inheritance as well as her husband's estate, and seems able to spend an extravagant £800 on a chimneypiece, that is, the entire fireplace, including mantel, tilework, hearth, and so forth.

A fair-sized edition of a two- or three-volume novel cost £100–200 to produce.

At its first publication, *Pride and Prejudice* sold for 18 shillings; her first novel, *Sense and Sensibility*, sold for 15 shillings. Building on Austen's reputation, Murray marketed *Emma* at £1, 1 shilling (one guinea).

In 1799, Jane Austen spent a little less than £2 for a cloak. In the same year, her brother Edward (adopted by the Knights) bought a pair of coach horses for 60 guineas (letter to Cassandra, 19 June 1799), that is £63. In 1799, a stable boy could be hired for £4 per year.

Edward Copeland gives the following reports ("Money," *The Cambridge Companion to Jane Austen*, ed. Copeland and Juliet McMaster: Cambridge, 1997):

- £200/year was needed to live as lower gentry (those able to maintain themselves without manual labor), and to afford a servant.
- £300/year allows for two servants, but is not comfortable for a marriage.
- £400/year affords comforts: a cook and a maid, at least.
- £500/year allows a cook, a maid, and a man, but not carriage and horses. Austen lived with her mother and her sister and one servant on a bit more than this, after her father's death.
- £700–1000/year is the range of the upper professional; one can afford a horse and carriage. Austen's father tried to maintain a carriage when his income reached £700 but found it

too expensive in the overall family budget. As today, having wheels not only was a convenience but signified wealth and status.

- In Austen's first published novel, *Sense and Sensibility*, Marianne Dashwood hopes to be established with £2000 a year, enabling a comfortable home with servants, a carriage or two, and hunters (for provision). Her sister Eleanor thinks £1000/year adequate for a clergyman's family (her goal).
- £2000/year (the landed-gentry income of Mr. Bennet in *Pride and Prejudice*) allows a prudently pleasant standard of living, depending on the size of the family and household economy.
- £4000/year and above allows genteel comforts, and allowed for a house in London for the social season.

# On Women and Men

In a conversation with Captain Harville in Chapter 11 (Vol. 2) Anne Elliot discusses male and female virtues, with attention to those of her "own sex." Such comparisons were a popular subject, especially in the "conduct" manuals written to guide the development of male and female character. Among the most influential of these were *An Enquiry into the Duties of Men in the Higher and Middle Classes of Society* (1794) and *An Enquiry into the Duties of Female Sex* (1797) by Anglican cleric and abolitionist Thomas Gisborne (1758–1846). There is evidence that Austen read *Duties of the Female Sex*; Gisborne's observations on marriage and the duties of a military wife fall across Anne's initial refusal of Captain Wentworth's proposal as well as the Croft and Musgrove marriages (however different). Lord Byron, who may have read *Persuasion* (John Murray published both authors), echoes many of Anne's observations on the different social fates of men and women through the character of Donna Julia in Canto I of *Don Juan*. Although Austen did not live long enough to read this great comic epic, she alludes to Byron's other poems throughout *Persuasion*, including his eastern tale *The Giaour*, which concludes with a paean to monogamy, which the Giaour, like Anne, regards as a missed opportunity.

## ♣ Thomas Gisborne
### From *An Enquiry into the Duties of the Female Sex* (London, 1792)

### C H A P.  I

#### PLAN OF THE WORK EXPLAINED

The sphere of domestic life, the sphere in which female exertion is chiefly occupied, and female excellence is best displayed, admits far less diversity of action, and consequently of temptation, than is to be found in the widely differing professions and employments into which private advantage and public good require that men should be distributed. The barrister and the physician have their respective duties, and their respective trials. The fundamental principles by which both the one and the other is to regulate his conduct are the same. The occasion, however, on which those principles are to operate, and the enticement, whether of pleasure or of interest, by which their present effect is impeded, and their future stability endangered, are continually presenting themselves to each in a shape adapted to the pursuits in which he is busied, and the objects most familiar to his attention and desire. But the wife and the daughter of the former are scarcely distinguished as such, by any peculiarities of moral obligation, from the persons standing in the same degree of relationship to the latter. The discriminating lines, unless their number or their strength be increased by circumstances not necessarily resulting from the profession of the husband or the father, are few, obscure, and inconstant. The same general truth might be exemplified in a variety of additional instances. Even the superiority of rank which elevates the peeress above her untitled neighbour, though it unquestionably creates a difference between their respective duties, is far from creating a difference equal to that which subsists between the duties of an hereditary legislator and those of a private gentleman. Such being the general similarity in the situation of women, differing in some respects from each other in outward circumstances, or even placed in separate classes of society; I purpose to couch in general terms the remarks about to be offered on the conduct of the female sex. But I shall at the same time be studiously solicitous to point out, whenever a fit occasion shall intervene, the most prominent of those instances in which the moral activity and the moral vigilance of the female mind are to be guided into particular channels, in consequence of some particularity, either in the station of the individual, or in the rank or profession of her nearest connections. The peculiar temptations of the capital, and those of the country, will also receive the distinct consideration which they deserve.

## CHAP. II

### General Grounds of the Importance of the Female Character Briefly Stated

In the course of a work which purposes to investigate somewhat at length the several duties of the female sex, the importance of the female character will naturally disclose itself. It is not by attending to formal and studied panegyric, but by considering in detail the various and momentous duties, to the discharge of which, women are called both by reason and revelation, that the influence of feminine virtues is rendered most conspicuous. It is thus too that the responsibility attached to that influence in all its branches, in all its minutest capacities of being beneficially employed, will be placed in the strongest light; a circumstance of no small weight with regard to precluding the emotions of arrogance and the confidence of self-sufficiency, which are ever likely to be produced by simple eulogium. The general contempt, therefore, which is sometimes manifested respecting women by persons of the other sex, and most frequently by persons who are unworthy or incapable of forming a judgement concerning those whom they profess to despise, would not have induced me to make any preliminary observations on the subject. There is, however, a prejudice which it is desirable to remove without delay, because it is found to exist in female minds, and unavoidably contributes, in proportion to its strength, to extinguish the desire of improvement, and to repress useful exertion. The fact is this. Young women endowed with good understandings, but desirous of justifying the mental indolence which they have permitted themselves to indulge; or disappointed at not perceiving a way open by which they, like their brothers, may distinguish themselves and rise to eminence; are occasionally heard to declare their opinion, that the sphere in which women are destined to move is so humble and so limited, as neither to require nor to reward assiduity; and under this impression, either do not discern, or will not be persuaded to consider, the real and deeply interesting effects which the conduct of their sex will always have on the happiness of society. In attempting to obviate this error, I should be very culpable were I to flatter the ambitious fondness for distinction, which may, in part at least, have given rise to it. To suggest motives to unassuming and virtuous activity, is the purpose of the following brief remarks.

Human happiness is on the whole much less affected by great but unfrequent events, whether of prosperity or of adversity, of benefit or of injury, than by small but perpetually recurring incidents of good or evil. The manner in which the influence of the female character is felt belongs to the latter description. It is not like the periodical inundation of a river, which overspreads once in a year a desert with transient plenty. It is like the dew of heaven which descends at all seasons, returns after short intervals, and permanently nourishes every herb of the field.

In three particulars, each of which is of extreme and never-ceasing concern to the welfare of mankind, the effect of the female character is most important.

First, In contributing daily and hourly to the comfort of husbands, of parents, of brothers and sisters, and of other relations, connections, and friends, in the intercourse of domestic life, under every vicissitude of sickness and health, of joy and affliction.

Secondly, In forming and improving the general manners, dispositions, and conduct of the other sex, by society and example.

Thirdly, In modelling the human mind during the early stages of its growth, and fixing, while it is yet ductile, its growing principles of action; children of each sex being, in general, under maternal tuition during their childhood, and girls until they become women.

Are these objects insufficient to excite virtuous exertion? Let it then be remembered, that there is another of supreme importance set before each individual; and one which she cannot accomplish without faithfully attending, according to her situation and ability, to those already enumerated; namely, the attainment of everlasting felicity, by her conduct during her present probationary state of existence.

In different countries, and at different periods, female excellence has been estimated by very different standards. At almost every period it has been rated among nations, deeply immersed in barbarism, by the scale of servile fear and capacity for toil. Examine the domestic proceedings of savage tribes in the old world and in the new, and ask who is the best daughter and the best wife. The answer is uniform. She who bears with superior perseverance the vicissitudes of seasons, the fervour of the fun, the dews of night. She who, after a march through woods and swamps from morn to eve, is the first to bring on her shoulders a burthen of fuel, and foremost in erecting the family wigwam, while the men stand around in listless unconcern: She who searches with the greatest activity for roots in the forest; prowls with the most success along the shore for limpets;[1] and dives with unequalled fortitude for sea-eggs in the creek: She who stands dripping and famished before her husband, while he devours, stretched at ease, the produce of her exertions; waits his

---

[1] Shellfish.

tardy permission without a word or a look of impatience; and feeds, with the humblest gratitude, and the shortest intermission of labour, on the scraps and offals which he disdains: She, in a word, who is most tolerant of hardship, and of unkindness. When nations begin to emerge from gross barbarism, every new step which they take towards refinement is commonly marked by a gentler treatment, and a more reasonable estimation of women; and every improvement in their opinions and conduct respecting the female sex, prepares the way for additional progress in civilisation. It is not, however, in the rudeness of uncivilised life, that female worth can either be fitly apprehended, or be displayed in its genuine colours. And we shall be the less inclined to wonder at the perversion of ideas which has been exemplified on this subject, amidst ignorance and necessity, among Hottentots[2] and Indians; when we consider the erroneous opinions on the same topic which have obtained more or less currency in our country, and even in modern times. It would perhaps be no unfair representation of the sentiment which prevailed in the last age, to affirm that she who was completely versed in the sciences of pickling and preserving, and in the mysteries of cross-stitch and embroidery; she who was thoroughly mistress of the family receipt-book and of her needle was deemed, in point of solid attainments, to have reached the measure of female perfection. Since that period, however, it has been universally acknowledged, that the intellectual powers of women are not restricted to the arts of the housekeeper and the sempstress. Genius, taste, and learning itself, have appeared in the number of female endowments and acquisitions. And we have heard, from time to time, some bold assertors of the rights of the weaker sex, stigmatizing, in terms of indignant complaint, the monopolising injustice of the other; laying claim, on behalf of their clients, to co-ordinate authority in every department of science and of erudition; and upholding the perfect equality of injured woman and usurping man in language so little guarded, as scarcely to permit the latter to confider the labours of the camp and of the senate as exclusively pertaining to himself.

The Power who called the human race into being has, with infinite wisdom, regarded, in the structure of the corporeal frame, the tasks which the different sexes were respectively destined to fulfil. To man, on whom the culture of the soil, the erection of dwellings,

---

[2] People of southern Africa.

and, in general, those operations of industry, and those measures of defence, which include difficult and dangerous exertion, were ultimately to devolve, He has imparted the strength of limb, and the robustness of constitution, requisite for the persevering endurance of toil. The female form, not commonly doomed, in countries where the progress of civilisation is far advanced, to labours more severe than the offices of domestic life, He has cast in a smaller mould, and bound together by a looser texture. But, to protect weakness from the oppression of domineering superiority, those whom He has not qualified to contend, He has enabled to fascinate; and has amply compensated the defect of muscular vigour by symmetry and expression, by elegance and grace. To me it appears, that He has adopted, and that He has adopted with the most conspicuous wisdom, a corresponding plan of discrimination between the mental powers and dispositions of the two sexes. The science of legislation, of jurisprudence, of political economy; the conduct of government in all its executive functions; the abstruse researches of erudition; the inexhaustible depths of philosophy; the acquirements subordinate to navigation; the knowledge indispensable in the wide field of commercial enterprise; the arts of defence, and of attack by land and by sea, which the violence or the fraud of unprincipled assailants render needful; these, and other studies, pursuits, and occupations, assigned chiefly or entirely to men, demand the efforts of a mind endued with the powers of close and comprehensive reasoning, and of intense and continued application, in a degree in which they are not requisite for the discharge of the customary offices of female duty. It would therefore seem natural to expect, and experience, I think, confirms the justice of the expectation, that the Giver of all good, after bestowing those powers on men with a liberality proportioned to the subsisting necessity, would impart them to the female mind with a more sparing hand. It was equally natural to expect, that in the dispensation of other qualities and talents, useful and important to both sexes, but particularly suited to the sphere in which women were intended to move, He would confer the larger portion of his bounty on those who needed it the most. It is accordingly manifest, that, in sprightliness and vivacity, in quickness of perception, in fertility of invention, in powers adapted to unbend the brow of the learned, to refresh the over-laboured faculties of the wife, and to diffuse, throughout the family circle, the enlivening and endearing smile of cheerfulness, the superiority of the female mind is unrivalled. Does man, vain of his pre-eminence in the track of profound investigation, boast that the result of the enquiry is in his favour? Let him check the premature triumph; and listen to the statement of another article in the account, which, in the judgement of prejudice itself, will be found to restore the balance. As yet the native worth of the female character has been imperfectly developed. To estimate it fairly, the view must be extended from the compass and shades of intellect, to the dispositions and feelings of the heart. Were we called upon to produce examples of the most amiable tendencies and affections implanted in human nature, of modesty, of delicacy, of sympathising sensibility, of prompt and active benevolence, of warmth and tenderness of attachment; whither should we at once turn our eyes? To the sister, to the daughter, to the wife. These endowments form the glory of the female sex. They shine amidst the darkness of uncultivated barbarism; they give to civilised society its brightest and most attractive luster. The priority of female excellence in the points now under consideration, man is seldom undiscerning enough to deny. But he not infrequently endeavours to aggrandise his own merits, by representing himself as characterized in return by superior fortitude. In the first place, however, the reality of the fact alleged is extremely problematical. Fortitude is not to be fought merely on the rampart, on the deck, on the field of battle. Its place is no less in the chamber of sickness and pain, in the retirements of anxiety, of grief, and of disappointment. The resolution which is displayed in braving the perils of war is, in most men, to a very considerable degree, the effect of habit and of other extraneous causes. Courage is esteemed the commonest qualification of a soldier. And why is it thus common? Not so much because the stock of native resolution, bestowed on the generality of men, is very large; as because that stock is capable of being increased by discipline, by habit, by sympathy, by encouragement, by the dread of shame, by the thirst of credit and renown, almost to an unlimited extent. But the influence of these causes is not restricted to men. In towns which have long sustained the horrors of a siege, the descending bomb has been found, in numberless instances, scarcely to excite more alarm in the female part of the families of private citizens, than among their brothers and husbands. In bearing vicissitudes of fortune, in exchanging wealth for penury, splendor for disgrace, women seem, as far as experience has decided the question, to have shewn themselves little inferior to men. With respect to supporting the languor and the acuteness of disease, the weight of testimony is wholly on the fide of the weaker sex. Ask the professors of the medical art, what description of the persons whom they attend exhibits the highest patterns of firmness, composure, and resignation under tedious and painful trials; and they name at once their female patients. It has, indeed, been asserted, that women, in consequence of the slighter texture of their frame, do not undergo, in the amputation of a limb, and in other cases of corporal suffering, the same degree of anguish which is endured by the rigid muscles and stubborn sinews of persons of the other sex under similar circumstances; and that a smaller portion of fortitude is sufficient to enable the former to bear the trial equally well with the latter. The assertion, however, appears to have been advanced not only without proof, but without the capability of proof. Who knows that the nerves are not as keenly sensible in a finer texture as in one more robust? Who knows that they are not more keenly sensible in the first than in the second? Who can estimate the degree of pain, whether of body or of mind, endured by any individual except himself? How can any person institute a comparison, when of necessity he is wholly ignorant of one of the points to be compared? If, in the external indications of mental resolution, women are not inferior to men; is a theory which admits not of experimental confirmation, a reasonable ground for pronouncing them inferior in the reality? Nor let it be deemed wonderful, that Providence should have conferred on women in general a portion of original fortitude, not much inferior, to speak of it in the lowest terms compatible with truth, to that commonly implanted in persons of the other sex, on whom many more scenes of danger and of strenuous exertion are devolved. If the natural tenderness of the female mind, cherished, too, as that tenderness is in civilised nations, by the established modes of ease, indulgence, and refinement, were not balanced by an ample share of latent resolution; how would it be capable of enduring the shocks and the sorrows to which, amid the uncertainties of life, it must be exposed? Finally, whatever may be the opinion adopted as to the precise amount of female fortitude, when compared with that of men, the former, I think, must at least be allowed this relative praise: that it is less derived from the mechanical influence of habit and example than the latter; less tinctured with ambition; less blended with insensibility; and more frequently drawn from the only source of genuine strength of mind, firm and active principles of religion.

# CHAP. XI

### Considerations Antecedent to Marriage

If an union about to take place, or recently contracted, between two young persons, is mentioned in conversation, the first question which we hear asked concerning it is, whether it be a good match. The very countenance and voice of the inquirer, and of the answerer, the terms of the answer returned, and the observations, whether expressive of satisfaction or of regret, which fall from the lips of the company present in the circle, all concur to shew what, in common estimation, is meant by being well married. If a young woman be described as thus married, the terms imply, that she is united to a man whose rank and fortune is such, when compared with her own or those of her parents, that in point of precedence, in point of command of finery and of money, she is, more or less, a gainer by the bargain. They imply, that she will now possess the enviable advantages of taking place of other ladies in the neighbourhood; of decking herself out with jewels and lace; of inhabiting splendid apartments; rolling in handsome carriages; gazing on numerous servants in gaudy liveries; and of going to London, and other fashionable scenes of resort, in a degree somewhat higher than that in which a calculating broker, after poring on her pedigree, summing up her property in hand, and computing, at the market price, what is contingent or in reversion, would have pronounced her entitled to them. But what do the terms imply as to the character of the man selected to be her husband? Probably nothing. His character is a matter which seldom enters into the consideration of the persons who use them, unless it, at length, appears in the shape of an after thought, or is awkwardly hitched into their remarks for the sake of decorum. If the terms imply any thing, they mean no more than that he is not scandalously and notoriously addicted to vice. He may be proud, he may be ambitious, he may be malignant, he may be devoid of Christian principles, practice, and belief; or, to say the very least, it may be totally unknown whether he does not fall, in every particular, under this description; and yet, in the language and in the opinion of the generality of both sexes, the match is excellent. In like manner a small diminution in the supposed advantages already enumerated, though counterpoised by the acquisition of a companion eminent for his virtues, is supposed to constitute a bad match; and is universally lamented in polite meetings with real or affected concern. The good or bad fortune of a young man in the choice of a wife is estimated according to the same rules.

From those who contract marriages, either chiefly, or in a considerable degree, through motives of interest or of ambition, it would be folly to expect previous solicitude respecting piety of heart. And it would be equal folly to expect that such marriages, however they may answer the purposes of interest or of ambition, should terminate otherwise than in wretchedness. Wealth may be secured, rank may be obtained; but if wealth and rank are to be main ingredients in the cup of matrimonial felicity, the sweetness of the wine will be exhausted at once, and nothing remain but bitter and corrosive dregs. When attachments are free from the contamination of such unworthy motives, it by no means always follows that much attention is paid to intrinsic excellence of moral character. Affection, quick-sighted in discerning, and diligent in scrutinising, the minutest circumstances which contribute to shew whether it is met with reciprocal sincerity and ardor, is, in other respects, purblind and inconsiderate. It magnifies good qualities which exist; it seems to itself to perceive merits which, to other eyes, are invisible; it gives credit for what it wishes to discover; it enquires not, where it fears a disappointment.

The truths which have been inculcated, are such as ought to be established in the mind while the affections are yet unengaged. When the heart has received an impression, reason acts feebly or treacherously. But let not the recent impression be permitted to sink deeper, ere the habitual principles and conduct of him who has made it shall have been ascertained. On these points in particular, points which a young woman cannot herself possess adequate means of investigating, let the advice and inquiries of virtuous relatives be solicited. Let not their opinions, though the purport of them should prove unacceptable, be undervalued; nor their remonstrances, if they should remonstrate, be construed as unkindness. Let it be remembered that, although parental authority can never be justified in constraining a daughter to marry against her will, there are many cases in which it may be justified in requiring her to pause. Let it be remembered, that if she should unite herself to a man who is unsettled as to the principles, or careless as to the practical duties of Christianity, she has to dread not only the risk of personal unhappiness from his conduct towards her, but the dangerous contagion of intimate example; she has to dread that his unsteadiness may render her unsteady, his carelessness may teach her to be careless. Does the prospect appear gloomy? Let her be wife, let her exert herself, before it is too late. It is better to encounter present anxiety, than to avoid it at the expense of greater and durable evils. And even if affection has already acquired such force, as not to be repressed without very painful struggles; let her be consoled and animated by the consciousness that the sacrifice is to prevent, while prevention is yet in her power, years of danger and of misery; that it is an act not only of ultimate kindness to herself, but of duty to God; and that every act of humble and persevering duty may hope to receive, in a better world, a reward proportioned to the severity of the trial.

In a union so intimate as that of matrimonial life, those diversities in temper, habits, and inclinations, which in a less close connection might not have been distinctly perceived, or would have attracted notice but seldom, unavoidably swell into importance. When surfaces are contiguous, every little prominence is mutually felt. Hence, among the qualifications which influence the probability of connubial comfort, a reasonable similarity of disposition between the two parties is one of especial moment. Where strong affection prevails, a spirit of accommodation will prevail also: but it is not desirable that the spirit of accommodation should be subjected to rigorous or very frequent experiments. Great disparity in age between a husband and a wife, or a wide difference in rank antecedently to marriage, is, on this account, liable to be productive of disquietude. The sprightliness of youth seems levity, and the sobriety of maturer years to be tinctured with moroseness, when closely contrasted. A sudden introduction to affluence, a sudden and great elevation in the scale of society, are apt to intoxicate; and a sudden reduction in outward appearance to be felt as degrading. Instances, however, are not very rare in which the force of affection, of good sense, and of good principles, shews itself permanently superior to the influence of causes, which, to minds less happily attempered, and less under the guidance of religious motives, prove sources of anxiety and vexation.

## CHAP. XII

### ON THE DUTIES OF MATRIMONIAL LIFE

Home is the center round which the influence of every married woman is principally accumulated. It is there that she will naturally be known and respected the most; it is there, at least, that she may be more known and more respected than she can be in any other place. It is there that the general character, the acknowledged property, and the established connections of her husband, will contribute with more force than they can possess elsewhere, to give weight and impressiveness to all her proceedings. Home, therefore, is the place where the pattern which she exhibits in personal manners, in domestic arrangements, and in every branch of her private conduct will be more carefully observed, and more willingly copied by her neighbours in a rank of life similar to her own, than it would be in a situation where she was a little known and transitory visitant. Home too is the place where she will possess peculiar means of doing good among the humbler classes of society. All the favorable circumstances already mentioned which surround her there, add singular efficacy to her persuasions, to her recommendations, to her advice. Her habitual insight into local events and local necessities, her acquaintance with the characters and the situations of individuals, enable her to adapt the relief which she affords to the merit and to the distress of the person assisted; and in the charitable expenditure of any specific sum, to accomplish purposes of greater and more durable utility than could have been attained in a place where she would not have enjoyed these advantages. They who are frequently absent from home, without an adequate cause, spontaneously abandon all these especial means of benefiting their equals, their inferiors, possibly even their superiors; means which Providence has committed to them, in order that each might be thus employed; means for the due employment of which they will be deemed responsible hereafter. Continually on the wing from one scene to another, they are like trees transplanted so often, that they take firm root no where. They appear covered with shewy verdure; but they bear little fruit. The ties of connection between them and the vicinity are broken. With the upper ranks, their intercourse is that of form and hurry; to the lower, they are become distant, cold, and estranged. When at their nominal home, they are there without attachment. They perch there, like a bird on a branch, rather as having found a convenient baiting-place, than from partiality to the spot. Every person who comes to see them expects to hear of another approaching expedition; and if he finds himself mistaken, surprises all whom he meets with the wonder. The habit grows by indulgence. Every trifle swells into a motive and a pretext for quitting their natural residence. In the winter, London is the magnet which attracts them. The desire of appearing polite, and the pride of being able to speak of having recently visited the metropolis, conspire with their impatience of home. If they hear that a neighboring family is going to town, to stay behind becomes intolerable. When stationed in the capital, some impending festivity, some approaching day of splendor at Court, affords an excuse for delaying their return. When summer commences, the center of attraction is transferred to some watering-place; and its force again proves irresistible. Neither are the intervals between these prominent periods in the system of wandering condemned wholly to the dreariness of the family seat. Little tours to see sights, long circuits of visits from the house of one acquaintance to that of another, and various incidental excursions, break the wearisome period into small parts; and aided by the cheering hope of longer expeditions, render life capable of being endured. When the rage of rambling has seized a woman, it is not always that the malady proceeds to the height which has been described. Like other maladies, it has its degrees.

The wife of an officer in the naval or in the military service is, in several respects, exposed to moral trials of considerable magnitude. In time of war she is left to endure the anxieties of a long separation from her husband, while he is toiling on the ocean, or contending in a distant quarter of the globe with the bullets of the enemy and the maladies of the climate. The state of tremulous suspense, when the mind is ignorant of the fate of the object which it holds most dear, and knows not but that the next post may confirm the most dreadful of its apprehensions, can be calmed only by those consolations which look beyond the present world. Let not despondency withhold the confidence due to the protecting Power of Him, "without whom, not "even a sparrow falleth to the ground[1]." Let not solicitude question the wisdom which uniformly marks the determinations of that Being, one of whose characteristic it is to be "wonderful in counsel:"[2] nor affliction forget that he has promised that "all things shall work together for good to "them that love Him."[3] When the husband is fighting the battles of his country, the whole management of the domestic economy of his family devolves upon his wife. Let her faithfully execute the trust, and shun even a distant approach towards extravagance. In her whole demeanour, let her guard against every symptom of levity, every trace of inadvertence, which might give rise to the misconceptions of ignorance, or awaken the censorious tongue

[1] Mathew on God's grace (Mathew 10: 29).

[2] Isaiah, **28**: 29.

[3] Romans, 7: 28.

of malice. Let it be her constant object that, if it shall please the divine Providence to restore her husband, she may present herself before him at least as worthy of his esteem and love as she was when he left her. The wife of the military officer has sometimes to encounter new and peculiar temptations, at times when she is not separated from her husband. Various circumstances frequently concur to lead her through the vicissitudes of a wandering life, in accompanying him successively from one country town where he is quartered to another; and occasionally fix her during the time of war in the vicinity of the camp where his regiment is posted. Disuse to a settled home, and the want of those domestic occupations and pleasures which no place of residence but a settled home can supply, tend to create a fondness for roving, an eagerness for amusement, an inveterate propensity to cardplaying, and an aversion to every kind of reading, except the perusal of the mischievous trash which the circulating library pours forth for the entertainment of a mind unaccustomed to reflection. It unfortunately happens too, that, in this situation, her society is not sufficiently composed of persons of her own sex. Feminine reserve, delicacy of manners, and even delicacy of sentiment, are in extreme danger of being worn away by living in habits of familiar intercourse with a crowd of officers; among whom it is to be expected that there will be some who are absolutely improper, and more who are very undesirable associates. Duty and affection may in certain cases render it necessary, that a married lady should stand the brunt of those temptations. But the consequent danger should excite her to unwearied and universal circumspection; and warn her to cultivate with unremitting vigilance those habits of privacy, and of useful and methodical employment, without which female diffidence, purity of heart, and a capacity for the enjoyment and the communication of domestic happiness, will scarcely be found to survive.

## ❧ Thomas Gisborne

### From *An Enquiry into the Duties of Men in the Higher and Middle Classes of Society in Great Britain*

## CHAP. VIII

### On the Duties of Naval and Military Officer

Whatever be the line of service or the rank in which an Officer is placed, the most obvious of all the moral obligations incumbent on him is that of faithfully performing the immediate duties of his post. A man of integrity and reflection will blush to receive a salary from the public, without making that return to his country, which, by accepting his commission, he has pledged himself to render. He will therefore apply with assiduity and perseverance to the several branches of military or naval service, in which his station requires him to bear a part. He will not think it sufficient barely to attain to such a degree of proficiency in the duties of his department, as may secure him from the reprehension of his superiors. He will not be contented with acquiring that facility in practice which is the result of habit; and neglect the study of the theoretical and scientific principles of his profession. He who regards his occupation as a mere mercenary trade, will aim only at doing what is absolutely necessary, and at doing that by rote. But he who feels an honest desire to distinguish himself by genuine merit, will be solicitous to be prepared for the various and sudden contingencies by which an Officer may be overtaken in the vicissitudes of war; and to be able to adapt the fundamental rules of the service to unforeseen and critical emergences. He will resolve to consider himself through life as a learner. He will not disregard the advice and suggestions of Experience, though they proceed from a person of rank inferior to his own. Too wise to contract a fondness for novelties only because they are new; he will shun the opposite extreme, more common among professional men, of pertinaciously adhering to antient practices, and resisting rational and seasonable improvements. He will study strict method in all branches of employment, as the only means of having business done well, at the cheapest rate, and in the shortest possible time. The latter circumstance is often essential to the success of warlike operations; and in many cases, as when troops encumbered with stores and baggage are to be removed from an approaching superiority of force, or a fleet is to be repaired in an insecure or unhealthy harbour, the delays which result from a confused and unsettled mode of proceeding may occasion the loss of multitudes by the sword or by disease. A good Officer will not trust to the inspection or agency of another what he ought to examine or conduct in person. Instead of declining what is actually comprehended within his own province, he will explore its utmost limits for proper opportunities of acquiring additional knowledge and skill, and of improving himself in all the different functions which he may be called upon to discharge. By accustoming himself on common occasions to alertness and activity, he will prevent greater exertions in more critical seasons from being difficult and oppressive to him. Habits of carelessness once contracted are continually encroaching more and more; and though at first extending only to trifles, gradually draw matters of the highest moment within the sphere of their influence. And whenever, by being unwarily indulged, they settle into confirmed indolence; they become the sources of every species of professional demerit, and of every kind of vice.

Steadiness of demeanour, and uniformity of conduct, are found by experience not only to secure the submission, but to conciliate the esteem of soldiers and seamen. How indeed shall that Officer be either feared or beloved, who shews himself the slave of levity, sickleness, and caprice? That happy union of firmness exempt from supercilious and tyrannical arrogance, with freedom guarded from indiscreet familiarity, which at once commands respect and wins the heart, is not to be attained without trouble, nor without an accurate observation of the character and manners of the different classes of society. It is however an attainment of such value, that it would deserve to be purchased even at a higher price. An affectionate attachment on the part of the private men towards their Officers, preserves them from being tempted to desert; disposes them to regular and cheerful obedience; encourages them to bear hardships with patience, to encounter dangers with alacrity; and contributes beyond most other circumstances to ensure victory in the day of battle.

He who is solicitous to be beloved by those under his command, will treat them on all occasions with justice and humanity. He will not seek personal advantages and emoluments for himself, at the expence either of their rights or of their comforts. Instead of ungenerously consulting his own ease and accommodation by disregarding their sufferings, he will alleviate the distresses which they undergo by bearing his share of them. He will not endeavour to gain the reputation of alertness, and thus to recommend himself to his superiors, by harassing his men with vexatious and unprofitable movements, or by needless encroachments on their hours of meals and rest. He will never expose their lives to unnecessary risk in action, or out of it; nor permit himself to acquire the horrid habit of being careless of human bloodshed. He will watch with incessant solicitude over their health; and will not forget how greatly its preservation depends on the salubrity of their food, the sufficiency of their clothing, their uniform regard to cleanliness, and the use of wholesome precautions against infection. He will gladly befriend them in their own little pecuniary concerns; as in establishing the validity of their wills by his attestation; in the transfer of a part of their gains to their absent families; in the recovering of wages or prize-money withheld from them; and in all those cases in which the private man finds the aid of his Officer necessary to enable him to secure or to dispose of the fruits of his labour. When sickness, casualties, or wounds, give them a peculiar claim to his tenderness, he will always adopt the most speedy, proper, and effectual method of assisting each individual; whether it be by taking care that he be supplied with every kind of succour which his situation requires, and existing circumstances admit of being furnished; or by supporting his claim to be received into some of the asylums provided by the public for those who are disabled in the defence of their country.

It remains to subjoin a few brief remarks relating to the conduct of an Officer in private life.

They who escape the vices peculiar to their profession, cannot avoid the habits which it naturally produces. It may be observed, with regard to the professions of which we are now treating (and a similar reflection might be applied to others), that some of the habits which they occasion, and even require, become vices when they are transferred from the camp and the quarter-deck to the walks of social and domestic life. And thither they will certainly, though perhaps imperceptibly, be transferred, unless active care be employed to confine them to their proper sphere. He who has been long accustomed to the exercise of undisputed command, is in danger of expecting from his family and dependents a mechanical submission to his inclinations, and an unbounded deference to his opinions; or at least of tarnishing the character of the Master, the Parent, and the Husband, by the authoritative demeanour and peremptory tone of the Officer. He who has been familiarised to the frequent change of place and company experienced by persons in the Navy and Army, is liable to harass those who are connected with him, by indulging a roving and unsettled disposition; to depress them by discontent at what he terms the dulness of retirement; or to ruin them by expensive efforts to enliven it. And he who has been used to pay that attention to personal air and appearance which is thought requisite on the parade, has but a step to take to the affectation and fopperies of dress; and it is well if he has not taken it already.

When an Officer is not called into employment, a portion of the leisure which he enjoys should be allotted to the study of his profession. Otherwise, when he returns into active service, his associates will probably perceive, if he should not make the discovery himself, that he has rapidly declined in knowledge, alacrity, and merit. This too is the time for storing his mind with other attainments in science, in history, in useful and elegant literature; which cannot be fully acquired, though they neither need nor ought to be neglected, during the shorter intermissions of professional avocations. In the intervals of garrison duty, and the quiet of a voyage, a package of well-chosen books, not bulky enough to occasion inconvenience, will impart much substantial information; and prevent the languor of many a tedious hour. As young men are frequently placed in the Navy and Army before their education is properly completed, every subsequent opportunity of improving the mind ought to be turned to the best advantage. A Military Officer in quarters in time of peace has many ample opportunities; and the due application of them will preserve him from the idle, finical, and dissipated habits, which otherwise he will scarcely fail to contract. He who belongs to the naval profession, when not engaged in real service, is generally detached altogether from professional business; and therefore feels himself at liberty to devote his thoughts and time to some other liberal employment, until his country calls again for his exertions in her defence. But the Military Officer is commonly exposed during peace to the disadvantage of being so far occupied by the duties, or at least by the forms, of his profession, as to be precluded from undertaking any other settled pursuit; while at the same time the greater part of his hours remains vacant, and open to the intrusion of indolence and vice.

## ♣ Lord Byron
### From *Don Juan, Canto I* (1819)—*Donna Julia's Letter to Don Juan*

The discovery of an adulterous affair between the married Donna Julia, a woman of twenty three, and the sixteen-year-old Juan has led to their separation. Julia is to be confined to a convent while Juan has been sent by his mother on a grand tour. More mature and more vulnerable, Julia is forced to reflect on her situation and on the situation of women in general.

### 191

She had resolved that he should travel through
All European climes, by land or sea,
To mend his former morals, and get new,

Especially in France and Italy,
1525 (At least this is the thing most people do).
Julia was sent into a convent; she
Grieved, but, perhaps, her feelings may be better
Shown in the following copy of her letter:

### 192

"They tell me 'tis decided; you depart:
1530 'Tis wise—'tis well, but not the less a pain;
I have no further claim on your young heart,
Mine is the victim, and would be again;
To love too much has been the only art
I used;—I write in haste, and if a stain
1535 Be on this sheet, 'tis not what it appears,
My eyeballs burn and throb, but have no tears.

### 193

"I loved, I love you, for this love have lost
State, station, heaven, mankind's, my own esteem,
And yet can not regret what it hath cost,
1540 So dear is still the memory of that dream;
Yet, if I name my guilt, 'tis not to boast,
None can deem harshlier of me than I deem:
I trace this scrawl because I cannot rest—
I've nothing to reproach, or to request.

### 194

1545 "Man's love is of man's life a thing apart,
'Tis woman's whole existence; man may range
The court, camp, church, the vessel, and the mart,
Sword, gown, gain, glory, offer in exchange
Pride, fame, ambition, to fill up his heart,
1550 And few there are whom these can not estrange;
Men have all these resources, we but one.
To love again, and be again undone.

### 195

"You will proceed in pleasure, and in pride,
Beloved and loving many; all is o'er
1555 For me on earth, except some years to hide
My shame and sorrow deep in my heart's core;
These I could bear, but cannot cast aside

The passion which still rages as before,
And so farewell—forgive me, love me—No,
1560    That word is idle now—but let it go.

### 196

"My breast has been all weakness, is so yet;
But still I think I can collect my mind;
My blood still rushes where my spirit's set,
As roll the waves before the settled wind;
1565    My heart is feminine, nor can forget—
To all, except one image, madly blind;
So shakes the needle, and so stands the pole,
As vibrates my fond heart to my fix'd soul.

### 197

"I have no more to say, but linger still,
1570    And dare not set my seal upon this sheet,
And yet I may as well the task fulfil,
My misery can scarce be more complete:
I had not lived till now, could sorrow kill;
Death shuns the wretch who fain the blow would meet,
1575    And I must even survive this last adieu,
And bear with life, to love and pray for you!"

### 198

This note was written upon gilt-edged paper
With a neat little crow-quill, slight and new;
Her small white hand could hardly reach the taper,
1580    It trembled as magnetic needles do,
And yet she did not let one tear escape her;
The seal a sunflower; "Elle vous suit partout,"[5]
The motto, cut upon a white cornelian;
The wax was superfine, its hue vermillion.

## ♣ Lord Byron
### From *The Giaour* (1813)

The Giaour (Arabic for "non-Muslim") was deeply in love with Leila, the favorite harem slave of Hassan, who had her murdered upon discovering the love affair. At the end of the poem, the Giaour

---

[5] French: she follows you everywhere. The sunflower is a heliotrope; the seal imprints the wax that fastens the letter.

has retreated to a monastery, where he launches a paean to monogamy as the ideal complement to passionate, erotic love.

> To me she gave her heart, that all
> Which Tyranny can ne'er enthrall;
> 1070 And I, alas! too late to save!
> Yet all I then could give, I gave—
> 'Twas some relief—our foe a grave.
> His death sits lightly; but her fate
> Has made me—what thou well mayst hate.
> 1075 His doom was sealed—he knew it well,
> Warned by the voice of stern Taheer,
> Deep in whose darkly boding ear
> The deathshot pealed of murder near,
> As filed the troop to where they fell!
> 1080 He died too in the battle broil,
> A time that heeds nor pain nor toil;
> One cry to Mahomet for aid,
> One prayer to Alla all he made:
> He knew and crossed me in the fray—
> 1085 I gazed upon him where he lay,
> And watched his spirit ebb away:
> Though pierced like pard by hunter's steel,
> He felt not half that now I feel.
> I searched, but vainly searched, to find
> 1090 The workings of a wounded mind;
> Each feature of that sullen corse
> Betrayed his rage, but no remorse.
> Oh, what had Vengeance given to trace
> Despair upon his dying face!
> 1095 The late repentance of that hour
> When Penitence hath lost her power
> To tear one terror from the grave,
> And will not soothe, and cannot save.
>
> "The cold in clime are cold in blood,
> 1100 Their love can scarce deserve the name;
> But mine was like the lava flood
> That boils in Ætna's breast of flame.
> I cannot prate in puling strain
> Of Ladye-love, and Beauty's chain:
> 1105 If changing cheek, and scorching vein,
> Lips taught to writhe, but not complain,
> If bursting heart, and maddening brain,
> And daring deed, and vengeful steel,

And all that I have felt, and feel,
1110     Betoken love—that love was mine,
And shown by many a bitter sign.
'Tis true, I could not whine nor sigh,
I knew but to obtain or die.
I die—but first I have possessed,
1115     And come what may, I have been blessed.
Shall I the doom I sought upbraid?
No—reft of all, yet undismayed
But for the thought of Leila slain,
Give me the pleasure with the pain,
1120     So would I live and love again.
I grieve, but not, my holy Guide!
For him who dies, but her who died:
She sleeps beneath the wandering wave—
Ah! had she but an earthly grave,
1125     This breaking heart and throbbing head
Should seek and share her narrow bed.
She was a form of Life and Light,
That, seen, became a part of sight;
And rose, where'er I turned mine eye,
1130     The Morning-star of Memory!

"Yes, Love indeed is light from heaven;
A spark of that immortal fire
With angels shared, by Alla given,
To lift from earth our low desire.
1135     Devotion wafts the mind above,
But Heaven itself descends in Love;
A feeling from the Godhead caught,
To wean from self each sordid thought;
A ray of Him who formed the whole;
1140     A Glory circling round the soul!
I grant my love imperfect, all
That mortals by the name miscall;
Then deem it evil, what thou wilt;
But say, oh say, hers was not Guilt!
1145     She was my Life's unerring Light:
That quenched—what beam shall break my night?
Oh! would it shone to lead me still,
Although to death or deadliest ill!
Why marvel ye, if they who lose
1150     This present joy, this future hope,
No more with Sorrow meekly cope;
In phrensy then their fate accuse;

In madness do those fearful deeds
That seem to add but Guilt to Woe?
1155    Alas! the breast that inly bleeds
Hath nought to dread from outward blow:
Who falls from all he knows of bliss,
Cares little into what abyss.
Fierce as the gloomy vulture's now
1160    To thee, old man, my deeds appear:
I read abhorrence on thy brow,
And this too was I born to bear!
'Tis true, that, like that bird of prey,
With havock have I marked my way:
1165    But this was taught me by the dove,
To die—and know no second love.
This lesson yet hath man to learn,
Taught by the thing he dares to spurn:
The bird that sings within the brake,
1170    The swan that swims upon the lake,
One mate, and one alone, will take.
And let the fool still prone to range,
And sneer on all who cannot change,
Partake his jest with boasting boys;
1175    I envy not his varied joys,
But deem such feeble, heartless man,
Less than yon solitary swan;
Far, far beneath the shallow maid
He left believing and betrayed.
1180    Such shame at least was never mine—
Leila! each thought was only thine!
My good, my guilt, my weal, my woe,
My hope on high—my all below.
Each holds no other like to thee,
1185    Or, if it doth, in vain for me:
For worlds I dare not view the dame
Resembling thee, yet not the same.
The very crimes that mar my youth,
This bed of death—attest my truth!
1190    'Tis all too late—thou wert, thou art
The cherished madness of my heart!

# The Novel and Romance

As Walter Scott observed in his 1816 review of *Emma*, the "new style" of novel that came into being in the latter part of the eighteenth century, which he saw typified in Austen, differed from previous models in "presenting to the reader, instead of splendid scenes of an imaginary world, a correct and striking representation of that which is daily taking place around him." This judgment had been anticipated by two novelists on Austen's bookshelf, Frances Burney and Clara Reeve. In the preface to her first and most successful novel *Evelina* (1778), Burney argues that the fate of the genre rests with novelists like herself, whose goal is to retrieve both the novel and its readers from the "fantastic regions of Romance," rife with unrealistic expectations that can lead to "injury," and in sore need of "aid from sober Probability." Reeve offered similar advice in *The Progress of Romance* (1785), a critical work, in the form of a conversation, which traces developments in fiction-writing over the centuries. "Romance," observes one conversant, "is an heroic fable, which treats . . . fabulous persons and things" whereas the "Novel is a picture of real life" and "of such things, as pass every day before our eyes." Of Reeve's several novels, the most important is her gothic novel, *The Old English Baron* (1777). Many of the issues raised by Burney and Reeve are echoed by Austen in *Northanger Abbey*, both its treatment of gothic romance generally and in its famous digression on novels and novelists in Chapter 5.

## ✤ Frances Burney
### Preface to *Evelina, or the History of a Young Lady's Entrance into the World* (1778)

In the republic of letters, there is no member of such inferior rank, or who is so much disdained by his brethren of the quill, as the humble

Novelist: nor is his fate less hard in the world at large, since, among the whole class of writers, perhaps not one can be named of which the votaries are more numerous but less respectable.

Yet, while in the annals of those few of our predecessors, to whom this species of writing is indebted for being saved from contempt, and rescued from depravity, we can trace such names as Rousseau, Johnson,[1] Marivaux, Fielding, Richardson, and Smollett, no man need blush at starting from the same post, though many, nay, most men, may sigh at finding themselves distanced.

The following letters are presented to the Public—for such, by novel writers, novel readers will be called,—with a very singular mixture of timidity and confidence, resulting from the peculiar situation of the editor; who, though trembling for their success from a consciousness of their imperfections, yet fears not being involved in their disgrace, while happily wrapped up in a mantle of impenetrable obscurity.

To draw characters from nature, though not from life, and to mark the manners of the times, is the attempted plan of the following letters. For this purpose, a young female, educated in the most secluded retirement, makes, at the age of seventeen, her first appearance upon the great and busy stage of life; with a virtuous mind, a cultivated understanding, and a feeling heart, her ignorance of the forms, and inexperience in the manners of the world, occasion all the little incidents which these volumes record, and which form the natural progression of the life of a young woman of obscure birth, but conspicuous beauty, for the first six months after her Entrance into the world.

Perhaps, were it possible to effect the total extirpation of novels, our young ladies in general, and boarding-school damsels in particular, might profit from their annihilation; but since the distemper they have spread seems incurable, since their contagion bids defiance to the medicine of advice or reprehension, and since they are found to baffle all the mental art of physic, save what is prescribed by the slow regimen of Time, and bitter diet of Experience; surely all attempts to contribute to the number of those which may be read, if not with advantage, at least without injury, ought rather to be encouraged than contemned.

---

[1] "However superior the capacities in which these great writers deserve to be considered, they must pardon me that, for the dignity of my subject, I here rank the authors of Rasselas and Eloise as Novelists" (Burney's note in the preface of *Evelina*). Burney is alluding here to Johnson's satire *Rasselas* (1759) and to Jean-Jacques Rousseau's *Julie ou la nouvelle Heolise* (1761), both of which are quite didactic. Burney also names the eighteenth-century playwright Pierre de Marivaux (1688–1763), whose early career was spent writing novels.

Let me, therefore, prepare for disappointment those who, in the perusal of these sheets, entertain the gentle expectation of being transported to the fantastic regions of Romance, where Fiction is coloured by all the gay tints of luxurious Imagination, where Reason is an outcast, and where the sublimity of the Marvellous rejects all aid from sober Probability. The heroine of these memoirs, young, artless, and inexperienced, is no faultless Monster that the world ne'er saw;[2] but the offspring of Nature, and of Nature in her simplest attire.

In all the Arts, the value of copies can only be proportioned to the scarcity of originals: among sculptors and painters, a fine statue, or a beautiful picture, of some great master, may deservedly employ the imitative talents of young and inferior artists, that their appropriation to one spot may not wholly prevent the more general expansion of their excellence; but, among authors, the reverse is the case, since the noblest productions of literature are almost equally attainable with the meanest. In books, therefore, imitation cannot be shunned too sedulously; for the very perfection of a model which is frequently seen, serves but more forcibly to mark the inferiority of a copy.

To avoid what is common, without adopting what is unnatural, must limit the ambition of the vulgar herd of authors: however zealous, therefore, my veneration of the great writers I have mentioned, however I may feel myself enlightened by the knowledge of Johnson, charmed with the eloquence of Rousseau, softened by the pathetic powers of Richardson, and exhilarated by the wit of Fielding and humour of Smollett; I yet presume not to attempt pursuing the same ground which they have tracked; whence, though they may have cleared the weeds, they have also culled the flowers; and, though they have rendered the path plain, they have left it barren.

The candour of my readers I have not the impertinence to doubt, and to their indulgence I am sensible I have no claim; I have, therefore, only to intreat, that my own words may not pronounce my condemnation; and that what I have here ventured to say in regard to imitation, may be understood as it is meant, in a general sense, and not be imputed to an opinion of my own originality, which I have not the vanity, the folly, or the blindness, to entertain.

Whatever may be the fate of these letters, the editor is satisfied they will meet with justice; and commits them to the press, though hopeless of fame, yet not regardless of censure.

---

[2] From *Essay on Poetry* by John Sheffield Duke of Buckingham. The actual quote is "A faultless monster, which the World ne'er saw."

## ♣ Clara Reeve
### From *The Progress of Romance, through Times, Countries, and Manners; With Remarks on the Good and Bad Effects of it, on them Respectively: In a Course of Evening Conversations* (1785)

EUPHRASIA. The word *Novel* in all languages signifies something new. It was first used to distinguish these works from Romance, though they have lately been confounded together and are frequently mistaken for each other.

SOPHRONIA. But how will you draw the line of distinction, so as to separate them effectually, and prevent future mistakes?

EUPHRASIA. I will attempt this distinction, and I presume if it is properly done it will be followed,—If not, you are but where you were before. The Romance is an heroic fable, which treats of fabulous persons and things.—The Novel is a picture of real life and manners, and of the times in which it is written. The Romance in lofty and elevated language, describes what never happened nor is likely to happen.—The Novel gives a familiar relation of such things, as pass every day before our eyes, such as may happen to our friend, or to ourselves; and the perfection of it, is to represent every scene, in so easy and natural a manner, and to make them appear so probable, as to deceive us into a persuasion (at least while we are reading) that all is real, until we are affected by the joys or distresses, of the persons in the story, as if they were our own.

HORTENSIUS. You have well distinguished, and it is necessary to make this distinction.—I clearly perceive the difference between the Romance and Novel, and am surprized they should be confounded together.

EUPHRASIA. I have sometimes thought it has been done insidiously, by those who endeavour to render all writings of both kinds contemptible.

SOPHRONIA. I have generally observed that men of learning have spoken of them with the greatest disdain, especially collegians.

EUPHRASIA. Take care what you say my friend, they are a set of men who are not to be offended with impunity. Yet they deal in Romances, though of a different kind.—Some have taken up an opinion upon trust in others whose judgment they prefer to their own.—Others having seen a few of the worst or dullest among them, have judged of all the rest by them;—just as some men affect to despise our sex, because they have only conversed with the worst part of it. . . . Let us next consider some of the early Novels of our own country.

We had early translations of the best Novels of all other Countries, but for a long time produced very few of our own. One of the earliest I know of is the *Cyprian Academy*, by *Robert Baron* in the reign of Charles the First.[3] —Among our early Novel-writers we must reckon Mrs. *Behn*.—There are strong marks of Genius in all this lady's works, but unhappily, there are some parts of them, very improper to be read by, or recommended to virtuous minds, and especially to youth. —She wrote in an age, and to a court of licentious manners, and perhaps we ought to ascribe to these causes the loose turn of her stories.—Let us do justice to her merits, and cast the veil of compassion over her faults.—She died in the year 1689, and lies buried in the cloisters of Westminster Abbey.—The inscription will shew how high she stood in estimation at that time.

HORTENSIUS. Are you not partial to the sex of this Genius?—when you excuse in her, what you would not to a man?

EUPHRASIA. Perhaps I may, and you must excuse me if I am so, especially as this lady had many fine and amiable qualities, besides her genius for writing.

SOPHRONIA. Pray let her rest in peace,—you were speaking of the inscription on her monument, I do not remember it.

EUPHRASIA. It is as follows:

> Mrs. APHRA BEHN, 1689.
>
> Here lies a proof that wit can never be Defence enough against mortality.
>
> Let me add that Mrs. Behn will not be forgotten, so long as the Tragedy of *Oroonoko* is acted, it was from her story of that illustrious African, that Mr. Southern wrote that play, and the most affecting parts of it are taken almost literally from her.

HORTENSIUS. Peace be to her *manes*!—I shall not disturb her, or her works.

EUPHRASIA. I shall not recommend them to your perusal *Hortensius*.

The next female writer of this class is Mrs. *Manley*,[4] whose works are still more exceptionable than Mrs. *Behn*'s, and as much inferior to them in point of merit.—She hoarded up all the public and private scandal within her reach, and poured it forth,

---

[3] Robert Baron's *Cyprian Academy* (1648)?

[4] Mary Delarivier Manley (1663–1724) wrote both fiction and political pamphlets. She was a member, along with Aphra Behn and Eliza Haywood (see below), of the so-called "fair triumvirate of wit."

in a work too well known in the last age, though almost forgotten in the present; a work that partakes of the style of the Romance, and the Novel. I forbear the name, and further observations on it, as Mrs. *Manley*'s works are sinking gradually into oblivion. I am sorry to say they were once in fashion, which obliges me to mention them, otherwise I had rather be spared the pain of disgracing an Author of my own sex.

SOPHRONIA. It must be confessed that these books of the last age, were of worse tendency than any of those of the present.

EUPHRASIA. My dear friend, there were bad books at all times, for those who fought for them.—Let us pass them over in silence.

HORTENSIUS. No not yet.—Let me help your memory to one more Lady-Author of the fame class.—Mrs. *Heywood*.[5] She has the same claim upon you as those you have last mentioned.

EUPHRASIA. I had intended to have mentioned Mrs. *Heywood* though in a different way, but I find you will not suffer any part of her character to escape you.

HORTENSIUS. Why should she be spared any more than the others?

EUPHRASIA. Because she repented of her faults, and employed the latter part of her life in expiating the offences of the former.—There is reason to believe that the examples of the two ladies we have spoken of, seduced Mrs. *Heywood* into the same track; she certainly wrote some amorous novels in her youth, and also two books of the same kind as Mrs. *Manley*'s capital work, all of which I hope are forgotten.

HORTENSIUS. I fear they will not be so fortunate, they will be known to posterity by the infamous immortality, conferred upon them by *Pope* in his Dunciad.

EUPHRASIA. Mr. *Pope* was severe in his castigations, but let us be just to merit of every kind. Mrs. *Heywood* had the singular good fortune to recover a lost reputation, and the yet greater honour to atone for her errors.—She devoted the remainder of her life and labours to the service of virtue. Mrs. *Heywood* was one of the most voluminous female writers that ever England produced, none of her latter works are destitute of merit, though they do not rise to the highest pitch of excellence.—*Betsey Thoughtless* is

[5] Eliza Haywood (1693–1756) was a novelist, actress, poet, playwright, and essayist, and is best known, as Reeve indicates, for her journalistic efforts in both the *Female Spectator*, which she began in 1744, and *The Invisible Spy* (1755) as well as for her many novels, including *The History of Miss Betsey Thoughtless* (1751) and *The Fortunate Foundlings* (1744).

reckoned her best Novel; but those works by which she is most likely to be known to posterity, are the *Female Spectator*, and the *Invisible Spy*.—this lady died so lately as the year 1758.

SOPHRONIA. I have heard it often said that Mr. *Pope* was too severe in his treatment of this lady, it was supposed that she had given some private offence, which he resented publicly as was too much his way.

HORTENSIUS. That is very likely, for he was not of a forgiving disposition.—If I have been too severe also, you ladies must forgive me in behalf of your sex.

EUPHRASIA. Truth is sometimes severe.—Mrs. *Heywood's* wit and ingenuity were never denied. I would be the last to vindicate her faults, but the first to celebrate her return to virtue, and her atonement for them.

SOPHRONIA. May her first writings be forgotten, and the last survive to do her honour!

EUPHRASIA. Let us proceed to other writers.—As I purpose in future to take notice only of such Novels as are originals, or else of extraordinary merit, I must beg your allowance for all trifling flips of memory, for errors in chronology, and all other mistakes of equal consequence.—I must also have leave to mention English and Foreign books indifferently, just as they happen to rise to my memory, and observation.

HORTENSIUS. It is but just that you should have these, and every other allowance you can require, we have already laid a heavy tax upon you.

SOPHRONIA. This is an indisputable truth,—there are many objectionable scenes in *Fielding's* works, which I think *Hortensius* will not defend.

HORTENSIUS. My objections were in character, and yours are so likewise; as you have defended *Richardson*, so I will defend *Fielding*.—I allow there is some foundation for your remarks, nevertheless in all *Fielding's* works, virtue has always the superiority she ought to have, and challenges the honours that are justly due to her, the general tenor of them is in her favour, and it were happy for us, if our language had no greater cause of complaint in her behalf.

EUPHRASIA. There we will agree with you.—Have you any further observations to make upon *Fielding's* writings?

HORTENSIUS. Since you refer this part of your task to me, I will offer a few more remarks.—*Fielding's Amelia* is in much lower estimation than his *Joseph Andrews*, or *Tom Jones*; which have both received the stamp of public applause.—He likewise wrote several dramatic pieces of various merits, but these and his other works have no place in our present retrospect.—Lest you should think me too partial to the merits of this writer, I will give you the sentence of an historian upon him.

> "The Genius of *Cervantes* (says Dr. *Smollet*) was transfused into the Novels of *Fielding*, who painted the characters, and ridiculed the follies of life, with equal strength, humour and propriety."

EUPHRASIA.  We are willing to join with you in paying the tribute due to *Fielding*'s Genius, humour, and knowledge of mankind, but he certainly painted human nature as *it is*, rather than as *it ought to be*.

## ✤ Jane Austen
### From *Northanger Abbey*

[*The heroine Catherine Morland, an avid reader of novels, has made a new friend in Isabella Thorpe, who shares her passion.*]
The progress of the friendship between Catherine and Isabella was quick as its beginning had been warm, and they passed so rapidly through every gradation of increasing tenderness that there was shortly no fresh proof of it to be given to their friends or themselves. They called each other by their Christian name,[6] were always arm in arm when they walked, pinned up each other's train for the dance, and were not to be divided in the set; and if a rainy morning deprived them of other enjoyments, they were still resolute in meeting in defiance of wet and dirt, and shut themselves up, to read novels together. Yes, novels; for I will not adopt that ungenerous and impolitic custom so common with novel-writers, of degrading by their contemptuous censure the very performances, to the number of which they are themselves adding—joining with their greatest enemies in bestowing the harshest epithets on such works, and scarcely ever permitting them to be read by their own heroine, who, if she accidentally take up a novel, is sure to turn over its insipid pages with disgust. Alas! If the heroine of one novel be not patronized by the heroine of another, from whom can she expect protection and regard? I cannot approve of it. Let us leave it to the reviewers to abuse such effusions of fancy at their leisure, and over every new novel to talk in threadbare strains of the trash with which the press now groans. Let us not desert one another; we are an injured

---

[6] A sign of their intimacy; Christian names were used most commonly only by one's family.

body. Although our productions have afforded more extensive and unaffected pleasure than those of any other literary corporation in the world, no species of composition has been so much decried. From pride, ignorance, or fashion, our foes are almost as many as our readers. And while the abilities of the nine-hundredth abridger of the History of England,[7] or of the man who collects and publishes in a volume some dozen lines of Milton, Pope, and Prior, with a paper from the Spectator, and a chapter from Sterne, are eulogized by a thousand pens[8]—there seems almost a general wish of decrying the capacity and undervaluing the labour of the novelist, and of slighting the performances which have only genius, wit, and taste to recommend them. "I am no novel-reader—I seldom look into novels—Do not imagine that I often read novels—It is really very well for a novel." Such is the common cant. "And what are you reading, Miss—?" "Oh! It is only a novel!" replies the young lady, while she lays down her book with affected indifference, or momentary shame. "It is only Cecilia, or Camilla, or Belinda";[9] or, in short, only some work in which the greatest powers of the mind are displayed, in which the most thorough knowledge of human nature, the happiest delineation of its varieties, the liveliest effusions of wit and humour, are conveyed to the world in the best-chosen language. Now, had the same young lady been engaged with a volume of the Spectator, instead of such a work, how proudly would she have produced the book, and told its name; though the chances must be against her being occupied by any part of that voluminous publication, of which either the matter or manner would not disgust a young person of taste: the substance of its papers so often consisting in the statement of improbable circumstances, unnatural characters, and topics of conversation which no longer concern anyone living; and their language, too, frequently so coarse as to give no very favourable idea of the age that could endure it.

[7] Oliver Goldsmith's widely admired *History of England* (1771) was abridged in 1774, preceded by David Hume's *History of England* (1754–61); Austen wrote her own parody of the genre in 1791.

[8] An early form of anthology, quite successful in the marketplace. Matthew Prior is a poet, Laurence Sterne is another novelist, most famous for *Tristram Shandy*. The *Spectator* was a popular daily publication from 1711–1714, with various essays on manners, morals and mores, literature, and amusing character sketches.

[9] Heroines of popular novels, Frances Burney's *Cecilia, or Memoirs of an Heiress* (1782) and *Camilla, or a Picture of Youth* (1796), and Maria Edgeworth's *Belinda, A Moral Tale* (1801). Editor Claire Grogan reports that Austen was among many subscribers (paying in advance of publication) for *Camilla*—a list that included Edgeworth and other notable women of letters.

# Reviews and Other Nineteenth-Century Responses

✤ **From the *Quarterly Review* (Walter Scott) and *The Champion* on *Emma***

The reviews of *Emma* in both the *Quarterly Review* (where Scott's unsigned review appeared) and *The Champion* are probably the two most sophisticated assessments of Austen's achievement published in her lifetime. By the time *Emma* appeared in 1815, Austen had already published *Sense and Sensibility* (1811), *Pride and Prejudice* (1813) and *Mansfield Park* (1814)—a fact to which readers were alerted on the title page of *Emma* even as the author was identified only as "a lady." In the wake of four novels all by the same author, Scott was able to widen his assessment to Austen's accomplishment overall, which he saw as remarkably uniform and contributing substantially to the rise of what he described as a new "style of novel," which "draws the characters and incidents introduced more immediately from the current of ordinary life than was permitted by the former rules of the novel." *The Champion*, which focused entirely on *Emma,* was also moved by Austen's achievement to generalize about the new novel or what it called "fictitious biography" in order to distinguish works like Austen's from more extravagant "romances" or "fictitious history," where the "recesses of domestic life" are rarely plumbed. Although *The Champion* is particularly impressed by the "microscopic detail" characteristic of Austen's practice as a novelist of everyday life, Scott is not. The "faults of the author," he notes, "arise from the minute detail which the author's plan comprehends."

WALTER SCOTT REVIEW OF *EMMA, QUARTERLY REVIEW* (OCTOBER 1815, ISSUED MARCH 1816, XIV, 188–201)

There are some vices in civilized society so common that they are hardly acknowledged as stains upon the moral character, the propensity to which is nevertheless carefully concealed, even by those who most frequently give way to them; since no man of pleasure would willingly assume the gross epithet of a debauchee or a drunkard. One would almost think that novel-reading fell under this class of frailties, since among the crowds who read little else, it is not common to find an individual of hardihood sufficient to avow his taste for these frivolous studies. A novel, therefore, is frequently 'bread eaten in secret'; and it is not upon Lydia Languish's toilet alone that Tom Jones and Peregrine Pickle[1] are to be found ambushed behind works of a more grave and instructive character. And hence it has happened, that in no branch of composition, not even in poetry itself, have so many writers, and of such varied talents, exerted their powers. It may perhaps be added, that although the composition of these works admits of being exalted and decorated by the higher exertions of genius; yet such is the universal charm of narrative, that the worst novel ever written will find some gentle reader content to yawn over it, rather than to open the page of the historian, moralist, or poet. . . . but in truth, when we consider how many hours of languor and anxiety, of deserted age and solitary celibacy, of pain even and poverty, are beguiled by the perusal of these light volumes, we cannot austerely condemn the source from which is drawn the alleviation of such a portion of human misery, or consider the regulation of this department as beneath the sober consideration of the critic.

If such apologies may be admitted in judging the labours of ordinary novelists, it becomes doubly the duty of the critic to treat with kindness as well as candour works which, like this before us, proclaim a knowledge of the human heart, with the power and resolution to bring that knowledge to the service of honour and virtue.

---

[1] Lydia Languish is the overly romantic heroine in Richard Brinsley Sheridan's play, *The Rivals* (1775) and Peregrine Pickle, the egotistical dandy in Tobias Smollett's picaresque and satiric novel, *The Adventures of Peregrine Pickle* (1751).

The author is already known to the public by the two novels announced in her title-page, and both, the last especially, attracted, with justice, an attention from the public far superior to what is granted to the ephemeral productions which supply the regular demand of watering-places and circulating libraries. They belong to a class of fictions which has arisen almost in our own times, and which draws the characters and incidents introduced more immediately from the current of ordinary life than was permitted by the former rules of the novel.

In its first appearance, the novel was the legitimate child of the romance; and though the manners and general turn of the composition were altered so as to suit modern times, the author remained fettered by many peculiarities derived from the original style of romantic fiction. These may be chiefly traced in the conduct of the narrative, and the tone of sentiment attributed to the fictitious personages. . . . the author of novels was, in former times, expected to tread pretty much in the limits between the concentric circles of probability and possibility; and as he was not permitted to transgress the latter, his narrative, to make amends, almost always went beyond the bounds of the former. Now, although it may be urged that the vicissitudes of human life have occasionally led an individual through as many scenes of singular fortune as are represented in the most extravagant of these fictions, still the causes and personages acting on these changes have varied with the progress of the adventurer's fortune, and do not present that combined plot, (the object of every skilful novelist,) in which all the more interesting individuals of the dramatis personæ have their appropriate share in the action and in bringing about the catastrophe. Here, even more than in its various and violent changes of fortune, rests the improbability of the novel. The life of man rolls forth like a stream from the fountain, or it spreads out into tranquillity like a placid or stagnant lake. In the latter case, the individual grows old among the characters with whom he was born, and is contemporary,—shares precisely the sort of weal and woe to which his birth destined him,—moves in the same circle,—and, allowing for the change of seasons, is influenced by, and influences the same class of persons by which be was originally surrounded. The man of mark and of adventure, on the contrary, resembles, in the course of his life, the river whose mid-current and discharge into the ocean are widely removed from each other, as well as from the rocks and wild flowers which its fountains first reflected; violent changes of time, of place, and of circumstances, hurry him forward from one scene to another, and his adventures will usually be found only connected with each other because they have happened to the same individual. Such a history resembles an ingenious, fictitious narrative, exactly in the degree in which an old dramatic chronicle of the life and death of some distinguished character, where all the various agents appear and disappear as in the page of history, approaches a regular drama, in which every person introduced plays an appropriate part, and every point of the action tends to one common catastrophe . . . there can be no doubt that, by the studied involution and extrication of the story, by the combination of incidents new, striking and wonderful beyond the course of ordinary life, the former authors opened that obvious and strong sense of interest which arises from curiosity; as by the pure, elevated, and romantic cast of the sentiment, they conciliated those better propensities of our nature which loves to contemplate the picture of virtue, even when confessedly unable to imitate its excellences.

But strong and powerful as these sources of emotion and interest may be, they are, like all others, capable of being exhausted by habit. The imitators who rushed in crowds upon each path in which the great masters of the art had successively led the way, produced upon the public mind the usual effect of satiety. The first writer of a new class is, as it were, placed on a pinnacle of excellence, to which, at the earliest glance of a surprized admirer, his ascent seems little less than miraculous. Time and imitation speedily diminish the wonder, and each successive attempt establishes a kind of progressive scale of ascent between the lately deified author, and the reader, who had deemed his excellence inaccessible. The stupidity, the mediocrity, the merit of his imitators, are alike fatal to the first inventor, by shewing how possible it is to exaggerate his faults and to come within a certain point of his beauties.

Materials also (and the man of genius as well as his wretched imitator must work with the same) become stale and familiar. Social life, in our civilized days, affords few instances capable of being painted in the strong dark colours which excite surprize and horror; and robbers, smugglers, bailiffs, caverns, dungeons, and madhouses, have been all introduced until they ceased to interest. And thus in the novel, as in every style of composition which appeals to the public taste, the more rich and easily worked mines being exhausted, the adventurous author must, if he is desirous of success, have recourse to those which were disdained by his predecessors as unproductive, or avoided as only capable of being turned to profit by great skill and labour.

Accordingly a style of novel has arisen, within the last fifteen or twenty years, differing from the former in the points upon which the interest hinges; neither alarming our credulity nor amusing our imagination by wild variety of incident, or by those pictures of romantic affection and sensibility, which were formerly as certain attributes of fictitious characters as they are of rare occurrence among those who actually live and die. The substitute for these excitements, which had lost much of their poignancy by the repeated and injudicious use of them, was the art of copying from nature as she really exists in the common walks of life, and presenting to the reader, instead of the splendid scenes of an imaginary world, a correct and striking representation of that which is daily taking place around him.

In adventuring upon this task, the author makes obvious sacrifices, and encounters peculiar difficulty. He who paints from *le beau idéal*, if his scenes and sentiments are striking and interesting, is in a great measure exempted from the difficult task of reconciling them with the ordinary probabilities of life: but he who paints a scene of common occurrence, places his composition within that extensive range of criticism which general experience offers to every reader. The resemblance of a statue of Hercules we must take on the artist's judgment; but every one can criticize that which is presented as the portrait of a friend, or neighbour. Something more than a mere sign-post likeness is also demanded. The portrait must have spirit and character, as well as resemblance; and being deprived of all that, according to Bayes, goes 'to elevate and surprise,' it must make amends by displaying depth of knowledge and dexterity of execution. We, therefore, bestow no mean compliment upon the author of *Emma*, when we say that, keeping close to common incidents, and to such characters as occupy the ordinary walks of life, she has produced sketches of such spirit and originality, that we never miss the excitation which depends upon a narrative of uncommon events, arising from the consideration of minds, manners, and sentiments, greatly above our own. In this class she stands almost alone; for the scenes of Miss Edgeworth are laid in higher life, varied by more romantic incident, and by her remarkable power of embodying and illustrating national character. But the author of *Emma* confines herself chiefly to the middling classes of society; her most distinguished characters do not rise greatly above well-bred country gentlemen and ladies; and those which are sketched with most originality and precision, belong to a class rather below that standard. The narrative of all her novels is composed of such common occurrences as may have fallen under the observation of most folks; and her dramatis personæ conduct themselves upon the motives and principles which the readers may recognize as ruling their own and that of most of their acquaintances. The kind of moral, also, which these novels inculcate, applies equally to the paths of common life, as will best appear from a short notice of the author's former works, with a more full abstract of that which we at present have under consideration.

*Sense and Sensibility*, the first of these compositions, contains the history of two sisters. The elder, a young lady of prudence and regulated feelings, becomes gradually attached to a man of an excellent heart and limited talents, who happens unfortunately to be fettered by a rash and ill-assorted engagement. In the younger sister, the influence of sensibility and imagination predominates; and she, as was to be expected, also falls in love, but with more unbridled and wilful passion. Her lover, gifted with all the qualities of exterior polish and vivacity, proves faithless, and marries a woman of large fortune. The interest and merit of the piece depend altogether upon the behaviour of the elder sister, while obliged at once to sustain her own disappointment with fortitude, and to support her sister, who abandons herself, with unsuppressed feelings, to the indulgence of grief. The marriage of the unworthy rival at length relieves her own lover from his imprudent engagement, while her sister, turned wise by precept, example, and experience, transfers her affection to a very respectable and somewhat too serious admirer, who had nourished an unsuccessful passion through the three volumes.

In *Pride and Prejudice* the author presents us with a family of young women, bred up under a foolish and vulgar mother, and a father whose good abilities lay hid under such a load of indolence and insensibility, that he had become contented to make the foibles and follies of his wife and daughters the subject of dry and humorous sarcasm, rather than of admonition, or restraint. This is one of the portraits from ordinary life which shews our author's talents in a very strong point of view. A friend of ours, whom the author never saw or heard of, was at once recognized by his own family as the original of Mr. Bennet, and we do not know if he has yet got rid of the nickname. A Mr. Collins, too, a formal, conceited, yet servile young sprig of divinity, is drawn with the same force and precision. The story of the piece consists chiefly in the fates of the second sister, to whom a man of high birth, large fortune, but haughty and reserved manners, becomes attached, in spite of the discredit thrown upon the object of his affection by the vulgarity and ill-conduct of her relations. The lady, on the contrary, hurt at the contempt of her connections, which the lover does not even attempt to suppress, and prejudiced against him on other accounts, refuses the hand which he ungraciously offers, and does not perceive that she has done a foolish thing until she accidentally visits a very handsome seat and grounds belonging to her admirer. They chance to meet exactly as her prudence had begun to subdue her prejudice; and after some essential services rendered to her family, the lover becomes encouraged to renew his addresses, and the novel ends happily.

*Emma* has even less story than either of the preceding novels. Miss Emma Woodhouse, from whom the book takes its name, is the daughter of a gentleman of wealth and consequence residing at his seat in the immediate vicinage of a country village called Highbury. The father, a good-natured, silly valetudinary, abandons the management of his household to Emma, he himself being only occupied by his summer and winter walk, his apothecary, his gruel, and his whist table. The latter is supplied from the neighbouring village of Highbury with precisely the sort of persons who occupy the vacant corners of a regular whist table, when a village is in the neighbourhood, and better cannot be found within the family. We have the smiling and courteous vicar, who nourishes the ambitious hope of obtaining Miss Woodhouse's hand. We have Mrs. Bates, the wife of a former rector, past every thing but tea and whist; her daughter, Miss Bates, a good-natured, vulgar, and foolish old maid; Mr. Weston, a gentleman of a frank disposition and moderate fortune, in the vicinity, and his wife an amiable and accomplished person, who had been Emma's governess, and is devotedly attached to her. Amongst all these personages, Miss Woodhouse walks forth, the princess paramount, superior to all her companions in wit, beauty, fortune, and accomplishments, doated upon by her father and the Westons, admired, and almost worshipped by the more humble companions of the whist table. The object of most young ladies is, or at least is usually supposed to be, a desirable connection in marriage. But Emma Woodhouse, either anticipating the taste of a later period of life, or, like a good sovereign, preferring the weal of her subjects of Highbury to her own private interest, sets generously about making matches for her friends without thinking of matrimony on her own account. We are informed that she had been eminently successful in the case of Mr. and Miss Weston; and when the novel commences she is exerting her influence in favour of Miss Harriet Smith, a boarding-school girl without family or fortune, very good humoured, very pretty, very silly, and, what suited Miss Woodhouse's purpose best of all, very much disposed to be married.

In these conjugal machinations Emma is frequently interrupted, not only by the cautions of her father, who had a particular objection to any body committing the rash act of matrimony, but also by the sturdy reproof and remonstrances of Mr. Knightley, the elder brother of her sister's husband, a sensible country gentleman of thirty-five, who had known Emma from her cradle, and was the only person who ventured to find fault with her. In spite, however, of his censure and warning, Emma lays a plan of marrying Harriet Smith to the vicar; and though she succeeds perfectly in diverting her simple friend's thoughts from an honest farmer who had made her a very suitable offer, and in flattering her into a passion for Mr. Elton, yet, on the other hand, that conceited divine totally mistakes the nature of the encouragement held out to him, and attributes the favour which he found in Miss Woodhouse's eyes to a lurking affection on her own part. This at length encourages him to a presumptuous declaration of his sentiments; upon receiving a repulse, he looks abroad elsewhere, and enriches the Highbury society by uniting himself to a dashing young woman with as many thousands as are usually called ten, and a corresponding quantity of presumption and ill breeding.

While Emma is thus vainly engaged in forging wedlock-fetters for others, her friends have views of the same kind upon her, in favour of a son of Mr. Weston by a former marriage, who bears the name, lives under the patronage, and is to inherit the fortune of a rich uncle. Unfortunately Mr. Frank Churchill had already settled his affections on Miss Jane Fairfax, a young lady of reduced fortune; but as this was a concealed affair, Emma, when Mr. Churchill first appears on the stage, has some thoughts of being in love with him herself; speedily, however, recovering from that dangerous propensity, she is disposed to confer him upon her deserted friend Harriet Smith. Harriet has, in the interim, fallen desperately in love with Mr. Knightley, the sturdy, advice-giving bachelor; and, as all the village supposes Frank Churchill and Emma to be attached to each other, there are cross purposes enough (were the novel of a more romantic cast) for cutting half the men's throats and breaking all the women's hearts. But at Highbury Cupid walks decorously, and with good discretion, bearing his torch under a lanthorn, instead of flourishing it around to set the house on fire. All these entanglements bring on only a train of mistakes and embarrassing situations, and dialogues at balls and parties of pleasure, in which the author displays her peculiar powers of humour and knowledge of human life. The plot is extricated with great simplicity. The aunt of Frank Churchill dies; his uncle, no longer under her baneful influence, consents to his marriage with Jane Fairfax. Mr. Knightley and Emma are led, by this unexpected incident, to discover that they had been in love with each other all along. Mr. Woodhouse's objections to the marriage of his daughter are overpowered by the fears of housebreakers, and the comfort which he hopes to derive from having a stout son-in-law resident in the family; and the facile affections of Harriet Smith are transferred, like a bank bill by indorsation, to her former suitor, the honest farmer, who had obtained a favourable opportunity of renewing his addresses. Such is the simple plan of a story which we peruse with pleasure, if not with deep interest, and which perhaps we might more willingly resume than one of those narratives where the attention is strongly riveted, during the first perusal, by the powerful excitement of curiosity.

The author's knowledge of the world, and the peculiar tact with which she presents characters that the reader cannot fail to recognize, reminds us something of the merits of the Flemish school of painting. The subjects are not often elegant, and certainly never grand; but they are finished up to nature, and with a precision which delights the reader. This is a merit which it is very difficult to illustrate by extracts, because it pervades the whole work, and is not to be comprehended from a single passage. . . . The faults, on the contrary, arise from the minute detail which the author's plan comprehends. Characters of folly or simplicity, such as those of old Woodhouse and Miss Bates, are ridiculous when first presented, but if too often brought forward or too long dwelt upon, their prosing is apt to become as tiresome in fiction as in real society. Upon the whole, the turn of this author's novels bears the same relation to that of the sentimental and romantic cast, that cornfields and cottages and meadows bear to the highly adorned grounds of a show mansion, or the rugged sublimities of a mountain landscape. It is neither so captivating as the one, nor so grand as the other, but it affords to those who frequent it a pleasure nearly allied with the experience of their own social habits; and what is of some importance, the youthful wanderer may return from his promenade to the ordinary business of life, without any chance of having his head turned by the recollection of the scene through which he has been wandering.

One word, however, we must say in behalf of that once powerful divinity, Cupid, king of gods and men, who in these times of revolution, has been assailed, even in his own kingdom of romance, by the authors who were formerly his devoted priests. We are quite aware that there are few instances of first attachment being brought to a happy conclusion, and that it seldom can be so in a state of society so highly advanced as to render early marriages among the better class, acts, generally speaking, of imprudence. But the youth of this realm need not at present be taught the doctrine of selfishness. It is by no means their error to give the world or the good things of the world all for love; and before the authors of moral fiction couple Cupid indivisibly with calculating prudence, we would have them reflect, that they may sometimes lend their aid to substitute more mean, more sordid, and more selfish motives of conduct, for the romantic feelings which their predecessors perhaps fanned into too powerful a flame. Who is it, that in his youth has felt a virtuous attachment, however romantic or however unfortunate, but can trace back to its influence much that his character may possess of what is honourable, dignified, and disinterested? If he recollects hours wasted in unavailing hope, or saddened by doubt and disappointment; he may also dwell on many which have been snatched from folly or libertinism, and dedicated to studies which might render him worthy of the object of his affection, or pave the way perhaps to that distinction necessary to raise him to an equality with her. Even the habitual indulgence of feelings totally unconnected with ourself and our own immediate interest, softens, graces, and amends the human mind; and after the pain of disappointment is past, those who survive (and by good fortune those are the greater number) are neither less wise nor less worthy members of society for having felt, for a time, the influence of a passion which has been well qualified as the 'tenderest, noblest and best.'

UNSIGNED REVIEW OF *EMMA, IN THE CHAMPION*,
31 MARCH 1816, PP. 102–103.

The imitative arts—and novel-writing is the art of imitating in a narrative the scenes of life—are productive of two distinct gratifications;—one, arising from the intrinsic beauty of grandeur of the objects represented, and the other, from the skill of the artist, shown in representing objects of an ordinary, and at the same time so familiar a nature, as to invite an easy comparison between the prototype and the imitation, and to draw the intellectual faculties into a pleasing criticism on the merits of his imitative efforts. The latter, rather than the former, is the principal attraction which we hold out to our readers in recommending to them the volumes before us. One rare merit which they possess, is an entire freedom from anything like the pretence or technicality of authorship.— Their style is easy, unaffected, and fluent. Simple elementary affections of middling life, and the little obvious peculiarities of character, are all which the authoress (for they are the work of a lady) pretends or professes to exhibit. Those who exclusively estimate the value of a work of fiction by its appeals to the more elevated feelings, and its display of the complex machinery of dark passions and imaginative sensations, will find very little to their taste, we fear, in the homely pictures of these volumes. Even of the sober pathos of domestic affliction, there is very little for the sentimental reader.—Lively sketches of comfortable home-scenes— graphic details of the localities of provincial life—pictures of worthy affections, unassuming amusements and occupations, and most spirited and racy touches of the grotesque peculiarities which diversify human character, are the claims which our authoress puts forth to popularity. She presents nature and society in very unornamented hues; and yet, so strong is the force of nature, that we will venture to say, few can take up her work without finding a rational pleasure in the recognitions which cannot fail to flash upon them of the modes of thinking and feeling which experience every day presents in real life. Her scenes have the advantage of being of that middling stamp, which come within the observation of a very large proportion of readers. The country house is no castle or hall of honour,—but a plain mansion, with a shrubbery and large gates, such as every one knows at the top of a populous village, looked up to as the great house of the place; and when we are occasionally transported to London, our authoress has the originality to waive Grosvenor or Berkeley-squares, and set us down in humble Brunswick-square. There is a corresponding modesty in her characters. If we take her own description of them, one is "rational and unaffected," another, "straight-forward and open-hearted;" and the heroine herself, who gives title to the work, is content with being "handsome, clever, and rich;"—to which we will add, lively, conceited, and rather proud, but benevolent, amiable, volatile,—and addicted to a very extraordinary occupation for a young lady, by no means hors de combat—being only twenty-one—viz. that of matchmaking. The scrapes and entanglements in which she involves herself in the pursuit of this dangerous amusement, are ingeniously managed, and give great life and interest to some parts of the work.

Our authoress excels also in characters of another stamp. Mr. and Mrs. John Knightley, are a picture of an estimable pair. The husband of dignified sense and rather reserved disposition: English in his faults, English in his virtues,—warm in his affections, and very intolerant of heartlessness and frivolity of all sorts: the wife, just perhaps what a wife ought to be—a pattern of affectionate and devoted zeal for her husband and children—sufficiently sensible—not at all clever—of a small mind which the ties and duties of domestic life abundantly fill—with qualities which rather endear than adorn, and are grounded in pure and ardent feelings, rather than in superior intellect.—Such characters as these are by no means to be included in the sweeping sentence of insipidity, with which some persons are inclined to banish all unpretending goodness from the dramatis personae of a novel.—The whole weight of this sentence should be kept for those monsters of romantic and incongruous virtues, who have escaped the Taygetan mount they deserve.[2] Life and identity are all that characters want—it is undoubtedly difficult, though not impossible to give these to characters of pretty uniform virtue. In history, goodness frequently makes but a dull figure,—because in the wide survey of events, little attention can be allotted to any thing but actions which immediately operate upon these.—But novels are rather fictitious biography, as romances may be called fictitious history.—To the historian's generalizing eye, unobtrusive virtue presents few features of prominence or splendour;—but the novelist has the licence of ranging into the recesses of domestic life, and of distinguishing the actions of the mind, the temper, and the feelings. Surveyed in this microscopic detail, characters which, to a more sweeping observer, furnish only the uniform outlines of virtue and worth, will always be found to exhibit sufficiently distinctive traits of mental and moral individuality, to

---

[2] An allusion to the mythological figure Taygeta, who hid herself under Mount Taygetus in order to escape Zeus' advances.

answer all an author's objects of giving them a personal identity and relief. The same observations which apply to history, apply more strongly, though on the same principle, to poetry,—for history is poetical as it deals in the grand, the general, and the aggregate,—without alluding to their primitive connection, the earliest poems being historical, and the earliest histories poetical.

We must shut up these amusing volumes, which plainly manifest the author to be a woman of good sense, knowledge of the world, discriminating perception and acute observation, and we are only sorry that our space will not permit us to give our readers a more exact idea of their contents.

Our authoress, though no great dabbler in poetry or quotations, quotes Cooper [*sic*]—It would perhaps not be difficult to account for the fact of every lady's admiring Cooper.

## ♣ Contemporary Reviews of *Persuasion*

Published posthumously in 1817 with the much earlier *Northanger Abbey* and with a prefatory "biographical notice" by Austen's brother Henry, the first reviews of *Persuasion* were forced to deal not only with two novels that had relatively little in common beyond their Bath setting, but also with Henry's characterization of his sister "as thoroughly religious and devout." Richard Whately, archbishop of Dublin, whose 1821 review in the *Quarterly* was, like that of his predecessor Walter Scott, a wide-ranging assessment of Austen's achievement overall, echoed Henry Austen in observing that Austen was "evidently a Christian writer," whose writings had imparted "moral lessons" in a uniquely palatable way by "combining . . . instruction with amusement." *Blackwood's Edinburgh Magazine* similarly pursued the theme of Austen's Christianity in its 1818 review, noting at the same time that her works "will appear very defective to that class of readers who are constantly hunting after the broad display of religious sentiments and opinions." And the *British Critic*, which quoted extensively from the biographical notice, focused, as did many early readers of Austen, on "her remarkable talent for observation . . . in recording the customs and manners of commonplace people in the commonplace intercourse of life." Regrettably, neither *Blackwood's* nor the *British Critic* devotes much space to *Persuasion* itself. However, all three reviews echo previous assessments in stressing the naturalness, realism, and probability of Austen's representations overall.

## ♣ Unsigned review, *British Critic* (March 1818, n.s. ix, 293–301)

In order to impart some degree of variety to our journal, and select matter suited to all tastes, we have generally made it a point to notice one or two of the better sort of novels; but, did our fair readers know, what a vast quantity of useful spirits and patience, we are for this purpose generally forced to exhaust, before we are able to stumble upon any thing that we can at all recommend to their approbation; what innumerable letters we are compelled to read from the witty Lady Harriet F———to the pathetic Miss Lucretia G———; through what an endless series of gloomy caverns, long and winding passages, secret trap doors, we are forced to pass— now in the Inquisition, now in a gay modern assembly—this moment in the cast wing of an old castle in the Pyrenees; in the next, among banditti; and so on, through all the changes and chances of this transitory life, acquiescing in every thing, with an imperturbable confidence, that he or she, who has brought us into all these difficulties, will, in their own good time, release us from them: sure we are, that even the most resolute foes to all the solid parts of learning, will agree with us in admitting, that the sound and orthodox divinity with which so considerable a portion of our pages is usually filled, and of which we have so often had the mortification to hear many sensible young ladies complain, is nevertheless very far from being quite so dull and exhausting, as are their own favourite studies, when indiscriminately pursued. In return for this concession on their part, we on our's will frankly allow, that a good novel, such, for example, as that at present before us, is, perhaps, among the most fascinating productions of modern literature, though we cannot say, that it is quite so improving as some others.

*Northanger Abbey* and *Persuasion*, are the productions of a pen, from which our readers have already received several admired productions; and it is with most unfeigned regret, that we are forced to add, they will be the last . . .

With respect to the talents of Jane Austen, they need no other voucher, than the works which she has left behind her; which in some of the best qualities of the best sort of novels, display a degree of excellence that has not been often surpassed. In imagination, of all kinds, she appears to have been extremely deficient; not only her stories are utterly and entirely devoid of invention, but her characters, her incidents, her sentiments, are obviously all drawn exclusively from experience. The sentiments which she puts into the mouths of her actors, are the sentiments, which we are every day in the habit of hearing; and as to her actors themselves, we are persuaded that fancy, strictly so called, has had much less to do with them, than with the characters of Julius Caesar, Hannibal, or Alexander, as represented to us by historians. At description she seldom aims; at that vivid and poetical sort of description, which we have of late been accustomed to, (in the novels of a celebrated anonymous writer) never; she seems to have no other object in view, than simply to paint some of those scenes which she has herself seen, and which every one, indeed, may witness daily. Not only her characters are all of them belonging to the middle size, and with a tendency, in fact, rather to fall below, than to rise above the common standard, but even the incidents of her novels, are of the same description. Her heroes and heroines, make love and are married, just as her readers make love, and were or will be, married; no unexpected ill fortune occurs to prevent, nor any unexpected good fortune, to bring about the events on which her novels hinge. She seems to be describing such people as meet together every night, in every respectable house in London; and to relate such incidents as have probably happened, one time or other, to half the families in the United Kingdom. And yet, by a singular good judgment, almost every individual represents a class; not a class of humourists, or of any of the rarer specimens of our species, but one of those classes to which we ourselves, and every acquaintance we have, in all probability belong. The fidelity with which these are distinguished is often admirable. It would have been impossible to discriminate the characters of the common-place people, whom she employs as the instruments of her novels, by any set and formal descriptions; for the greater part of them, are such as we generally describe by saying that they are persons of 'no characters at all.' Accordingly our authoress gives no definitions; but she makes her *dramatis personæ* talk; and the sentiments which she places in their mouths, the little phrases which she makes them use, strike so familiarly upon our memory as soon as we hear them repeated, that we instantly recognize among some of our acquaintance, the sort of persons she intends to signify, as accurately as if we had heard their voices. This is the forte of our authoress; as soon as ever she leaves the shore of her own experience, and attempts to delineate fancy characters, or such as she may perhaps have often heard of, but possibly never seen, she falls at once to the level of mere ordinary novellists. Her merit consists altogether in her remarkable talent for observation; no ridiculous phrase, no affected sentiment, no foolish pretension seems to escape her notice. It is scarcely possible to read her novels, without meeting with some of one's own absurdities reflected back upon one's conscience; and this, just in the light in which they ought to appear. For in recording the customs and manners of commonplace people in the commonplace intercourse of life, our authoress never dips her pen in satire; the follies which she holds up to us, are, for the most part, mere follies, or else natural imperfections; and she treats them, as such, with good-humoured pleasantry; mimicking them so exactly, that we always laugh at the ridiculous truth of the imitation, but without ever being incited to indulge in feelings, that might tend to render us ill-natured, and intolerant in society. This is the result of that good sense which seems ever to keep complete possession over all the other qualities of the mind of our authoress; she sees every thing just as it is; even her want of imagination (which is the principal defect of her writings) is useful to her in this respect, that it enables her to keep clear of all exaggeration, in a mode of writing where the least exaggeration would be fatal; for if the people and the scenes which she has chosen, as the subjects of her composition, be not painted with perfect truth, with exact and striking resemblance, the whole effect ceases; her characters have no kind of merit in themselves, and whatever interest they excite in the mind of the reader, results almost entirely, from the unaccountable pleasure, which, by a peculiarity in our nature, we derive from a simple imitation of any object, without any reference to the abstract value of importance of the object itself. This fact is notorious in painting; and the novels of Miss Austen alone, would be sufficient to prove, were proof required, that the same is true in the department of literature, which she has adorned. For our readers will perceive (from the instance which we are now about to present, in the case of the novels before us,) that be their merit what it may, it is not founded upon the interest of a narrative. In fact, so little narrative is there in either of the two novels of which the publication before us consists, that it is difficult to give any thing like an abstract of their contents.

*Northanger Abbey*, is one of the very best of Miss Austen's productions, and will every way repay the time and trouble of perusing it. Some of the incidents in it are rather improbable, and the character of General Tilney seems to have been drawn from imagination, for it is not a very probable character, and is not pourtrayed with our authoress's usual taste and judgment. There is also a considerable want of delicacy in all the circumstances of Catherine's visit to the Abbey; but it is useless to point them out; the interest of the novel, is so little founded upon the ingenuity or probability of the story, that any criticism upon the management of it, falls with no weight upon that which constitutes its appropriate praise, considered as a literary product. With respect to the second of the novels, which the present publication contains, it will be necessary to say but little. It is in every respect a much less fortunate performance than that which we have just been considering. It is manifestly the work of the same mind, and contains parts of very great merit; among them, however, we certainly should not number its moral, which seems to be, that young people should always marry according to their own inclinations and upon their own judgment; for that if in consequence of listening to grave counsels, they defer their marriage, till they have wherewith to live upon, they will be laying the foundation for years of misery, such as only the heroes and heroines of novels can reasonably hope ever to see the end of.

## ✤ Unsigned notice of *Northanger Abbey* and *Persuasion, Blackwood's Edinburgh Magazine* (May 1818, n.s.ii, 453–5)

We are happy to receive two other novels from the pen of this amiable and agreeable authoress, though our satisfaction is much alloyed, from the feeling, that they must be the last. We have always regarded her works as possessing a higher claim to public estimation than perhaps they have yet attained. They have fallen, indeed, upon an age whose taste can only be gratified with the highest seasoned food. This, as we have already hinted, may be partly owing to the wonderful realities which it has been our lot to witness. We have been spoiled for the tranquil enjoyment of common interests, and nothing now will satisfy us in fiction, any more than in real life, but grand movements and striking characters. A singular union has, accordingly, been attempted between history, and poetry. The periods of great events have been seized on as a ground work for the display of powerful or fantastic characters: correct and instructive pictures of national peculiarities have been exhibited; and even in those fictions which are altogether wild and monstrous, some insight has been given into the passions and theories which have convulsed and bewildered this our 'age of Reason.' In the poetry of Mr. Scott and Lord Byron, in the novels of Miss Edgeworth,

Mr. Godwin, and the author of *Waverley*, we see exemplified in different forms this influence of the spirit of the times,—the prevailing love of historical, and at the same time romantic incident,—dark and high-wrought passions,—the delineations, chiefly of national character,—the pursuit of some substance, in short, yet of an existence more fanciful often than absolute fiction,—the dislike of a cloud, yet the form which is embraced, nothing short of a Juno. In this raised state of our imaginations, we cannot, it may be supposed, all at once descend to the simple representations of common life, to incidents which have no truth, except that of universal nature, and have nothing of fiction except in not having really happened,—yet the time, probably, will return, when we shall take a more permanent delight in those familiar cabinet pictures, than even in the great historical pieces of our more eminent modern masters; when our sons and daughters will deign once more to laugh over the Partridges and the Trullibers, and to weep over the Clementinas and Clarissas of pass times, as we have some distant recollection of having been able to do ourselves, before we were so entirely engrossed with the Napoleons of real life, or the Corsairs of poetry; and while we could enjoy a work that was all written in pure English, without ever dreaming how great would be the embellishment to have at least one half of it in the dialect of Scotland or of Ireland.

When this period arrives, we have no hesitation in saying, that the delightful writer of the works now before us, will be one of the most popular of English novelists, and if, indeed, we could point out the individual who, within a certain limited range, has attained the highest perfection of the art of novel writing, we should have little scruple in fixing upon her. She has confined herself, no doubt, to a narrow walk. She never operates among deep interests, uncommon characters, or vehement passions. The singular merit of her writings is, that we could conceive, without the slightest strain of imagination, any one of her fictions to be realized in any town or village in England, (for it is only English manners that she paints,) that we think we are reading the history of people whom we have seen thousands of times, and that with all this perfect commonness, both of incident and character, perhaps not one of her characters is to be found in any other book, portrayed at least in so lively and interesting a manner. She has much observation,—much fine sense,—much delicate humour,—many pathetic touches,—and throughout all her works, a most charitable view of human nature and a tone of gentleness and purity that are almost unequalled. It is unnecessary to give a particular account of the stories here presented to us. They have quite the same kind of merit with the preceding works of their author. As stories they are nothing in themselves, though beautiful and simple in their combination with the characters. The first is the more lively, and the second the more pathetic; but such is the facility and the seemingly exhaustless invention of this lady, that, we think, like a complete mistress of a musical instrument, she could have gone on in the same strain for ever, and her happy talent of seeing something to interest in the most common scenes of life, could evidently never have been without a field to work upon. But death has deprived us of this most fascinating companion, and the few prefatory pages which contain a sketch of her life, almost come upon us like the melancholy invitation to the funeral of one whom we had long known and loved.

She was the daughter of a clergyman of the name of Austen, 'a scholar and a ripe one,' whose care of her education was soon rewarded by the early promise which she displayed. It was not, however, till after his death that she published any of her works; 'for though in composition she was equally rapid and correct, yet an invincible distrust of her own judgment induced her to withhold her writings from the public till time and many perusals had satisfied her that the charm of recent composition was dissolved.' She lived a quite and retired life with her mother and sister, in the neighbourhood of Southampton, when early in 1816 she was attacked by the disease which carried her off. It was a decline, at first deceitfully slow, and which her natural good constitution and regular habits, had given little room to dread. 'She supported all the varying pain, irksomeness and tedium attendant on decaying nature, with more than resignation,—with a truly elastic cheerfulness. She retained her faculties, her memory, her fancy, her temper, and her affections warm, clear, and unimpaired to the last. Neither her love of God nor of her fellow creatures flagged for a moment.' The following passages from a letter written a few weeks before her death, are the best representation of her happy state of mind. 'My attendant is encouraging, and talks of making me quite well. I live chiefly on the sofa, but am allowed to walk from one room to another. I have been out once in a sedan chair, and am to repeat it, and be promoted to a wheel chair as the weather serves. On this subject I will only say further, that my dearest sister, my tender, watchful, indefatigable nurse, has not been made ill by her exertions. As to what I owe to her, and to the anxious affection of all my beloved family on this occasion, I can only cry over it, and pray to God to bless them more and more.' She then turns off in her lively way to another subject. 'You will find Captain———a very respectable, well meaning man, without much manners,—his wife and sister all good humour and obligingness, and, I hope, (since the fashion allows it,) with rather longer petticoats than last year.'

Such was this admirable person, the character of whose life fully corresponds with that of her writings. There is the same good sense, happiness, and purity in both. Yet they will appear very defective to that class of readers who are constantly hunting after the broad display of religious sentiments and opinions. It has been left for this age to discover that Mr. Addison himself was scarcely a Christian:[3] but we are very certain, that neither the temper of his writings, nor even that of Miss Austen's, (novels as they are, and filled with accounts of balls and plays, and such abominations,) could well have been formed without a feeling of the spirit of Christianity.

### ❧ Richard Whately on Jane Austen, unsigned review of *Northanger Abbey* and *Persuasion*, *Quarterly Review* (January 1821, xxiv, 352–76)

The times seem to be past when an apology was requisite from reviewers for condescending to notice a novel; when they felt themselves bound in dignity to deprecate the suspicion of paying much regard to such trifles, and pleaded the necessity of occasionally stooping to humour the taste of their fair readers. The delights of fiction, if not more keenly or more generally relished, are at least more readily acknowledged by men of sense and taste; and we have lived to hear the merits of the best of this class of writings earnestly discussed by some of the ablest scholars and soundest reasoners of the present day.

We are inclined to attribute this change, not so much to an alteration in the public taste, as in the character of the productions in question. Novels may not, perhaps, display more genius now than formerly, but they contain more solid sense; they may not afford

---

[3] Joseph Addison (1672–1719) was a famous politician and writer, who collaborated with Richard Steele in establishing *The Spectator* magazine in 1711. He also wrote a play, *Cato, A Tragedy* (1712).

higher gratification, but it is of a nature which men are less disposed to be ashamed of avowing. We remarked, in a former Number, in reviewing a work of the author now before us, that 'a new style of novel has arisen, within the last fifteen or twenty years, differing from the former in the points upon which the interest hinges; neither alarming our credulity nor amusing our imagination by wild variety of incident, or by those pictures of romantic affection and sensibility, which were formerly as certain attributes of fictitious characters as they are of rare occurrence among those who actually live and die. The substitute for these excitements, which had lost much of their poignancy by the repeated and injudicious use of them, was the art of copying from nature as she really exists in the common walks of life, and presenting to the reader, instead of the splendid scenes of an imaginary world, a correct and striking representation of that which is daily taking place around him.'[4]

Now, though the origin of this new school of fiction may probably be traced, as we there suggested, to the exhaustion of the mines from which materials for entertainment had been hitherto extracted, and the necessity of gratifying the natural craving of the reader for variety, by striking into an untrodden path; the consequences resulting from this change have been far greater than the mere supply of this demand. When this Flemish painting, as it were, is introduced— this accurate and unexaggerated delineation of events and characters—it necessarily follows, that a novel, which makes good its pretensions of giving a perfectly correct picture of common life, becomes a far more *instructive* work than one of equal or superior merit of the other class; it guides the judgment, and supplies a kind of artificial experience. It is a remark of the great father of criticism, that poetry (i.e. narrative, and dramatic poetry) is of a more philosophical character than history; inasmuch as the latter details what has actually happened, of which many parts may chance to be exceptions to the general rules of probability, and consequently illustrate no general principles; whereas the former shews us what must naturally, or would probably, happen under given circumstances; and thus displays to us a comprehensive view of human nature, and furnishes general rules of practical wisdom. It is evident, that this will apply only to such fictions as are quite *perfect* in respect of the probability of their story; and that he, therefore, who resorts to the

---

[4] This is from Scott's review of *Emma*, which appeared previously in the same journal.

fabulist rather than the historian, for instruction in human character and conduct, must throw himself entirely on the judgment and skill of his teacher, and give him credit for talents much more rare than the accuracy and veracity which are the chief requisites in history. We fear, therefore, that the exultation which we can conceive some of our gentle readers to feel, at having Aristotle's warrant for (what probably they had never dreamed of) the *philosophical character* of their studies, must, in practice, be somewhat qualified, by those sundry little violations of probability which are to be met with in most novels; and which so far lower their value, as models of real life, that a person who had no other preparation for the world than is afforded by them, would form, probably, a less accurate idea of things as they are, than he would of a lion from studying merely the representations on China tea-pots.

Accordingly, a heavy complaint has long lain against works of fiction, as giving a false picture of what they profess to imitate, and disqualifying their readers for the ordinary scenes and everyday duties of life. And this charge applies, we apprehend, to the generality of what are strictly called novels, with even more justice than to romances. When all the characters and events are very far removed from what we see around us,—when, perhaps, even supernatural agents are introduced, the reader may indulge, indeed, in occasional day-dreams, but will be so little reminded of what he has been reading, by any thing that occurs in actual life, that though he may perhaps feel some disrelish for the tameness of the scene before him, compared with the fairy-land he has been visiting, yet at least his judgment will not be depraved, nor his expectations misled; he will not apprehend a meeting with Algerine[5] banditti on English shores, nor regard the old woman who shews him about an antique country seat, as either an enchantress or the keeper of an imprisoned damsel. But it is otherwise with those fictions which differ from common life in little or nothing but the improbability of the occurrences: the reader is insensibly led to calculate upon some of those lucky incidents and opportune coincidences of which he has been so much accustomed to read, and which, it is undeniable, *may* take place in real life; and to feel a sort of confidence, that however romantic his conduct may be, and in whatever difficulties it may involve him, all will be sure to come right at last, as is invariably the case with the hero of a novel.

[5] Algerian.

On the other hand, so far as these pernicious effects fail to be produced, so far does the example lose its influence, and the exercise of poetical justice is rendered vain. The reward of virtuous conduct being brought about by fortunate accidents, he who abstains (taught, perhaps, by bitter disappointments) from reckoning on such accidents, wants that encouragement to virtue, which alone has been held out to him. 'If I were *a man in a novel*,' we remember to have heard an ingenious friend observe, 'I should certainly act so and so, because I should be sure of being no loser by the most heroic self-devotion, and of ultimately succeeding in the most daring enterprises.'

It may be said, in answer, that these objections apply only to the *unskilful* novelist, who, from ignorance of the world, gives an unnatural representation of what he professes to delineate. This is partly true, and partly not; for there is a distinction to be made between the *unnatural* and the merely *improbable*: a fiction is unnatural when there is some assignable reason against the events taking place as described,—when men are represented as acting contrary to the character assigned them, or to human nature in general; as when a young lady of seventeen, brought up in ease, luxury and retirement, with no companions but the narrow-minded and illiterate, displays (as a heroine usually does) under the most trying circumstances, such wisdom, fortitude, and knowledge of the world, as the best instructors and the best examples can rarely produce without the aid of more mature age and longer experience.— On the other hand, a fiction is still *improbable*, though *not unnatural*, when there is no reason to be assigned why things should not take place as represented, except that the *overbalance of chances* is against it; the hero meets, in his utmost distress, most opportunely, with the very person to whom he had formerly done a signal service, and who happens to communicate to him a piece of intelligence which sets all to rights. Why should he not meet him as well as any one else? all that can be said is, that there is no reason why he should. The infant who is saved from a wreck, and who afterwards becomes such a constellation of virtues and accomplishments, turns out to be no other than the nephew of the very gentleman, on whose estate the waves had cast him, and whose lovely daughter he had so long sighed for in vain: there is no reason to be given, except from the calculation of chances, why he should not have been thrown on one part of the coast as well as another. Nay, it would be nothing unnatural, though the most determined novel-reader would be shocked at its improbability, if all the hero's enemies, while they were conspiring his ruin, were to be struck dead together by a lucky flash of lightning: yet many denouements which *are* decidedly unnatural, are better tolerated than this would be. The distinction which we have been pointing out may be plainly perceived in the events of real life; when any thing takes place of such a nature as we should call, in a fiction, merely improbable, because there are many chances against it, we call it a lucky or unlucky accident, a singular coincidence, something very extraordinary, odd, curious, &c.; whereas any thing which, in a fiction, would be called unnatural, when it actually occurs, (and such things do occur,) is still called unnatural, inexplicable, unaccountable, inconceivable, &c. epithets which are not applied to events that have merely the balance of chances against them.

When, therefore, the generality, even of the most approved novels, were of this character, (to say nothing of the heavier charges brought, of inflaming the passions of young persons by warm descriptions, weakening their abhorrence of profligacy by exhibiting it in combination with the most engaging qualities, and presenting vice in all its allurements, while setting forth the triumphs of 'virtue rewarded') it is not to be wondered that the grave guardians of youth should have generally stigmatized the whole class, as 'serving only to fill young people's heads with romantic love-stories, and rendering them unfit to mind any thing else.' That this censure and caution should in many instances be indiscriminate, can surprize no one, who recollects how rare a quality discrimination is; and how much better it suits indolence, as well as ignorance, to lay down a rule, than to ascertain the exceptions to it: we are acquainted with a careful mother whose daughters, while they never in their lives read a *novel* of any kind, are permitted to peruse, without reserve, any *plays* that happen to fall in their way; and with another, from whom no lessons, however excellent, of wisdom and piety, contained in a *prose-fiction*, can obtain quarter; but who, on the other hand, is no less indiscriminately indulgent to her children in the article of tales in *verse*, of whatever character.

The change, however, which we have already noticed, as having taken place in the character of several modern novels, has operated in a considerable degree to do away this prejudice; and has elevated this species of composition, in some respects at least, into a much higher class. For most of that instruction which used to be presented to the world in the shape of formal dissertations, or shorter and more desultory moral essays, such as those of *The Spectator* and

*Rambler,*[6] we may now resort to the pages of the acute and judicious, but not less amusing, novelists who have lately appeared. If
their views of men and manners are no less just than those of the
essayists who preceded them, are they to be rated lower because
they present to us these views, not in the language of general
description, but in the form of well-constructed fictitious narrative?
If the practical lessons they inculcate are no less sound and useful, it
is surely no diminution of their merit that they are conveyed by
example instead of precept: nor, if their remarks are neither less
wise nor less important, are they the less valuable for being represented as thrown out in the course of conversations suggested by
the circumstances of the speakers, and perfectly in character. The
praise and blame of the moralist are surely not the less effectual for
being bestowed, not in general declamation, on classes of men, but
on individuals representing those classes, who are so clearly delin-
eated and brought into action before us, that we seem to be
acquainted with them, and feel an interest in their fate.

Biography is allowed, on all hands, to be one of the most attractive and profitable kinds of reading: now such novels as we have been
speaking of, being a kind of fictitious biography, bear the same relation to the real, that epic and tragic poetry, according to Aristotle,
bear to history: they present us (supposing, of course, each perfect in
its kind) with the general, instead of the particular,—the probable,
instead of the true; and, by leaving out those accidental irregularities,
and exceptions to general rules, which constitute the many improba-
bilites of real narrative, present us with a clear and *abstracted* view of
the general rules themselves; and thus concentrate, as it were, into a
small compass, the net result of wide experience.

Among the authors of this school there is no one superior, if
equal, to the lady whose last production is now before us, and
whom we have much regret in finally taking leave of: her death (in
the prime of life, considered as a writer) being announced in this the
first publication to which her name is prefixed. We regret the failure
not only of a source of innocent amusement, but also of that supply
of practical good sense and instructive example, which she would
probably have continued to furnish better than any of her contemporaries:—Miss Edgeworth, indeed, draws characters and details
conversations, such as they occur in real life, with a spirit and

---

[6] *The Rambler* was semi-weekly periodical featuring essays on morality, politics,
religion, and society written by Samuel Johnson. It ran from 1750 to 1752.

fidelity not to be surpassed; but her stories are most romantically improbable, (in the sense above explained,) almost all the important events of them being brought about by most *providential coincidences*; and this, as we have already remarked, is not merely faulty, inasmuch as it evinces a want of skill in the writer, and gives an air of clumsiness to the fiction, but is a very considerable drawback on its practical utility: the personages either of fiction or history being then only profitable examples, when their good or ill conduct meets its appropriate reward, not from a sort of independent machinery of accidents, but as a necessary or probable result, according to the ordinary course of affairs.

Miss Austin has the merit (in our judgment most essential) of being evidently a Christian writer: a merit which is much enhanced, both on the score of good taste, and of practical utility, by her religion being not at all obtrusive. She might defy the most fastidious critic to call any of her novels, Coelebs was designated, we will not say altogether without reason,[7] a 'dramatic sermon.' The subject is rather alluded to, and that incidentally, than studiously brought forward and dwelt upon. In fact she is more sparing of it than would be thought desirable by some persons; perhaps even by herself, had she consulted merely her own sentiments; but she probably introduced it as far as she thought would be generally acceptable and profitable: for when the purpose of inculcating a religious principle is made too palpably prominent, many readers, if they do not throw aside the book with disgust, are apt to fortify themselves with that respectful kind of apathy with which they undergo a regular sermon, and prepare themselves as they do to swallow a dose of medicine, endeavouring to *get it down* in large gulps, without tasting it more than is necessary.

The moral lessons also of this lady's novels, though clearly and impressively conveyed, are not offensively put forward, but spring incidentally from the circumstances of the story; they are not forced upon the reader, but he is left to collect them (though without any difficulty) for himself: her's is that unpretending kind of instruction which is furnished by real life; and certainly no author has ever conformed more closely to real life, as well in the incidents, as in the characters and descriptions. Her fables appear to us to be, in their own way, nearly faultless; they do not consist (like those of some of

---

[7] Hannah More (1745–1833), a religious writer, wrote the didactic novel *Coelebs in Search of Wife* (1809).

the writers who have attempted this kind of common-life novel writing) of a string of unconnected events which have little or no bearing on one main plot, and are introduced evidently for the sole purpose of bringing in characters and conversations; but have all that compactness of plan and unity of action which is generally produced by a sacrifice of probability: yet they have little or nothing that is not probable; the story proceeds without the aid of extraordinary accidents; the events which take place are the necessary or natural consequences of what has preceded: and yet (which is a very rare merit indeed) the final catastrophe is scarcely ever clearly foreseen from the beginning, and very often comes, upon the generality of readers at least, quite unexpected. We know not whether Miss Austin ever had access to the precepts of Aristotle; but there are few, if any, writers of fiction who have illustrated them more successfully.

The vivid distinctness of description, the minute fidelity of detail, and air of unstudied ease in the scenes represented, which are no less necessary than probability of incident, to carry the reader's imagination along with the story, and give fiction the perfect appearance of reality, she possesses in a high degree; and the object is accomplished without resorting to those deviations from the ordinary plan of narrative in the third person, which have been patronized by some eminent masters. We allude to the two other methods of conducting a fictitious story, viz. either by narrative in the first person, when the hero is made to tell his own tale, or by a series of letters; both of which we conceive have been adopted with a view of heightening the resemblance of the fiction to reality. At first sight, indeed, there might appear no reason why a story told in the first person should have more the air of a real history than in the third; especially as the majority of real histories actually are in the third person; nevertheless, experience seems to show that such is the case: provided there be no want of skill in the writer, the resemblance to real life, of a fiction thus conducted, will approach much the nearest (other points being equal) to a deception, and the interest felt in it, to that which we feel in real transactions.

Nevertheless novels in the first person have not succeeded so well as to make that mode of writing become very general. It is objected to them, not without reason, that they want a *hero*: the person intended to occupy that post being the narrator himself, who of course cannot so describe his own conduct and character as to make the reader thoroughly acquainted with him; though the attempt frequently produces an offensive appearance of egotism.

The plan of a fictitious correspondence seems calculated in some measure to combine the advantages of the other two; since, by allowing each personage to be the speaker in turn, the feelings of each may be described by himself, and his character and conduct by another. But these novels are apt to become excessively tedious; since, to give the letters the appearance of reality, (without which the main object proposed would be defeated,) they must contain a very large proportion of matter which has no bearing at all upon the story. There is also generally a sort of awkward disjointed appearance in a novel which proceeds entirely in letters, and holds together, as it were, by continual spicing.

Miss Austin, though she has in a few places introduced letters with great effect, has on the whole conducted her novels on the ordinary plan, describing, without scruple, private conversations and uncommunicated feelings: but she has not been forgetful of the important maxim, so long ago illustrated by Homer, and afterwards enforced by Aristotle, of saying as little as possible in her own person, and giving a dramatic air to the narrative, by introducing frequent conversations; which she conducts with a regard to character hardly exceeded even by Shakspeare himself. Like him, she shows as admirable a discrimination in the characters of fools as of people of sense; a merit which is far from common. To invent, indeed, a conversation full of wisdom or of wit, requires that the writer should himself possess ability; but the converse does not hold good: it is no fool that can describe fools well; and many who have succeeded pretty well in painting superior characters, have failed in giving individuality to those weaker ones, which it is necessary to introduce in order to give a faithful representation of real life: they exhibit to us mere folly in the abstract, forgetting that to the eye of a skilful naturalist the insects on a leaf present as wide differences as exist between the elephant and the lion. Slender, and Shallow, and Aguecheek, as Shakspeare has painted them, though equally fools, resemble one another no more than Richard, and Macbeth, and Julius Caesar; and Miss Austin's Mrs. Bennet, Mr. Rushworth, and Miss Bates, are no more alike than her Darcy, Knightley, and Edmund Bertram. Some have complained, indeed, of finding her fools too much like nature, and consequently tiresome; there is no disputing about tastes; all we can say is, that such critics must (whatever deference they may outwardly pay to received opinions) find the *Merry Wives of Windsor* and *Twelfth Night* very tiresome; and that those who look with pleasure at Wilkie's pictures, or those of the Dutch school, must admit that excellence of imitation may confer attraction on that which would be insipid or disagreeable in the reality.

Her minuteness of detail has also been found fault with; but even where it produces, at the time, a degree of tediousness, we know not whether that can justly be reckoned a blemish, which is absolutely essential to a very high excellence. Now, it is absolutely impossible, without this, to produce that thorough acquaintance with the characters, which is necessary to make the reader heartily interested in them. Let any one cut out from the Iliad or from Shakspeare's plays every thing (we are far from saying that either might not lose some parts with advantage, but let him reject every thing) which is absolutely devoid of importance and of interest *in itself*; and he will find that what is left will have lost more than half its charms. We are convinced that some writers have diminished the effect of their works by being scrupulous to admit nothing into them which had not some absolute, intrinsic, and independent merit. They have acted like those who strip off the leaves of a fruit tree, as being of themselves good for nothing, with the view of securing more nourishment to the fruit, which in fact cannot attain its full maturity and flavour without them. . . .

To say the truth, we suspect one of Miss Austin's great merits in our eyes to be, the insight she gives us into the peculiarities of female character. . . . Her heroines are what one knows women must be, though one never can get them to acknowledge it. As liable to 'fall in love first,' as anxious to attract the attention of agreeable men, as much taken with a striking manner, or a handsome face, as unequally gifted with constancy and firmness, as liable to have their affections biassed by convenience or fashion, as we, on our part, will admit men to be. . . .

But we must proceed to the publication of which the title is prefixed to this article. It contains, it seems, the earliest and the latest productions of the author; the first of them having been purchased, we are told, many years back by a bookseller, who, for some reason unexplained, thought proper to alter his mind and withhold it. We do not much applaud his taste; for though it is decidedly inferior to her other works, having less plot, and what there is, less artificially wrought up, and also less exquisite nicety of moral painting; yet the same kind of excellences which characterise the other novels may be perceived in this, in a degree which would have been highly creditable to most other writers of the same school, and which would have entitled the author to considerable praise, had she written nothing better. . . .

The latter of these novels, however, *Persuasion*, which is more strictly to be considered as a posthumous work, possesses that superiority which might be expected from the more mature age at which it was written, and is second, we think, to none of the former ones, if not superior to all. In the humorous delineation of character it does not abound quite so much as some of the others, though it has great merit even on that score; but it has more of that tender and yet elevated kind of interest which is aimed at by the generality of novels, and in pursuit of which they seldom fail of running into romantic extravagance: on the whole, it is one of the most elegant fictions of common life we ever remember to have met with.

Sir Walter Elliot, a silly and conceited baronet, has three daughters, the eldest two, unmarried, and the third, Mary, the wife of a neighbouring gentleman, Mr. Charles Musgrove, heir to a considerable fortune, and living in a genteel cottage in the neighbourhood of the Great house which he is hereafter to inherit. The second daughter, Anne, who is the heroine, and the only one of the family possessed of good sense, (a quality which Miss Austin is as sparing of in her novels, as we fear her great mistress, Nature, has been in real life,) when on a visit to her sister, is, by that sort of instinct which generally points out to all parties the person on whose judgment and temper they may rely, appealed to in all the little family differences which arise, and which are described with infinite spirit and detail.

The following touch reminds us, in its minute fidelity to nature, of some of the happiest strokes in the subordinate parts of Hogarth's prints: Mr. C. Musgrove has an aunt whom he wishes to treat with becoming attention, but who, from being of a somewhat inferior class in point of family and fashion, is studiously shunned by his wife, who has all the family pride of her father and eldest sister: he takes the opportunity of a walk with a large party on a fine day, to visit this despised relation, but cannot persuade his wife to accompany him; she pleads fatigue, and remains with the rest to await his return; and he walks home with her, not much pleased at the incivility she has shown. . . .

But the principal interest arises from a combination of events which cannot be better explained than by a part of the prefatory narrative, which forms, in general, an Euripidean prologue to Miss Austin's novels. . . .

After an absence of eight years, he returns to her neighbour-hood, and circumstances throw them frequently in contact. Noth-ing can be more exquisitely painted than her feelings on such occasions. First, dread of the meeting,—then, as that is removed by custom, renewed regret for the happiness she has thrown away, and the constantly recurring contrast, though known only to herself, between the distance of their intercourse and her involuntary sym-pathy with all his feelings, and instant comprehension of all his thoughts, of the meaning of every glance of his eye, and curl of his lip, and intonation of his voice. In him her mild good sense and ele-gance gradually re-awake long-forgotten attachment: but with it return the usual accompaniments of undeclared love, distrust of her sentiments towards him, and suspicions of their being favourable to another. In this state of regretful jealousy he overhears, while writing a letter, a conversation she is holding with his friend Cap-tain Harville, respecting another naval friend, Captain Benwick, who had been engaged to the sister of the former, and very speedily after her death had formed a fresh engagement: we cannot refrain from inserting an extract from this conversation, which is exqui-sitely beautiful. . . .

While this conversation has been going on, he has been replying to it on paper, under the appearance of finishing his letter: he puts the paper into her hand, and hurries away. . . .

We ventured, in a former article, to remonstrate against the dethronement of the once powerful God of Love, in his own most especial domain, the novel; and to suggest that, in shunning the ordinary fault of recommending by examples a romantic and uncal-culating extravagance of passion, Miss Austin had rather fallen into the opposite extreme of exclusively patronizing what are called pru-dent matches, and too much disparaging sentimental enthusiasm. We urged, that, mischievous as is the extreme on this side, it is not the one into which the young folks of the present day are the most likely to run: the prevailing fault is not now, whatever it may have been, to sacrifice all for love. . . .

We may now, without retracting our opinion, bestow unquali-fied approbation; for the distresses of the present heroine all arise from her prudent refusal to listen to the suggestions of her heart. The catastrophe however is happy, and we are left in doubt whether it would have been better for her or not, to accept the first proposal; and this we conceive is precisely the proper medium; for, though we would not have prudential calculations the sole principle to be regarded in marriage, we are far from advocating their exclusion. To disregard the advice of sober-minded friends on an important point of conduct, is an imprudence we would by no means recommend; indeed, it is a species of selfishness, if, in listening only to the dictates of passion, a man sacrifices to its gratification the happiness of those most dear to him as well as his own; though it is not now-a-days the most prevalent form of selfishness. But it is no condemnation of a sentiment to say, that it becomes blameable when it interferes with duty, and is uncontrouled by conscience: the desire of riches, power, or distinction,—the taste for ease and comfort,—are to be condemned when they transgress these bounds; and love, if it keep within them, even though it be somewhat tinged with enthusiasm, and a little at variance with what the worldly call prudence, i.e. regard for pecuniary advantage, may afford a better moral discipline to the mind than most other passions. It will not at least be denied, that it has often proved a powerful stimulus to exertion where others have failed, and has called forth talents unknown before even to the possessor. What, though the pursuit may be fruitless, and the hopes visionary? The result may be a real and substantial benefit, though of another kind; the vineyard may have been cultivated by digging in it for the treasure which is never to be found. What, though the perfections with which imagination has decorated the beloved object, may, in fact, exist but in a slender degree? still they are believed in and admired as real; if not, the love is such as does not merit the name; and it is proverbially true that men become assimilated to the character (i.e. what they *think* the character) of the being they fervently adore: thus, as in the noblest exhibitions of the stage, though that which is contemplated be but a fiction, it may be realized in the mind of the beholder; and, though grasping at a cloud, he may become worthy of possessing a real goddess. Many a generous sentiment, and many a virtuous resolution, have been called forth and matured by admiration of one, who may herself perhaps have been incapable of either. It matters not what the object is that a man aspires to be worthy of, and proposes as a model for imitation, if he does but *believe* it to be excellent. Moreover, all doubts of success (and they are seldom, if ever, entirely wanting) must either produce or exercise humility; and the endeavour to study another's interests and inclinations, and prefer them to one's own, may outlast the present occasion. Every thing, in short, which tends to abstract a man in any degree, or in any way, from self,—from self-admiration and self-interest, has, so far at least, a beneficial influence in forming the character.

On the whole, Miss Austin's works may safely be recommended, not only as among the most unexceptionable of their class, but as combining, in an eminent degree, instruction with amusement, though without the direct effort at the former, of which we have complained, as sometimes defeating its object. For those who cannot, or will not, *learn* any thing from productions of this kind, she has provided entertainment which entitles her to thanks; for mere innocent amusement is in itself a good, when it interferes with no greater; especially as it may occupy the place of some other that may *not* be innocent. The Eastern monarch who proclaimed a reward to him who should discover a new pleasure, would have deserved well of mankind had he stipulated that it should be blameless. Those, again, who delight in the study of human nature may improve in the knowledge of it, and in the profitable application of that knowledge, by the perusal of such fictions as those before us.

# *Later Responses*

Later responses in the nineteenth century also emphasized what Julia Kavanagh described as Austen's ability "to show life in its everyday aspect" and, following *The Champion*, "to make so much out of so little." But where both Kavanagh and her contemporary Charlotte Brontë were struck by the absence of "strong contrasts" and "bold flights" in Austen's novels, the *Retrospective Review* anticipated other aspects of the Victorian response to Austen's writings, in recruiting both the novels' heroines and their passions to a largely didactic purpose in conjunction with the woman's growing role in society (see Gisborne) as a moral guide and model.

## ✤ By an anonymous reviewer
### From an unsigned review of the Life and Adventures of Peter Wilkins, *Retrospective Review* (no month, 1823, vii, 131–35)

But two female writers there are, each the favourite of her generation, whom we would particularly specify, as illustrating in their works the opposite tastes of two successive ages; one still, we believe, in existence, but belonging, as a writer, to the last century; and the other, though coeval with ourselves, now no more, cut short by that early doom, which Heaven has ordained for all of the porcelain clay of human kind. In the lively and spirited caricatures of the author of *Evelina* and *Cecilia*,[1] we may see the style of portrait-painting relished by our fathers. Turning from them to the soberly coloured and faithful likenesses of Jane Austen, we may behold that approved by ourselves.

---

[1] Two novels by Frances Burney to whom Austen is favorably compared here.

Over the works of the first, we laugh abundantly; but this is an expression which an author should be least anxious to extort. Do we ever experience that agreeable serenity and complacency, which is diffused over the mind by the sensible and pleasant conversation of persons with whose feelings we sympathise? There are a great many turns and changes in the eventful course of the narrative; but do we see, are we at the trouble to see, what produced them? and if we are so happy as to discern the cause, does it always appear a probable or a sufficiently important one? The hero and the heroine—the lover and the beloved—fall out and in, and out again, through the whole five volumes—do they always know, or even care to understand why? The heroine is constantly in distress—poor lady! does the hard-hearted reader ever take his share of the burden? The hero is always a very respectable young man—we have no fault to find with his moral qualities—but do we ever take a jot more interest in him, than in any well-behaved, insipid young gentleman, with whom it may be our hard lot to ride fifty miles or so on a rainy day? Then there are your villains—marvellous, shrewd, calculating villains—but do they ever plot with the least probability of success? And gay deceivers, too, there are, with whom no woman can be safe in heart or reputation. But are they your men, 'to love, fight, banter, in a breath,' and stay by a torrent of wit the angry speech just kindling in the blushing cheek, and glancing eye, and half-opened lip? O no!—mere conquerors they of hearts that beat against the shop-board. Whatever a man's cue is, that he never forgets for an instant. The miser is always most miserly, and always showing it. The proud man has the pride of Lucifer, and that in perpetuity. The book-worm, again, has a trick of absence of mind, and he forgets his dinner till it is clear he ought to die of starvation. The vulgar man is broad, irredeemably, intensely vulgar. The gay, dissipated man rides down hill to the devil, with unlocked wheels, and never spends a thought as to whither he is speeding. But is there not, in this medley of all the vices, follies, and absurdities personified, some intermixture of tenderness and sentiment? Yes; two persons are set apart to talk it—two soft-sighing sentimental souls, who whine and cry through the drama; and then, heart-broken for the loss of the objects of their separate affection, at the end of the play, club together each other's fragments, and become heart-whole again.

We ask the reader's pardon for speaking with so much levity of works, which, after all that can be said in detraction, are monuments of genius. The exaggeration of nature—the everlasting sameness of character—the perpetual acting—the want of truth in the incidents—of simplicity in the structure, and above all, of moral beauty in the tone and sentiments of the story, are the faults of that bad taste which she derived from her contemporaries. . . .

Born in the same rank of life, familiar with the same description of people, equally precocious, and equally possessed of a lively fancy, and an acute perception of character, with the single advantage of belonging to a later generation, the author of *Persuasion* and *Mansfield Park* has produced works of much fresher verdure, much sweeter flavour, and much purer spirit. Without any wish to surprise us into attention, by strangeness of incident, or complication of adventure,—with no great ambition of being amazingly facetious, or remarkably brilliant,—laboriously witty, or profoundly sentimental,—of dealing out wise saws and deep reflections, or keeping us on the broad grin, and killing us with laughter;—the stream of her Tale flows on in an easy, natural, but spring tide, which carries us out of ourselves, and bears our feelings, affections, and deepest interest, irresistably along with it. She has not been at the trouble to look out for subjects for her pencil of a peculiar and eccentric cast, nor cared to outstep the modesty of nature, by spicing with a too rich vein of humour, such as fell in her way in the ordinary intercourse of life. The people with whom her works bring us acquainted were, we feel certain, like those among whom she herself shared the good and ill of life,—with whom she thought and talked—danced and sung—laughed and wept—joked and reasoned. They are not the productions of an ingenious fancy, but beings instinct with life;—they breathe and move, and think and speak, and act, before our mind's eye, with a distinctness, that rivals the pictures we see in memory of scenes we ourselves have beheld, and upon the recollections of which we love to dwell. They mingle in our remembrances with those, whom we ourselves have known and loved, but whom accident, or coldness, or death, have separated from us before the end of our pilgrimage.

Into those of her characters in particular, who engage our best affections, and with whom we sympathise most deeply, she seems to have transfused the very essence of life. These are, doubtless, the finest of her compositions, and with reason; for she had only, on any supposed interesting occurrence of life, to set her own kind and amiable feelings in motion, and the tide sprang up from the heart to the pen, and flowed in a rich stream of nature and truth over the page. Into one particular character, indeed, she has breathed her whole soul and being; and in this we please ourselves with thinking, we see and know herself.

And what is this character?—A mind beautifully framed, graceful, imaginative, and feminine, but penetrating, sagacious, and profound.—A soul harmonious, gentle, and most sweetly attuned,—susceptible of all that is beautiful in nature, pure in morals, sublime in religion;—a soul—on which, if, by any accidental contact with the vulgar, or the vicious, the slightest shade of impurity was ever thrown, it vanished instantaneously, like man's breath from the polished mirror; and, retreating, left it in undiminished lustre.—A heart large and expansive, the seat of deep, kind, honest, and benevolent feelings.—A bosom capacious of universal love, but through which there flowed a deeper stream of domestic and holy affections,—as a river through the lake's broad expanse, whose basin it supplies with its overflowing waters; and through which its course is marked only by a stronger current.—A temper even, cheerful, gladdening, and serene as the mild evening of summer's loveliest day, in which the very insect that lives but an hour, doth desport and enjoy existence.—Feelings generous and candid,—quick, but not irritable,—sensitive to the slightest degree of coolness in friend or lover, but not easily damped;—or, if overwhelmed by any heart-rending affliction, rallying, collecting, settling into repose again, like some still and deep waters disturbed by the fall of an impending rock.—Modest in hope, sober in joy, gay in innocence,—sweet soother of others' affliction,—most resigned and patient bearer of her own. With a sunny eye to reflect the glad smiles of happy friends,—dim and cloudy at the sight of others' grief; but not revealing the deep seated woes of the remote chambers of her own breast, by aught but that wild, pensive, regardful, profound expression, which tells nothing to a stranger or acquaintance, but, if a parent or friend, might break your heart but to look upon.—The beloved confidante of the young and infantine—at once playmate and preceptress;—the patient nurser of their little fretful ailments;—the more patient bearer of their rude and noisy mirth, in her own moments of illness or dejection;—exchanging smiles, that would arrest an angel on his winged way, for obstreperous laughs;—and sweet low accents, for shrill treble screams. The friend of the humble, lowly, and indigent; respecting in them, as much as in those of highest degree and lordliest bearing, the image of their common Maker. Easy, pleasant, amusing, playful, and kind in the intercourse of equals—an attentive hearer, considerate, patient, cheerfully sedate, and affectionate in that of elders. In scenes of distress or difficulty, self-dependent, collected, deliberate, and provident,—the one to whom all instinctively turned for counsel, sympathy, and consolation. Strong in innocence as a tower, with a face of serenity, and a collectedness of demeanour, from which danger and misery—the very tawny lion in his rage—might flee discomfited,—a fragile, delicate, feeble, and most feminine woman!

Whether, in this enumeration of female excellencies, one of those deeply attached friends, of whom she was sure to have had many, might recognize some, or most of the admirable qualities of JANE AUSTEN, we cannot say;—but sure we are, if our memory have not failed us, or our fancy deceived us, or our hearts betrayed us, such, or nearly such, are those, of which she has herself compounded one of the most beautiful female characters ever drawn;—we mean, the heroine of *Persuasion*.

But we have digressed farther than we intended.—Indeed, so fast and thick do recollections of what is beautiful and good in the works of this admirable woman, throng into our mind, that we are borne away involuntarily and irresistibly. They stole into the world without noise,—they circulated in quiet,—they were far from being much extolled,—and very seldom noticed in the journals of the day,—they came into our hands, as nothing different from ordinary novels,—and they have enshrined themselves in the heart, and live for ever in the thoughts,—along with the recollections of all that is best and purest in our own experience of life. Their author we, ourselves, had not the happiness of knowing,—a scanty and insufficient memoir, prefixed to her posthumous work, not written in the best taste, is all the history of her life, that we or the world have before us; but, perhaps, that history is not wanted,—her own works furnish that history. Those imaginary people, to whom she gave their most beautiful ideal existence, survive to speak for her, now that she herself is gone.

The mention of her works happened to fall in our way as the noblest illustration we could give of that improvement in this department of literature, which we are fond to believe in; but we frankly confess, we would, at any time, have travelled far out of it to pay our humble tribute of respect to the memory of Jane Austen. Nor is it so foreign to our regular speculations, as the reader may be apt to imagine. Our conversation, as one of our own number has well observed, is among the tombs; and there dwells all that once enshrined in a form of beauty a soul of exceeding and surpassing brightness.—O lost too soon to us!—but our loss has been thy immortal gain.

## ♣ Julia Kavanagh on Jane Austen[2]
### (From Chapter 18, 'Miss Austen's Six Novels,')
### in *English Women of Letters* (1862), pp. 251–74)

The writings of women are betrayed by their merits as well as by their faults. If weakness and vagueness often characterize them, they also possess when excellent, or simply good, three great redeeming qualities, which have frequently betrayed anonymous female writers. These qualities are: Delicacy, Tenderness, and Sympathy. We do not know if there exists, for instance, a novel of any merit written by a woman, which fails in one of these three attributes. Delicacy is the most common—delicacy in its broadest sense, not in its conventional meaning. Where that fails, which is a rare case, one of the other qualities assuredly steps in. Aphra Behn had no delicacy of intellect or of heart, but she had sympathy. Perhaps only a woman could have written *Oroonoko*, as only another woman could have written *Uncle Tom's Cabin* two hundred years later.[3] Man has the sense of injustice, but woman has essentially pity for suffering and sorrow. Her side is the vanquished side, amongst men or nations, and when she violates that law of her nature she rarely fails to exceed man in cruelty and revenge.

Delicacy was the great attribute of the writer under our notice. Mademoiselle de Scudéry[4] alone equalled Miss Austen in delicacy, with this difference, however, that one applied hers to thought, feeling, and intellectual speculation, and that the other turned hers to the broader and more living field of character and human nature. The method, too, was as different as the application. One analyzed, the other painted.

Miss Austen, however, though she adopted the pictorial method, is not an effective writer. Her stories are moderately interesting—her heroes and heroines are not such as to charm away our hearts, or to fascinate our judgment; but never has character been displayed in

---

[2] Julia Kavanagh (1824–77), was a novelist and literary critic. In addition to *English Women of Letters*, she wrote *French Women of Letters* (1862), *Women in France during the Eighteenth Century* (1850) and *Women of Christianity* (1852). Her novels include *Adele* (1837) and *Queen Mab* (1863).

[3] Both Aphra Behn's novel *Oroonoko* (1688) and Harriet Beecher Stowe's *Uncle Tom's Cabin* (1851) protest slavery in the Americas.

[4] Madeleine de Scudéry (1607–1701) wrote novels under the pseudonym of Sappho and is generally regarded as the first French feminist writer.

such delicate variety as in her tales; never have commonplace men and women been invested with so much reality. She cannot be said to have created or invented; Jane Austen had an infinitely rarer gift—she saw.

Not without cause did the faith and superstition of our forefathers invest with veneration and awe that mysterious word—a seer. The poet, the painter, are no more—they see. To see well is one of the greatest, and strange, too, of the rarest attributes of the mind. Commonplace people see little or nothing. Beauty and truth escape their dull perceptions. Character does not exist for them; for them life is no story—Nature no wonderful poem.

That great gift Miss Austen possessed, not in its fulness, for her range of vision was limited, but in all its keenness. The grand, the heroic, the generous, the devoted, escaped her, or, at least, were beyond her power; but the simply good, the dull, the lively, the mean, the coarse, the selfish, the frivolous, she saw and painted with a touch so fine that we often do not preceive its severity. Yet inexorable it is, for it is true. To this rare power Miss Austen added another equally rare—she knew where to stop. Two qualities are required to write a good book: to know what to say and what to withhold. She had the latter gift, one which is rarely appreciated: it seems so natural not to say more than is needed! In this respect she must have exercised great judgment, or possessed great tact, since her very qualities are those that lead to minuteness. Mademoiselle de Scudéry's prolixity was the result of a delicate and subtle mind, and that prolixity ruined her, for it made her well-nigh unreadable. Her fame decreased with time; steady progress has marked that of Jane Austen. In vain every year sees the birth of works of fiction that prove her deficiencies. She has remained unequalled in her own region—a wide one, the region of commonplace.

Persons who care to think on literary subjects, as well as to enjoy literature, must often be struck with the want of truth which tragedy and comedy display, whether on the stage or in fiction. There is nothing so unlike life as either. Life as we see it around us is not cast in sorrow or in mirth—it is not all stately or ridiculous—but a strange compound in which commonplace acts a far more striking part than heroic events or comic incidents. This middle region Jane Austen painted with a master-hand. Great calamities, heroic sorrows, adventures, and all that hangs upon them, she left to more gifted or to more ambitious painters. Neither did she trench on that other world of fiction where satire, ridicule, and exaggerated character are needed. She was satisfied with life and society, as she saw them around her, without endless sorrows, without great passions or unbecoming follies, and especially without exaggeration. Her men and women are neither very good nor very bad; nothing singular or very dramatic falls to their lot; they move in the circle of friends and home, and the slight incidents of their life are not worked up to gloomy interest, in order to suit the purposes of a tale. Indeed, if Miss Austen's merit, and it is a great one, is to have painted simply and naturally such people as we meet with daily, her fault is to have subdued life and its feelings into even more than their own tameness. The stillness of her books is not natural, and never, whilst love and death endure, will human lives flow so calmly as in her pages.

The impression life produced on Miss Austen was peculiar. She seems to have been struck especially with its small vanities and small false-hoods, equally remote from the ridiculous or the tragic. She refused to build herself, or to help to build for others, any romantic ideal of love, virtue, or sorrow. . . .

[S]he could not paint happy love. Did she believe in it? If we look under the shrewdness and quiet satire of her stories, we shall find a much keener sense of disappointment than of joy fulfilled. Sometimes we find more than disappointment.

Beyond any other of Miss Austen's tales, *Persuasion* shows us the phase of her literary character which she chose to keep most in the shade: the tender and the sad. In this work, as in *Sense and Sensibility*, and in *Mansfield Park*, but with more power than in either, she showed what can be the feelings of a woman compelled to see the love she most longs for, leaving her day by day. The judicious Elinor is, indeed, conscious that she is beloved; but her lover is not free, and she long thinks him lost. Fanny is her lover's *confidante*, and must be miserable when he is blest, or happy when he is wretched. The position of Anne Elliot has something more desolate still. The opposition of her relatives, and the advice of friends, induce her to break with a young naval officer, Captain Frederick Wentworth, to whom she is engaged, and the only man whom she can love. They part, he in anger, she in sorrow; he to rise in his profession, become a rich man, and outlive his grief; she to pine at home, and lose youth and beauty in unavailing regret. Years have passed when they meet again. Captain Wentworth is still young, still handsome and agreeable. He wishes to marry, and is looking for a wife. Anne Elliot, pale, faded, and sad, knows it, and sees it—she sees the looks, the smiles of fresher and younger beauties seeking him, and apparently not seeking him in vain.

Here we see the first genuine picture of that silent torture of an unloved woman, condemned to suffer thus because she is a woman and must not speak, and which, many years later, was wakened into such passionate eloquence by the author of *Jane Eyre*. Subdued though the picture is in Miss Austen's pages, it is not the less keen, not the less painful. The tale ends happily. Captain Wentworth's coldness yields to old love, Anne's beauty returns, they are married, yet the sorrowful tone of the tale is not effaced by that happy close. The shadow of a long disappointment, of secret grief, and ill-repressed jealousy will ever hang over Anne Elliot.

This melancholy cast, the result, perhaps, of some secret personal disappointment, distinguishes *Persuasion* from Miss Austen's other tales. They were never cheerful, for even the gentlest of satire precludes cheerfulness; but this is sad.

Of the popularity of Miss Austen's six novels, of the estimation in which they are held, we need not speak. It is honourable to the public that she should be so thoroughly appreciated, not merely by men like Sir Walter Scott and Lord Macaulay, but by all who take up her books for mere amusement. Wonderful, indeed, is the power that out of materials so slender, out of characters so imperfectly marked, could fashion a story. This is her great, her prevailing merit, and yet, it cannot be denied, it is one that injures her with many readers. It seems so natural that she should have told things and painted people as they are, so natural and so easy, that we are apt to forget the performance in the sense of its reality. The literary taste of the majority is always tinged with coarseness; it loves exaggeration, and slights the modesty of truth.

Another of Miss Austen's excellencies is also a disadvantage. She does not paint or analyze her characters; they speak for themselves. Her people have never those set sayings or phrases which we may refer to the author, and of which we may think, how clever! They talk as people talk in the world, and quietly betray their inner being in their folly, falsehood, or assumption. For instance, Sir Walter Elliot is handsome; we are merely told so; but we never forget it, for he does not. He considers men born to be handsome, and, deploring the fatal effect of a seafaring life on manly beauty, he candidly regrets that 'naval gentlemen are not knocked on the head at once,' so disgusted has he been with Admiral Baldwin's mahogany complexion and dilapidated appearance. And this worship of personal appearance is perfectly unaffected and sincere. Sir Walter Elliot's good looks have acted on him internally; his own daughter Anne rises in his opinion as her complexion grows clearer, and his first inquiry concerning his married daughter, Mary, is, 'How is she looking? The last time he, Sir Walter, saw her, she had a red nose, and he hopes that may not happen every day.' He is assured that the red nose must have been accidental, upon which the affectionate father exclaims kindly: ' "If I thought it would not tempt her to go out in sharp winds, and grow coarse, I would send her a new hat and pelisse." '

But it was natural that powers so great should fail somewhere, and there were some things which Miss Austen could not do. She could not speak the language of any strong feeling, even though that feeling were ridiculous and unjust. A rumour of Mr. Darcy's marriage with Elizabeth Bennet having reached his aunt, Lady Catherine de Bourgh, she hurries down to Longbourn to tax and upbraid Miss Bennet with her audacity, and to exact from her a promise that she will not marry Mr. Darcy. Elizabeth refuses, and there is a scene, but not a good one. Lady Catherine's interference is insolent and foolish, but it is the result of a strong feeling, and, to her, it is an important, a mighty matter, and this we do not feel as we read. Her assertions of her own importance, her surprise at Elizabeth's independence, are in keeping, but we want something more, and that something never appears. The delicate mind that could evolve, so shrewdly, foolishness from its deepest recesses, was powerless when strong feelings had to be summoned. They heard her, but did not obey the call.

This want of certain important faculties is the only defect, or rather causes the only defect, of Miss Austen's works: that everything is told in the same tone. An elopement, a death, seduction, are related as placidly as a dinner or ball, but with much less spirit. As she is, however, we must take her, and what her extraordinary powers wanted in extent, they made up in depth. In her own range, and admitting her cold views of life to be true, she is faultless, or almost faultless. By choosing to be all but perfect, she sometimes became monotonous, but rarely. The value of light and shade, as a means of success, she discarded. Strong contrasts, bold flights, she shunned. To be true, to show life in its everyday aspect, was her ambition. To hope to make so much out of so little showed no common confidence in her own powers, and more than common daring. Of the thousands who take up a pen to write a story meant to amuse, how many are there who can, or who dare, be true, like Jane Austen?

# Further Reading

## Jane Austen's Writings

*The Novels of Jane Austen.* Ed. R.W. Chapman. 5 vols. 3rd edition. London: Oxford UP. 1932–34.

*Minor Works.* Ed. R.W. Chapman. Vol. 6 of *The Novels of Jane Austen.* London: Oxford UP. 1954.

*Jane Austen's Letters.* Ed. Deirdre Le Faye. 3rd edition. Oxford: Oxford UP. 1995.

## Biographical Studies

Austen-Leigh, J.E. *A Memoir of Jane Austen.* London, 1870.

Fergus, Jan S. *Jane Austen: A Literary Life.* London: Macmillan; New York: St. Martins, 1991.

Halperin, John. *The Life of Jane Austen.* Baltimore: Johns Hopkins UP, 1996.

Honan, Park. *Jane Austen: Her Life.* London: Weidenfeld and Nicholson, 1987.

Jenkins, Elizabeth. *Jane Austen: A Biography.* London: Gollancz, 1938.

Lane, Maggie. *Jane Austen's World: The Life and Times of England's Most Popular Author.* London: Carlton, 1996.

Nokes, David. *Jane Austen: A Life.* London: Fourth Estate, 1997.

Tomalin, Claire. *Jane Austen: A Life.* Harmondsworth: Viking Press, 1997.

Wilks, Brian. *The Life and Times of Jane Austen.* 1978; London: Chancellor Press, 1997.

## Critical Studies

Armstrong, Nancy. *Desire and Domestic Fiction: A Political History of the Novel.* New York and London: Oxford UP, 1987.

Auerbach, Nina. *Romantic Imprisonment: Women and other Glorified Outcasts*. New York: Columbia UP, 1985.

Bradbrook, Frank, W. *Jane Austen and Her Predecessors*. Cambridge: Cambridge UP, 1966.

Brown, Julia Prewitt. *Jane Austen's Novels: Social Change and Literary Form*. Cambridge: Harvard UP, 1979.

————. *A Reader's Guide to the Nineteenth-Century English Novel*. London: Macmillan, 1985.

Brown, Lloyd. *Bits of Ivory: Narrative Techniques in Jane Austen's Fiction*. Baton Rouge: Louisiana State UP, 1973.

Burrows, J. F. *Computation into Criticism: A Study of Jane Austen's Novels and an Experiment in Method*. Oxford: Clarendon, 1987.

Butler, Marilyn. *Jane Austen and the War of Ideas*. Oxford: Oxford UP, 1975. Reprinted with new introduction 1987.

————. *Romantics, Rebels, and Reactionaries English Literature and its Backgrounds. 1760–1830*. Oxford: Oxford UP, 1981.

Collins, Irene. *Jane Austen and the Clergy*. London: Hambledon Press, 1994.

Copeland, Edward. *Women Writing about Money: Women's Fiction in England 1790–1820*. Cambridge: Cambridge UP, 1995.

Copeland, Edward and Juliet McMaster, eds. *The Cambridge Companion to Jane Austen*. Cambridge: Cambridge UP, 1997.

Dames, Nicholas. "Austen's Nostalgics." *Representations* 73 (Winter 2001): 117–43.

Deresiewicz, William. *Jane Austen and the Romantic Poets*. New York: Columbia UP, 2004.

Devlin, David. *Jane Austen and Education*. Totowa: Barnes and Noble, 1975.

Duckworth, Alistair M. *The Improvement of the Estate: A Study of Jane Austen's Novels*. Baltimore: Johns Hopkins UP, 1971.

Favret, Mary A. "Everyday War." *ELH* 72 (2005): 605–33.

————. Romantic Correspondence: Women, Politics, and the Fiction of Letters. Cambridge: Cambridge UP, 1993.

Fergus, Jan. *Jane Austen and the Didactic Novel: Northanger Abbey, Sense and Sensibility, and Pride and Prejudice*. London: Macmillan; Totowa: Barnes and Noble, 1983.

Gallagher, Catherine. *Nobody's Story: The Vanishing Act of Women Writers in the Marketplace 1670–1820*. Berkeley: University of California Press, 1994.

Galperin, William H. "'Describing What Never Happened': Jane Austen and the History of Missed Opportunities." *ELH* 73 (2006): 355–82.

———. *The Historical Austen*. Philadelphia: University of Pennsylvania Press, 2003.

Gaull, Marilyn. *English Romanticism*. New York: Norton, 1988.

Gard, Roger. *Jane Austen's Novels: The Art of Clarity*. 1936; New Haven: Yale UP, 1992.

Gilbert, Sandra M. and Susan Gubar. *The Madwoman in the Attic: The Woman Writer and the Nineteenth-Century Literary Imagination*. New Haven: Yale UP, 1979.

Grey, J. David, ed. *The Jane Austen Companion*. New York: Macmillan, 1986.

Harding, D.W. "Regulated Hatred: An Aspect of the Work of Jane Austen," *Scrutiny* 8 (1940): 346–62.

Hardwick, Michael. *A Guide to Jane Austen/The Osprey Guide to Jane Austen*. 1924; New York: Scribner, 1973.

Hardy, Barbara Nathan. *A Reading of Jane Austen*. London: Owen, 1975.

Harris, Jocelyn. *Jane Austen's Art of Memory*. Cambridge: Cambridge UP, 1989.

Johnson, Claudia L. *Jane Austen: Women, Politics, and the Novel*. Chicago: University of Chicago Press, 1988.

———. *Equivocal Beings: Politics, Gender, and Sentimentality in the 1790s. Wollstonecraft, Radcliffe, Burney, Austen*. Chicago: University of Chicago Press, 1995.

Jones, Darryl. *Jane Austen*. London: Palgrave, 2004.

Kaplan, Deborah. *Jane Austen among Women*. Baltimore: Johns Hopkins UP, 1992.

Kelly, Gary. *English Fiction of the Romantic Period, 1798–1830*. London: Longman, 1989.

Kirkham, Margaret. *Jane Austen, Feminism and Fiction*. Totowa: Barnes & Noble, 1983.

Knox-Shaw, Peter. *Jane Austen and the Enlightenment*. Cambridge: Cambridge UP, 2004.

Koppel, Gene. *The Religious Dimension of Jane Austen's Novels*. UMI Research Press, 1988.

Kroeber, Karl. *Styles in Fictional Structures: The Art of Jane Austen, Charlotte Brontë, and George Eliot*. Princeton: Princeton UP, 1971.

Lascelles, Mary. *Jane Austen and Her Art*. Oxford: Oxford UP, 1939.

Lane, Maggie. *Jane Austen's England*. London: R. Hale, 1986.

Litz, A. Walton. *Jane Austen: A Study of Her Artistic Development*. New York: Oxford UP, 1965.

Looser, Devoney, ed. *Jane Austen and Discourses of Feminism*. New York: St. Martin's Press, 1995.

Lynch, Deidre Shauna. *The Economy of Character: Novels, Market Culture, and the Business of Inner Meaning*. Chicago: University of Chicago Press, 1998.

MacDonagh, Oliver. *Jane Austen: Real and Imagined Worlds*, New Haven: Yale UP, 1991.

McKeon, Michael. *The Origins of the English Novel, 1600–1740*. Baltimore: Johns Hopkins UP, 1987.

McMaster, Juliet. *Jane Austen on Love*. Victoria: University of Victoria Press, 1978.

———. *Jane Austen the Novelist*. New York: St. Martin's Press, 1996.

———, ed. *Jane Austen's Achievement*. London: Macmillan, 1973.

——— and Bruce Stovel, eds. *Jane Austen's Business: Her World and Her Profession*. London: Macmillan, 1996.

Miller, D. A. *Jane Austen, or The Secret of Style*. Princeton: Princeton UP, 2003.

———. *Narrative and its Discontents: Problems of Closure in the Traditional Novel*. Princeton: Princeton UP, 1981.

———. "The Late Jane Austen." *Raritan* 10 (Summer 1990): 55–70.

Moler, Kenneth L. *Jane Austen's Art of Allusion*. Lincoln: University of Nebraska Press, 1968.

Monaghan, David, ed. *Jane Austen in a Social Context*. London: Macmillan; Totowa: Barnes and Noble, 1981.

———. *Jane Austen, Structure and Social Vision*. London: Macmillan, 1980.

Mooneyham, Laura. *Romance, Language and Education in Jane Austen's Novels*. London: Macmillan, 1988.

Morgan, Susan. *In the Meantime: Character and Perception in Jane Austen's Fiction*. Chicago: University of Chicago Press, 1980.

Mudrick, Marvin. *Jane Austen: Irony as Defense and Discovery*. Princeton: Princeton UP, 1952.

Nardin, Jane. *Those Elegant Decorums: The Concept of Propriety in Jane Austen's Novels*. Albany: State University of New York Press, 1973.

Ousby, Ian. *The Englishman's England*. Cambridge: Cambridge UP, 1990.

Page, Norman. *The Language of Jane Austen*. Oxford: Blackwell, 1972.

Phillips, K.C. *Jane Austen's English*. London: André Deutsch Ltd., 1970.

Pinch, Adela. *Strange Fits of Passion: Epistemologies of Emotion, Hume to Austen*. Stanford: Stanford UP, 1996.

Poovey, Mary. *The Proper Lady and the Woman Writer: Ideology as Style in the Works of Mary Wollstonecraft, Mary Shelley, and Jane Austen*. Chicago: University of Chicago Press, 1984.

Rzepka, Charles J. "Making It in a Brave New World: Marriage, Profession, and Anti-Romantic *Ekstasis* in Austen's *Persuasion*." *Studies in the Novel* 26 (1994): 99–120.

Sales, Roger. *Jane Austen and Representations of Regency England*. London: Routledge, 1996.

Sedgwick, Eve Kosofsky. "Jane Austen and the Masturbating Girl," in *Tendencies* (Durham: Duke UP, 1993), 113–26.

Southam, B.C., ed. *Critical Essays on Jane Austen*. London: Routledge, 1968.

———. *Jane Austen: The Critical Heritage*. Vol. 1. London: Routledge, 1968; Vol. 2. London and New York: Routledge, 1987.

———. *Jane Austen and the Navy*. London: Hambledon and London, 2003.

———. *Jane Austen's Literary Manuscripts*. London: Oxford UP, 1964.

Spacks, Patricia Meyer. *Desire and Truth: Functions of Plot in Eighteenth-Century English Novels*. Chicago: University of Chicago Press, 1990.

Spring, David. "Interpreters of Jane Austen's Social World: Literary Critics and Historians." In *Jane Austen: New Perspectives*. Ed. Janet Todd. New York: Holmes and Meier, 1983. pp. 53–72.

Stewart, Maaja. *Domestic Realities and Imperial Fictions: Jane Austen's Novels in Eighteenth-Century Contexts*. Athens: University of Georgia Press, 1993.

Sulloway, Alison. *Jane Austen and the Province of Womanhood*. Philadelphia: University of Pennsylvania Press, 1989.

Tanner, Tony. *Jane Austen*. Cambridge: Harvard UP, 1986.

Tave, Stuart. *Some Words of Jane Austen*. Chicago: University of Chicago Press, 1973.

Thomas, Keith G. "Jane Austen and the Romantic Lyric: *Persuasion* and Coleridge's Conversation Poems." *ELH* (1987): 893–924.

Thompson, James. *Between Self and World: The Novels of Jane Austen*. University Park: Pennsylvania State UP, 1988.

Tinniswood, Adrian. *A History of Country House Visiting: Five Centuries of Tourism and Taste*. Oxford and New York: Blackwell and the National Trust, 1989.

Todd, Janet, ed. *Jane Austen: New Perspectives. Women & Literature*, n.s. 3. New York: Holmes & Meier, 1983.

Troost, Linda and Sayre Greenfield, eds. *Jane Austen in Hollywood*. Lexington: UP of Kentucky, 1998.

Tuite, Claire. *Romantic Austen: Sexual Politics and the Literary Canon*. Cambridge: Cambridge UP, 2002.

Wallace, Tara Ghoshal. *Jane Austen and Narrative Authority*. New York: St. Martin's Press, 1995.

Warhol, Robyn R. "The Look, the Body, and the Heroine: A Feminist-Narratological Reading of *Persuasion*." *Novel* 26 (1992): 5–19.

Watt, Ian, ed. *Jane Austen: A Collection of Critical Essays*. Englewood Cliffs, N.J.: Prentice-Hall, 1963.

———. *The Rise of the Novel*. Berkeley: University of California Press, 1957.

Wiesenfarth, John. *The Errand of Form*. New York: Fordham UP, 1967.

Wilson, Edmund. "A Long Talk about Jane Austen," *Classics and Commercials*. New York: Farrar, 1950. 196–203.

Wiltshire, John. *Jane Austen and the Body: "The Picture of Health."* Cambridge: Cambridge UP, 1992.

———. *Recreating Jane Austen*. Cambridge: Cambridge UP, 2001.

## Some Web Resources and Websites

The Chawton House Library: http://www.chawton.org/

The Jane Austen Centre in Bath: http://www.janeausten.co.uk/

The Jane Austen Society [of England]: http://www.janeaustensoci.freeuk.com/

The Jane Austen Society of North America: http://www.jasna.org/

*Persuasions*: the Jane Austen Journal On_Line: http://www.jasna.org/persuasions/index.html

The Republic of Pemberley: http://www.pemberley.com/